VANITY FAIR'S

WOMEN
ON
WOMEN

VANITY FAIR'S

WOMEN ON WOMEN

EDITED BY RADHIKA JONES

WITH DAVID FRIEND

PENGUIN PRESS
NEW YORK
2019

PENGUIN PRESS
An imprint of Penguin Random House LLC
penguinrandomhouse.com

All essays in this collection were previously published in *Vanity Fair* or on vanityfair.com.
The following essay is used by permission:

LIBRARY OF CONGRESS CATALOGING-IN-PUBLICATION DATA

Names: Jones, Radhika, editor.
Title: Vanity fair's women on women / edited by Radhika Jones ; with David Friend.
Other titles: Vanity fair (New York, N.Y. : 1983)
Description: New York : Penguin Press, 2019.
Identifiers: LCCN 2019009993 (print) | LCCN 2019981398 (ebook) |
ISBN 9780525562146 (hardcover) | ISBN 9780525562153 (ebook)
Subjects: LCSH: Women--Biography. | Women--Attitudes--Case studies.
Classification: LCC CT3235 .V36 2019 (print) | LCC CT3235 (ebook) |
DDC 920.72--dc23
LC record available at https://lccn.loc.gov/2019009993
LC ebook record available at https://lccn.loc.gov/2019981398

Printed in the United States of America
1 3 5 7 9 10 8 6 4 2

Designed by Gretchen Achilles

CONTENTS

THE RENEGADES

THE MUSICIANS

THE HOUSE OF WINDSOR

THE STARS

IN THEIR OWN WORDS

INTRODUCTION

By Radhika Jones

anity Fair profiles set themselves apart through the bracing, un-flinching nature of the writer's gaze. This is especially powerful and poignant when the gaze is female. Who could prepare for the scene in Maureen Orth's 1993 portrait of Tina Turner when Turner pulls the hem of her dress from her legs all the way up to her shoulders—no bra—and turns to show off her curves in profile. A showstopper, you'd think—but Orth doesn't stop there. Instead, she looks past the silhouette to note that the thing she can't see is just as important, if not more. "What's *really* remarkable about Tina Turner's face," she writes, "is how few scars it bears from the years of beatings she took." A difficult, at times contentious discussion of brutal do-mestic violence ensues. This is no glossed-over celebrity profile; this is a deep, dark dive. *(See page 224.)*

But since this is also the resilient Tina Turner, she comes up singing. And at one point, Turner circles back to an almost confrontational question that Orth posed during their sessions together: Have you ever stood up for any-thing? Turner, with strength and vulnerability on display, revisits the ques-tion and responds, "I am happy that I'm not like anybody else. Because I really do believe that if I was different I might not be where I am today. You asked me if I ever stood up for anything. Yeah, I stood up for my life."

This book is full of women who are not like anybody else—women who, in their singular ways, stood up for their lives, as they envisioned them, and in so doing, shaped the lives of multitudes. *Vanity Fair's Women on Women* is a collection of classic profiles and essays about women by women. All these pieces appeared in the modern incarnation of the magazine, during the past thirty-six years, though some travel further back, into the lives of icons such as Frida Kahlo and Grace Kelly, whose work and legacy endure.

Since its inception during the Jazz Age, more than a century ago, *Vanity Fair* has covered historically significant women, focusing on their pursuits and passions, their trials and triumphs, and their evolving roles in society. When the magazine's inaugural editor, Frank Crowninshield, took the helm in 1914, one of the cornerstones of his mission statement for the publication declared: "We hereby announce ourselves as determined and bigoted feminists." The magazine would go on to be a vital cultural bellwether until the Great Depression, when it suspended publication and was folded into *Vogue*, only to be resurrected in 1983.

Crowninshield—a social dynamo, art connoisseur, and uncanny arbiter of magazine talent—employed dozens of women writers and editors. Among his earliest hires was a budding essayist, humorist, and contrarian named Dorothy Rothschild (later Dorothy Parker). Among the most influential editors in Crowninshield's crew was Clare Boothe (Brokaw) Luce, who, after helping conceive what would become *Life* magazine in the 1930s, became a renowned playwright, member of Congress, U.S. ambassador to Italy, and an advisor to presidents.

Vanity Fair's literary roster during the Jazz Age included many of the luminaries of the era: Djuna Barnes, Helen Brown Norden, Margaret Case Harriman, Willa Cather, Colette, Janet Flanner, Anita Loos, Vita Sackville-West, Edna St. Vincent Millay, Gertrude Stein, Helen Wells, and Elinor Wylie among them. Illustrators such as Thelma Cudlipp, (Regina) Aline Farrelly, Ethel M. Plummer, Ethel Rundquist, and Rita Senger—along with the prolific Anne Harriet Fish—created scores of memorable covers. Women also filled *Vanity Fair*'s photographer ranks, including some of the emerging portraitists of the time, such as Berenice Abbott, Imogen Cunningham, Louise Dahl-Wolfe, Helen Macgregor, Florence Vandamm, and Toni von Horn.

Women contributed essays and columns about the suffrage movement and social norms, sexual mores and modern manners, crime and scandal, nightlife and high society, the workplace and the home, art criticism and theater reviews. In 1915, Crowninshield decided to assign one of the magazine's most popular early pieces after he was ridiculed for asserting that he knew a dozen women in New York who earned more than $50,000 a year—and fifty more who made over $10,000 (more than $250,000 in current dollars). The writer, Anne O'Hagan, conducted her own investigation, surveying a range of female entrepreneurs and arts figures, and discovered that Crowninshield's estimate was far too low.

Some seventy years later, Tina Brown, who turned the magazine into a cultural mainstay in the 1980s and early 1990s, continued in this tradition, realizing that the voice of the intrepid woman writer—along with the vision of women photographers and illustrators—were part of *Vanity Fair*'s DNA. One need only consider how integral the work of Annie Leibovitz, the magazine's principal photographer for its entire modern era, has been to its identity to understand the role women have played in *Vanity Fair*'s staying power, whether through the inaugural Hollywood Issue cover in 1995 (featuring a young Sandra Bullock, Gwyneth Paltrow, and Julianne Moore, among others), Leibovitz's portrait of Queen Elizabeth II in 2016, or her picture of a wry, knowing Lena Waithe, the actor-screenwriter-producer, in 2018.

Graydon Carter, who edited the magazine for twenty-five years, and who assigned the lion's share of the stories in this anthology, once described *Vanity Fair* as "the biography of our age, one month at a time." Like the best biographies, the stories in *Vanity Fair* gain power from their contemporary resonance. Magazines are cultural arbiters, and their editors unabashedly seek to predict the future—or even help determine it. The only problem is that by the time that future comes to pass, the magazine has often been relegated to the recycling heap. It is striking, therefore, in this collection, to come across past moments of prescience one, two, even three decades old. A remark from Gail Sheehy's profile of Hillary Clinton in the spring of 1992: "Hillary could—and should—be our first woman president." (Were we governed by the popular vote, she would have been.) An observation from Ingrid Sischy's profile of Nicole Kidman ten years later: "She's proved herself to be a star with a capital *S*, the one-in-a-generation kind who, like Elizabeth Taylor, is bigger than the Hollywood system." (Kidman's almost-complete takeover of big and small screens can attest to this.) A passage from Janet Coleman's profile of Whoopi Goldberg in 1984: "Among her fans was the Pulitzer Prize–winning novelist

Alice Walker. ('I loved her work,' Walker says. 'I thought she was just great.') They discussed the film version of Walker's novel *The Color Purple*. 'Honey, in *The Color Purple*,' Whoopi says, 'I'd play the dirt.'" In fact, she played the lead, Celie, in the 1985 film directed by Steven Spielberg, a performance that earned her an Oscar nomination and a Golden Globe for Best Actress in a Drama.

But signaling the future isn't *Vanity Fair*'s only function. Also in its house codes is a fascination with nostalgia, those forays into the past that help us interpret the present and remind us how we got from there to here. There was Julia Child, an ad-industry copywriter turned employee of the O.S.S. (precursor to the C.I.A.), who, after acquiring a knack for fine cuisine while living in Paris and Provence, would eventually elevate the palate, taste, and cooking regimens of millions of Americans. There was Emily Post, the former debutante who dabbled unremarkably in Edith Wharton–style fiction before turning her attention at the age of forty-eight to a bible of manners—a book that still sells hundreds of thousands of copies. (Laura Jacobs writes, "The very qualities that made Post's fiction a bit simplistic—her endless optimism, her ingrained sense of fair play, her authorial presence too much in the room— were exactly the qualities that made *Etiquette* embraceable, accessible, intimate.") There was Cher—no, no, Cher is still here; she is very much still here. Cher is forever.

In a sense, they all are forever, as long as their stories remain. To spend time with these women—subjects and writers alike—is to be reminded of how indelibly they continue to shape our culture, our politics, the way we live now. It is something of a magazine maxim that the most compelling stories expand out from their subjects to capture something fleeting about the world around them—the ways they make their moment, and the ways their moment makes them. This is a moment for women's voices, and we are proud and delighted to bring them forward.

THE
COMEDIANS

MAKING WHOOPI

By Janet Coleman | July 1984

The bombilation started in New York on February 3, 1984, when the headline WHOOPI GOLDBERG DOES "THE SPOOK SHOW" exploded in the "Weekend" section of the *Times* above a picture of a grinning black woman and Mel Gussow's rave review. Whoopi Goldberg was described as a cross between Lily Tomlin and Richard Pryor, "not simply a stand-up comedian but a satirist with a cutting edge and an actress with a wry attitude toward life and public performance."

At the Dance Theater Workshop, in Chelsea, early the following Saturday night, the lines on the staircase included college kids, agents, middle-aged black men in tweed sport coats, old women in minks, and sisters in cornrows. To a dignified experimental theater like D.T.W., *The Spook Show* was obviously more than just a mild sensation. Twenty minutes before curtain, the only seats were on the floor.

For her New York debut, Whoopi Goldberg selected four haunting characters—"spooks"—to appear as a quartet: a dope fiend, a knocked-up surfer chick, a cripple, and a little girl. The dope fiend, Fontaine, opened the show, singing, "Around the world in ay-tee muh'fuckin' days." Scratching his crotch, Fontaine moved into the audience and at once put the crowd at ease and on edge: "How you doin', mama. That's a bad ring you're wearin'. Want me to hold it for you?"

Back in the spotlight, Fontaine blithely discussed every conceivable controversial subject, from legalized marijuana and Abraham Lincoln to Mr. T ("A guy with a Mohawk I'm supposed to relate to. This motherfucker is a throwback, man") and AIDS ("A government conspiracy—they put germs in the discos"). He panned *The Big Chill* as "a lot of motherfuckers sitting around crying about the sixties. I could have saved them a whole lot of money, Jack. 'Cause I know what happened in the sixties, CETA"—the Comprehensive Employment and Training Act—"You could get a CETA job and learn to part your hair. I see you had one of those jobs."

Next, this funky Don Quixote ran down a European trip. His spiel was accompanied by a series of eye-popping physical transformations: into a stewardess steering a quivering beverage cart; a microwaved airplane string bean; a German burgher ogling "the *Schwarze*" making his way down narrow Amsterdam streets and thanking God for legal hashish.

The anxiety in the theater was tangible when Fontaine's itinerary stopped at the house of Anne Frank. There seemed nothing here to be funny about. But Whoopi Goldberg didn't plan to amuse. From empty space she created the room where Anne Frank and her family hid from the Nazis—the table, the wallpaper, the stillness, the fifteen-year-old girl's note to posterity: "In spite of everything I still believe that people are really good at heart." Fontaine relived a moment of enlightenment, and we were moved. "It kicked my ass," he said. "I discovered what I didn't think I had: a heart. Now if someone breaks into my house to steal my stereo, I will break his legs, but I will remember that *in spite of everything,* there is goodness in people. And *that* will save his life."

When Fontaine turned upstage, the back view of Whoopi Goldberg transformed into that of a teenage girl who was "like a surfer chick, like *not* a Valley Girl. Moon Zappa has wrecked our lives." With jerky teenage mannerisms and studied nonchalance, she told of an unwanted pregnancy and her first attempt to abort the child with "a mixture of Comet and Johnnie Walker Red, and, you know, like jump up and down fifty-six times." She had resorted to the hanger only after being rejected by her mother and the church. The surfer chick described the grisly procedure and unsentimentally shrugged off the way it would have affected her life: "Like you can't go surfing with a baby on your back."

Next, Whoopi Goldberg distorted her voice and contorted her body into a character so handicapped one wondered whether she could make it work without veering into bathos, or bad taste. Like Lily Tomlin, who has walked a similar tightrope, she brought it off.

The last character, the little girl, looked so young that one observer swore Whoopi Goldberg was thirteen. She wore an old white skirt draped over her head and called it "long blond hair." She said her ambition was to sail on the Love Boat, but with a headful of pigtails that "don't do nuffin', don't blow in the wind," she wouldn't be welcomed aboard. She had tried other ways not to be black, but bathing in Clorox didn't work. This night the little girl approached a black woman in the audience. "Do you go out with a skirt on your head?" The answer was no, but the little girl pressed on, asking, "Can I touch your hair?" She was so clever and charming, her victim couldn't refuse.

Mike Nichols did not become famous for sentimentality, but when he embraced Whoopi Goldberg and called her "a true artist," he was in tears.

I had not seen Whoopi Goldberg since 1980, when she and I and a group of Second City actors were working for a La Jolla, California, shrink tank on a state-funded PBS show about loneliness and isolation. Unlike the rest of us, Whoopi had been hired locally. She was not just the token black member of the cast. Like a seltzer bottle in the desert, she was the only black comedienne in all of San Diego County.

She was born in a Chelsea housing project not far from the Dance Theater Workshop. "Whoopi" was her invention, but, yes, "a real Goldberg" was in her mother's ancestral line. She moved to San Diego in 1974 because "someone paid my fare." At twenty-four, she was a divorced mother with a one-year-old daughter. She was also a terrible but dogged driver, grinding her gears along the freeway in a beat-up VW bug and scuffling to support herself and Alexandrea. As a licensed beautician, she had worked in a mortuary, and the last head she'd beautified had belonged to a stiff. "When you work in a beauty parlor," she says, "you can't talk back and you can't talk mean. Dead folks, you can have conversations with 'em and tell 'em how you really feel: 'I'm glad you're dead. I think you're a bitch.' You can grab their head and go, 'Hey, come on. Sit up here. Let's try the Joan Crawford look on you. Nah, that doesn't work. Let's try Lucille Ball.'"

Her decision to do "this comedy stuff" was one of desperation: "I got tired of people in dinner theaters saying, 'We can't put you and a white guy together, because the folks from Texas can't handle it.' And 'You *are* good, but our economy rides on people coming to see what they expect. And they're not expecting you.'"

She became the toast as well as the scourge of San Diego. When she introduced her piece on teenage abortion, the right-to-lifers picketed her act. "I had Nazis on my back," says Whoopi. She got threatening letters. "Thanks for the free publicity," she said.

Moving north to Berkeley, to perform with its oldest avant-garde theater troupe, the Blake Street Hawkeyes, she fell in love with one of its founders, the writer and performance artist David Schein. "Before, there was just me and Alex, and anything I got to do was always just a little bit, because I always had to be Mommy. Now I'm a woman with a great man. He said, 'Go for it.' And here I am."

First performed at 2019 Blake Street, Whoopi's *The Spook Show* got raves. "The critics hadn't seen any black woman doin' what I'm doin'. I did three *Spook Shows*, with thirteen characters. The name Whoopi Goldberg was a godsend. That's what brought 'em out."

Among her fans was the Pulitzer Prize–winning novelist Alice Walker. ("I loved her work," Walker says. "I thought she was just great.") They discussed the film version of Walker's novel *The Color Purple.* "Honey, in *The Color Purple*," Whoopi says, "I'd play the dirt." [In 1985, in fact, Goldberg would play the lead, Celie, winning a Golden Globe and earning an Academy Award nomination. She would go on to win a best-supporting-actress Oscar and a Golden Globe for her portrayal of Oda Mae Brown in the 1990 feature *Ghost.*]

Touring Europe with Schein, she was referred to by the Germans as "*die schwarze Schauspielerin*," or "the black actress." When they returned to Berkeley, Schein recalls, Fontaine's European monologue was dashed off the top of her head in one inspired night.

Using the material of the late Moms Mabley, the great black comedienne, Whoopi opened another show, called *Moms*, viewing it as both a tribute and a potential annuity. "I got fabulous, amazing reviews," says Whoopi. "Everyone came out to see if I could pull it off. I did."

Over a year ago, she signed up for the gig in New York. She had no agent, no manager, no professional advisers. With Schein on the home front in Berkeley, her daughter, the staff of D.T.W., and Danny Osman, an actor she has known since San Diego, were her entire entourage. She thought it would be a nice way to see her hometown and her mother, Emma Johnson, a teacher with Head Start. The rest was a "fluke." "I figured they wanted my picture so they could put an arrow on it and say, 'Don't see her, she stinks.' "

"Girl, I've never seen anything like this before," said New York African-American psychotherapist Constance Carr-Shepherd after Whoopi Goldberg wiped imaginary snot from her finger and ran it through Connie Carr–from–Philadelphia's hair.

Unlike the characters of Lily Tomlin, Richard Pryor, and even Lenny Bruce, who deliver interior monologues essentially uninfluenced by audience reaction, Whoopi's "spooks" talk directly to the audience, and in these conversations the characters will bend dramatically to meet the audience's reactions. No two shows are the same. I saw seven. The soul of the Whoopi Goldberg variations is improvisation, the illumination of the moment, as in a revival meeting or in jazz.

"I came expecting comedy," remarked Sue Mingus, widow of the jazz great Charles. "She's deadly serious. She's not a comedian. She's a philosopher. Or a saint."

On the word of a San Francisco theater colleague, the D.T.W. had booked Whoopi Goldberg sight unseen. Suddenly, her show was successful beyond an avant-garde theater's most surrealistic dreams. Its star had been reviewed twice in the *Village Voice*, a full-page story about her was about to be published in *Newsweek*, and after a week of Liz Smith's promos, she was finally seen chatting behind dark glasses with Jack Cafferty on *Live at Five*.

Since the D.T.W. was helpless to capitalize on the bonanza—its season was already booked—the journalist-tummeler Bob Weiner took it upon himself to convince a bunch of club owners and show-business honchos that a trip downtown to see *The Spook Show* was better than watching movie stars eat blinis at the Russian Tea Room.

"Everybody knows I hate everything and everybody," says Weiner. "But I thought Whoopi Goldberg was the funniest, most moving performer I'd ever seen."

Following Weiner's tip, Greg Dawson promptly offered her a space at the Ballroom, on Twenty-eighth Street, for an extended run. Joe Cates offered to produce her in a "regular situation," where she could "build as a theater artist" in a "classy Off Broadway venue." Larry Josephson, WBAI's sour gourmand, asked her to write material for the Radio Foundation, which produces *The Bob and Ray Show*.

It is possible there were even more spectacular offers: strangers pressed their phone numbers on Whoopi Goldberg until her pockets were stuffed. Her backstage visitors included Bette Midler, Burt Bacharach, Carole Bayer Sager, Jerry Stiller, Anne Meara, Warner Bros. vice president Diane Sokolow, Mrs. Oscar Hammerstein II, Norma Kamali, supermanager Sandy Gallin, and superagent Sam Cohn. After the penultimate performance, one of her idols, Mike Nichols, stood before her for a speechless five minutes. Mike Nichols did not become famous for sentimentality, but when he embraced Whoopi Goldberg and called her "a true artist," he was in tears.

No celebrities were present at Whoopi Goldberg's two great shows at Manhattan Community College, on Chambers Street. In front of a student body of which 70 percent belonged to a minority [group], Whoopi really let it rip. Among the smart and sophisticated middle-class crowd at D.T.W., she was the dangerous one, with her provocative language, her forays into the audience, and her threats to steal rings. Here, the most galvanic laugh of the afternoon was at the dope fiend Fontaine's discovery that a French bathroom attendant wants money for the toilet paper. Here, when she sassed the audience, the audience sassed back.

Describing his trip into the Schwarzwald, Fontaine observed, "There was me and it. The last black person these folks seen was Hannibal." Instantly, Whoopi figured out why the kids didn't laugh. "You don't know who Hannibal is!" Fontaine gasped. "Is this a college? Hannibal crossed the Alps on an elephant! He was a very dark-skinned man!" Horrified, Fontaine scratched his crotch and adjusted his shades. "Check out the libraries, y'all," he said.

At the Odeon that night, she ordered, as Fontaine would have, a filet mignon "done-done." She explained to the waiter that she got freaked eating blood.

The steak arrived oozing red. Conversations with show-business mavens that week, she was saying, had yielded this advice: "Get a good writer"; "Don't do a sitcom right away"; "Develop a strong New York cult following"; and "Say you're twenty-nine." Her flicker of hesitation gave way to defiance, and Whoopi pushed away the twenty-one-dollar dish. She looked blankly at her steak and said, "Save it for the dog." One wondered how anyone, including Moms Mabley, could tell her how to direct this sort of success. Over lemon dacquoise, her options sounded less freewheeling than choosing a hairdo for a corpse.

Whoopi Goldberg left New York hoping things would simmer down. But Diane Sokolow was sending a big Warner Bros. contingent to join the crowds catching her performance at L.A.'s Wallenboyd Center on a double bill with David Schein. Warner Bros. is producing *The Color Purple*. "Cross your fingers," says Diane Sokolow. "She could be Celie." "She's a real crossover artist," reports her actor friend Tom Mack. "Hollywood wants her, and so does the L.A. Museum of Contemporary Art."

She called Sandy Gallin, one of her most ardent fans, whose stable includes such stars as Dolly Parton, Mac Davis, Paul Rodriguez, of the defunct *a.k.a. Pablo*, and Debbie Allen, of *Fame*. "Sandy Gallin is a top-notch, big-time Hollywood manager," one producer says. "Better at getting money than anyone. All the clichés. He negotiated Joan Rivers's multimillion-dollar Johnny Carson deal. You wouldn't think this was his cup of tea."

In New York, Sandy Gallin had "dragged everyone from dress designers to high-school friends" to see Whoopi's show. And his partners in Hollywood heard reports that he had seen "the greatest black actress of our lifetime." At the Russian Tea Room, Gallin asked Whoopi to consider signing with Katz-Gallin-Morey & Addis, promised to read *The Color Purple*, and then had her driven to the projects in a limousine.

Now, after Mac Davis's Vegas show at the MGM Grand, Whoopi grilled Davis about signing with Sandy Gallin, while Gallin grilled David Schein, who said, "Just let her do what she wants. She's very surprising when she does what she wants." She wanted to sign.

"She belongs in New York. She's a theater artist," said Joe Cates, who hoped to be Whoopi Goldberg's producer. "Marcel Marceau isn't managed by Sandy Gallin, but he still works." "She needs an editor. She needs to build an audience. She needs a workshop situation," said Bob Weiner, "like Bette Midler at the Continental Baths." "Let's face it, she could play Las Vegas. She might not like it, but she could do it," Joe Cates admitted. "She could get the laughs."

"Whoopi Goldberg," Sandy Gallin said simply, "is going to be a very big star."

At the South Street Seaport, Whoopi Goldberg was talking in the seventy-seven-year-old voice of Inez Beaverman, whose performing milieu is a Las Vegas lounge. In this voice, which she claimed was raspy from venereal disease and Jack Daniel's and cranberry juice, she lamented the consequences of [the Rev.] Jesse Jackson [having called New York City] "Hymietown" [earlier that year while he was running in the presidential primaries]. ("He blew it, dolling. Jesse blew it. He blew it even more because he didn't cop to it. He tried to tippy-tip-tip around. What a shame. It was in the palm of his hand.") Inez said, "I'm insulted that I haven't heard from Frank [Sinatra]. Frankie knows I'm here. That's how people get. That's why I never got big. I could never crawl over people the way that Frank does. I turned him on to Jack Daniel's and cranberry juice. Frank's voice gave out when he stopped drinking it. He thought he knew it all."

In her own voice, Whoopi was less flippant. "It's like babies," she said. "You say, 'I'll have one when I'm ready.' But you're never ready for stuff like this when it looks like it's going to break."

She envisioned a cruise for her mother. Treats for her daughter. A word processor for David Schein. Besides a limo, all she wanted for herself was new leather pants. She was wearing a black cashmere coat that had belonged to her grandfather. A knitted Rasta tarn covered the pigtails she wears in corkscrews all over her head. "The scariest thing about starting to make it is the Ten Best-Dressed List," she said. "This is the best you'll see me dressed till I die."

On Water Street, with our thumbs in the air, we were watching the traffic whiz by. You forget how inconvenient life can be until you wait for a cab with a black woman in her grandfather's clothes. "Maybe they don't know that I'm a woman," Whoopi said. "If I wasn't wearing pants, I could pull up my dress."

The avant-garde theater and the nightclub stage had been a haven, a sanctuary for expressing "thoughts that could get you arrested or taken to Bellevue." She had never yet been censored and was concerned for her integrity. "I read all these biographies about what drove folks nuts. People change toward you. I want to do good work. I don't think I can compromise that and live. 'Cause if I have to shake my tits or play somebody's fuckin' maid for the rest of my life, it isn't worth it. My stuff, that's the one thing I know no amount of money can stop me from doin'. 'Cause that's the reason why I'm here on earth. I like to think that Moms and Lenny are leading me. Moms and Lenny are saying, 'Do it. It's going to piss a lot of people off.'"

(Whoopi Goldberg is among the handful of artists to have received Academy, Emmy, Grammy, and Tony Awards.)

WHAT TINA WANTS

By Maureen Dowd | January 2009

Tina Fey has never dated a bad boy.

She didn't even let boys she dated do anything bad.

"I remember the biggest trouble I ever got into—" says her husband, Jeff Richmond, a short, puckish man of 48 in jeans and a T-shirt, cutting himself off mid-thought at the mere memory of Tina's wrath. "Oh, my God." (He calls himself "the Joe Biden of husbands" because he's prone to "drop the bomb" in interviews.)

Fey is sitting across from Richmond in their comfy, vintage-y Upper West Side apartment, where a lavender exercise ball lolls next to the flat-screen TV, a pink tricycle is parked under a black grand piano, and golden award statuettes abound. When I arrived, at 9:30 p.m., Fey had already put her three-year-old daughter, Alice, to bed and was tapping away on a silver Mac laptop at the kitchen counter on a script for *30 Rock*, her slyly hilarious NBC comedy about an NBC comedy. She'll return to the script when I leave, near midnight.

Fey shoots Richmond a warning look. It's undercut by the fact that she's wedged into her daughter's miniature red armchair, joking about squeezing her butt in and looking like Alice in Wonderland grown big in navy velour sweatpants and pink slippers.

The 38-year-old Fey sips a glass of white wine and eats some cheese and crackers—all her food-obsessed doppelgänger on *30 Rock*, Liz Lemon, longs to do is go home and eat a big block of cheese—while Richmond and I drink vodka martinis he has made.

"What are you gonna tell?" she teases her husband. "Think this through."

Richmond wades in. "When we were first dating," he says, harking back to Chicago in 1994, "some of the guys at Second City said, 'Hey, wouldn't it be a hoot if we go over—'"

"'—over to the Doll House,'" Fey finishes. "'We'll go to this strip club *ironically.*' I was like, 'The fuck you will.'"

Their conversation is woven with intimacy, the easy banter of a couple who knew each other long before fame hit. They fell in love quickly, soon after a Sunday afternoon spent together at Chicago's Museum of Science and Industry. ("We walked into a model of the human heart," Fey deadpans.) The writer-comedian and the musician-director dated for seven years, have been married for another seven, and have worked together in improv theater in Chicago, on *Saturday Night Live,* and on *30 Rock.* (He composed the bouncy retro theme music.) Richmond still reassures her, all these years later: "Nothing happened. We were there for like an hour. We ate chicken, really good pasta."

And Fey still recoils. "It didn't go great when you came back, did it? I was very angry. It was disrespectful."

I mention that in the pilot of *30 Rock* Liz Lemon puts on a Laura Bush–style pink suit from her show-within-a-show's wardrobe department to go to lunch with Tracy Jordan (Tracy Morgan), to try to sign him, and he takes her to a strip club in the Bronx, where she gets drunk and dances onstage with a stripper named Charisma.

"I love to play strippers and to imitate them," says Fey. "I love using that idea for comedy, but the idea of actually going there? I feel like we all need to be better than that. That industry needs to die, by all of us being a little bit better than that."

There's a reason her former *S.N.L.* pal Colin Quinn dubbed Tina Fey "Herman the German." She's a sprite with a Rommel battle plan.

Elizabeth Stamatina Fey started as a writer and performer with a bad short haircut in Chicago improv. Then she retreated backstage at *S.N.L.,* wore a ski hat, and gained weight writing sharp, funny jokes and eating junk food. Then she lost 30 pounds, fixed her hair, put on a pair of hot-teacher glasses, and made her name throwing lightning-bolt zingers on "Weekend Update." Speeding through the comedy galaxy, she wrote the hit *Mean Girls* and created her own show based on an *S.N.L.*-type show: *30 Rock*. The comedy struggled in the ratings for two years but was a critical success, winning seven Emmys last fall and catapulting Fey into red-hot territory. Before she even had a chance to take a breath, a freakish twist of fate turned her from red- to white-hot, and enabled her, at long last, to boost the ratings of *30 Rock*: Fey was a ringer for another hot-teacher-in-glasses, Sarah Palin, the comely but woefully unprepared Alaska governor, who bounded out of the woods with her own special language to become not only the first Republican woman to run on a national ticket [as Senator John McCain's would-be vice president] but also God's gift to comedy and journalism. So where does Fey go from white-hot?

"Tina is not clay," says Lorne Michaels, the impresario of *Saturday Night Live*, *Mean Girls*, and *30 Rock*, when I ask him how he helped shape her career. Steve Higgins, an *S.N.L.* producer, observes, "When she got here she was kind of goofy-looking, but everyone had a crush on her because she was so funny and bitingly mean. How did she go from ugly duckling into swan? It's the Leni Riefenstahl in her. She has such a German work ethic even though she's half Greek. It's superhuman, the German thing of 'This will happen and I am going to make this happen.' It's just sheer force of will."

As it turns out, the 669-page autobiography of Leni Riefenstahl—chronicling her time as Hitler's favorite filmmaker and the creation of the propaganda movie *Triumph of the Will*—is one of Fey's favorite (cautionary) books. "If she hadn't been so brilliant at what she did, she wouldn't have been so evil," Fey says. "She was like, in the book, 'He was the leader of the country. Who was I not to go?' And it's like, Note to self: Think through the invite from the leader of your country."

Tina Fey speaks what she calls "less than first-grade" German and so does Liz Lemon of *30 Rock*, which Fey thinks is fun because German is "so uncool." (Lemon's cell-phone ring is the Wagnerian "Kill da Wabbit" from Bugs Bunny's *What's Opera, Doc?*) Fey is a rules girl—"I don't like assertions of status or line cutting"—and she's made Lemon one, too. Far from the John

Belushi model—the only drug packets scattered around *S.N.L.* these days are Emergen-C—Fey drinks sparingly, is proud that she has never taken drugs, and calls her husband's ex–smoking habit "disgusting."

Her true vice is cupcakes. I've brought her a box, one frosted with the face of Sarah Palin. She chooses that one, which is bigger, joking that it's O.K. if she gains weight before her Annie Leibovitz photo shoot in a few days, because "Annie's going to photograph my soul, right?" When it comes to her looks, she's both forgiving and self-deprecating. "The most I've changed pictures out of vanity was to edit around any shot where you can see my butt," she says. "I like to look goofy, but I also don't want to get canceled because of my big old butt." Frowning and rubbing the lines between her eyes, she adds that she might also tell the *30 Rock* postproduction team, "'Can you digitally take this out?' Because I don't have Botox or anything."

Fey's friend Kay Cannon, a *30 Rock* writer, says that Tina has remained self-deprecating even as she has glammed up. "She'll always see herself as that other, the thing she came from."

Rules are Tina's "Achilles' heel in some ways," Richmond says. "She's half German, half Greek. That is just like loosey-goosey-crazy, and then you get, 'Do the trains run on time?'" It is Fey's fierce clarity about rules that allows Richmond to feel secure now that he's suddenly in celebrity-magazine features with titles such as "I Married a Star" and is living with the woman the *New Yorker* staff writer Michael Specter calls "the sex symbol for every man who reads without moving his lips."

"I know how she feels about some things," Richmond tells me over coffee one day at an Italian place around the corner from his house. "Like, we never had to deal with any of this, but: adultery. Just looking at examples from other people's lives, we know that anything like that, messing around, is just such a complete 'No' to her. And she has her principles and she sticks to her principles more than anybody I've ever met in my life. Like that whole idea of, if you are in a relationship, there are deal breakers. There's not a lot of gray area in being flirty with somebody. She's very black-and-white: 'We're married—you can't.'" He calls their marriage "borderline boring—in a good way." And she concurs: "I don't enjoy any kind of danger or volatility. I don't have that kind of 'I love the bad guys' thing. No, no thank you. I like nice people."

"She used to wear crazy boots," Richmond recalls, "knee-length frumpy dresses with thrift-store sweaters."

Rip Torn, the wonderful 77-year-old actor who plays the C.E.O. of G.E. on *30 Rock*, told me he was "gazing admiringly" at Fey one day, and she said, "I'm married, you know. I love my husband and I have a child."

S.N.L.'s Amy Poehler has described Fey as "monastic," the type who sits on the side and watches everybody else belly-flop in the pool, and then writes about it.

During cocktails at her apartment, I ask Fey, What's the wildest thing you've ever done?

"Nothing," she replies blithely.

Did she ever use the Sarah Palin voice to entice her own First Dude?

No, she said, but once, when she did a voice-over for a pinball machine in Chicago, she used an Elly May Clampett voice. "These critters need some attention," she says in a soft southern drawl, giving her husband a sexy glance. She's as pitch-perfect channeling Elly May as she is channeling Palin. "And that was the only time Jeff has kind of hinted that maybe I should talk like that all the time."

Last September, when Fey saw Mary Tyler Moore and Betty White giving out the Emmy for outstanding comedy series, she says, "I had this visceral thing of, like, I want them to gimme that! I want to get that from those ladies!"

And within moments *30 Rock* was called and she went up onstage, glowing in a strapless eggplant mermaid David Meister gown, to take the Emmy from the two women who had provided the template for her own show. In fact, *30 Rock* would rock the Emmys, tying the record held by *All in the Family*. Given her frumpy start in comedy and her wooden start on *30 Rock*, it was a dazzling Cinderella moment (except for Fey's purse getting stolen while she was onstage). She got her own slipper, writing and willing herself into the role, and the shoe wasn't glass. It was a silver Manolo Blahnik.

"I don't like my feet," she says. "I'm not crazy about anybody's feet. But I have flat feet."

Liz Lemon sleeps in socks and tells Oprah she hates her feet. Robert

Carlock, who wrote for *S.N.L.* and now is co-show-runner of *30 Rock*, told me that Fey, too, is "not willing to have people see her feet. I come in to talk about scripts when she's getting pedicures and have been summarily dismissed." Jack McBrayer, the former Second City comic who plays Kenneth, the Goody Two-Shoes NBC page, laughs: "They're normal feet. She's just a loony bird."

Fey has unleashed her inner Sally Bowles, the role she played in a student production of *Cabaret* at the University of Virginia. (Yes, she sings, too, with what she calls "a birthday-party-quality voice.") Her makeover is the stuff of legend. The Hollywood agent Sue Mengers warned her pal Lorne Michaels that he simply could not bring Fey out of the writers' room and put her on-air for "Weekend Update."

"She doesn't have the looks," Mengers told him.

"Lorne brought her over to my house when she was head writer," Mengers recalls. "She was very mousy. I thought, Well, they gotta be having an affair. But they weren't. He just appreciated her talent. And now, suddenly, she's become this sexy, showing-tit, hot-looking woman. I said to Lorne, 'What the fuck did she do?'"

Far from holding Mengers's brutal candor against her, Tina spent the Friday night before the Emmys hanging at Mengers's house, thanked her when she won, and came back with Jeff the next day for a celebratory brunch. "She's quietly smart," Mengers says. "You know that she doesn't miss anything, right down to the buckle on your shoe."

Fey's father (the German side) is an affable Clint Eastwood look-alike who loves reading books about comedy and often drives up from the Philly area to visit Tina and Alice on the set. (His artwork fills their apartment.) Fey's acerbity comes from her mother (the Greek side), who has what Richmond calls "drag-queen humor—that bitter, extremely caustic kind of stab-you-in-the-heart humor." Mrs. Fey played a weekly poker game with her friends. "I loved hanging out with the ladies, because they were very funny, and a little bit mean, and had lots of Entenmann's products," Fey says. There's an additional legacy: "Because of the Greek-girl thing, I have, like, boobs and butt," so "I only have two speeds—either matronly or a little too slutty. I have to be steered away from cheetah print."

30 Rock features many shots of Liz Lemon's younger life, when she looks like a nerd in goofy clothes and frizzy hair. "I really wasn't heavy in high school," Fey recalls over lunch one afternoon at Café Luxembourg, where she dutifully switches her order from a B.L.T. to a salad. "But no one feels right in their own skin, particularly in high school." Her love life in school was, she says, a "famine": "I really didn't have very many dates at all. And that's not an exaggeration. But also, I don't think we should discount the fact that unplucked eyebrows and short hair with a perm may not have been the best offering, either." Liz Lemon tells Oprah on *30 Rock* that she was a virgin until she was 25. Tina Fey confesses much the same to me, noting, "I remember bringing people over in high school to play—that's how cool I am—that game Celebrity. That's how I successfully remained a virgin well into my 20s, bringing gay boys over to play Celebrity."

Adam McKay, the former *S.N.L.* head writer who hired Fey and taught her first improv class in Chicago, remembers one night when a bunch of comics were having drinks after a performance at the Upright Citizens Brigade. "I asked her who she lost her virginity to and she blushed, and I said, 'Tina, I'm really surprised, who cares?'" He loved her "prim and proper" Philly reserve combined with the "chord of anger running through her humor," the way she could throw down the fastest, meanest joke referencing everything from Allen Ginsberg to poop and still be shy.

That prude/lewd split personality had already been defined during her adolescence in Upper Darby, a suburb of Philadelphia, where, Fey says, she had "a dash of high-school bitchy," as one of her *S.N.L.* skits described Palin. Her friend Damian Holbrook, a *TV Guide* writer who attended a nearby high school and whose first name she took for the gay character in *Mean Girls*, says she was like the Janis character in that movie, the sweet girl in an oversize Shaker sweater who didn't run with the cool crowd or strut around to get guys, yet had the wit to burn the mean girls if she wanted to. Fey liked to watch *The Love Boat* and old Gene Kelly movies; she was involved in choir, theater, and the newspaper, for which she wrote a tart, anonymous column under the byline "The Colonel." In middle school, she was a flutist, which came in handy for her imitation of Sarah Palin's beauty-contest skills. She didn't have great athletic ability but played tennis, and, citing Kay Cannon, says that team sports breed "a different kind of woman," with a "game-on, let's-do-it work ethic"; she hopes her daughter will grow up to play sports. ("I want Alice to play professional football.") She also wants her daughter to go through "a character-building puberty" with some frizzy, zit-filled years. ("It's going to be heartbreaking when we have to see that kid with a unibrow, when all that Greek stuff kicks in," Richmond observes.)

Liz Lemon favors her right side. That's because a faint scar runs across Tina Fey's left cheek, the result of a violent cutting attack by a stranger when Fey was five. Her husband says, "It was in, like, the front yard of her house, and somebody who just came up, and she just thought somebody marked her with a pen." You can hardly see the scar in person. But I agree with Richmond that it makes Fey more lovely, like a hint of Marlene Dietrich *noir* glamour in a Preston Sturges heroine.

"That scar was fascinating to me," Richmond recalls. "This is somebody who, no matter what it was, has gone through something. And I think it really informs the way she thinks about her life. When you have that kind of thing happen to you, that makes you scared of certain things, that makes you frightened of different things, your comedy comes out in a different kind of way, and it also makes you feel for people."

I wonder how the scar affected Fey in high school. "She wasn't Rocky Dennis developing a sense of humor because of her looks, like in *Mask*," says Damian Holbrook, laughing. Liz Lemon's blustery Republican boss, Jack Donaghy, played with comic genius by Alec Baldwin, tells Lemon, "I don't know what happened in your life that caused you to develop a sense of humor as a coping mechanism. Maybe it was some sort of brace or corrective boot you wore during childhood, but in any case I'm glad you're on my team."

Marci Klein—the cool, tall, blond executive producer of *30 Rock* and producer of *S.N.L.*, and the daughter of Calvin Klein—who was kidnapped for 10 hours when she was 11, remembers, "Tina said to me, 'Well, you know, Marci, we had the Bad Thing happen to us. We know what it's like.'"

Fey herself rarely mentions the episode. "It's impossible to talk about it without somehow seemingly exploiting it and glorifying it," she says. Did she feel less attractive growing up because of it? "I don't think so," she says.

"Because I proceeded unaware of it. I was a very confident little kid. It's really almost like I'm kind of able to forget about it, until I was on-camera, and it became a thing of 'Oh, I guess we should use this side' or whatever. Everybody's got a better side."

She used therapy to cope with her extremely fearful reaction to the anthrax attack at 30 Rock shortly after 9/11—the first time her co-workers had seen her vulnerable. The therapist talked to her about 9/11 and the anthrax delivered to Tom Brokaw's office, linking them to the crime against her when she was little. "It's the attack out of nowhere," Fey says. "Something comes out of nowhere, it's horrifying."

I asked her how the childhood attack affected her as a mother.

"Supposedly, I will go crazy," she replies evenly. "My therapist says, 'When Alice is the age that you were, you may go crazy.'"

Over coffee with Richmond, I ask him to describe Fey in her pre-glamour-puss days, back in Chicago. "She was quite round," he says, "in a lovely, turn-of-the-century kind of round—that beautiful, Rubenesque kind of beauty." And as for her clothes: "Things that didn't match. She used to wear crazy boots. She would wear just a lot of knee-length frumpy dresses with thrift-store sweaters and kind of what was comfortable. It still looked kind of cool on her. I used to get all my suits in thrift stores, because I realized I was the size of little old men who were dying." The five-foot-three-and-a-half Richmond says they bonded over hot veal sandwiches and their appreciation of "sarcastic humor and Garry Shandling shows."

Fey recalls she was at her heaviest in Chicago and, later, sitting at a desk at *S.N.L.* "I'm five four and a half, and I think I was maxing out at just short of 150 pounds, which isn't so big. But when you move to New York from Chicago, you feel really big. Because everyone is pulled together, small, and Asian. Everyone's Asian."

She saw herself on an *S.N.L.* monitor as an extra, "and I was like, 'Ooogh.' I was starting to look unhealthy. I looked like a behemoth, a little bit. It was probably a bad sweater or something. Maybe cutting from Gwyneth Paltrow to me." She wanted to be "PBS pretty"—pretty for a smart writer. She called

Jeff, who was directing a show at Second City in Chicago, and said, "O.K., I'm starting Weight Watchers."

Fey says, "I got to that thing that's so enjoyable where people tell you, 'Oh, you're thin, you've gotten too thin.' Lorne was like, 'Please, please make sure you're eating.'" McKay recalls Fey telling a story about her heavier days. "Steve Martin walked right past her at the coffee table, and then, after the makeover, he was like, 'Well, hel-looo—who are you?'"

The newly svelte Fey took over the "Weekend Update" anchor desk with Jimmy Fallon and made her name writing zingers for herself and jokes for Fallon, like this one about Demi Moore going with Ashton Kutcher: "Actress Demi Moore turned 40 on Tuesday, but she feels like a 25-year-old inside."

30 Rock made its debut in 2006, with *Washington Post* critic Tom Shales acidly noting that Fey was "not Orson Welles." I ask Baldwin if he coached Fey, whose acting background was improv and "Weekend Update," on how to do longer-form comedy. No, he says, only on what Richmond dryly calls "knockers shots." "I would say things to her, never giving advice: she's a woman you don't easily give advice to—she's very self-reliant. I'd say to her, 'You know, you're a really beautiful girl. You've got to play that. It's a visual medium. This is not Upright Citizens Brigade, where we're doing sketch comedy at nine o'clock at night on a Sunday for a bunch of drunken college graduate students. You are a very attractive woman and you've got to work that. You've got to pop one more button on that blouse and you've got to get that hair done and you've got to go! Glamour it up.'"

Ah, I say, so you're the one who encouraged Fey to wear so many low-cut tops, even though Lemon seems like the crewneck-sweater type. "There is Liz Lemon and there is Liz Lemon as portrayed by a leading actress in a TV show," Baldwin responds with amused and amusing disdain. "It's not a documentary. Tina's a beautiful girl. We needed to get the pillows fluffed on the sofa and we needed to get the drapes steamed, and we needed to get everything all nice and get the presentation just right. Tina always played the cute, nerdy girl. Tina on the news, the glasses. There was not a big glamour quotient for her. Now there is.

"The collective consciousness has said, 'Tina, *dahling*, where have you been? Where on earth have you been?'"

30 Rock struggled at first. The network made Fey drop her old friend Rachel Dratch from one of the leads, and the show was locked in a sibling rivalry with NBC's other show-within-a-show, Aaron Sorkin's *Studio 60 on the Sunset Strip*. Fey lured the viewers she craved only when she started moonlighting on *S.N.L.* as the look-alike Alaska governor who sometimes talks, as Fey puts it, as if she's lost in a corn maze. Sarah Palin's debut left conservative men salivating—"Babies, guns, Jesus: hot damn!" Rush Limbaugh thundered—and left Fey little choice. There had not been such a unanimous national casting decision since Clark Gable as Rhett Butler in *Gone with the Wind*. Besides, she and Michaels knew it could be good for *30 Rock* and *S.N.L.* Her Palin mimicry—with sketches written mainly by Seth Meyers—convulsed the nation and propelled *S.N.L.* into relevance again. The show got its biggest ratings since Nancy Kerrigan hosted in 1994, after having had her leg busted up by Tonya Harding's henchman.

Even the pros were blown away by Fey. "I've never seen a better impression," the *S.N.L.* master of the art, Darrell Hammond, says. "If they put those two on a sonar, they would match up electronically." Jon Stewart—her "Dear Diary," as she calls it, teenage crush (replacing Danny Kaye) from his days at *Short Attention Span Theater* on Comedy Central—told *The New York Times*'s Bill Carter that Fey "had the single best line of this campaign year," one she wrote herself and delivered in the role of Palin during the debate: "I believe marriage is a sacred institution between two unwilling teenagers."

I n October, it seemed that Tina Fey *was* the campaign, with journalists writing that she had "swift-butted" Palin and derailed her future. Two weeks before the election, Fey's Palin and Palin's Palin met cute: the two women walked past each other wordlessly in *S.N.L.*'s opening sketch. As cast member Casey Wilson, standing next to a giggling Secret Service agent backstage, looked at Palin on a monitor raising the roof to Amy Poehler's racy Wasilla rap, she blurted out, "Oh, my God!" Watching a parade consisting of Mark Wahlberg, a donkey, Palin, and her Secret Service agents, a visiting screenwriter observed, "This is like a Fellini movie."

The McCain camp was on hand to ride herd, cutting out Poehler's rap line about how, in the Palins' bedroom, it's "drill, baby, drilla."

There were passionate arguments leading up to Palin's appearance. Some connected with the show did not want to give the Alaska governor a platform. Neither did bloggers on the Huffington Post. "The people on the left were like, 'No, you can't do that!'" Fey recalls. "And it's like, 'We don't work for you.'" The famously liberal Baldwin also found that line of liberal reasoning silly, saying he was outraged that commenters on the Huffington Post compared Palin to David Duke: "Palin came there to get thrown in the dunk tank. She knew it and she was gracious."

Still, the debate raged about the politics of Sarah Palin's appearance on *S.N.L.* Did it help her? Did it hurt her? Was it demeaning to politics? Were late-night shows determining the election? Should a comedian care? (Similar questions had arisen after Fey's "Weekend Update" comment about Hillary Clinton: "Bitch is the new black.") After weeks of appearing on *S.N.L.* as Palin, Fey opted to minimize the onstage interaction when the real Palin finally showed up, and despite reams of speculation the reason wasn't fundamentally political. "Tina was agonizing about it, and I'm drawn to anybody who agonizes about things," says her friend Conan O'Brien. "She told me, 'When I fly, I don't like to meet the pilot.' On the one hand, she knew: It's my job to sort of go after this person in a way, but at the same time I know when I meet her, she's a human being and a mom. She's not the Devil incarnate or Antichrist."

After the mock and real Palins do their walk-by—in identical red jackets and black skirts the *S.N.L.* seamstresses whipped up for the two women, with flag pins provided by Palin—Fey seems relieved. She changes and comes back to the small room offstage where Lorne Michaels's guests are hanging out. There are some drinks on ice by the monitor in Lorne's cubbyhole, and Fey has a glass of white wine in a plastic cup. "At least I can have one of these now," she says, smiling, to Jeff Zucker, the NBC president, who crows that she is "the hottest thing in American culture." She's wearing a purple-and-white checked Steven Alan shirt, and black Seven for All Mankind pants. She has taken off her Palin-streaked beehive wig, and her dark-brown hair is pulled back in a thick ponytail. She looks like a really pretty graduate student, and she has a soft voice and reserve that Matthew Broderick says cause people to "lean in to her." (Like Daisy Buchanan, except her voice is full of funny rather than money.) She says the moments with Palin—which she has been dreading because it has been an ugly week on the Republican campaign, and because you don't like to meet someone you're "goofing" on— have gone fine. "She asked me where my daughter was," Fey says. (Alice had been there earlier at the rehearsal, pointing at the monitor showing Palin and thinking it was somehow her mommy, even though Mommy was with her.) "She said Bristol could have babysat."

Fey chats about the election for a moment, wondering if Obama could be "another Jimmy Carter." She tells Zucker, who is leaning against the wall, taking it all in, that she hasn't yet called her "Republican parents" to see how they feel about tonight's skit. Later, she tells me, "I grew up in a family of Republicans. And when I was 18 and registering to vote, my mom's only instruction was 'You just go in and pull the big Republican lever.' That's my welcome to adulthood. She's like, 'No, don't even read it. Just pull the Republican lever.'" (Fey made a call to arrange for Richmond's excited Republican parents and sister to meet Palin at a rally in Erie, Pennsylvania.)

Although some considered it a missed comedic opportunity, Fey says she didn't want to do what Jim Downey, the burly writer who has done many of *S.N.L.*'s renowned political skits, calls "a classic sneaker-upper" with Palin. "I just didn't want to have to do the impression at the same time with her," she said. "One, it would shine a light on the inaccuracies of the impression, and, two, it's just always . . . the only word I can think of is 'sweaty.' It just always feels sweaty."

Two weeks after the appearance with Palin, Fey does another scorchingly funny Palin skit, this time with John McCain, a bit where Fey's Palin goes "rogue" and starts selling "Palin in 2012" T-shirts on QVC. "A man running for president of the United States onstage with a woman playing his running mate—isn't that a great moment in our country's history?," Lorne Michaels says in wonder as he leaves 30 Rock, wading through a throng of reporters, at 1:30 a.m. Adam McKay, Will Ferrell's writing partner in Hollywood, wrote the *S.N.L.* sketch where Ferrell's fumbling W. gives Fey's flirtatious Palin an endorsement. "It is the most ridiculous, borderline-dangerous thing that the Republican vice-presidential nominee happened to look like the funniest woman working in America," McKay says. "What if the next Republican presidential nominee looks exactly like Seth Rogen?"

Around the same time, Fey saw an entertainment reporter on TV say that Palin had been gracious toward Fey, but Fey hadn't been gracious toward Palin. "What made me super-mad about it," Fey says later, "was that it seemed very sexist toward me and her. The implication was that she's so fragile, which she is not. She's a strong woman. And then, also, it was sexist because, like, who would ever go on the news and say, 'Well, I thought it was sort of mean to Richard Nixon when Dan Aykroyd played him,' and 'That seemed awful mean to George Bush when Will Ferrell did it.' And it's like, No, that's not the thing. This is a comedy sketch on a comedy show." "Mean," we agreed, was a word that tends to get used on women who do satirical humor and, as she says, "gay guys."

"I feel clean about it," she says. "All these jokes were fair hits."

When Fey and her clever band of writers conjure up Liz Lemon, her 21st-century Mary Tyler Moore New York career girl, they put in a lot of Rhoda-like neuroses and insecurity about looks and food jokes and epically bad dates—though this season she's upgraded to *Mad Men*'s sexy Jon Hamm, who plays a pediatrician who impresses Lemon with his love of pie-making documentaries and ice-cream makers. Liz is more like *Seinfeld*'s Elaine—bossy/awkward on the outside and meek/insecure at her core—than *The Mary Tyler Moore Show*'s poised Mary Richards. Fey borrows much of the material from her own life and her writers' and actors' lives, and then heightens it. Baldwin's character has an obsessive relationship with an ex, and hers dates a little person she had initially mistaken for a child. Richmond wonders serenely if he inspired it.

Lemon noshes on "off-brand" Mexican cheese curls called "Sabor de Soledad"—"taste of solitude." When forced to choose between a great man and a great sandwich, she puts the sandwich first. "No one has it harder in this country today than women," Liz complains to her friend Jenna. "It turns out we can't be president. We can't be network news anchors. Madonna's arms look crazy."

But in her own life, Fey is the stable one, just as Mary Richards was on TV, anchored among oddballs in her Minneapolis newsroom. Outside her comedy, Fey does not want drama. When I ask her if she ever gets the urge to straighten out Lindsay Lohan, who starred in Fey's movie *Mean Girls*, or to counsel Tracy Morgan or Alec Baldwin when they hit tempestuous passages in their personal lives, she says, "I have no enabler bone in my body—not one. I'm sort of like, 'Oh, are you going crazy? I'll be back in an hour.'" She is the Obedient Daughter, the German taskmistress, the kind but firm maker and keeper of rules. And what Tina wants, Tina gets, sooner or later, because she works and works and works for it.

So what does she do with what she calls her "15 minutes," now that she's got America's attention and a $5 million deal for a humor book?

Her manager, David Miner, whom she met when he was in the coatroom at Second City, has no doubt she'll continue to call on the way up to his office and get a latte for his assistant. "She never looks at the world and says, 'Give me this,'" he says. "She adapts and rolls up her sleeves."

She'd like to "mono-task" for a change and pull *30 Rock* into syndication. She'd like a slightly bigger apartment, so they can entertain more. (Jeff cooks *and* sews.) "I feel like the window is closing—I'm 38," she says about having more kids. "Obviously you want the best chance of the baby being healthy, and I think with our life and jobs right as they are at this moment, it doesn't seem possible. It's the year after the baby comes that is like someone hitting you every day in the face with a hammer."

Fey's idea of an ideal day off is still the same: she and Jeff take Alice to the playground and go to the Neptune Room, a fish place around the corner, or the Shake Shack on the Upper West Side for shakes and burgers and fries.

Everybody wants to be Tina Fey, I tell her. Who do you want to be?

"I don't want to be somebody else," she says.

And why would she?

THE
WHITE
HOUSE

BARBARA'S BACKLASH

By Marjorie Williams | August 1992

E ven Barbara Bush's stepmother is afraid of her. Over the course of a half-hour interview, Willa Pierce, the South Carolina painter the First La-dy's widowed father married in 1952, hasn't commented on anything much more controversial than her famous stepdaughter's shoe size. But now, in a quavering voice, she is re-evaluating her decision to say anything at all.

"I could get in so much trouble if I said something she didn't agree with," the elderly widow says pleadingly. "Because you know how she is: she knows how she wants to appear to the world."

Indeed: Barbara Bush is America's grandmother, casual, capable, down-to-earth; she is fake pearls and real family. "I'm not a competitive person," she once said, "and I think women like me because they don't think I'm compet-itive, just nice." She bakes cookies, knits, needlepoints. She is funny, but mostly at her own expense. She is a woman so modest that she writes in the voice of a dog.

At a time when George Herbert Walker Bush has slid almost fifty points in most polls in a little more than a year, Barbara Bush stands as close to uni-versal popularity as any figure in American life. Her approval rating is forty, even fifty points higher than her husband's, and she gets as many as eight thousand letters a month. Aides call her "the National Treasure"—"the treasure" for short—in sly tribute to the qualities that make her an awesome asset to her husband.

The First Lady's hard work on causes ranging from AIDS to illiteracy has been justly praised, but it has also helped to obscure the void of the Bush domestic policy with a theater of activism. She is, first and foremost, her husband's alter ego, charged with showing his compassion in the areas that an aide merrily summarizes as "poverty, pain, and degradation, basically."

"In the thirty-some years I've been around American politics, she's far and away the greatest political spouse I've seen," says political strategist Edward J. Rollins, one of the managers of [independent presidential candidate] Ross Perot's campaign. And her help has never been more important than at the current moment, when political advisers to Bush have taken to joking that every one of the president's speeches should include the phrase "Barbara and I . . ."

It is an extra stroke of luck for the president that the Democrats' answer to Barbara Bush is Hillary Clinton. "I'll take a matchup between George and Barbara Bush and Bill and Hillary Clinton any day," says a senior Bush adviser. "People like Barbara Bush. And people don't like Hillary Clinton." Even if Ross Perot, not Bill Clinton, proves to be the greater threat to Bush's re-election, Margot Perot seems unlikely to divert much attention from the symbolic face-off between her more famous counterparts. Republican strategists will be working overtime to remind us that the Arkansas governor's controversial wife is the perfect foil for the First Lady's image as the embodiment of all cardinal virtues.

It is an image that has been perfectly honed through almost four years at the White House. "Short of ax murder," says former Bush spokeswoman Sheila Tate, "I think she could get away with anything. She's so benign."

Then why are people so scared of her?

Current and former associates inevitably set anonymity as the price of any statement at variance with the myth.

"People always said Nancy Reagan would kill you if you said bad stuff about her," says one staff aide who worked closely with the Bushes during his vice presidency. "But I always thought Mrs. Bush was the one who would kill you. . . . No one sat around and gossiped about Mrs. Bush. I don't think it was that people loved her; I think everyone was scared of her. It was just like when your mother said, 'I have eyes in the back of my head.'"

People who have worked with the Bushes use words and phrases like "difficult" . . . "tough as nails" . . . "demanding" . . . "autocratic." A 1988-campaign staffer recalls that "when she frowned it had the capacity to send shudders through a lot of people."

And one longtime associate explained his refusal to talk—even to describe his most positive feelings about Mrs. Bush—by saying, straight-faced, "I don't want to be dead. . . . I really like her, but I don't go anywhere near her."

Some of the fear she inspires is a function of her position: no one wants to piss off a president by crossing his wife. But the widespread apprehension that Barbara Bush creates is also a fear of the woman herself.

The same reporters who spin misty reports of Barbara Bush toiling in soup kitchens discuss a different reality among themselves: the flinty stare she fixes on the source of a question she doesn't like; the humorous dig; the chilly put-down. For behind her rampart of pearls, the nation's most self-effacing celebrity is in fact a combative politician. Always there, not far below the surface, is the Barbara Bush who briefly emerged in 1984 to denounce Geraldine Ferraro as "that $4 million—I can't say it, but it rhymes with 'rich.'"

This Barbara Bush has a brilliant grasp of image, and has always understood a chief source of her appeal: that she is—as folks in Washington never tire of pointing out—Not Nancy [Reagan].

During inaugural week in 1989 she made unmistakable digs at her predecessor, especially by spoofing her own new clothes: "Please notice—hairdo, makeup, designer dress," she said at one event. "Look at me good this week, because it's the only week."

Washington lapped it up—despite the fact that Barbara Bush had been wearing makeup, designer dresses, and "hairdos" for years. True, her earlier instincts had run to shirtwaists and circle pins. But by the time George Bush became president, his wife was a faithful customer of Arnold Scaasi and Bill Blass. Similarly, she has commissioned interior designer Mark Hampton to work on every house in which the Bushes have lived since 1981, both private and official.

Yet, today, she has successfully established her image as one too down-to-earth for fashion. "Personally, I think she's tougher than Nancy, but in a much more sophisticated way. . . . She's a pretty slick lady," says one sharp-eyed former Reagan aide, who counts such details as the $1,245 Judith Leiber bag that was a gift from the designer.

While she has excelled by poking fun at herself—her hair, her age, her waistline—aides have learned that they cannot count on this self-abasement: the First Lady is not amused when someone else tries to inject this note into a speech written for her.

Barbara Bush controls her press more tightly than Nancy Reagan ever dreamed of doing. She uses publicity to good effect when she sees an opportunity to deliver a useful message. In one of her first public events as First Lady, for example, she arranged to be photographed holding an AIDS baby, to convey the message that the disease can't be contracted through casual contact.

But she almost never sits down alone with news reporters who cover the White House regularly. Instead, she speaks to them a few times a year over ladylike luncheons in the family quarters, where they feel constrained by her hospitality. Reporters are social creatures, too, and are far less likely to lob a hostile question over the zucchini soup. (Mrs. Bush declined to be interviewed for this article, and most of her family, including her children, followed suit.)

Privately, she is a caustic and judgmental woman, who has labored to keep her sarcasm in check—with incomplete success. And once she notes a soft spot, says a longtime associate, "she hangs on forever. She never, ever, ever, ever lets go. She can just get under your skin and needle you."

"I mean," elaborates a former aide, "she's a good person, she talks about AIDS and stuff. But she's not this nice person."

One Washington regular—the second wife of a prominent man—tells of meeting the First Lady at a recent party. Mrs. Bush, who had a slight friendship with the man's first wife, seemed "hostile" to the couple, "her vibes, the look on her face, everything. . . . She looked at me, and if looks could kill, I'd be dead," the woman relates. Hoping at least to make the conversation smooth, the second wife mentioned a mutual acquaintance, a Bush-family friend. She had met him, she said, through political circles, and had supported him in a recent, unsuccessful bid for office.

"Well," retorted the First Lady, "that is undoubtedly why he lost."

On a personal level, she can be domineering. Aides, old friends, even family members give eerily similar accounts of her offering unsolicited advice on appearance: "You've got to do something about your hair," she told one aide; to another, who had just grown a mustache, she said, "Has George seen that? Shave it off!" She is full of admonitions about smoking, now that she has given it up, and diet—especially diet.

Peggy Stanton, a friend from the years when Bush served in Congress, remembers being embarrassed at lunches of the congressional wives' club. "I was a pretty healthy eater, and Bar would say, 'Now, watch Peggy, she's going up for her third helping.' Which was true, but I didn't necessarily want the world to know."

"You're too fat," Barbara tells her younger brother, Scott Pierce, when he puts on weight. And when Bush was vice president, according to an aide, Barbara boiled over one day at the sight of the staffers eating junk food on Air Force Two. "She said we were all fat, we all ate too much, and from then on we would only get fruit and so on," a change that was instituted immediately.

The more people talk about Barbara Bush, the more confusing grows the disjunction between the image and the woman. Two apparently contradictory threads run through her history. The first is her rigorous fealty to the gender roles of her day. And the second is the clear force of her personality—the commanding will that has been diverted and disguised, but never extinguished, by her life as the humble helpmate of George Herbert Walker Bush. The two threads of her life come together in an uneasy suspicion that she has paid a heavy price for the image she has lived.

I f this is Tuesday, it must be Miami Beach. Clean white limousines are packed like Chiclets at the curb of the convention center, where a thousand loyal Republicans have gathered to salute First Lady Barbara Bush as "National Statesman of the Year." They have forked over a little more than $800,000 to their state party, in amounts ranging from $500 to $10,000, for the privilege of eating a chicken dinner in her presence.

At seven o'clock they are herded into a curtained-off area of the huge exhibition space, its concrete floor and cavernous ceiling wanly cheered by a few potted ferns draped in Christmas lights. Like all political dinners, this one is interminable, with a dozen separate speeches, an invocation, the Pledge of Allegiance, a twelve-piece band, and a rendering of "God Bless America" by a choir of overmiked children.

The First Lady has been up since 5:30 in the morning, and has already flown to San Antonio (for a lunch-hour fund-raiser) and then back East to Miami. But to judge by her facial expressions, greatly magnified on a huge video monitor suspended over the crowd, she would rather be spending this night with a thousand rich Florida strangers in an echoing exhibition hall than spend it anywhere else on earth. She rewards every speaker's peroration with emphatic nods of agreement; she traverses even the dullest bits with her attentive, First Lady–listening expression firmly in place.

And these men do talk. The hour is ticking past 9:30 when Barbara Bush finally rises to speak.

She is *over-whelmed* by this whole evening, she tells the crowd.

She thanks the priest for his *bee-ooo-ti-ful* prayer.

She comments on the *won-der-ful* music.

She does so in a rich, cultured, carefully modulated voice that is still soaked, after forty-five years of Texas and politics, in the affluent air of her childhood. A slight shock attends anything she says: for all the familiarity of her image, you suddenly realize that you have almost no memory of hearing her voice. It is one of the chief requirements of her job that she say as few genuinely memorable things as possible.

"I've known for years that I was the luckiest woman in the world," she says. "I do have the most marvelous husband, children, and grandchildren. We live in the greatest country in the world. And tonight you have honored me with such a great honor," she says. "I don't deserve it. Of course I'm going to accept it, but I don't deserve it."

To some degree, Barbara Bush's persona is a simple function of beautiful manners. I have watched her over and over in these First Lady tableaux: at a

White House tea, cuddling a child who has a brain tumor; in New Hampshire, choking down yet another chicken breast at a Keene senior citizens' center; at the home of a grandmother in D.C.'s drug corridor, where she escorted the Queen of England—and where she actually made good enough small talk to bridge the gap between the hostess and her royal visitor.

Her exigent private manner is balanced, in public, by a universal graciousness. The only way to reconcile these two facets of Barbara Bush is to understand her as a woman of her class: the American social stratum that has always raised its children to assume their own superiority—and also to mask that assumption at all times.

Her roots are in Rye, New York, the kind of town that imparts an unconscious confidence: not quite so rich as Greenwich, Connecticut, just up the way, where George Bush was raised, but secure and Waspy and well-to-do.

The Pierces lived on Onondaga Street, in a five-bedroom brick house almost at the border of the Apawamis gold club. They didn't have a fortune, but they had a large social inheritance: Pauline Pierce was the daughter of an Ohio Supreme Court justice, and Marvin, a member of a once wealthy Pennsylvania iron clan, was a distant relative of President Franklin Pierce.

"We weren't rich" compared with some of the neighbors, says Scott Pierce, who still lives in Rye. "But we were certainly upper-middle-class."

Barbara, the third of four children, had a caustic tongue even as a child. June Biedler, who was one of Barbara's best friends, remembers her as "very articulate, very witty," and as "kind of a gang leader." When the girls boarded the school bus in the morning, "Barbara would have decided 'Let's not speak to June today.' Or Barbara would decide 'Let's not speak to Posy today,' and so the rest of us would obediently follow along and give that person a miserable time. And I don't remember that there was ever a 'Let's not speak to Barbara today' arrangement." Biedler stresses today that she loves and admires Barbara Bush, and believes that her friend grew up to be a kind and generous woman. But as a teenager, she recalls, "I thought Barbara was really mean and sarcastic." Among other things, she teased Biedler about her painful childhood stammer.

This cruelty, Biedler suggests, may have been the result of having "a mother that was a little mean to her." Pauline Pierce was a beautiful woman, but an exacting observer of social status. She was rather humorless, "austere," according to Biedler; "formal," in Scott Pierce's memory. She was particularly critical of Barbara, according to Donnie Radcliffe's biography, *Simply Barbara Bush*. In several of the stories Barbara tells of her childhood, one makes out Pauline's unpleasant concern that her younger daughter—a big girl, who by the age of twelve was five feet eight inches and weighed 148 pounds—might not cut it in the marriage market.

For her junior year in high school, Barbara followed her sister, Martha, to Ashley Hall, a genteel ladies' prep school in Charleston, South Carolina, the kind of place where a chaperone accompanied the girls to dances at the Citadel.

As photos attest, she had by then developed into a slim and pretty teenager, with pale skin and large, dark eyes. She was "at her prettiest," muses Biedler, "probably in her early twenties or in her late teens," but even then "she always had somebody who was prettier, like her sister." Martha, five years older, was devastating competition, a knockout who during college appeared on the cover of *Vogue*. Rosanne M. (Posy) Clarke, one of Barbara's friends, remembers that Martha "was gorgeous—tall and skinny and beautiful. Barbara . . . was pretty, but Martha was glamour."

Barbara was far closer to her father, a well-liked, genial man, than to her mother. From these parents, she learned her earliest lessons in gender politics, a model of how moms rule the roost but dads win the popularity contests. "Mother was kind of the glue of the family," says Scott Pierce, "although my dad was the one everybody admired."

By 1941, the year Barbara turned sixteen, Marvin Pierce was nearing the top of McCall Corp., publisher of *McCall's* and *Redbook*, among other magazines. The company's flagship magazine, which his younger daughter read avidly in her dorm room, had by then developed the blueprint of her life. Amid cautionary tales about women who were not humble or kind or careful enough to land and keep a man, ads advised that the goal of life was to tie the knot ("She's engaged! She's lovely! She uses Pond's!").

Within weeks of Pearl Harbor, while home from school on Christmas break, Barbara met her destiny. It was at a dance at the Round Hill Club in Greenwich, the kind of tame affair designed so that boys home from Taft and Andover and Deerfield could practice their mating calls on suitable girls home from Miss Porter's and Saint Tim's.

Barbara and George Bush, only sixteen and seventeen years old, locked onto each other with a striking seriousness, an intense mixture of teenage crush and wartime gravity that is almost unimaginable today. Three years would go by before the wedding, but the outcome was never seriously in doubt.

Most of their friends are at a loss when asked what so quickly cemented this couple. The answer often boils down to social class—that they were, as George's redoubtable mother put it, "sensible and well suited to each other."

On her side, there was the glamour of his enlistment, his string-bean handsomeness, his reputation as a big man on the Andover campus. "He was a real catch," emphasizes Posy Clarke. "He was terribly attractive—this young naval officer—and the Bush family was certainly prestigious."

On his side, the most intriguing account comes from his brother Jonathan, who once said, "She was wild about him. And for George, if anyone wants to be wild about him, it's fine with him."

Barbara went—again in Martha's footsteps—to Smith, but even while she attended classes she seemed hardly there at all. "She was different from the rest of us in that her destiny was already fixed," says Margaret Barrett, a roommate. "Her whole life was bound up in [George]." She made plans to return sophomore year but canceled at the last minute, in August, dropping out for good. "I was just interested in George," Barbara has said.

They married, with all the trimmings, while he was home on leave in January 1945. Their plan was that after the war he would take up his education at Yale, and she would take up the life of his young bride. They honeymooned on Sea Island, Georgia, where George dashed off a magisterial bulletin to his sister, Nancy: "Married life exceeds all expectations. Barbara is a fine wife!"

"It was a real storybook romance," says Posy Clarke in wry summary.

"They married and went to New Haven, and she worked her tail off the rest of her life."

Meet Mr. and Mrs. Bush, the Wasp patriarch and wife: He is lanky and spare, with sharp bones and a youthful hardness to his jaw, graying but still handsome. She, though, is lined and bowed, snow-topped, spreading at the middle. So unfair, what nature can do to men and women, and what society makes of the results.

By the time George and Barbara Bush reached their early forties, she was conscious of the disparity in their looks. Over time she tried different strategies for dealing with this painful contract—including, for a while, unsuccessfully dyeing her hair—until finally she settled on a rollicking self-satire that firmly beat observers to the punch.

These days, no one admits to being among the advisers and hangers-on who once carped about her looks (Can't we do something about Barbara?). Each and every one of her courtiers understood all along how fabulously refreshing she was. The White House had the power to turn her hair from gray to "silver," and her style from matronly to "natural."

And still, the contrast between her and her husband remains, insistently pointing to another possibility: that she is his picture of Dorian Gray, the one who wears the life they have lived together.

"She's tougher than he is," runs the standard refrain of friends and aides of George and Barbara Bush. For decades, going back almost to the start of their marriage, Barbara bore the hardest parts of this couple's lot.

The division of the burdens was subtle initially, not untypical of family life in the late forties and early fifties. In almost every account of their first years together in Texas, George Bush is out doing and being—starting his own company, raising money back East, enjoying what he would always describe nostalgically as a great adventure. And Barbara is living a parallel life of grinding hard work.

In the first six years of their marriage they moved at least eleven times, first in the service, then to New Haven, and then out West, into the oil business: from Odessa, Texas, to Huntington Park, California, Bakersfield to

Whittier to Ventura to Compton, then back to Texas, where they settled in Midland. Over fourteen years Barbara bore six children: George, Robin, Jeb, Neil, Marvin, and Dorothy.

For long periods Barbara managed the family alone, while George traveled. "I remember Mom saying she spent so many lonely, lonely hours with us kids," the Bushes' daughter Doro told Ann Grimes, author of the book *Running Mates*. "I can understand how she felt. She did it all. She brought us up."

"The kids were much more afraid of their mother than their father, I think," says Susan Morrison, who got to know the family well as a press secretary during the 1980 campaign. "If she said it, it went. And if he said it, maybe there was a way around it." His natural aversion to conflict, his great eagerness to be liked, made him the quintessential good cop; her basic toughness, her acid wit and strong will, made her the perfect disciplinarian.

As with Barbara's parents, Mother was the glue, and Dad was the fun.

To this day, says one who knows the family well, "he uses her to throw some bombs, while he sits back and calms the waters."

The greatest burden of Barbara's young life, though, was the death of her second child, Robin, at the age of three. Here, too, one can see the Bushes dividing roles in a way that assigned Barbara the more painful tasks.

In the spring of 1953, Robin, then the Bushes' only daughter, was diagnosed as having leukemia. "You should take her home, make life as easy as possible for her, and in three weeks' time, she'll be gone," the doctor told the Bushes.

But this was not their style. Instead they flew Robin to New York, where George's uncle was a big wheel at Memorial Hospital, and where doctors from the Sloan-Kettering Institute agreed to treat her aggressively. They managed to gain seven months of life.

At almost exactly the time of Robin's diagnosis George had begun a new business partnership, hugely increasing his business stakes, and the demands of his work presented a welcome escape. It was Barbara who sat with Robin every day in the hospital, she who was a daily witness to her daughter's pain, the torment of treatment with drugs and needles. She laid down the law: no crying in front of the girl, who was not to know how sick she was. Thomas "Lud" Ashley, a Yale friend of George Bush's, was then living in New York and saw a lot of Barbara during the ordeal. "It was the most remarkable performance of that kind I've ever seen," he says. "It took its toll. She was very human later, after the death. But not until then."

Only twenty-eight years old, she was alone when she made the final decision of her daughter's life: while the prognosis was hopeless, the doctors offered a chance to arrest the internal bleeding caused by all the drugs Robin had been given. It was a risky operation, but might buy more time. George, who was on his way to New York, couldn't be reached.

George's uncle advised against the surgery, but Barbara decided to go ahead. Thirty-six years later, she cried when talking to a reporter about this lonely decision. Robin never came out of the operation, though George reached the hospital before she died.

In defining herself solely as a wife and mother, Barbara Bush was like millions of other women of her generation, sold on a romantic vision of domesticity. Even so, she seems to have pursued the whole package more emphatically than most, working at homemaking like the strong-willed woman she is. "Bar was the leader of the pack," says Marion Chambers, a friend from Barbara's Midland years. "She set the example for us." Her children had the best, most elaborate birthday parties in the neighborhood, as well as the most carefully nametagged clothes. Her house was spotless; others felt, in contrast, like slackers.

She ground her teeth at night and smoked Newports by the pack.

Every year, a week before Christmas, she made an elaborate gift of cookies to her friends' children—a decorative packet for each child, containing a differently shaped cookie for each day before Christmas; the idea was to tie it onto the tree so the child could work his or her way toward the big day. She also threw herself into charity work, the hospital, the local women's league.

Above all, her rule was to accommodate her husband. "The one thing she made sure of was that George Bush was comfortable—she's been very clear about that," says Susan Morrison. At first glance this, too, seems an unremarkable policy for a woman of Barbara Bush's generation. But women who have known her in different stages of their married life say that she went even further to cater to her husband than most of her peers did in their marriages.

"She was very thoughtful of him in every way," says Peggy Stanton, who befriended Barbara in the congressional wives' club after Bush was elected to Congress in 1966. "Probably more so than most of us . . . I just remember that she wouldn't impose on him in any way."

George Bush is famously frenetic, "desperate to be in constant motion," in the words of one of his oldest friends, FitzGerald Bemiss. His omnivorous sociability has meant constant hard work for his wife. Peter Teeley, a longtime adviser, says, "Look, he is very boyish in the sense that he would say, 'Let's have fifty people over this weekend, we'll serve 'em so-and-so and so-and-so,' and then not worry about how the food is going to be purchased, and who's going to get it there, and who's going to cook it, and so on. He'd say, 'Well, I've got to go golfing.' Or 'play tennis.' "

Barbara would sometimes grumble about this, but she never seemed to say no. By 1974, when other women were discovering the wounded, angry sister who had so often shadowed the bouncing figure in the women's magazines, Barbara could still send this description of her activities to the *Smith Alumnae Quarterly*: "I play tennis, do vol. work and admire George Bush!"

From the very beginning, George Bush's political career was simply a larger canvas on which to paint her domestic destiny. All that discipline she had; why, sacrifice was her middle name—of course she was happy to visit all 189 precincts in Harris County, Texas, in 1962, to help him win the post of Republican Party county chairman in his first race ever. By the time he ran for Congress, of course she would listen to the same speech, over and over and over and over, while madly needlepointing red, white, and blue patches bearing his name for the good ladies of Houston to sport on their purses.

Her iron manners, too, made her a champion political wife. Admiral Dan Murphy, who was Bush's first vice-presidential chief of staff, remembers sitting next to Barbara at an official dinner somewhere in Africa. "We had been warned by the doctors not to eat any salads, anything that hadn't been cooked. So I didn't, but she was going along eating the salad. I said, 'Mrs. Bush, the doctors told us we shouldn't eat things like that.' And she said, 'This is their country, and they're serving salad, so I'm going to eat it.' "

She soldiered her way through a losing Senate race, two terms in Congress, and a painful second Senate loss. She smiled at George Bush's side through his stints as Richard Nixon's ambassador to the U.N. and then as chairman of the Republican Party—though she had strongly counseled him to avoid the G.O.P. post, which was offered him in the midst of the Watergate cover-up. They spent fourteen months in Beijing, where he was special envoy to the People's Republic of China.

And suddenly, after their return to the U.S. in late 1975, she fell into a black depression—the only time that Barbara's will openly rebelled against Barbara's life.

would feel like crying a lot and I really, painfully hurt," she later told *U.S. News & World Report*. "And I would think bad thoughts, I will tell you. It was not nice."

In some interviews, she has attributed her depression to "a small chemical imbalance." In some, she laid it at the door of the women's movement, saying, "Suddenly women's lib had made me feel my life had been wasted."

But in others she has hinted that it was the classic mid-life crisis of the woman who had been raised to gain all her identity through the service of others, whose lives had now left the cozy orbit of her care. Not only was 1976 the year her youngest child, Doro, turned seventeen, but it also marked a devastating shift in her relationship with her husband.

She had suddenly gone from feast to famine. In Beijing, with the younger children off in boarding school, the Bushes were alone for the first time since their marriage, exploring their strange new world together. "I loved it there," she has said over and over. "I had George all to myself."

When he was called back to Washington to become director of the C.I.A., he was all at once in a job whose very nature reinforced the old divide in the Bushes' daily lives: this time, he couldn't talk about his job at night.

But if 1976 was the year Barbara's frustration reached a crisis, it was not the only time she expressed it. The Bushes' history is full of poignant references to her unrequited desire for his company.

Even if his work didn't draw him away from home, his frenzied social life did. "His attitude is 'If you want to see me, great, get your clubs.' I think she's constantly trying to make the marriage work that way," says a former aide.

"Do you think they ever sit alone and have dinner? I think she'd like that, but she knows it's never going to happen."

Barbara Bush took up golf last year, she told reporters, in the hope of spending more time with the president. But he declined to play with her—just as he had stopped playing tennis doubles with her years before, because he didn't think she was a good enough player.

In what one person on the scene described as a "pathetic" tableau, Barbara and her friend Betsy Heminway went "tagging after him" while he and three buddies played Kennebunkport's Cape Arundel Golf Club. As Maureen Dowd of *The New York Times* reported then, the president gleefully announced to the press that his wife's game "stunk."

"When the president, pressed by journalists, finally agreed to play with his wife, the disillusioned First Lady shot back, 'When? Just like he's going to garden with me one day.'"

"The joking wasn't pleasant," reports one person who saw the scene. "It wasn't fun, Nick-and-Nora repartee."

Even at times when the Bushes' lives meshed more closely, there was an undercurrent of insecurity in Barbara. "She was very aware that he was so young-looking," says a friend from the late sixties. By then Barbara was already hardening her defenses, beginning to make jokes that lanced the wound before someone else could press on it. "I noticed that years back, that she would joke about her appearance," says Peggy Stanton.

Bush often seems to treat Barbara more like a buddy than a wife. In public they present their relationship as a partnership that had transcended sex, entering the realm of teasing friendship. Last summer, on Barbara Bush's sixty-sixth birthday, the millionaire president gave her twenty pairs of Keds as a gift. When he was vice president, says a former aide, his advance teams would joke about having to remind him to open doors for her.

With other women, however—the dozens of attractive young women he meets in his work—George Bush is famously flirtatious. "A biiiiiig flirt," says a female former aide.

Rumors have circulated since 1980 that Bush has had extramarital affairs. But they are unlikely to be proved unless a party involved chooses to talk about it. All we can intuit, through outward signs, is Barbara Bush's long, more subtle struggle to remain as important a part of her husband's life as he has been of hers.

In this regard, his sporting relationships with his male buddies, his manic insistence on constant motion and the presence of crowds, seem as great a challenge as other women do. During the Thanksgiving weekend after his election, the Bushes invited the reporters covering them in Kennebunkport to come to the house for wine and cheese. When *USA Today* reporter Jessica Lee burbled her thanks to Barbara, the future First Lady responded grimly, "Don't thank me. Thank George Bush. He invited you." (In these moments of exasperation or pain she often refers to him by both his first and last names.)

"I think there's an essence of sadness about her, way deep down," says someone who has worked with Barbara Bush in politics. "Maybe a lot of who she is developed in reaction to sadness."

When her depression hit, she was not the type to deal with it introspectively. Her husband urged her to talk to someone about it, but her style was to tough it out. She was helped, paradoxically, by Bush's growing political ambitions. His entry into presidential politics opened up a new world, and a more expansive role for her beyond the threshold of their house. The higher George Bush rose, the more he needed Barbara in his political life.

In pictures taken of the early planning meetings for the '88 campaign, there are seven or eight advisers lounging around the pretty green living room of the Bushes' Kennebunkport home. In the background, intent on a jigsaw puzzle or a knitting project, hardly paying any attention at all, is Barbara Bush. She is doing what she once did as a young bride at Yale, sitting for long hours behind home plate while George played ball—keeping score.

This is the first of her two roles in his career: the watchful monitor of internal politics who judges each man and woman by the standard of his or her devotion to George Bush. This role is mysterious to almost everyone who works with Bush, for she is infinitely careful. Yet no one around them doubts that she has great power to influence her husband, especially in his views of people. Some go as far as to suggest that she is his number-one political adviser, "first among equals."

But at almost all times she maintains the ultra-traditional façade of the old-style political wife, who is there only to see to her husband's comfort. Aides and associates from every period of his political career hasten to explain that Barbara Bush is not Nancy Reagan. She does not carry her own agenda, or choose political goals for her husband; she doesn't muck around with policy or sit in on Cabinet meetings. Aides to Sam Skinner and John Sununu say that neither chief of staff, even in the most troubled passages of his tenure, heard often from the First Lady.

But every successful politician has a quasi-official "family" around him, an inner circle in which personality has a great impact on politics and policy. It is in this realm that Barbara Bush is influential. Here, staffers learn that Barbara is always "just within earshot, just out of sight," in the words of one campaign staffer. Courtiers tread very, very carefully in this domain, knowing, in the words of media adviser Roger Ailes, that "she wants what's best for her husband, and boy, she's strong."

Her second role in George Bush's career is a version of the role she played in their family life—the disciplinarian.

Bush is skilled at surrounding himself with others who will draw the heat away from him. Says Ed Rollins, "George Bush is a man who wants to be loved. As opposed to respected. It's very important to him that everybody like him." Thus Bush works harder than most at delegating the more unpleasant parts of his job.

In 1988, for example, Bush assigned the role of bad cop to Lee Atwater; for the first three years of his presidency, John Sununu played the heavy. (The effectiveness of having such a tool has become clearer than ever since December, when Sununu left. Lacking this essential foil, Bush has assigned the role piecemeal to various aides, as when spokesman Marlin Fitzwater was sent out to blame the Los Angeles riots on the programs of the Great Society. But because the men who now fill the White House seem too bland to personify evil, responsibility seems to get laid at Bush's door faster than it used to.)

On a subtler level, Bush has always cast family members in similar roles. Today his son George W. Bush plays the role of enforcer or executioner when a tough call must be made: it was the younger Bush, for example, who told Sununu that his time had run out.

And many suggest that, especially during a political race, Barbara plays a more light-handed version of the same role. "She definitely is the institutional memory of slights," says one former political staffer. "She is one distinct other level of the Praetorian Guard."

"I think George Bush has gotten a whole lot of mileage out of letting Bar be thought of as the heavy," says a former political associate. For example, several reporters have been casually told by the president, during one-on-one interviews, that Barbara was angry over something they wrote about him. "Look out, the Silver Fox is really mad at you . . . ," he'll say, effectively delivering the warning that the reporter's copy has offended, without having to risk any personal conflict himself with the reporter.

Whether Barbara's role is conscious and deliberate, or something that evolved wordlessly out of a long marriage, only the Bushes know. Some believe that it is more conscious on her part than on his. "She knows this man very, very well, and his strengths and weaknesses, and I think she probably compensates for his weaknesses," says Rollins. "She's probably a better judge of character than he is."

"I think she's much more judgmental about people than he is," says another longtime associate. "I think she really takes a bead on someone, and for good or for bad, you're in that box; she's got you pigeonholed."

It is widely believed in Washington that Barbara Bush got fed up with John Sununu earlier than her husband did. But "she's wily in that regard," says a former staffer. "She knows how things work, and if she doesn't want to read about what she did, she won't do it in that way."

Sometimes, however, her intercession is in a staffer's favor. When Transportation Secretary Sam Skinner took over from Sununu, one of his first instincts—clearly communicated, through the grapevine of leaks, to the newspapers—was to replace David Demarest as communications director. But Demarest kept his job—reportedly because Barbara defended him. "Word around the White House was she liked him a lot," says one senior White House aide. It was an important bureaucratic defeat for Skinner, contributing to an early perception that he couldn't follow up on his own intentions.

Typically, Barbara works at the margins, letting staffers know obliquely—

but unmistakably—when they are coming up short. In one legendary story, Barbara clipped the wings of Craig Fuller, chief of staff in Bush's second term as vice president. Word got back to her from friends and supporters around the country that Fuller was out of touch, hard to reach. So one day on Air Force Two, seeing him leaf through an inches-high stack of phone messages, she told him—in a voice carefully modulated to reach her husband—"Keep looking . . . you'll find a couple from me."

She uses humor, too, to keep staffers on their toes. In '88, she closely monitored the negative campaign tactics of Atwater and Ailes, because she was concerned they would bring too much criticism down on Bush. When Ailes entered a room in which she was present, she would sometimes greet him jovially, "Here's my bad boy." Coming from Barbara, it's hard to read as anything but a reminder: *I'm watching.*

If George Bush walks a fine line in his political tactics, Barbara is the line referee—making sure that he doesn't cut it too close. Aides expect her to have a large role in monitoring the propriety of the Bush campaign this fall. While she has not yet shown a strong influence on campaign strategy, she has expressed concern over how tight—and negative—a race is shaping up. Campaign operatives have been warned that the First Lady will not tolerate tactics so inflammatory that they will provoke retaliatory attacks on the Bush family—especially on her sons.

In talking about Barbara Bush's great influence, however, almost everyone agrees that its boundary is clear. All of her vigilance is directed solely to the greater glory of George Bush. Aides who have tried to draw her into the open on substantive matters have been firmly turned down. Deborah Steelman, Bush's adviser on domestic affairs in the '88 campaign, tried to draft Barbara Bush as an ally on issues like child care, health care, and early education. "It just was rebuffed, officially, at every turn," Steelman recalls. "You only had to do that to her a couple of times to realize that was off bounds."

To the extent that Barbara weighs in on policy, it is in the dimension of taste—as a protector of her husband's reputation. She is said to disagree with the president's stated opinions in several areas; White House aides are especially eager to suggest that she differs from him on abortion and gun control, fanning some faint hope among Republican moderates that she is fighting a good fight over morning coffee every day.

But it seems unlikely that Barbara Bush actually works to change her husband's mind on such issues: his positions in those areas are dictated by politics, and she is as shrewd a politician as anyone around him.

Her role in placating moderates may be more important this year than ever before. In a three-way race that includes Perot, the two major-party candidates will likely be forced to defend their traditional bases, which means they will have to appease the most extreme elements in their coalitions. For Bush, this means waging a fall campaign that offers lots of red meat to social-issue conservatives. Barbara Bush's help will be crucial in telegraphing a contradictory message to more liberal Republicans, especially women angry at Bush over [his nomination of Supreme Court justice] Clarence Thomas and the issue of abortion.

U p to now, Barbara Bush has been able to have it both ways. She has offered herself as evidence of her husband's good intentions, while going out of her way to disclaim any power at all to shape the policies that affect the lives—the squalid schools, the threadbare health care, the marginal services—of the unfortunates who people her photo ops.

When Bush decided, in the late seventies, to run for president, Barbara pondered what her major "issue" should be and came up with literacy, a canny choice. On the one hand, as she often explains, it touches on every problem in society, ranging from crime to childhood poverty; on the other hand, it doesn't invite any controversy.

As the vice president's wife she joined the board of the child-oriented Reading Is Fundamental, and as First Lady she founded the Barbara Bush Foundation for Family Literacy, to which she has donated all the profits from *Millie's Book*. It gives away half a million dollars in grants every year to programs that address illiteracy as a self-perpetuating problem passed from parents to children.

But if her signature issue was chosen with calculation, there has been nothing artificial about her good works. Even before Bush's political career began, she was a dedicated volunteer in hospitals; over the years, she has quietly worked at such places as the Washington Home for Incurables, and has served on boards ranging from that of the Ronald McDonald House to that of the predominantly black Morehouse School of Medicine.

Today you can easily see that she has a greater capacity than her husband has to look death and pain in the face. To cancer wards and AIDS clinics, she brings not only helpful publicity but a full self, a capacity to let in the suffering around her and give it its due, which is one of the few gifts any stranger can confer. The president, on the other hand, is famous for squirming through visits to hospitals. When he visited the bed of a Los Angeles firefighter shot during the riots, the only consolation he could think to offer was for himself: "I'm sorry Barbara's not here," he said miserably.

Every afternoon the First Lady has her staff send up to her office in the family quarters a clip file of stories related to poverty, education, literacy, child care—her issues. And sometimes she reacts quickly to what she reads. In 1989, for example, she was angered by reports that the Salvation Army had been barred from making Christmas collections at some of the snootier local shopping malls. She made a trip to a mall that did permit the solicitations and took along a press pool to capture her dropping some change into the bucket, which successfully shamed most of the Scrooge-ish merchants into line.

This is as good a use of celebrity as exists in America. It is, by the accounts of Democrats and Republicans, blacks and whites, all of those who have fallen in love with the grandmotherly image of the First Lady, the very best of Barbara Bush.

But even in the uprightness of this image lies a certain moral complexity. For the past three and a half years, the First Lady had almost single-handedly symbolized her husband's good intentions in the realm of domestic affairs. Extended to a society's breadth, the Bush model implies a return to an era in which women relieved their powerful men—relieved government—of responsibility for the disadvantaged. It is the old Victorian contract, in which life was divided into two spheres, male and female; while men ran the world, their women ran the soup kitchens.

Bush advisers have worked hard over the years to suggest that Barbara's compassion will one day rub off on her husband, to imply that she can (and should) be relied on to police his interest in social services. "Every time he says 'Head Start,' that's Bar," spokeswoman Sheila Tate told reporters at the dawn of his administration. And for some time the country seemed to accept the idea that Barbara was a facet of George—a reliable indicator of his goals. At the time of Bush's inauguration, columnists raved about how Barbara would be "the conscience of the White House."

But without Barbara, Americans might have noticed sooner that the self-styled "education president" had offered nothing meaningful in the way of education reform.

Without Barbara, voters might have noticed from the start how disengaged Bush seemed from domestic concerns.

Barbara Bush successfully silenced the logical question that called out for response: Isn't the president supposed to be the conscience of the White House?

As George Bush campaigns for a second term, a lot rides on Barbara Bush's careful balancing act. She is the answer to a frightened campaign's prayers, a surrogate campaigner who can command almost as much press and hoopla as the president can—while incurring comparatively little risk. As early as last winter one could trace the dawning importance of her role. She was sent to New Hampshire to file the papers for Bush's candidacy, "because nobody would dare to boo Barbara," in the words of a strategist. She spent more time campaigning in the state than the president did.

And when Bush officially announced his candidacy, it was Barbara Bush who introduced him. In a classic reversal of roles, the candidate quoted his wife, referring to "my favorite political philosopher, Barbara Bush."

All through the spring, once the threat of Buchanan's primary campaign had faded, she traveled far more than her husband did, headlining as many as thirty major fund-raisers around the country.

Republican strategists go as far as to say that they believe voters ambivalent about George Bush may think twice about voting his wife out of the White House. It's an extraordinary exception to the normal wisdom, which suggests that the best most spouses can do is adhere to the Hippocratic oath of politics: Just do no harm.

Opinions differ about how badly Barbara Bush wants to stay in the White House. She is said to blame the presidency for the problems of her son Neil, implicated in the Silverado Banking, Savings and Loan Association debacle.

Friends also surmise she has had a more difficult time than she lets on dealing with Graves' disease, the thyroid condition that has tired her and painfully distended her eyes.

But by most accounts she has reveled in her time as First Lady. Even as the president floundered through the spring and early summer, his polls in free-fall, Barbara Bush lived in a charmed circle within her control. She has reached the apotheosis of the life she read about in her daddy's magazines, a victory she presents as grand affirmation of the ultra-traditional plan she has lived by.

"My mail tells me that a lot of fat, white-haired, wrinkled ladies are tickled pink," she said on the eve of Bush's inauguration. "I mean, look at me—if I can be a success, so can they."

But only one person gets to be married to the president of the United States. It is a rare full-time homemaker and college dropout who receives an honorary degree from Smith, who is asked to speak to the graduating class at Wellesley, who appears on the covers of *Time* and *Life*.

George Bush's political ascent allowed her to enact her role of helpmate on a vast, symbolic scale—one that offered more ego gratification than the same role performed as an anonymous daily sacrament.

This was how she staved off the fated collision between her cramped idea of women's role and her great strength of personality. It is also how she tamed the most turbulent themes of her own life.

Toward the end of the Republicans' May dinner in Miami Beach, two videos about Barbara Bush were shown on the giant screen that hung above the diners. Together they suggested just how far she has traveled.

The first was a brief, condescending biography prepared by the state party. It showed more events from George Bush's life than from his wife's and included all the same photos that appear in standard Bush biographies—showing handsome young politician George Bush surrounded by his happy brood of children and, standing at the back of the picture, his stocky, weathered wife with her oddly dyed hair and uncertain smile.

But then, with the second videotape, a spectral George Bush appeared on the screen to salute his popular spouse.

"Remember her Wellesley commencement speech?" he asked rhetorically. "Some students protested, saying she's just a woman who followed her husband. Well, they got it wrong. In countless ways, I've followed Barbara.

"I think it's appropriate," he continued, "that Barbara would be honored at the Statesman's Dinner. Someone once said that a politician thinks of the next election, but a statesman thinks of the next generation. Well, that's Barbara Bush, in so many ways."

It seemed an unconsciously honest moment, alluding not only to the reasons America loves her but also to the reasons America now scorns him. Suddenly, it was strangely poignant to watch his video-blurred face, to hear his canned voice, as he talked about the famous, widely loved woman being celebrated in the flesh.

The moment seemed to summarize the ironic reversal being played out before the nation: Now he is the burdened one, she is the butterfly. He can no longer maintain the buoyancy that has been the hallmark of his life, while for her, public goodwill remains at flood tide, affirming her life's choices.

How impossibly sweet it must feel to her. Today she helps her husband most by embodying the levity that was always, until this hour, his to claim.

(George and Barbara Bush would depart the White House in 1993 when Bill Clinton assumed the presidency. Their son George W. Bush would succeed Clinton eight years later. Barbara Bush died in April 2018; her husband, seven months later.)

WHAT HILLARY WANTS

By Gail Sheehy | May 1992

n May of 1990, Bill Clinton was running for his fifth term as governor of Arkansas. While he was conveniently out of town, a challenger in the Democratic primary, Tom McCrae, called a press conference in the echo chamber of the Capitol rotunda. He was in the middle of telling everyone who would listen that Bill Clinton was a chicken—"and since the governor will not debate . . ."—when all at once another voice chewed into his sound bite. "Tom, who was the one person who didn't show up in Springdale? Give me a break! I mean, I think that we oughta get the record straight . . ."

The camera swung around to a small, yellow-haired woman in a houndstooth-check suit—literally *in his face*. Having crashed McCrae's photo op, she planted herself directly opposite him, just spoiling for a fight. She looked quite pale without studio makeup, but her eyes flashed in the lights of the television camera. "Many of the reports you issued," she charged, "not only praised the governor on his environmental record, but his education record *and* his economic record!"

The camera spun again to reveal the hapless man's grit-eating smile, his eyes bobbling around in his head as if he'd just been zapped by a stun gun. His stammering response was trampled by the woman ticking off her points, reading embarrassing passages from the candidate's own earlier handouts.

"You now turn around and as a candidate have a very short memory," she finished. As they say in Arkansas, *she ate his lunch.*

The Eyewitness News man wound up his thrilled coverage with the tag line "Hillary Clinton showed again that she may be the best debater in the family."

I t is the Year of the Political Woman. [Presidential candidate] Paul Tsongas [the former Massachusetts congressman and senator], whose least appealing quality was his mopey personality, said with a grateful nod to his attorney wife, Niki, "If you don't have charisma, you marry it." Ruth Harkin, a former prosecutor, assumed the role of her husband [the Iowa senator Tom Harkin]'s unofficial political adviser for his six-month run. Marilyn Quayle, who told *The Washington Post* through clenched teeth that politicians in the past never acknowledged that "your little wifey . . . helps you," commands entry into the Office of Vice President [Dan Quayle] from a six-office suite across the hall, passing judgment on lobbyists and other supplicants. (Marilyn says she raises a subject with the vice president "if I think it's important enough." Otherwise, staffers "let me make the decision instead.") President [George H. W.] Bush, who often leans on his vastly more popular wife [Barbara] at public appearances, has recently brought on board his rudderless re-election team wordsmith Peggy Noonan. Her job description: "Message development." Even bullyboy Pat Buchanan, Beltway pundits say, wouldn't have run [as a Republican challenger to President Bush] if it hadn't been for his sister—who is also his campaign chairwoman.

And it is Hillary Rodham Clinton, lawyer–activist–teacher–author–corporate boardwoman–mother and wife of Billsomething, who is the diesel engine powering the front-running Democratic campaign. In the space of one week in late January, Hillary fast-forwarded from being introduced as "wife of" (*60 Minutes*) to the victim of "the other woman" (*PrimeTime Live*) to "Trapped in a Spotlight, Hillary Clinton Uses It" (*The New York Times*), the last illustrated by a picture which said it all: Hillary with her arm thrust in the air and wearing a big campaign smile, out in front of her husband.

The forty-four-year-old wife and mother still shows flashes of the sweet ingenue smile of her college years, and has maintained her size 8 by touching little more than a lettuce leaf and water during campaign fund-raisers (her less disciplined husband has put on twenty-five pounds). When the cameras dolly in, however, one can detect the calculation in the f-stop click of Hillary's eyes. Lips pulled back over her slightly jutting teeth, the public smile is practiced; the small frown establishes an air of superiority; her hair looks lifelessly doll-like.

But there is no mistaking the passion in her words or the impact of her presence. "The *instant* she came in the door of the ballroom, I knew it," said a savvy pol, Patricia Derian, an assistant secretary of state under Jimmy Carter, who saw Hillary sway a big-ticket Washington crowd at a benefit in March. There was no fanfare, no spotlight, the lady isn't even much taller than a podium microphone. "But there was no missing her," said Derian, "and that's really rare. She's a spectacular candidate in her own right. She's got my vote."

In Los Angeles, at a March 26 salmon-and-spinach luncheon hosted by Hollywood producer Dawn Steel and television producer Linda Bloodworth-Thomason (among others), Hillary dazzled an audience that is usually ho-hum about stars and plenty impressed with themselves. "We need to be against brain-dead politics wherever we find it!" she thundered, looking fierce in a fire-engine-red suit. "We need to forge a new consensus about [our] new political direction . . . that doesn't jerk us to the right, jerk us to the left, prey on our emotions, engender paranoia and insecurity . . . but instead moves us forward together." Producer Sherry Lansing pronounced it "an extraordinary speech, *extraordinary*."

The sold-out luncheon—her most successful of the season, raising $50,000—came off in the heat of the controversy over Hillary's role in her husband's campaign. Her snappish response to [former governor of California and Democratic presidential candidate] Jerry Brown's broadside on her career—"I suppose I could have stayed home and baked cookies and had teas"—had offended millions of women who have chosen to be full-time home-makers, reinvoking the arrogance of the Tammy Wynette quote that so irritated the country-music vote. That very morning, *New York Times* columnist William Safire had written about what he called "the Hillary problem," describing her as a "political bumbler" who suffers from "foot-in-mouth disease."

In a private interview after the luncheon, I asked Hillary how she felt about being labeled "the problem." Uncharacteristically, she squirmed and stammered. "I don't know how to feel about it. . . . I think I'll just have to be more . . . *careful* in the way I express my feelings, so I don't inadvertently hurt anybody.

"I think the only legitimate concern is around the misconstruction of what I said about baking cookies and having tea. I can understand why some people thought that I was criticizing women who made different choices than the one I had—in fact, criticizing the choice that my mother and a lot of dear friends have made. Nothing could be further from what I believe."

Did she, then, agree with Barbara Bush, who stirred up a hornet's nest at Hillary's alma mater, Wellesley College, when she told students that a working mother should always put family before career? "For *me*, I believe that," Hillary replied fervently. "*Personally*, I believe that a woman should put her family and her relationships—which are really at the root of who you are and how you relate to the world—at the top of your priority list." She hastened to add, "But I don't believe that I, or Barbara Bush, should tell all women that's what *they* have to put first. . . . What we have to get away from is the idea that there's only one right choice."

Hillary seems to understand why she has become a lightning rod in her husband's presidential campaign. "What they're trying to figure out is 'How will she be able to influence him? Who is this person?' Well, Bill Clinton is the kind of person who asks advice from literally dozens of people. If you look at George Bush, he's advised by a coterie of men . . . who are, frankly, all of one mind, a very narrow, all-white coterie of, exclusively, men."

The president is one of Hillary's favorite targets, and she pillories him mercilessly in her speeches. "When it's all stripped away," she told the L.A. crowd, "at bottom what we see is a failure of leadership, rooted in a very hollow sense of what politics is and can be." As one listener put it, "She's unbelievably articulate and connects with her audience with a message that hits home." Then she joined the buzz heard all over the room: "You can't help but think, Why isn't *she* the candidate?'"

She almost was. Two years ago, when Bill Clinton considered forgoing his fifth gubernatorial contest in order to build an early base for his lifelong presidential ambitions, Hillary called up a friend and former newspaper publisher in the state, Dorothy Stuck, and asked, "What would happen if *I* ran for governor?"

"After all this time Bill's been in office, you'd be hung with his baggage," answered the veteran newspaperwoman. She pledged her support, but advised Hillary to wait a few more years. "She thought she had a good chance," remembers Stuck, who adds that Hillary Clinton is revered by many women in Arkansas. Hillary's closest confidante, Carolyn Huber, confirms, "She got very enthusiastic about the prospect of running for governor." Hushing her voice, as if telling a little tale out of school, Huber says, "I think she'd like to be governor, but she wasn't about to try if Bill wanted to again."

"Some say the wrong Clinton is in the statehouse," the governor himself drawled at a charity roast of Hillary four years ago, "and I wouldn't disagree with them." On February 7, when I asked if he was concerned about being upstaged by his wife, Clinton was unfazed. "I've always liked strong women. . . . It doesn't bother me for people to see her and get excited and say she could be president. I always say she could be president, too." At his own fund-raisers he has often quipped, "Buy one, get one free!"

In fact, fewer people seem to have negative feelings toward Hillary than toward her husband. According to a national survey conducted from March 27 to 29 by Yankelovich Clancy Shulman for *Vanity Fair*, 41 percent of those surveyed have a generally favorable impression of Hillary, while 24 percent have an unfavorable one. Fifty-five percent think she is an asset to her husband's campaign; 24 percent think she's a liability. A whopping 84 percent say they would not object to a First Lady with a separate career. Those surveyed use the following descriptions of Hillary: intelligent (75 percent); tough-minded (65 percent); a good role model for women (48 percent); a feminist in the best possible sense (44 percent). The negatives: power-hungry (44 percent); too intense (36 percent); a wife who dominates her husband (28 percent). Most disturbing for the Clintons, however, is the skepticism over their relationship: 53 percent think it is more a "professional arrangement" than a "real marriage" (22 percent).

The raised eyebrows are due in part to the way Hillary has seized the stage at certain public appearances. Even the normally unflappable Tom Brokaw was startled when, in the triumphal glow of the southern stomp on Super Tuesday, she shot past her husband to man the microphone. "What I would like to do, in introducing . . . *someone* . . ." she began, while her husband danced in the background like a prizefighter trying to stay warm. Soon she was booming, "We believe *passionately* in this country and we cannot stand by for ONE MORE YEAR and watch what is happening to it!" Over the applause, Brokaw observed dryly, "Not just an introduction, this is a *speech* by Mrs. Clinton."

Hillary barely referred to her husband—and then only as "the messenger." If he is the messenger, she may be the message. Those who keep asking "Why isn't *she* running?" miss the point. Hillary Clinton *is* running. She and her husband have been a political team for more than twenty years. And now they are, despite protestations to the contrary, *co-candidates* for president of the United States. Asked at the L.A. luncheon if she wanted to be her husband's vice president, Hillary brushed off the question. "I'm not interested in attending a lot of funerals around the world," she cracked. She got a laugh, but when she continued it was with serious intent. "I want maneuverability . . . I want to get deeply involved in solving problems." She later told me that she doesn't see herself as a Cabinet officer but as an all-around adviser. And she doesn't see what all the fuss is about. "No one gives George Bush a hard time when he gets advice from Jim Baker," she'd complained to me earlier in the campaign.

Before he was forced to retreat on the subject of Hillary's possible role in a Clinton administration on NBC's *Meet the Press*, Bill told me, "If I get elected president, it will be an unprecedented partnership, far more than Franklin Roosevelt and Eleanor. They were two great people, but on different tracks. If I get elected, we'll do things together like we always have."

Which would make Hillary Clinton one of the most formidable women in the world, a model of a full partner in public life. Friends go even further, touting Hillary as the next attorney general by pointing out that she would be better qualified than Robert Kennedy was when his brother named him to the post. Hillary's own brother Hugh Rodham, a public defender in Dade

County, Florida, foresees even higher callings. "Attorney general is only local lawmaking," he says dismissively. "There's treaty negotiations she could do. There's labor stuff. There's secretary of state . . ."

The Clinton camp had planned "a slow build for Hillary," according to her campaign manager, Richard Mintz. That was until all hell broke loose—until the day Bill Clinton was "deflowered" by a cabaret singer who once headlined at the Pinnacle Lounge in Little Rock, [insisting that she and the Arkansas governor had maintained a long-term relationship].

The candidate's strategists huddled in panicky planning sessions. One significant piece of information: polls showed that 39 percent of voters would have reservations about voting for a candidate who had been unfaithful—but that the number diminishes if the wife knows about it and accepts it. The clear conclusion was that Gennifer [Flowers]'s unforgettable slot-machine eyes and hydraulic lips and indelible black roots required an immediate visual challenge: the apple-cheeked, moon-eyed wife of the governor, staggeringly poised, effortlessly articulate, primly silk-scarved. Blond, too—in fact, Hillary looked like a *Town & Country* version of Gennifer Flowers, but not with a *G*, with a good little Wellesley girl's hair band covering her brown roots.

Hillary rendezvoused with Bill in Boston the night before the Clintons' extraordinary "Checkers speech" on *60 Minutes.* She conferred with the television crew on colors and camera angles. "You can quote me as saying that my sense of it was that she was in control," says Steve Kroft, the interviewer. "We fiddled around with who should sit on which side, and they fiddled around with chair heights and things like that. You didn't know she was his wife, you'd have thought she was a media consultant. She didn't do it in a dictatorial sort of way. . . . She was very delightful and charming. When they left the room, everybody pretty much said, 'Boy, she's terrific' "

The next day, before airtime, tension was reportedly running high in the control room, with [*60 Minutes*] producer Don Hewitt ranting to Clinton advisers George Stephanopoulos and Harold Ickes, "He's gotta come clean! He's got to say yes!" Once Bill and Hillary were seated, Mrs. Clinton stared intently at Bill as he responded to the grilling. This was no Nancy Reagan glaze—this was the look of the *consigliere* sitting vigil over a member of the family.

Kroft's impression was that Hillary was "tougher and more disciplined than he is. And analytical. Among his faults, he has a tendency not to think of the consequences of the things he says. I think she knows. She's got a ten-second delay. If something comes to her mind she doesn't think will play right, she cuts it off before anybody knows she's thinking it."

"I have acknowledged wrongdoing," Bill offered when the cameras were rolling. "I have acknowledged causing pain in my marriage." At another point when Kroft pressed him—"I am assuming from your answer that you're categorically denying that you ever had an affair with Gennifer Flowers"—he took the bait. "I've said that before," he replied quickly. "And so has she . . ."

In jumped Hillary the litigator: "I don't want to be any more specific. I don't think being any more specific about what's happened in the privacy of our life together is relevant to anybody besides us."

It was a signal for her husband to button up. "Having made the mistake of denying Gennifer Flowers, he was undoing what they had decided to do," explains senior campaign adviser Susan Thomases. "So she was reminding him, 'Hey, buddy, remember our strategy: if you say you're not going to talk about *any* specific case, and then you talk about one case, you're blowing the strategy.'"

Hillary's presence was so strong, in fact, that, according to Kroft, "we found ourselves rationing her sound bites to keep her from becoming the dominant force in the interview."

But some people think it has become obvious that Hillary is the dominant force in the Clinton campaign. Even those awed by her commented after her Super Tuesday speech, "There's something a little scary, a little Al Haig–ish about her." Her closest counterparts, high-striving professional women, often react viscerally: she's "too intense," they say, or she's "missing something feminine"—as if they can't forgive her for appearing to have it all.

The slings and arrows never seem to pierce Hillary's armor-plated determination. "Hillary is convinced the way she does things is the right way," attests her brother Hugh. Carolyn Huber, the woman who may know her best, having served as Hillary's "mansion administrator," day-to-day logistical helper, and surrogate grandmother to her child, affirms that Hillary will simply not be deterred. "She wants to win as bad as he does." Is she tougher than he is? "I think so," laughs Huber. "She's more clear about what she wants and the way she wants it done. I don't think there's ever been a time when Hillary set her mind to something she wanted to happen that it hasn't happened."

Hillary is widely regarded by their closest associates as the tougher, cooler, and more intellectually tart of the two. Her favorite recreation is standing with friends and talking ideas around the kitchen counter in the governor's mansion, one long *Big Chill* party, people helping themselves out of the fridge. (Hillary rarely cooks, and the state dining room is scarcely used.) She might mimic one of her hillbilly witnesses spitting tobacco from the stand while she cross-examines him. Or she'll burst into a high-pitched Ozark honk—hee hee hee—over one of her husband's Bubba lines. But come 10:30 she'll announce, "That's it for me, I'm goin' to bed." Bill is the night owl, the eternal schmoozer; Hillary is the emotionally disciplined one.

Sometimes this causes dissonance. "Hillary's hard to know," concedes a close family friend, Carolyn Y. Staley. Another family friend, assured she wouldn't be identified, is more candid: "I never know from one day to the next how I'm going to be received by Hillary. She's very busy, she knows exactly where she wants to go and how to get there. You're either useful or extraneous to her." Finally she blurts, "Look, Hillary's tough as nails. *Bill has always deferred to women to fight his battles.*"

Indeed, throughout his career Bill Clinton has surrounded himself with exceptionally strong-willed, capable women. Following his first and only loss as governor, he drafted the rough-and-tumble George McGovern operative Betsey Wright as his campaign manager; she devoted the next ten years of her life to protecting and re-electing him. (Wright, who quit as Arkansas Democratic Party chair just before Clinton announced, says that she was "fried" by the time this presidential race came around.) He persuaded the flinty Susan Thomases, who had cut her teeth on Bill Bradley's first Senate campaign, to join his current brain trust. And his top staff in the Arkansas statehouse has been predominantly female. "The only two men I know in American politics who are capable of treating women as real equals," says Thomases, "are Bill Bradley and Bill Clinton."

Part of Clinton's dependence on his wife is financial. As one of the chief litigating partners in the Rose Law Firm and a director on five corporate boards (including a position as the only woman on the board of Wal-Mart) Hillary earned—based on her own figures—an estimated $160,000 in 1990. Twice voted one of the hundred most influential lawyers in America by *The National Law Journal*, "she could command the top salary for a litigator in any law firm in New York or Los Angeles," claims her partner Herb Rule. (The going rate is $500,000 and up.) Instead, she has committed much of her energy to pro bono work, such as chairing the Children's Defense Fund, and serving on the boards of nearly a dozen other educational and social-justice organizations.

"If Hillary were doing what she most wanted to do in this world, she would not be a partner in a corporate law firm," confides her close friend and former Wellesley dormmate Jan Piercey. "That's what she's had to do—she's responsible for the revenue in the family." (Bill has increased his salary from $25,000 at the age of twenty-nine to the princely sum of $35,000 almost twenty years later.)

Bill Clinton is the *puer aeternus*, suggests one of their older, wiser friends—the eternal boy, a Jungian archetype, who remains stuck in an adolescent orientation toward life, often prompted by an exaggerated dependence on his mother. Seductive to men as well as women, the prototypical eternal boy often hopes to redeem mankind; in the archetype he is meant to replace the old king as a symbol of the renewal of life. But the "winged youth" often falls, psychologically, and in crisis turns to strong female figures to raise him up again. "Bill has achieved enormous success, but he's still reaching," says an Arkansas friend. "It's the young man who's been a star and who is, I hope, not locked in adolescence. We don't know that yet—he's only forty-five."

George Fisher cartooned Bill Clinton in the guise of a boy for fourteen years at the old *Arkansas Gazette,* starting him off in his first term in a baby buggy, later graduating him to a tricycle and a ten-speed bike. (In real life Bill Clinton plays with a '64 Mustang—Hillary calls it his "boy's toy.") In the mid-eighties Fisher penned a striking drawing that captures Bill Clinton's dependence on his delivering angels. The cartoon, which was never published, shows three winged, spear-carrying women—Hillary, Betsey, and Clinton's former press secretary—lifting their barefoot boy from the battlefield. They are meant to be Valkyries, "awful and beautiful," who gather up the worthy and fly them to Valhalla.

I saw Fisher's cartoon come to life during what the campaign calls "the incredible week" after the *60 Minutes* appearance, a week I referred to once as a "crisis" only to have Hillary correct me: "This is not a crisis, not a *personal* crisis anyway." Flying with her, knee-to-knee, I watched while she fashioned the strategy to bring her husband "back from the dead," as he now describes it.

It was in a nondescript motel in Pierre, South Dakota, where she had twenty minutes of downtime, that Hillary flipped on the TV on Monday, January 27, and caught the end of Gennifer Flowers on CNN playing tapes of her phone conversations with the governor. They were devastating.

"Let's get Bill on the phone," Hillary coolly directed her campaign manager, Mintz, who was himself fighting back tears. According to Hillary, Clinton told his wife he wasn't concerned—after all, who was going to believe this woman? "Everybody knows you can be paid to do anything," the governor said.

"Everybody *doesn't* know that," she insisted. "Bill, people who don't know you are going to say, 'Why were you even talking to this person?'"

At 6:25 P.M. Central time, Hillary was pressing the flesh at a Pork Producers Rib Feed in Pierre when her campaign manager whispered in her ear, "All three nets led with the Flowers press conference." She excused herself and made a beeline for the one pay phone in the hall, pursued by a camera crew from *PrimeTime Live.* Mintz appealed to them not to shoot her. "I promise I'll give you a shot of her on the phone, but this is not the time."

I watched as a terrible shrug went down Hillary's face. Little Rock was telling her about the latest deal—a young woman had been offered half a million dollars to say she'd had a one-night stand with Bill Clinton. Where would it stop?

Back in her six-seat charter plane, Hillary vented her frustration above the grinding hum: "If we'd been in front of a jury I'd say, 'Miss Flowers, isn't it true you were asked this by A.P. in June of 1990 and you said no? Weren't you asked by the *Arkansas Democrat* and you said no?' I mean, *I would crucify her.*"

Hillary boils over at what she perceives as a double standard—that the press has shied away from investigating long-standing rumors about George Bush. "I had tea with Anne Cox Chambers [the heiress who is chairwoman of her media empire's Atlanta newspaper group]," Hillary recalled to me in a later interview, "and she's sittin' there in her sun-room saying, 'You know, I just don't understand why they think they can get away with this—everybody knows about George Bush,' and then launches into this long description of, you know, Bush and his carrying on, all of which is apparently well known in Washington. But I'm convinced part of it is that the Establishment— regardless of party—sticks together. They're gonna circle the wagons on Jennifer _____ and all these other people." (Anne Cox Chambers remembers telling Hillary, "I don't understand why nothing's ever been said about a George Bush girlfriend—I understand he has a Jennifer, too.")

The reference is to a decade-long Bush staffer who now enjoys a senior State Department position. She has been persistently linked with the president in rumors that have never been proved. When I interviewed her in 1987 in Bush's Senate office, the amply built middle-aged woman, a born-again Christian, was discreet about her work and travel with Bush. (In June of 1987, George Bush Jr. told *Newsweek* that when he asked his father if he'd ever committed adultery he replied, "The answer to the Big A question is N.O.")

On the tiny plane, Hillary focused on the problem at hand. "I'm just not going to sit by anymore and say, 'Well, it's the press's responsibility.' If we can destroy people with paid stories, what's next? . . . I don't think Bill appreciates how TV really doesn't give the other side. It's like negative advertising." A light bulb switched on behind her eyes. "*That's* what I should have told him. In 1980 the Republicans started the negative advertising; in 1992 we have paid political character assassination. What Bill doesn't understand is you've *gotta* do the same thing in response as you do with negative advertising—[the 1988 Democratic presidential nominee, Michael] Dukakis didn't understand that." Suddenly, a brainstorm. "This is the daughter of Willie Horton!" Now she had the outlines of a proactive, not reactive, strategy: pound the "Republican attack machine" and run against the press.

Just before landing, she recited a prayer she says often: *Dear Lord, be good to me. The sea is so wide and my boat is so small.* Thump, bump, the plane skated through the blackness toward a shack with the sign RAPID CITY. Within minutes, Hillary was clicking across the concrete airfield, coatless, eager to coach her husband and rev up the campaign staff on a conference call. "Who's getting information on the *Star*?" she demanded. "Who's tracking down all the research on Gennifer? Where is our surrogate program? Who's going to be out there speaking for us?" She let the fragile young staffers who had not experienced a Hiroshima in a campaign know that she and Bill were going to be out there fighting, "and I want you all to be putting this stuff together."

"It was," says deputy campaign manager George Stephanopoulos, "inspirational."

To Hillary Clinton, the stories of her husband's sexual infidelities seem to register, consciously at least, as having nothing to do with her, or with their marriage, but rather as evidence of the depths of degradation to which the hit men behind George Bush will stoop. Rarely does anyone in her audiences dare to bring up the question of infidelity, and when someone does, Hillary usually knocks it out of the park, leaving people cheering. Her refrain has become something of a mantra, protecting her from ever seeming to take the whole ugly business personally: "This is a much bigger issue than just Bill and me—I just hope for the sake of the country we'll set some boundaries for others coming along."

Not only is her altruistic defense politically astute, it also serves to buffer her psychologically from the feelings that would send most women off on an emotional roller coaster. "It doesn't make any difference what people say about her," says her friend Stuck, "whatever criticism or belittling, she doesn't take it personally, because the cause is always more important. It may very well be the way she insulates herself from hurt. And I think in the past ten or twelve years with Bill she may have done that, to protect her sanity."

In all the time I traveled with Hillary, and in sixty interviews with her friends, family, and associates, there was just one hint of a deep emotional reaction. "She never shows her personal feelings on the surface," attests Carolyn Huber, but that week, when the governor's wife phoned her confidante and Huber broke into sobs, a fissure opened in the protective coating of equanimity. "I know, Carolyn, it's hurting so bad," Hillary said. "The press doesn't believe you have any feelings. They sure don't believe in the Bible."

But Hillary is also an avowed pragmatist, accustomed to life in the political fishbowl. "She knew this day would come," says Jan Piercey, her former college dormmate, "and she wasn't going to put anybody in the position of lying." Another friend says of the media frenzy over Clinton's nocturnal peccadilloes, "None of this came as a surprise to her."

I asked Hillary if she thought her husband had told her everything she needed to know. "Yes. I have absolutely no doubt about that," she replied, her light-blue eyes unblinking beneath the dark hedgerow of brows. "I don't think I could be sitting here otherwise. That's been, over years, part of the development of trust."

I asked if she thought Gary Hart was qualified to be president, or did she think his problems revealed something disturbing about his character? "He was not yet at a point where he could be honest with himself, that's my perception," she said. "People in his campaign said they confronted him and said, 'Have you ever?' and he said 'No.'"

She praised Bill Clinton for being honest with the people he loves, admitting his problems, and declaring he wanted to do better. "I think as he got older, as he became a father, he began to let his breath out a little bit," observes Hillary. Her husband believes that trauma and mistakes are all tests that help one grow. For him, says Hillary, "it's a constant coming to grips with who you are and what stage of life you can grow beyond."

The Clintons' friends fiercely idealize their marriage, seeing in it a remarkable integration of strong personalities and sheer guts. "Most of us have thrown in the towel," says one friend, the thoughtful actress Mary Steenburgen. "These people didn't. It's exciting to be around them and to see how it *can* be to be a married couple." Another member of the "Arkansas diaspora" in L.A., television producer Linda Bloodworth-Thomason, is one of Hillary's most loyal intimates. "Look, this isn't Lurleen Wallace," says Bloodworth-Thomason. "Hillary doesn't have to stay with Bill Clinton. She could get to the Senate or possibly the White House on her own—and she knows it. . . . But these two people are intertwined on every level, as a man and woman, as friends, as lovers, as parents, as politicians. . . . This is a love story." Huber agrees, describing how "Bill and Hillary are always smooching." Their pals call the Clintons "soul mates," saying they confide fully in nobody, not even family, only in each other.

"She also has an investment in this marriage and his career," points out the practical Wright, who says Hillary never considered divorce. "It absolutely was not an alternative that she gave him."

The only area of vulnerability friends spot in Hillary is her daughter, Chelsea. The longest periods of silence she maintains are in hotel rooms, a phone cradled to her ear, often dead tired but listening without interruption to the stream-of-consciousness account of the twelve-year-old's day. Before the campaign, Hillary was out of town on law or board work two or three nights a week. She does homework with Chelsea by fax.

"Whenever Hillary was there, she always sat with Chelsea while she had dinner," recalls Melinda Martin, the resident baby-sitter from '85 to '87. (Most of the Clintons' baby-sitters are fresh out of the University of Arkansas, with names like Melinda, Melissa, and Michelle.)

I asked Melinda how often Bill and Hillary went out together. "Just the two of them? Very, very seldom. . . . Hillary took Chelsea on vacations. Bill would promise to catch up, but usually he'd come a couple of days late, or not at all."

Hillary's protectiveness of her daughter took precedence one evening, at the peak of the bimbomania, when she was facing a command performance as the "candidate's wife" before a backbiting Washington audience at a roast of Ron Brown, chairman of the Democratic National Committee. Bill was scheduled to take Chelsea to a father-daughter dance at the Little Rock Y.W.C.A. Their friend Linda Bloodworth-Thomason had an inspiration: "Let's do a live remote to Little Rock—it will be a nice image for them to see Bill dancing with his daughter."

Hillary didn't think twice. "No," she said. "This is Chelsea's night."

It is one of Hillary's philosophical tenets that children should be spoken to just like adults. This explains how Hillary is able to pass the supermarket checkout counter in the company of her adored daughter without gagging. Indeed, Hillary is the first to point out the lurid tabloid headlines screaming about multiple affairs or a love child, instructing Chelsea that "this is what's to be expected in a political campaign." Chelsea follows the political horse race avidly, but "when they talk bad about my daddy" on TV, she leaves the room.

For women who have been betrayed by unfaithful husbands, Hillary Clinton is a Rorschach test. Some grimace at the prospect of having their hearts broken by a man whose story you never know whether to believe: "I don't want another charmer." Others admire her stoicism and buy the strength-through-adversity story.

Still, any wife subjected to embarrassing, detailed reports of infidelity must register searing pain at some level. It is quite possible that Hillary is so focused on power agendas that she is disconnected from her feelings, able to compartmentalize her pain: she codes it, labels it, and puts it away in the deep freeze. What does that leave? An unresolved hurt so profound that it may not surface until all the sound and fury of campaigning is over.

The secret behind Hillary's boldness goes back to the torch passed from a silent generation of mothers to the daughters of the feminist movement. "I was determined that no daughter of mine was going to have to go through the agony of being afraid to say what she had on her mind," says Dorothy Rodham, Hillary's mother, who hadn't finished college before marrying Hugh Rodham, a rough-edged Chicago salesman and later owner of a small textile business. Mrs. Rodham made raising her three children her full-time occupation. They played endless word games and rarely watched television. Thus, Hillary was an especially sheltered four-year-old when the Welsh-English family moved to Park Ridge, a middle-class, white-collar suburb out near O'Hare airport.

The new neighborhood was dominated by a family with a daughter, Suzy, who regularly decked the beribboned little Hillary, watching in triumph as she ran home sobbing.

"There's no room in this house for cowards," Hillary's mother announced one day. "You're going to have to stand up to her. The next time she hits you, I want you to hit her back."

Out trudged the trembling four-year-old. A circle of scowling boys and the pugilistic girl closed around her. Suddenly, Hillary threw out her fist, knocking Suzy off her pins. The boys' mouths dropped open. Flushed with victory, Hillary ran home to exclaim to her proud mother, "I can play with the boys now!"

The lesson sank in deep. "Boys responded well to Hillary," clucks her mother. "She just took charge, and they let her." Even as a child she thought in terms of mobilizing constituents for her causes, organizing neighborhood carnivals or clothing drives for migrant workers. As a young teen she helped her youth minister, the Reverend Don Jones, in counseling black and Hispanic teens from the South Side. "She would think things through to see what would be appealing to the group," recalls her brother Hugh. "We would just follow along as little brothers."

The other formative experience for Hillary was competitive sports. A keen though terminally mediocre athlete, Hillary now appreciates having learned the lesson few girls did in those days: "You win one day, you lose the next day, you don't take it personally. You get up every day and you go on." It became the pattern of her life, a pattern that has fortified her in the topsy-turvy days of the current campaign.

To go east in 1965 to Wellesley College—"all very rich and fancy and very intimidating to my way of thinking"—was a big stretch. She started out a Goldwater Girl. Though instant conversions to radicalism were common at the time, Hillary had a slower, more thoughtful evolution in her political views, working her way through the moderate Rockefeller wing of the Republican Party to campaigning for Eugene McCarthy by '68.

Jeff Shields, her Harvard boyfriend in those days, who is now a Chicago lawyer, fell in love with her earnestness. "The thing that I remember most were the conversations," he recalls. "She would rather sit around and talk about current events or politics or ideas than to go bicycle riding or to a football game."

Hillary's charisma was strong enough to attract a half-dozen girls to move into the Gothic dorm, Stone Davis, to be near her. They all ate together in a cloistered stone-and-glass gazebo. "You were surrounded by role models," remembers Jan Piercey of the all-female college. "We came away just assuming that everyone had serious aspirations." Hillary became president of her college government and graduated with high honors.

Coming to political consciousness in the late 1960s, Hillary saw these as "years dominated by men with dreams, men in the civil-rights movement and the Peace Corps, the space program." As an ambitious fourteen-year-old Hillary had written to NASA asking what it took to be an astronaut. She was told girls need not apply. Still, "growing up in the fifties, a lot of us sensed that we could redefine what women do." Her mother had hoped Hillary would be the first woman on the Supreme Court, "but Sandra Day O'Connor beat her to it," she jokes. Friends along the way have told her what Dorothy Stuck says today: "Regardless of what happens to Bill, the nation will be exposed to Hillary Clinton, and Hillary could—and should—be our first woman president."

Bill Clinton's childhood, as tumultuous as Hillary's was stable, helps illuminate his complicated relationship with his wife and the mistakes that have tested their political and personal partnerships.

Three months prior to his birth, his mother, a high-spirited, part–Native American, part-Irish woman by the maiden name of Virginia Cassidy, lost Bill's father, the first of her four husbands. William Jefferson Blythe III, a traveling salesman, swerved across the highway driving home from Chicago and drowned in a rain-filled ditch at the age of twenty-nine. The tragedy meant that Bill was left with his grandparents in the tiny town of Hope, Arkansas, for his first four years while his mother went off to New Orleans to pursue nurse's training in anesthesiology. Young Billy adored his grandfather, a six-day-a-week storekeeper who died when the boy was eleven. From then on he was bereft of family male role models.

When I asked Bill Clinton who was the first man who endorsed him as worthwhile, there was a very long pause. He stared out the plane window at the bleak, snow-blistered New England terrain. After mentioning his grandfather, he spoke stiffly of his stepfather Roger Clinton. "He took me to St. Louis in a train once, I remember that." He dredged up one family vacation, one fishing trip. "Literally, all those years and I can count on one hand—there just weren't many times. It was sort of sad. . . . I missed it."

When Bill was seven, the family moved to Hot Springs, a tingly place notorious for its racetrack, illegal gambling clubs, whorehouses, and gangster glamour. Every winter the high rollers would come from New York and Chicago and Miami Beach, looking for action. "The Clintons fit in with all that," says Carolyn Staley, the local preacher's daughter, who introduced herself to me at Clinton headquarters as "Bill's 'girl next door.'" Staley says Virginia Clinton was at the races every day—still is—she has her own box. "She loves it, it's in her blood. She wrote her own rules."

Clinton's mother also worked at being glamorous. With a silver streak dyed down the middle of her dark hair and three shades of eye shadow, "she'd put on tailored men's pajamas and mules and hang around with a cigarette in her hand, real Hollywood," says Staley. "She was a good-lookin' lady and hilarious. . . . One-liners are her trademark, like a walking female Will Rogers."

Virginia Clinton remained emotionally stoic through the abuse of Bill's alcoholic stepfather, who went on rampages that sometimes ended with a bullet hole shot in the wall or a beating of Bill's mother or younger brother. Finally, at fourteen, Clinton put an end to the violence in a shocking confrontation that marked the turning point of his adolescence. Hearing a fight, he broke down the door of his parents' bedroom. "[I] told him that I was bigger than him now, and there would never be any more of this while I was there," Clinton recalled to political writer Joe Klein.

Virginia Clinton temporarily threw Roger out of the house—a brief divorce—and began taking her teenage son along to a nightclub she frequented called the Vapors. During racing season the club ran fast and loose with lusty Vegas entertainers singing over the raucous *chi-ching* of slot machines and the squeals at the blackjack tables—an experience which seems to have simultaneously intrigued and repelled the boy. "It was fascinating," Bill told me. But he added, "I didn't like to be around dark smoky places where people were drinking too much. . . . I had a real negative association with alcoholism. I think subconsciously I was afraid it would happen to me." Bill later became president of his Baptist Sunday-school class.

"Some of the mistakes I made later in life were rooted in all those things that were unsaid or unexplored when we were growing up," Bill told me. Virginia Clinton made no attempt to explain or analyze behavior. "My mother was trying to keep peace and survive in an explosive situation." Bill never rebelled, adds Staley. "He had to be the shining light in his mother's life."

The fact that his reality as a child was completely defined by a woman may explain his later dependence on Hillary and other strong women. Young Bill also developed the pleasing style of many children from alcoholic homes, who reason, as Betsey Wright describes it, "'If I'm really nice, and I make this person feel better, then maybe this [behavior] will stop.'" Wright adds, "I can see that in Bill now. *He* sees it."

Another common result in families where parents are weak, narcissistic, or alcoholic is that the growing child either copies the immature habits he sees at home or leaps ahead to become a premature grown-up. The missed childhood can later trigger immature behavior as an adult. "I always wondered if I'd want to be sixteen when I was forty because I never felt like I got to complete my childhood," Bill Clinton has said.

Carolyn Staley confides that "Virginia and Bill and Hillary have taken what might otherwise have been made out to be a debilitating background and they've carefully developed a spin to their lives to make Bill the conquering hero."

Bill Clinton first laid eyes on Hillary Rodham at Yale Law School in a class they shared in political and civil liberties. He thought she was "the greatest thing on two legs," but there was more to the attraction. They belonged to a new generation, where everything was supposed to be equitable between the sexes. Hillary had come to Yale already a star, renowned as a multiple winner on the TV quiz show *College Bowl*, and as the college senior who delivered an extraordinary counter-commencement speech at Wellesley College in 1969. The address, which earned her national publicity, including her picture in *Life*, had struck a very sixties tone: "We feel that our prevailing, acquisitive and competitive corporate life . . . is not the way of life for us. We're searching for more immediate, ecstatic . . . modes of living."

What does Hillary remember as the most ecstatic experience of her twenties? She ponders, then laughs, conjuring up the sunny southerner with Elvis sideburns who entered Yale Law School a year after she did. "Falling in love with Bill Clinton," she answers.

What attracted her to him? "He wasn't afraid of me," says Hillary.

"But I was afraid of *us*, I tell you that," admits Bill.

He trailed her out of the class they shared, following her so close he could smell her hair, and then he stopped dead in his tracks. *No, this is nothing but trouble*, he told himself. "I could just look at her and tell that she was interesting and deep." He walked away. For the next couple of weeks he stared at her, he stalked her, but he couldn't bring himself to make the first move.

One night, huddled at the end of the library, he watched the object of his gaze stand up and march the full length of the Yale Law School library until she stood face-to-face with him. "Look, if you're going to keep staring at me, then I'm going to keep looking back," Hillary said, "and I think we ought to know each other's names. I'm Hillary Rodham."

"I was dumbstruck," says Bill Clinton. "I couldn't think of my name."

They have been looking at each other with mixed feelings of fascination and apprehension ever since.

Studious, solemn, dynamic, substantive—these are the adjectives her classmates use to describe Hillary Rodham at Yale Law School. Hillary gave no thought to "getting herself up," and was in fact mousy-haired, makeupless, and somewhat intimidating behind her oversize, Steinem-like glasses. Big Bill Clinton, by contrast, was "Mr. Aura"—a good time, funny, intense, a very quick study. Bill shared a famous beach house for the first two years with an African-American from a family of Philadelphia Republicans, Bill Coleman.

He remembers Clinton partying, reading Camus, dating several women (including an African-American classmate). But he spent most of his time working on political campaigns. "He did not spend lots of time trying to master *Marbury* v. *Madison*," snickers Coleman.

Professor Burke Marshall remembers Hillary vividly. "She was even then forceful, very smart, very articulate. Some very good lawyers ramble, but that's not Hillary. Her mind is an organized mind." Of Bill Clinton he says, "He was a very good student, he's very, very smart. But I'd never have thought Bill Clinton was law-firm material. He was obviously going to be a candidate."

To Clinton, law school was just a credential. He had a single-track focus. Even when he and Hillary took a house together, a baby Colonial, and "he was totally consumed by somebody else's being," as Coleman recalls, Clinton did not take his eye off his soaring political ambitions. As a result, doubts about the match lingered for Bill and Hillary. "I loved being with her, but I had very ambivalent feelings about getting involved with her," Bill admits. He insists he warned Hillary from their earliest dates, "You know, I'm really worried about falling in love with you, because you're a great person, you could have a great life. If you wanted to run for public office you could be elected, but I've got to go home. It's just who I am."

When Hillary and Bill joined the Barristers' Union, to put on a competitive trial before a real jury, she whipped him into shape as her partner. Alan Bersin, a fellow student, now a partner at Munger, Tolles & Olson in L.A., chuckles as he remembers Bill, "who was superb at presenting. But Hillary was definitely the serious one about getting work done and thinking through the position." They did not, however, win the prize trial. "I just had a bad day," Bill told me sheepishly, adding that it didn't help when "Hillary wore this bright-orange outfit."

But the dynamic duo made a lasting impression on one of the judges, John Doar, a hero of the civil-rights movement. Six months after they graduated, Doar was shopping for crack young lawyers to staff the House Judiciary Committee inquiry that would prepare the impeachment case against President Richard Nixon. Bill excused himself; he was already geared up for his 1974 congressional race. But what about Hillary? "If he hadn't suggested her, I would have called her anyway," says Doar.

The work was thrilling and grueling, twenty hours a day for six months. In August, treed by the committee's work and public opinion, Nixon resigned. By the end of her first year out of law school, Hillary Rodham had become part of history.

W*hy would she marry him?* That was what her Wellesley classmates and the feminists who knew Hillary from the McGovern campaign demanded to know. Most thought Bill was terrific. *But move to Arkansas? You gotta be kidding*, the subtext clearly being *buncha redneck racists*.

"I kept struggling between my head and my heart," Hillary remembers. Head said: gold-plated law firm in New York or Washington, public-interest law, or government. Heart won. Later in the summer of 1974, she "took a leap of faith" and moved to Fayetteville. "I just knew I wanted to be part of changing the world," she says now. "Bill's desire to be in public life was much more specific than my desire to do good."

Hillary and Bill taught at the University of Arkansas Law School, eschewing living together "because of the local mores." After a year of trying on Arkansas life, Hillary decided to see what all her friends were doing that she might be missing. "I went to Boston, New York, Washington, Chicago," she recalls. "I didn't see anything out there that I thought was more exciting or challenging than what I had in front of me."

When Bill picked her up at the midget airport, he was ebullient. "You know that house you liked?" Hillary looked blank. "What house?"

As Bill tells the story, she'd made a passing comment about a pretty little glazed-brick house. He'd gone out and bought it, feathering the nest with an antique bed and flowered sheets from Wal-Mart. "So you're going to have to marry me," he declared, winding up his pitch as he pulled into the driveway of the house. Two months later she did.

"I was disappointed when they married," admits Betsey Wright, who had met the dating couple when they came to her home state of Texas to work for the McGovern campaign in 1972. "She has been absolutely critical to Bill's success but, then, I had images in my mind that she could be the first woman president."

Mack McLarty, a childhood friend of Bill's who now serves with Hillary on the board of the yogurt giant TCBY Enterprises, adds candidly, "I married above myself in terms of intellect, like Bill did."

For Hillary, Arkansas was a different world. Even in Little Rock, where they moved in 1976 when Bill became attorney general, women were expected to be content with curling their eyelashes and selecting china patterns—especially political wives.

Instead, Hillary was recruited as one of the first women in the state to join a mainline law practice, the Rose Law Firm, after several partners were impressed by the way she set up the University of Arkansas's legal-aid clinic. "I think initially there were some [clients] who might put her into a stereotype . . . the pushy, Yankee female," says her law partner Webb Hubbell, "but I don't think anybody after fifteen minutes with Hillary would think that. . . . She can tell if the client is very nervous or concerned about something and can put them at ease."

In 1978 the Clintons swept into the governor's office with the promise of youth and purity. "Arrogant" was the outcry of the Establishment, and the governor's spouse became the lightning rod for people's resentment. To southerners expecting a more decorative First Lady, Hillary Rodham was almost an eyesore. She rejected makeup, glared through thick glasses, drowned herself in big shapeless fisherman's sweaters, and adamantly stuck to her maiden name.

Two years later, at the age of thirty-two, Hillary produced her "one perfect child" the same month she made law partner. According to Carolyn Huber, Hillary believed the baby came three weeks early because she was under the emotional stress of litigating a tough child-custody case. There were harrowing hours until Hillary underwent a cesarean. Finally, Bill emerged from the delivery room in green scrubs, cradling a seven-pound baby, saying he was "bonding" with his new daughter, and generally acting "like he'd invented fatherhood," says Diane Blair, a political-science professor in Fayetteville.

But it was also an election year. When the newspapers reported that "Governor Bill Clinton and Hillary Rodham had a daughter," the voters were outraged at their First Lady's blatant feminism.

His defeat that November was devastating for the Wunderkind governor, who was written off as having no political future. "There are a couple of periods in my adult life that were pretty tough," says Bill, and this was the first one. Observant friends think Bill also felt as if he had failed Hillary. "The mutual admiration that creates the closeness in their marriage also produced difficulties," says Piercey.

At the time of his disorienting loss, Hillary's own career was soaring. "Subconsciously, that's hard for all of us," sympathizes Herb Rule, another of Hillary's partners. "You always want your friends and spouse to do well. But not at a time when you're failing."

For the next six months, according to friends, the governor "went a little crazy." They suggest that the Clintons' marital problems began around this time, and lasted until a few years ago. Before the couple purchased a small house, Betsey Wright was summoned to move into the mansion and see what was salvageable of Bill's career and his political records. "He got crazy in the incessant quest for understanding what he did wrong, which was masochistic," remembers Wright.

The ousted governor stalked around the state apologizing for himself—and seeking solace. "The frustrations I went through in the seven years of being his chief of staff," moans Wright, "of watching the groupie girls hanging around and the fawning all over him. But I always laughed at them on the inside, because I knew no dumb bimbo was ever going to be able to provide to him all of the dimensions that Hillary does."

According to Wright, Clinton resisted the aphrodisiac effect of his powerful position more than many men. But, she admits, "Bill was always very careless, out of an unbelievable naïveté. He has a defective shit detector about personal relationships sometimes. He just thinks everyone is wonderful. He is also careless about appearances."

Bill remembers during this dark period being so haunted by a sense of imminent death, "I would seize everything." Hillary thinks he "viewed his father's death as so irrational—so out of the blue—that it really did set a tone for his own sense of mortality. . . . Not just in his political career. It was reading everything he could read, talking to everybody he could talk to, staying up all night, because life was passing him by." Uncharacteristically, her narrative begins to skip at this juncture: "I mean it was . . . it was an intense sense of . . . what he might miss at any moment."

Some say Hillary took the political defeat harder than her husband did. When she gets down for brief periods, she withdraws into reading, playing dress-up with Chelsea, or trudging off to the Y to work out. She also prays. "Hillary has an unbelievable ability to control her personality and her moods," marvels Wright. Sometimes, she pops off, not often, but stingingly. "The person on the receiving end never gets over it," says Huber.

Hillary determined to do whatever it took to put her husband back in power. So, without a word from Bill, she shed her name for his. She also dyed her hair, traded her thick glasses for contacts, and feigned an interest in fashion.

The Clintons campaigned nonstop those next two years—on top of their jobs at respective law firms. The first of a series of baby-sitters was hired to live on the premises and be on twenty-four-hour call. Once their daughter began speaking, at age two, "Chelsea would say, 'I want my mama,'" recalls Huber, but she soon learned to answer her own question: "Mommy go make 'peech."

Commonly, a chief of staff and willful wife are natural enemies, but "Hillary made herself absolutely indispensable," says Betsey Wright. She sat in on their strategy sessions. "Her own performance in selling and implementing his government programs was extraordinary. There were so many ways he needed her."

Hillary also acted as his conscience. "I think that there have been many times when he would have liked to go home and turn on the TV and escape or just read a book," concedes Wright, "and she would be in with a list of things people had called her about that day or that had to be done. He would be 'Ah, couldn't you just be a sweet little wife?' instead of being this person helping me be what I'm supposed to be.

"Between Hillary at home and me at the office, pushing and pushing him, I know there was a point where he felt, *These people need to leave me alone. I just want to do what I want to do.* It was a rebellion."

By the time voters returned the Clintons to the governor's mansion in 1982, Hillary was ready with her beaded inauguration gown, Chantilly lace over charmeuse silk. And for Easter she made sure to pick out the sort of cartwheel-brimmed hat that would stir whispers of "Very nice" and "Just right." As Jan Piercey puts it, "Hillary made her tradeoffs early on, and I think she steeled herself not to look back."

The Clintons marched straight into the heat of public censure in '83 when the governor appointed Hillary to chair the state committee on educational standards. She spearheaded a requirement for a onetime teacher examination. "Lower than a snake's belly," one school librarian called her. It was typical of the insults she faced for the next several years.

Hillary pushed on to introduce a consumer-rights approach to education, and the concept of continuing education for educators. She barnstormed around the state for hearings, stopping in all seventy-five counties. Her husband massaged his legislature until Arkansas was eventually tunneling seventy cents out of every tax dollar into education programs. These improvements—plus the governor's timely hike last year in teachers' salaries—won over the teachers' union, which had been their bitterest foe. It was typical of the way their political partnership worked.

Hillary also injected her ideals into her corporate-board work. As a sort of resident sociologist on the board of Wal-Mart, a nonunion company with 380,000 employees, she contributed to the retailing giant's ranking in *The 100 Best Companies to Work for in America*. Named head of Wal-Mart's environmental committee, she reframed the question from waste disposal to education and launched the company on a recycling program. She "saved us from a false start on environmental policy," says Rob Walton, son of the company's founder.

The Clintons' partnership looked perfect, at least from the outside. And then Bill stepped on another land mine from his past.

He was thirty-seven when he went through the worst year of his life. It was 1984, during his second term as governor, when a colonel of the state police phoned Betsey Wright, who dashed out to track down Hillary in a nearby restaurant and tell her, "We need to talk to Bill." His twenty-seven-year-old half-brother, Roger, had been spotted selling cocaine. The state police wanted to inform Clinton about their undercover surveillance. Though he was pained by it, he told them to proceed. "It was," says Hillary, "a much greater crisis than anything we've had in this presidential campaign."

Bill's half-brother did more than a year in prison, then came out only to discover that he was cross-addicted to alcohol. A drug counselor rounded up Bill, Roger, their mother, and even occasionally Hillary for intense family therapy. She led them through discussions on co-dependency. Clinton says the process helped him to learn things he never knew about himself. The counselor told them that the line between wanting to be a rock star—Roger's dream—and a governor is a very thin one.

During "the next two or three years of discovery . . . they all came to grips with having grown up in the home of an abusive stepfather," says Wright.

"After my brother got into trouble in 1984, it really had a profound impact on me," explains Clinton. "I just couldn't imagine. . . . I kept asking myself, How could I not have known this?"

The unfinished business of his past threw him again into a period of dis-equilibrium. He feared he might not be able to live up to the great expectations of his political life and his life partner. The soulsearching, which coincided with Bill's mid-life passage from the age of thirty-seven to forty, also sparked a revival of the behavior that had earlier put strains on their marriage.

I n the summer of 1987 forty-year-old Bill Clinton was poised to launch his candidacy for the presidency. Political big shots flew into Little Rock for the announcement luncheon. Everything was ready.

But moments before the scheduled start, Bill backed out. He and Hillary had had a heart-to-heart talk about the longstanding rumors of his zipper problem. Chelsea was only seven. It was too soon. The press that July day caught a rare glimpse of Hillary Rodham Clinton spilling emotion: she stood behind Bill and wept.

The period that followed the climb-down from their joint national aspirations may have been the nadir of their marriage. A clue slipped out during the *60 Minutes* confessional. Bill told Steve Kroft humbly, "If we had given up on our marriage . . . three years ago, four years ago, you know . . . If we were divorced, I wouldn't be half the man I am today, without her and Chelsea."

So it was that Hillary Clinton woke up one morning last August in the Arkansas governor's mansion, looked over at her husband's sleepy face, and told him, "You almost have to do it," meaning run for president.

"Do you have any idea what we're getting into?" he asked.

"I know, it'll be tough," she replied. But she was ready to take her own platform national, as a campaign letter described it. And she was bored with the politics of Arkansas, where her husband has put in a full decade as governor. "She doesn't like all the duties of First Lady," confirmed her brother Hugh Rodham. "It's tiresome and too local."

Reflecting back on the personal journey he has made over the last four years, Bill says the fear of life running out at any moment has subsided. "It's all different now. I think—in the aftermath of my brother's encounter and all the stuff that Hillary and I went through, and where we are together now, and Chelsea—I'm so much more relaxed. I got into this race because I really felt I was strong enough and ready to be president . . . and because the things that Hillary and I have worked on together were more relevant to what has to be done in the country than anybody else."

"Every life has challenges," Hillary told me philosophically. "Life has become very unpredictable and scary for people. And the only insurance policy you've got against whatever comes down the pike is to be as ready as you personally can be. I think that's part of what the voters have been saying to me: Nobody could have predicted that all this would happen to you. You didn't ask for it. But you were ready. And, boy, we're glad you were."

If he loses, Hillary predicts, "Bill and I have great opportunities, we'll always be able to make a good living, we've got a wonderful daughter—we'll be fine." It doesn't usually work that way, however, particularly not for two driven people whose every axon and dendrite have been tingling for months as they crisscross the country in matching campaign planes, eager to deliver political redemption to the masses. If suddenly they land, SPLAT, back in Little Rock, and they wake up to the concern that their child has been necessarily neglected, and perhaps Hillary begins to thaw out the small, ex-cruciatingly painful little package in the deep freeze labeled "Bill's Marital Mistakes," this could be a very difficult period.

But Hillary Clinton also has developed her own form and substance, her survival instincts and resilience. Maybe the next gubernatorial election the other Clinton will run. There could be a role switch: Bill might find rewards in replicating his childhood—supporting the woman who defines and con-trols his existence.

And maybe the next presidential election, or several more down the line, the other Clinton will be on the ticket. As Hillary told a Los Angeles audience recently, "We'll have a woman president by 2010."

Would she consider running? she was pressed. "We'll talk later."

(Hillary Clinton would go on to become First Lady [1993], New York senator [2001], U.S. secretary of state [2009], and, in 2016, the first woman ever to be named the presidential nominee of a major American political party.)

MICHELLE OBAMA

FIRST LADY IN WAITING

By Leslie Bennetts | December 2007

A s Michelle Obama strolls around Mack's Apples Pick-Your-Own orchard greeting people at the Londonderry children's fair, she seems relaxed and friendly, her casual manner belying the pressing schedule that just whisked her from Chicago to New Hampshire and will soon rush her off to an afternoon packed with other events.

But when she addresses the crowd, there is no mistaking her sense of urgency as she makes an impassioned case for her husband's presidential candidacy. "I am desperate for change—now," she says, "not in 8 years or 12 years, but right now. We don't have time to wait. We need big change—not just the shifting of power among insiders. We need to change the game, because the game is broken. When I think about the country I want to give my children, it's not the world we have now. All I have to do is look into the faces of my children, and I realize how much work we need to do."

Right now the Obamas' daughters, six-year-old Sasha and nine-year-old Malia, are bouncing on the inflated castle at the fair, oblivious to the country's problems. But for some of the assembled voters, their father's youth is also an issue. Even his admirers acknowledge that, at 46, Barack Obama—a first-term senator and the youngest presidential contender in either party— has great potential but is relatively green. Most of his rivals are over 60, and many analysts have viewed the 2008 campaign as an exploratory run that could set the groundwork for a future race when Obama is more seasoned and the electorate has adjusted to the idea of America's first black president.

Michelle Obama, who turns 44 in mid-January, is also young, by First Lady standards. Regally tall, stunning, and city-chic in a triple strand of pearls atop her country-casual pants-and-sweater outfit, she manages to look as down to earth as any other soccer mom and as glamorous as a model while instantly commanding respect, even before she starts to speak.

But Mrs. Obama has no interest in an ongoing quest for the White House. "To me, it's now or never," she tells me a few days later, in Chicago, where we've met up again at the campaign's Michigan Avenue headquarters. "We're not going to keep running and running and running, because at some point you do get the life beaten out of you. It hasn't been beaten out of us yet. We need to be in there now, while we're still fresh and open and fearless and bold. You lose some of that over time. Barack is not cautious yet; he's ready to change the world, and we need that. So if we're going to be cautious, I'd rather let somebody else do it, because that's a big investment of time, just to do it the same way. There's an inconvenience factor there, and if we're going to uproot our lives, then let's hopefully make a real big dent in what it means to be president of the United States."

And what it means to Mrs. Obama is sacrificing many of the things she holds most dear, in favor of a larger goal. Although she has concluded that this mission is worth what it takes, achieving such acceptance has been diffi-cult, and the adjustments are ongoing.

Her husband's vaulting ambition was always a given. "She knew what she was getting into," says Craig Robinson, Michelle's brother, who is the men's basketball head coach at Brown University. "Ever since I've known Barack, he's said that he wanted to be in politics. He's never changed his interests; it just happened that he's turned out to be very good at it."

But Obama's accelerated timetable came as a shock, even to his spouse. As recently as 2000, Obama—then a little-known Illinois state senator—lost his first race for Congress. But in 2004 he ran for the U.S. Senate and won in a landslide victory, collecting more votes than any Illinois politician in history and becoming the nation's only black senator.

No sooner had his family adjusted to that development than he started to consider a run for the presidency in 2008. "This was a sudden decision," Mrs. Obama says. "He had just won his U.S. Senate seat. In my mind, it was 'O.K., here we are—you're a U.S. senator.'"

With Barack commuting to Washington while Michelle and the children remained in Chicago, the family's life was already complicated, and Michelle was stunned when Barack abruptly fast-forwarded his presidential aspirations. "I thought, Uhhhh—you're kidding! It was like, No, not right now—right? There was a period of 'Let's not do this now; let's press the "easy" button! Can we get a break, please?'"

She sighs and rolls her eyes. "So we had to talk about it. Before I signed on, I had to know, in my mind and my heart, how is this going to work for me, and would I be O.K. with that? He wouldn't have done this if he didn't feel confident that I felt good about it, because it is a huge sacrifice. The pressure and stress on the family isn't new. But we entered this thing knowing it was going to be really, really hard. For us, the question was: are we ready to do something really hard again, right after doing something that was really hard?"

Barack eventually managed to persuade the whole family that his quest justified the cost. "This is something that's bigger than everybody," says Craig Robinson. "This is so important that it's worth her saying, 'I've got to rethink the way my family is structured.'"

Although Mrs. Obama had recently been appointed as vice president at the University of Chicago Medical Center, her husband's announcement in February 2007 that he was entering the presidential race forced her to scale back her professional commitments. In May, she reduced her work schedule to 20 percent in order to meet the needs of her family while participating in the campaign.

"She was intending to take a full leave of absence, but she couldn't make herself separate from this professional career that's been so important to her," says Susan Sher, vice president for legal and governmental affairs at the University of Chicago Medical Center, where she is Mrs. Obama's boss. "Her involvement in her work life has been so serious that it's not easy to just say, 'Never mind.'"

Mrs. Obama has a long history of speaking out about the ways in which men's choices—particularly their professional ambitions—often leave their wives to pick up the slack, even when they have their own careers. "What I notice about men, all men, is that their order is me, my family, God is in there somewhere, but me is first," she told the *Chicago Tribune* in 2004. "And for women, me is fourth, and that's not healthy."

But for the moment, at least, Mrs. Obama has reconciled herself to putting her career on the back burner. "The way I look at it is, We're running for president of the United States. Me, Barack, Sasha, Malia, my mom, my brother, his sisters—we're all running," she says. "I can't hold down a full-time job as vice president of community and external affairs and be on the road three or four days a week. Barack has never asked me to stop doing my job; as far as he was concerned, 'You have to do whatever makes you feel comfortable.' But, for me, it was: How can I not be part of this? How can I go to work every day, when we're trying to do something I believe in? If I really felt it was more important for me to be vice president of community and external affairs full-time, I would do that. But the bigger goal here is to get a good president—somebody I believe in, like Barack, who's really going to be focused on the needs of ordinary people. For what I'm trying to do at the hospital, getting him elected is a better way for me to reach that goal. Part of doing this is that I would have felt guilty not doing it. I would have felt I was being selfish. We have this opportunity, and Barack could do amazing things, but I wanted help with the laundry? Now my conscience is clear."

That equanimity has been hard-won, however. Earlier in their 15-year marriage, she was often furious with her husband. "I have chosen a life with a ridiculous schedule, a life that requires me to be gone from Michelle and the girls for long stretches of time and that exposes Michelle to all sorts of stress," Barack wrote in his best-seller *The Audacity of Hope*. By the time their second child was born, he reported, "my wife's anger toward me seemed barely contained. 'You only think of yourself,' she would tell me. 'I never thought I'd have to raise a family alone.'"

Mrs. Obama finally got tired of being enraged and miserable. "One day I woke up and said, 'I can't live my life mad. This is just no fun,'" she reports. "For a period in my life, I thought the help I needed had to come from Barack. It wasn't that he didn't care, but he wasn't there. So I enlisted moms and babysitters and got help with the housecleaning, and I built that community myself."

She also had to re-evaluate the gap between her own expectations and her husband's far more flexible ideas about family life. "I came into our marriage with a more traditional notion of what a family is," she says. "It was what I knew growing up—the mother at home, the father works, you have dinner around the table. I had a very stable, conventional upbringing, and that felt very safe to me. And then I married a man who came from a very different kind of upbringing. He didn't grow up with a father; his mother traveled the world. So we both came to this marriage with very different notions about what children need, and what does a couple need to be happy."

She shrugs resignedly. "So I had to give up some of my notions, and so did he. That's part of being married; everyone makes compromises. Once I got a sense that the family we were creating was going to be good for our children, I realized that it wasn't exactly what I had, but our children are thriving and they feel loved. Part of my fear was: Are my kids going to be O.K.? If they don't see their dad at night, like I did, will they feel he loves them? Barack grew up not seeing his mother for months at a time. There was a period when his mother stayed in Indonesia and he came back to Hawaii, and he was living with his grandparents. And he experienced that fully feeling that 'my mother loves me deeply.' So he was more comfortable with those choices than I was, and that was an adjustment that I had to make."

I t was one of many. A graduate of Princeton University and Harvard Law School, Michelle Robinson met her future spouse when she was assigned to mentor him at the Chicago law firm of Sidley Austin; although he is three years older, he was still a law student at the time. In 1992 Michelle decided to leave the law firm and pursue a career in public service. "She just knew the private practice of law was not sufficiently satisfying, and she was willing to walk away from a huge salary potential and all the trappings of power that go along with it," says Valerie Jarrett, a longtime friend and former boss.

But even before Michelle married Barack, she was consulting him about her career decisions. Jarrett was Chicago mayor Richard M. Daley's deputy chief of staff when she first met Michelle and offered her a job—whereupon Michelle asked Jarrett to meet with her and Barack to discuss his reservations about the offer.

"He had some trepidation about her going to the mayor's office and joining the Daley administration," says Jarrett, who is now president and C.E.O. of the Habitat Company, a real-estate development-and-management company. Although she admits it was highly irregular for a job-seeker to request that a prospective boss meet with her fiancé, Jarrett says, "I think it's a sign of a real partnership, that they are friends and advisers who think through major decisions together."

One clue to Michelle's approach may lie in her relationship with her older brother, which was both close and competitive. As a high-school junior, she visited Craig at Princeton University, which had recruited him to play basketball. "I'm smarter than he is," she thought, and determined to attend Princeton herself—which she did.

Even as a child, however, Michelle had figured out how to wield power over an older, larger sibling while appearing to defer to him. "We had this game where we set up two rooms and played 'Office,'" says her brother, who grew up to be six feet six inches tall. "She was the secretary, and I was the boss. But she did everything. It was her game, and I kind of had nothing to do."

Her daughters are a major reason Mrs. Obama has tried to avoid that dynamic with her husband. "When he comes home, he's taking out the garbage and he's doing the laundry and he's making up the beds, because the girls need to see him doing that, and he knows I need him to do that," she says.

She grins, her eyes twinkling. "And that was a meeting of the minds that we had to reach. I wasn't content with saying, 'You're doing important things in the world, so go off and be important and I'll handle everything else here'—because the truth is, if I did that, I'd probably still be angry."

Their friends say that both Obamas have made significant sacrifices to accommodate each other's needs. "Sometimes one person compromises and sometimes the other one does," says Cindy Moelis, a former colleague of Michelle's in the Chicago mayor's office who is currently executive director of the Pritzker Traubert Family Foundation. Money worries were one issue, according to Moelis: "They had a lot of student loans, and there was a lot of tension around that. Barack's choices made her life harder." When Barack wrote a book that became a best-seller, the resulting income eased the Obamas' financial situation. Another example Moelis cites is Michelle's decision to stay in Chicago after Barack became a U.S. senator. "People said, 'He needs you in Washington,' but her friends and family and support system are here, and she said, 'This is where I'm going to be,'" Moelis reports.

Mrs. Obama does not affect the kind of pious deference favored by many other political wives. On the campaign trail, she takes pains not to exaggerate her husband's admittedly stellar qualities, and she has often startled observers with her sardonic sense of humor—including her admonition that her husband is "just a man."

Many voters are delighted by a degree of candor they find appealing and reassuring. "When Michelle Obama talks about Senator Obama, she makes you laugh, because he puts his dirty towels on the floor like any other husband," says Brenda MacLellan, co-chairman of New Hampshire's Henniker Democrats. "She talks with the dignity of a First Lady, but you don't have to be prim and proper to be First Lady. She's a real person, and we need real people in Washington. I don't want any more surprises. We can't afford any more surprises."

But others are put off by Mrs. Obama's tart-tongued irreverence, and some of her comments have attracted disproportionate attention. The media pounced on such innocuous remarks as Mrs. Obama's admission that her husband can be "snore-y and stinky" in the morning, as well as her wry complaint that Barack once rushed out of the house and left her to deal with an overflowing toilet.

When I ask Mrs. Obama if she is censoring herself these days, she gives me a rueful smile. "I'm kind of sarcastic, and I've felt that my sense of humor had to be subjugated on some level," she admits. "My husband loves my sense of humor, and we tease each other mercilessly. But if somebody doesn't get the joke, then you become a caricature of what the joke was. So it's like, Well, jeez—let me not joke, then, if it's going to be all that problematic. People get real worked up about some things I felt were really minor, funny, harmless observations about who we are as people."

Mrs. Obama nonetheless believes that it's better for voters to understand her husband and herself before deciding on their choice. "My hope is that Americans really want to know who the people who are going to be in the White House are," she says. "What's our sense of humor? What are we trying to accomplish? What are our values? My view is: know that now; make the judgment. I think people are ready for truth, if it's real—so that's what I'm banking on."

In any case, the American electorate won't be treated to any displays of the adoring-spouse pose perfected by Nancy Reagan, who never tweaked her husband in public and whose worshipful mask never slipped no matter how many times she sat through the same speech. "I can't do that," Mrs. Obama says. "That's not me. I love my husband. I think he's one of the most brilliant men I've ever met, and he knows that. But he's not perfect, and I don't want the world to want him to be perfect. If you look for that, then people can't try hard stuff, because you might mess up. We want leaders to be bold and to try some things that might not work, because they might work and be great. I think that's one of our failings as a nation—we're looking for our leaders to be something that's not realistic, and then we're deeply disappointed when they don't live up to those unrealistic standards. So let's shake that up a little bit. We're moving into the 21st century, and life is different. We've struggled; we've grown. Let's not be hypocrites about it, either. Let's not say we want one thing and then demand you be something you're not."

S ome voters contrast the Obamas' apparent openness with the hairsplitting evasions that alienated many of the Clintons' former admirers. "I trust Michelle to tell you how it is, good or bad," says one longtime Democratic activist at an Obama event in New Hampshire. "But I don't trust Hillary to tell me the truth, and I don't want to deal with all the history of Bill's infidelity. Why didn't she kick his ass out? I know many women who would be voting for her if she had kicked him out." She scowls, and then confides that her own unfaithful husband left her with two children and another on the way. "I don't need Hillary's baggage," she says. "I've got enough of my own."

The Clintons have long elicited such intensely personal reactions, and their marriage continues to occupy center stage despite decades of public scrutiny. Some voters see the Obamas as representing the chance for a fresh start with honest straight shooters—a prospect that Mrs. Obama deftly encourages. "Barack will not be a perfect president, but he will always tell you the truth," Mrs. Obama assures her audience in Londonderry. "You will always know where he stands."

Though she never mentions the Clintons, her emphasis on her husband's personal integrity implies a clear contrast between the Clintons' oft-tortured marriage and her own. Her husband has behaved honorably in his personal as well as his political life, she says: "He is a fabulous husband and father, and I think that is right up there with everything else you should look at."

Some of her husband's supporters give Mrs. Obama much of the credit. "She talks about Barack being a good husband, but it takes a strong wife to make a good husband," says Representative Paul Hodes, a New Hampshire Democrat who has endorsed Obama.

So far Mrs. Obama has avoided making any specific promises about what she would do as First Lady. But as for who she would be, her attitude is clear: what you see is what you get.

"I am really being as authentically me as I can be," she says. "When people ask, 'What kind of First Lady will you be?'—I'm going to try, in all this, to be honest, hopefully funny, and open, and share important parts of me with people, hopefully in a way that will help them think about their lives and avoid the mistakes we may have made in our lifetime. What you see on the trail is probably who I will be as First Lady, because that's really who I am."

But she has no illusions about maintaining an independent career if her husband reaches the White House. "Absolutely not," she says. "I don't think that's possible or realistic or desirable. Everything I do on my job would pose some huge conflict."

These days her very participation in the current campaign reflects the depth of her commitment to her husband's goal, according to her friends. "She hasn't taken this role every time he's run for office," says Cindy Moelis. "This is the first time in all these elections that I've seen her be as passionate and committed as she has been."

"I think they really struggled through it, but once the decision was made, she's totally gung-ho," says Susan Sher.

As for the outcome of this race, Mrs. Obama seems philosophical about her husband's prospects. "We're doing our best," she says. "I hand it over to people and say, 'O.K.—it's on you,' so I'm good."

Such earnestness proves too much of a temptation, however, and she quickly succumbs to a characteristic flash of mischievous humor. "I'm good," she repeats, her voice starting to quaver. "No, really—really! Can't you tell? I'm great with it!" She buries her head in her hands and pretends to sob.

But then she straightens up in her chair and gives a blank, faux-happy smile, as if beaming mindlessly for the camera. Nobody's perfect, and Michelle Obama—lawyer, soccer mom, hospital executive, Senate wife, potential First Lady—is the last person who would ever want you to think she considers herself a finished product who has it all together.

"I think I'm 60 percent there," she says. "I'm still a work in progress, too."

(Michelle Obama would serve as First Lady from 2009 to 2017. Her best-selling 2018 memoir, Becoming, *has broken numerous publishing milestones.)*

SOCIETY
AND
STYLE

EMILY POST'S SOCIAL REVOLUTION

By Laura Jacobs | December 2001

n 1921 the writer Edith Wharton published a novel called *The Age of Innocence*. It was set in the highest, mightiest circle of New York society in the late 1800s, a time known as the Gilded Age. Here was Society with a capital *S*, a world of Astors and Van Rensselaers, calling cards on silver trays, ancestral portraits on drawing-room walls. Wharton's book was an elegy to a lost era of rectitude and reticence, unwritten rules and unspoken understandings. The people of this world, Wharton wrote, "lived in an atmosphere of faint implications and pale delicacies." And when they spoke, they spoke as one.

A year later, in 1922, as if to smack closed the coffin on Wharton's rose-colored era, Sinclair Lewis brought out *Babbitt*. In fact, he dedicated his novel, the story of a real-estate salesman in a boomtown called Zenith, to Edith Wharton. When the book begins, George F. Babbitt is hungover, and his first spoken word is "Damn!" Behold the climbing Everyman of postwar America. The name Babbitt soon symbolized the melting-pot, free-market Babel our country had become, a rising clamor of conflicting voices.

Another book was published in 1922. This one, however, was poised between Edith Wharton's Gilded Age and Sinclair Lewis's Jazz Age. Looking both backward and forward, it took Society's unwritten rules (not to mention those faint implications and pale delicacies) and wrote them down in black and white so that anyone—new marrieds in the boonies, newly minted millionaires, even Mr. and Mrs. George F. Babbitt—could know the rules, too. And it wasn't a silver spoon talking, but a voice of sterling character, wit, and wisdom. One of the 20th century's great acts of democracy, 619 pages carried forth on a deeply ethical undercurrent, this $4 book was a masterpiece in its own right—a how-to and a self-help and an Old Testament and a constitution, with here and there dashes of satire. It would go on to 10 revisions and 89 printings in the author's lifetime, never selling fewer than 30,000 copies a year. The book was titled *Etiquette: In Society, in Business, in Politics and at Home*. But it swept America as "Emily Post."

She was born Emily Price in Baltimore in 1873, a 10-times great-granddaughter of John Alden, one of the *Mayflower* Pilgrim fathers of 1620. Emily's mother was Josephine Lee, daughter of a coal baron from Wilkes-Barre, Pennsylvania. Josephine was sent to Baltimore for finishing school, and while not the prettiest girl in her class, she was shrewd and knew exactly what she wanted. When Josephine met young Bruce Price, an up-and-coming architect with aristocratic good looks, a good background, but no money beyond a modest salary, she determined to have him. His talent, her drive—they were on their way.

Bruce Price's career carried the family to New York City, where he was soon one of the golden boys of late-19th-century architecture. "He is thought of as one of the artistic architects," says Christopher Gray, who writes about the history of New York City for *The New York Times*. "If you had to compare him either to [architects Charles Follen] McKim or Stanford White, you'd say Stanford White, more of a designy type with great artistic flair." Price won plum assignments, one of his biggest coming in 1885 when Pierre Lorillard III asked him to design Tuxedo Park, a 6,000-acre private sporting community about 30 miles north of Manhattan in Orange County. Tuxedo, as members called it, took its place alongside Bar Harbor, Maine, and Newport, Rhode Island, as a posh playground for the rich. Of the three, Tuxedo was the most inconspicuous in its luxury, correct yet rustic. Price was given four "cottages" at the club, and the family, having previously summered in Bar Harbor, switched allegiance to Tuxedo.

———

Emily was an only child and a daddy's girl, doted on by her father and devoted to him in return. When his American Surety Building was going up at Broadway and Pine—"a sophisticated skyscraper," remarks Gray—Emily would visit the Wall Street site with her father, taking in every word he had to say about scale, proportion, and the classical line. "The rules are all there," he told her. "Living is building. If you know the laws and respect them, you can't help building well." In later life she would refer to the American Surety Building with pride, explaining that it contained construction innovations that led to ever higher skyscrapers. More important historically was its aesthetic advance. Price designed it in the round, with a finished facade on all four sides so that no blank walls would blight the view. Just as Tuxedo Park suggested a way of life—the comfort of shared values—the American Surety Building was a monument to a way of being: upstanding on the inside, and, on the outside, gracious to all no matter what their angle.

Coming of age in the Prices' red-brick town house at 12 West 10th Street, Emily absorbed the clockwork decorum of her day, the rituals of social expectation, all the while encouraged by her father to study art, history, literature. For Emily, who could herself have been the ingenue in a novel by Edith Wharton, it was indeed a life of surety. First, she was a beauty, tall and straight, her complexion famously alabaster, her delphinium-blue eyes often remarked upon. Second, she was self-possessed. In her debutante year of 1890, she was named by Ward McAllister, gadfly arbiter of Society, who coined the term "Four Hundred" (the number of Society's chosen who could fit into Mrs. Astor's ballroom), as one of the 10 ladies in New York who could gracefully cross a ballroom floor alone. Third, she was quick and clever. And yet, in Emily's set, too much cleverness was cause for concern. As with entertainer Ruth Draper and actress (then decorator) Elsie de Wolfe, it could lead a woman into ego, exhibitionism, i.e., into the arts or onto—gasp!—the stage. When Emily made a sensation in a Tuxedo Park amateur theatrical, she was forbidden to act again. Emily's destiny—what she and her finishing-school friends were groomed for from birth—was marriage to a man of her own class or higher, to be followed by children, preferably sons. Emily began to fulfill this destiny on June 1, 1892. She married Edwin Main Post of the Long Island Posts, manufacturers of railway equipment.

It was a brilliant match—Emily, the season's most radiant debutante; Edwin, the handsomest of bachelors and moving successfully into finance. The courtship commenced with their first polka, a giddy beginning for two who loved to dance. They felt made for each other. And in many ways the Society marriage of that time was a kind of dance, a formal round in which you did not jar your partner or step on toes. While her husband rose on Wall Street, Mrs. Edwin Post mastered her role, teaching herself to be the perfect wife and hostess, and giving birth to two sons, Edwin junior and Bruce. She was also learning something else: her husband was not like her father.

Leafing through the Post-family scrapbook from the 1890s, one finds Emily in Victorian skirts, tightly corseted. Her boys are in curls and dresses until the age of two (the age of pants!), and poor Edwin junior must wear a cap, according to Emily's caption, "to flatten ears." The summers are pastoral, Emily in white linen framed by lawn and leaves, her hair up, her posture casting a glance of protection over her sons. Winters are silver, the Christmas tree great with mercury-glass garlands and balls, the toys underneath a fantasy of plenty. But absence is unmistakable. It is more than halfway through the scrapbook before the man who is Emily's husband appears, the man with membership in 35 clubs, who drove a red Pierce Arrow trimmed in brass and was one of America's 10 best bridge players. In the whole of Emily's scrapbook there is not one photograph of the couple together, and there are only two of Edwin Post—slim, dark-eyed, distant—and these two were taken within minutes of each other. In one photo a cigar hangs nonchalantly between two fingers; in the other, no cigar.

Well, Emily loved books; Edwin loved sailing, sports. She was happiest at home; he preferred parties, friends. She was idealistic; he was hedonistic.

"Since she could not share Edwin's enthusiasm for physical enjoyments, and he would, or could, not share her interests which were chiefly mental," writes Edwin Post Jr. in *Truly Emily Post*, a biography of his mother, "there was nothing but for each to go his own way without interfering with the other's pleasures. . . . Their private disappointments or failures to each other were of no importance to Society."

Nor were such disappointments discussed. In the summer of 1902, Emily was persuaded to go abroad to visit friends at their European estates. The boys would spend time on a farm in France, and Edwin could yacht the Eastern Seaboard to his heart's content. Emily, freed from the old routine, began a new one. Waking early, around six, she would sit up in bed and write letters—fresh, funny letters reporting the romantic intrigues, the human comedy, within these landed households ("A man who marries for money *earns* it! Every penny!"). Ten years into the marriage, it was not her husband to whom she sent these letters but her father. Emily was 29 and still clever. But now a different destiny was asking her to dance.

I t began later that year, when writer and family friend Frank Smith was visiting, and Josephine praised Emily's letters from Europe, saying, "They made me laugh." Smith asked to read them, and 10 days later Emily was invited to lunch with both Smith and George Barr Baker, the editor of *Ainslee's* magazine, one of the most popular periodicals in the nation. Baker felt the letters could be recast to tell a story—a light romance—which could be serialized in *Ainslee's* and then published as a book. Emily set to it, urged on by her father, who said, "You and I are alike. We are workers. We are only fully ourselves when we are working." In early 1903, just as Emily was finishing *The Flight of a Moth*, a novel in letter form, her father fell ill. That summer, mere months before Emily's words were in print, he died.

"The French say that the ideal condition for a woman would be to be born a widow; and that is nearly my case, as I am just now starting out upon what I feel to be a new life." Emily gives this line to Grace, the widowed heroine of *The Flight of a Moth*, but it certainly reflects Emily's own emotional terrain at that time. We see ambivalence about wifedom, her feeling of being alone within her marriage (she was known to call herself a "yacht-widow"), and perhaps even a wish to be a genuine widow. And there is the "new life" she is starting out upon—her life as a writer. In society she was Mrs. Edwin Post, but in print she had become her own property, Emily Post.

The Flight of a Moth was a hit, and Emily began work on *Purple and Fine Linen*, another romance, set among New York's gilded class, and a book whose theme of slow-stealing marital disillusion (husband holding on to his bachelor habits, wife feeling like a "doll-wife" to be put in a "show case") speaks of Emily's own experience: "Every now and then she longed for someone, not only to talk to, but someone who felt as she did—some one of her own kind." Of course, all ended well in Emily Post's early novels, with heroines and husbands reaching new levels of love and understanding. Already detectable is an urge to instruct, a hope for the way things could and should be. But Emily was not one to blind herself to the way things were. In 1905, when *Purple and Fine Linen* was published, her age of innocence ended.

Just as "Emily Post" was becoming a popular byline in national magazines, Edwin Post received a call from *Town Topics*, a New York weekly that specialized in scandal. *Town Topics* was not unlike the tabloids of today, except for one difference—it dug its dirt for blackmail. The basic M.O. was as follows: once a victim's indiscretion was substantiated with names, dates, and sometimes photos, the victim received a note or phone call requesting an interview. He (it was usually a he) was told that if he cared to take an ad in *Town Topics* or buy a subscription ($500 to $1,000) to a special volume the company was publishing, the paper wouldn't run the offending story. Edwin Post received his call on June 21, 1905. *Town Topics* suggested he buy a $500 subscription to its limited "edition de luxe of *America's Smart Set*." Edwin discussed it with his lawyer, who discussed it with Emily. She said fight.

GOT $500 FROM POST, THEN WAS ARRESTED. The story broke July 12, on the front page of both *The New York Times* and *The New York Tribune*. Right there for all to see was the threat made to Edwin: "Mr. Post . . . we have in our office some matter that you probably would not like to see printed. It is something, you know, about a white studio in Stamford and a fair charmer." The love nest, the showgirl, the usual. The papers then gave a step-by-step account of the days leading from threat to arrest, which took place when Post, in a men's room at the New York Stock Exchange, handed five marked $100 bills to Charles P. Ahle, a man associated with *Town Topics*. A detective hiding in the next room apprehended not only Ahle but a briefcase full of receipts from other "subscribers," among them J.J. Astor, A. Van Rensselaer, and three (count 'em) Vanderbilts. The investigation later turned up the names of Stanford White, Isaac Guggenheim, and F. Ziegfeld (Flo). This scroll of shame was a veritable hall of fame, and Post, the *Times* reported, "received a regular ovation when he made his appearance on the floor of the Stock Exchange. One member shouted, 'Go for them, Post, my boy! We are with you, for we've all been through that mill ourselves!'"

But, as other New York papers pointed out, Edwin Post's action "was taken on the advice of Mrs. Post." She was the one with the nerve, for she was the one whose private injury would become public knowledge. When the dust settled, Emily did something even nervier, something she would never have put her fictional characters through. She filed for divorce. Believing her changed status—still a rarity at that time—demanded a changed name, she christened herself Mrs. Price Post, as if to reiterate "I am my father's daughter." One also suspects, given the names in Ahle's briefcase, that Emily felt no man could measure up to Bruce Price. In her early 30s, at the height of her beauty, she closed up shop, romantically speaking. For the rest of her life, Emily Post would cross all ballroom floors alone.

W e are workers," her father had said, and next to raising her two sons, work was all she wanted. In three years Post published three books, beginning in 1908 with *Woven in the Tapestry*, a slim volume of strange fables written in a perfumed Symbolist style, and dedicated to Bruce Price. Archaic and esoteric, it was not a success. *The Title Market*, in 1909, was. This bestseller about American heiresses in pursuit of titled Europeans made Post an instant authority on society marriages. The book showcases Post's strength—her keen feeling for the way character is revealed through manners (the content in form!). And it also betrays her weakness: good guys and bad guys who are simply too good and too bad. In 1910, with *The Eagle's Feather*, Post tried for complexity—a misogynist hero, a martyred heroine. And still the book ends with everyone illumined, forgiven. Post knew darkness—she just couldn't bow to it.

With the boys away at school at Pomfret, then Harvard, Post lived at Tuxedo and used the house on 10th Street when visiting editors and friends in the city. She was keeping meticulous scrapbooks of her reviews, marking particularly positive mentions with red (her favorite color) and negative comments in light blue. And now she was in the best magazines, including *Collier's,* edited by the bon vivant Frank Crowninshield, a close friend who was soon to become the editor of *Vanity Fair.* "Crownie" was full of ideas for Post, and in 1915 he came up with a doozy. Using the new Lincoln Highway—a dirt road in some states—would she motor from New York to San Francisco, dispatching reports to *Collier's* along the way?

Why not? Edwin junior took a leave from Harvard to be chauffeur, cousin Alice Beadleston squeezed in with the luggage, and the three were off—27 stops in 26 days. After the custom-made car's first breakdown 20 miles from Utica, Post wrote, "Is there anything more exhilarating than an automobile running smoothly along? Is there anything more dispiriting than the same automobile unable to go?" When an old man comes along in a buggy, she notes, "He grinned as the owner of a horse always does grin under such circumstances." This is the voice that emerges in *By Motor to the Golden Gate*— game, engaging, getting right to the heart of human nature. It is a voice tuning up for something larger.

Back in New York, Post watched her elder son, Edwin junior, leave for war, where in 1917 he was cited in French Army Orders for bravery. In these years, at the behest of friends who admired her eye for interiors, Post developed a second career helping these friends redesign their homes. She loved making cardboard dioramas of rooms, showing where a staircase should go, where a window. In a later era she might have followed her father into architecture, which she thought the highest of the arts. But it was still writing that paid the bills.

Post was pasting together a model of a house, a makeover for the daughter of Mrs. Stanley Mortimer, when she received another Crownie call—not actually from Crowninshield, but at his suggestion. Richard Duffy of Funk & Wagnalls felt there was a market for a good book on etiquette, and having called Crowninshield for advice, he was told, "If you want a book for the 10,000, get Edith Wharton. But if you want a book for the millions, I would suggest Emily Post."

Mrs. Price Post wanted no part of it (she thought Duffy was *selling* encyclopedias). When she finally understood what Duffy was proposing, she refused to consider it. Crownie, however, was not the Diaghilev of cultural New

York for nothing. He sent Post a lately published book on etiquette, a condescending work that stressed pinkie fingers and fish forks. Post read late into the night, then threw the book from bed. As she would later explain, "It was all so wrong. The ultimatums they laid down would merely have made people unpleasant. Their attitude was false and silly and cheap. At 3 o'clock in the morning, I called up Mr. Duffy." In 1921, at the age of 48, Emily Post began research on the book she was born to write.

Crowninshield had been onto something. As gifted a storyteller as Post was, her novels did read like second-rate Edith Wharton. The very qualities that made Post's fiction a bit simplistic—her endless optimism, her ingrained sense of fair play, her authorial presence too much in the room—were exactly the qualities that made *Etiquette* embracing, accessible, intimate. Here was Post's own American Surety Building, a site on which to apply those golden means (like golden rules) she'd lived with all her life—the Price ideals of scale and proportion. She wrote the book sitting on a high stool at an architect's drafting table, no doubt remembering her father's words "Living is building." It was 18 months in the making, 38 chapters, moving from "Introductions" ("Most people very much dislike being asked their names") to every aspect of social interaction, the last line pointing to "the Golden Age that is sure to be." Emily Post's *Etiquette* was monumental, a blueprint for a better civilization.

Chapter I—"What Is Best Society?"—sets the standard. "Etiquette must, if it is to be of more than trifling use, include ethics as well as manners. . . . Thus Best Society is not a fellowship of the wealthy, nor does it seek to exclude those who are not of exalted birth; but it *is* an association of gentle-folk, of which good form . . . and instinctive consideration for the feelings of others are the credentials by which society the world over recognizes its chosen members." Anyone could be of Emily Post's "Best Society," if only they understood the code. Correctness could be learned, but it rang hollow without kindness.

Still, there was nothing sweet or simpering about Post's text. Upon reading the 1922 edition, America's reigning literary critic, Edmund Wilson, wrote, "I had no conception of her extraordinary book till I looked into it recently,

[and] fell under its spell. . . . Mrs. Post is not merely the author of a comprehensive textbook on manners: she is a considerable imaginative writer, and her book has some of the excitement of a novel." Post had indeed brought her fictional skills to bear on the book, and her characters had names right out of Restoration drama: the Oldnames, the Toploftys, the Gildings, Clubwin Doe, the Kindharts, the Littlehouses, Mr. Richan Vulgar, the Upstarts. In other hands they might have been mere chess pieces, but instead, wrote Dorothy Parker in *The New Yorker*, "these people in Mrs. Post's book live and breathe; as Heywood Broun once said of characters in a play, 'they have souls and elbows.'"

And they elbowed their way into satire, sometimes even slapstick. There are scenes in *Etiquette* which once read can never be forgotten. Edmund Wilson's favorite is "The House Party in Camp," where Mrs. Worldly "looks at her napkin ring as though it were an insect." (Dorothy Parker writes of Mrs. Worldly, "I know of no character in the literature of the last quarter century who is such a complete pain in the neck.") The classic, though, is "How a Dinner Can Be Bungled." In this lesson an eager young wife ("You," the reader) oversteps herself, attempting a formal dinner before her household has proved itself on smaller occasions. Post achieves a mounting comic horror, the slow drip toward social disaster you get in Jane Austen. Example: "And then comes the soup. You don't have to taste it to see that it is wrong. It looks not at all as 'clear' soup should! Instead of being glass-clear amber, it is a greasy-looking brown. . . . You look around the table; Mr. Kindhart alone is trying to eat it." Drop into *Etiquette* anywhere and it's impossible not to keep reading.

"Etiquette books surface at different times in history," says Judith Martin (Miss Manners). "It's either in periods where life is so complicated that you can't possibly just imitate your parents and hope to get away with it. Or times like the Renaissance, when people want to develop aesthetics in behavior as well as in building and arts. And then the other big time—times of social upheaval. So, yes, you had an influx of new rich then. We have it now. America is founded on this idea, that you get ahead through your own merit."

As Duffy intuited, an authoritative guide was just what 1920s America— its economy booming, its classes in flux—wanted. In a kind of call and response unique in the history of American letters, *Babbitt* topped 1922's best-seller list for fiction while *Etiquette* leapt to the top of nonfiction, edging out Giovanni Papini's *Life of Christ*. Overnight, Emily Post was writing from the mountaintop. The new social arbiter of America, the first to be so accepted, she was, in the words of novelist Katherine Anne Porter, "the high priestess of good manners, expounding the scriptures even in the temples of the most high. She carries the word to the population, and is at once the interpreter and apologist—in the classic sense of that noble word—of society."

"She was the founder of this in America," says Letitia Baldrige, who writes etiquette books herself and served as chief of staff for Jacqueline Kennedy. "There had been many other writers on etiquette before her, but she was the first one who reached the popular vote. She did not talk in too starchy and cold a way, like the ones before her did. She didn't scare you." And the bungled dinner party? "How amusing that is and how it relaxes the reader."

"She's dealing very thoroughly with the subtext as well as the text," explains Judith Martin. "The outward rules of etiquette are not all that complicated, and one could set them down once and forever. It's the subtext, what it shows you about human conflict, that's fascinating."

"She's full of feeling," says Eleanor Elliott, who was social secretary to John Foster Dulles, Eisenhower's secretary of state. "There's an emotion to her. She explains certain relationships and how to do things very adroitly, and her philosophy was not the crooked little finger; it was about treating people correctly. The how-to-do-it may have changed somewhat, but the principles haven't. She's timeless."

Fifty when *Etiquette* was published, Emily Post rose to her new role without missing a beat. She finished the novel she had been working on when Duffy first phoned her—*Parade*, a story about a society beauty who is sexually cold (rather convincingly written, it may suggest Emily's own failing of Edwin way back when)—and with its publication in 1925 left novel writing forever. Her day, beginning as always around six, was focused on writing her newspaper column (syndicated in some 200 papers), answering letters (she received up to 6,000 a week), and planning revisions to the next printing of *Etiquette* (by 1945, the chapter "The Chaperon and Other Conventions" had become "The Vanished Chaperon and Other Lost Conventions"). She emerged at lunch, one on the dot, and her social life took place mostly at home within a closed circle of friends and family. She hated restaurants because she hated the waste of time waiting for food. "Punctuality at meals was a real fetish with her," recalls Emily's only grandchild, Bill Post Sr., the son of Edwin junior.

She was a household word, an institution—or as one newspaper observed, "Three great factors in American civilization: parcel post, *Saturday Evening Post*, Emily Post."

She was constantly queried for her opinion on issues of the day—from the length of Queen Mary's skirts (too long), to Prohibition ("I am a wet," she said, "a sopping wet!"), to corn pone, crumble or dunk? (depends on neighborhood custom). She was a role model constantly watched. When Post spilled a bowl of Swedish lingonberries at a Gourmet Society dinner, the event was reported in *The New York Times*. "Some regard me as a mechanical robot," she is quoted as saying. "I'm not at all, really, as you can see."

Perhaps the happiest period of Post's life was these years, the mid-1920s. After a few false starts, her younger son, Bruce, had become an architect, following in his grandfather's footsteps, much to Post's pride and joy. His career dovetailed with her need for a new home. Looking for a place to live in New York City, Post could find nothing suitable. The apartments didn't have enough windows, closets, or adequate rooms for the service staff, and the rents were outrageous. In 1925, over lunch with friends at the Colony Club (of which Post was an early member), she decided to build her own co-op, signing up friends as joint owners, including Bessie White (Stanford White's widow) and Mrs. James Roosevelt. It was a move that only the daughter of Bruce Price might dare to do, and the building that went up on the northeast corner of Madison Avenue and 79th remains one of the dozen or so tenant-sponsored co-operatives in New York City history. Post hired the esteemed firm of Kenneth M. Murchison, where Bruce was employed, and mother and son helped design the building. It was pure Price Post. "Very reserved and simple," says Christopher Gray. "Nothing show about it." The following year, on their own, Bruce and Emily renovated an old sea captain's house on Martha's Vineyard. Winters in Manhattan, summers in Edgartown.

The greatest sadness of Post's life hit in 1927. Just when her younger son, in the words of the *Times*, "had given evidence of inheriting the talent of his grandfather," Bruce Post died at 32, from peritonitis following an appendectomy. "She was devastated," says Bill Post Sr. Post did not openly grieve. She kept up with her work. But in the months following Bruce's death, in the blank spaces and empty edges, she made herself do puzzles, intricate jigsaw puzzles, to keep her mind off herself and her sorrow. And in *Etiquette* she revised her section on mourning, adding the line "Most of us merely do the best we can to continue to keep occupied and to avoid casting the shadow of our own sadness upon others." Nothing "show" about it.

Emily Post had no peer, and *Etiquette*'s new 1945 subtitle—"The Blue Book of Social Usage"—reflected that stature. This was the guide. During the 1930s, Post reached millions through weekly radio broadcasts, one of the first females on the air. And World War II brought yet another surge of popularity. With the country again experiencing upheaval, new decisions on decorum needed to be made. (Was it all right for women doing factory jobs to hitchhike to work? Post said yes.) Even servicemen were making a run on *Etiquette*. According to war correspondent Ernie Pyle, if boys wanted to be officers, they had to "know their Emily Post." The chapter Post added to the 1945 edition of *Etiquette*, titled "Concerning Military and Post-War Etiquette," is not only a rich slice of American history, but also unexpectedly moving. Under the heading "When the Disabled Man Is Her Son or Husband or Betrothed," Post writes of the moment when this man searches a woman's face "to measure the degree of his handicap by its effects on her": "She must above everything remember that abandonment to tears is not the way to help him. The one thing that does help is to make him realize that to her he is not any different from the man he was—and to assure him that in the years to come he is not to be set apart."

That "not" is pure Emily Post, a commandment of compassion: Thou shalt not break his heart. It is no coincidence that, soon after its publication, *Etiquette* ranked second to the Bible as the book most commonly lifted from bookstores and libraries.

S he really ruled," says Mrs. Howard Cox, archivist at the Colony Club (and mother-in-law of Tricia Nixon). "If you heard someone say, 'Oh, Emily Post wouldn't approve of that,' well, that was the rule, that was law.

Emily Post was taken very seriously." In fact, at this time the two most powerful women in America were Eleanor Roosevelt and Emily Post.

And what was the powerful Post, a woman making almost $100,000 a year at the age of 72, like in real life?

"She was a very natural person," says Yvonne Sylvia, Post's secretary in Edgartown for 15 years. "She was very generous. When I had my second son, I still went a full day, but she paid for a baby-sitter for my children. She seemed very content. I think she was perfectly happy with her grandson and great-grandchildren. She didn't need the companionship that other people do."

"She was a lovely, lovely person," says Isabel Paulantonio, Post's devoted secretary in New York City. "I was a little in awe of her, considering her background and *Etiquette*. But she immediately put me at ease."

"That was one of her charms, one of her talents," says Elizabeth Post, wife of Bill Post Sr. (and the woman who would take over *Etiquette* after Emily's death). "She made you feel totally at ease. She was imposing, a very large lady. She held herself very erect. But she had a very kind face. And she laughed a lot."

"She enjoyed being Emily Post," says Bill Post Sr. "She liked to tell stories on herself."

When *Vanity Fair* ran a full-page Covarrubias caricature of Emily in 1933—frizzy-haired, owl-eyed, bare feet propped on the table, pinkie crooked in a question mark—fans were aghast at the irreverence, while Post thought it "too giggle-making for words." (She had laughed at herself before in *Vanity Fair*, when in 1926 Crowninshield talked her into spoofing *Etiquette* with a quirky, anonymous serial called "How to Behave Though a Debutante.")

Post's great-grandchildren talk about her as if she were just like any other great-grandmother.

"She'd give us dimes so we could eat ice-cream cones at the local drugstore," says Allen Post.

"She was not formidable," says Peter Post.

"She was not pretentious in any way," agrees Bill Post Jr.

"To be pretentious was the worst faux pas you could make," continues Cindy Post Senning, who co-directs the Emily Post Institute in Burlington,

Vermont. Bill Post Sr. seconds that: "If she had to go to the bathroom, she'd say, 'I have to go where the king goes on foot.'"

She was down-to-earth.

"Almost to the day she died," says Bill Post Sr., "she could sit perfectly happy on the floor, bolt upright with her legs crossed. For me as a child that was neat."

In the last years of her life, in the late 1950s, Post became increasingly forgetful, and the family believes she may have been suffering from Alzheimer's disease. During those years her son Edwin junior wrote her column from Italy, where he had retired, and her faithful secretaries kept up the correspondence. Emily Post died of pneumonia on September 25, 1960, in her bedroom at 39 East 79th Street. She was 86. Her ashes were buried in Tuxedo Park, next to her son Bruce. Today, Post's *Etiquette* (which has sold more than 500,000 copies since 1984) is updated by feisty Peggy Post, wife of great-grandson Allen.

When those close to Emily Post speak of her, they invariably touch on her love of color, how she impulsively, happily re-painted furniture, radios, whatever struck her as needing new life, and how she adored red—bright Chinese red. And then they remember her shoes, red shoes—a closetful! It's a fascinating footnote. In Hans Christian Andersen's tale "The Red Shoes," a girl puts on scarlet slippers and cannot stop dancing, just as Post, having written *Etiquette*, could never stop being her book. But the similarity ends there. Emily Post loved the dance she was doing. And she did it with such joy. Who better to teach us the steps than the woman who wrote (under "Rules of Sportsmanship"), "If you are hurt, whether in mind or body, don't nurse your bruises. Get up and light-heartedly, courageously, good-temperedly get ready for the next encounter. This is the only way to take life—this is also 'playing' the game!"

TO WAR IN SILK STOCKINGS

By Marie Brenner | November 2011

O n May 16, 1941, Kathleen Harriman, the daughter of the new
American special envoy to Britain, W. Averell Harriman, was on a
train speeding to London for her first look at war. She would have
worn a hat, and probably gloves—that was the kind of girl she was, pretty and
very rich, a graduate of Foxcroft and Bennington who wanted to be taken seriously. She had with her a small black notebook and her father's New York
shopping requests: silk stockings and chiffon handkerchiefs for the Churchill
family, Stim-U-Dents, *Time* magazine, *The New York Times*, and six Guer-
lain lipsticks—which she knew better than to question. The notebook would
become indispensable—the only place where the 23-year-old would feel safe
to confide her thoughts—and she would fill pages from her seat at the center
of power. All that summer and autumn of 1941, she set down moments small
and large, then tucked the notebook away and never discussed its existence
or contents with anyone—including her children—for 70 years.

She gazed at the craters in the streets, the charred remains of towns, children playing in the rubble. "Perhaps someday I'll be able to figure out what
made me want to come . . . pluck has nothing to do with it," she wrote in
pencil in a boarding-school hand. The previous week in London had been an
unimaginable hell: the British Museum, Waterloo Station, and the House of

Commons had been almost destroyed by the *Luftwaffe*. Delayed in Lisbon, Kathy, as she was known, had been spared the thousands of buzz bombs dumped on central London, which killed 3,000 people.

"When are you Americans coming to help us? Because you know we can't win without you," she was asked by a woman in her compartment soon after the train left Bristol. Did Kathy let on who she was? By then, her father was already on page one of every newspaper. Averell Harriman was in London on a mission of desperation: to help save the British from Hitler. A senior partner of Brown Brothers Harriman, he was nicknamed "the crocodile" for his outbursts of sovereignty. But Harriman's own urgency about the need to go to war had given him bleeding ulcers. Months before Japan attacked America at Pearl Harbor, Roosevelt was still holding off on entering the war even as England was battered by the Blitz. Roosevelt's stopgap was to send Harriman, the lordly financier and a co-owner of *Newsweek*, as a personal liaison to implement the new aid program called Lend-Lease. It was understood inside Washington that Harriman's real task was to help forge an alliance between Churchill and Roosevelt, known for their chilly relationship.

"Are those silk stockings you're wearing? Are you American?" Startled by the cheerful conversation, Kathy wrote down the questions, as well as her new friend's zinger: "Looking at her own stockings of cotton lisle, she announced that hers were far more serviceable." When Kathy told her of the latest New York fashions—"hip-length jackets, apron skirts, the big competition for bigger and better hats"—the woman was dismissive: "Oh, well, we have all of that. You see, war or no war, we keep up."

Kathy had no real reporting experience, but her father had managed to pull a plum assignment for her: she would write of the heroics of the English-women. The series—for Hearst's International News Service—would be called "The British Woman at War." "Just give us everything you can observe and think of, sobbing all over the page," one editor would later instruct her. Her bona fides were that she was intelligent, stylish, and a Harriman. She was clearly worried about the entitlement. "I'm no Dorothy Thompson," she confided in her diary. She wouldn't have to be.

A n expert rider and an Olympic-level skier, she was called Kathy by her friends and Puff by her father, who was, in 1941, the fourth-richest man in America. A member of the elite circle of titans educated at Groton and Yale later known as the Wise Men, Harriman would become an architect of the American Century. Remote and often charm-free, Harriman in private was an affectionate father who pushed his two daughters to excel. He critiqued their schoolwork and encouraged their closeness with his favorite sister, Mary Rumsey, a member of Roosevelt's inner circle who was an early consumer advocate. She had inspired her younger brother to become a Democrat and helped transform him from a polo-playing rich boy. At 49 he was still dazzlingly handsome. The *New York Post*'s Dixie Tighe would tell Kathy, "For God's sake, tell your father the next time I have to cover his conference to wear a gas mask so I can concentrate on what he is saying." On the slopes, with his head tossed back and wearing sunglasses, Harriman exuded the effortless style of an American aristocrat. So did Kathy, who could out-ski him and out-shoot him. Harriman adored her.

THINGS OK HERE CABLE WHETHER YOU SERIOUSLY WANT TO COME, he had wired shortly after his arrival in England. Not long out of Bennington, Kathy was marooned in Sun Valley, the Idaho ski resort her father had built at the height of the Depression to be America's Saint-Moritz. Her favorite Austrian ski instructors had fled to join Hitler or were threatened with arrest as enemy aliens. Put to work writing press releases in the winter of 1940, Kathy wrote in her diary that she felt lost and melancholy. At a time when no reporters were easily cleared for London, Harriman had pressed hard to get her a passport and a job. IT IS HARD TO UNDERSTAND IN NEW YORK THE SIGNIFICANCE OF WHAT IS GOING ON HERE IT IS A UNIQUE PRIVILEGE TO BE HERE THEREFORE I AM GOING TO ENCOURAGE KATHLEEN TO COME . . . CAN GET NEWSWEEK APPOINT-MENT IF NONE OTHER AVAILABLE, he cabled home. Secretary of State Cordell Hull wrote back: PASSPORTS . . . HAVE HAD TO BE REFUSED TO THE FAMILIES OF OFFICIALS . . . MIGHT PROVE AN ADDED EMBARRASSMENT I STRONGLY ADVISE AGAINST. Other cables followed, to Assistant Secretary of State Dean Acheson and to John Gilbert Winant, the American ambassador to Britain, known as Gil. Harriman's final cable was to Kathy herself: GET IN TOUCH WITH HARRY.

There was no one more influential in America in 1941 than Roosevelt's top aide, Harry Hopkins, a hero to many, a Rasputin to others, and one of Harriman's closest friends. Soon Kathy could cable her father: PASSPORT OKAY LOVE KATHLEEN HARRIMAN.

For years Harriman had struggled to overcome his legacy as the son of the robber baron who started the Union Pacific Railroad, a man President Theodore Roosevelt had blasted as a "malefactor of great wealth." It was said of Harriman that he was forever trying to measure up to his stern and remote father, who had died when Averell was 17. Desperately ambitious, he had set out to make a fortune in minerals in Russia. He traveled on private Streamliners—America's first all-coach rail service—and counted among his close friends the *New Yorker* writer Alexander Woollcott and CBS head Bill Paley. His lust for power and his zeal had alienated America's old money— especially Franklin Roosevelt. As Washington filled with bankers during the New Deal, Harriman was placed on financial commissions, and not until March 1941 had he been allowed a seat at the table. London would be a test for both father and daughter.

Harriman knew that Kathy's poise and elegant presence would bring him luster. As slender as a model, she wore Worth suits that she could buy off a mannequin. With her wide smile and natural curiosity, she would be a perfect hostess for her father. Harriman's wife, Marie, an earthy art dealer, had severe vision problems, which kept her in America. For Kathy, "Ave," as she called him, had always been a bachelor father. Kathy's mother had filed for a divorce when Kathy was 12, and died seven years later. Kathy and her older sister, Mary, had been raised by a beloved governess, Elsie Marshall. An invitation to London to be with her father was a chance for her finally to have him all to herself—or so she thought.

Once off the train at Paddington, Kathy typed up her notes and telexed them to a Hearst re-write man. Her schmaltzy column closer was just what her editor had in mind: "These English women may not have my silk stockings, but they have something else, something I'd like to catch hold of." Captioned "N.Y. Girl Looks at War," a picture of her at the Stork Club occupied three columns in the *New York Journal-American*. Her story, "Silk Stockings Still Important in London," ran all over America and in London's *Evening Standard*. She soon discovered that even if she wasn't Dorothy Thompson she had a good ear for a quote. Her father wrote home immediately, "She is the center of attention among certain groups in London—if it weren't for her Spartan upbringing (for which I take no credit) she would become unbearably spoiled."

Her unstated role was as urgent as her father's mission—to boost sympathy for the need to help the British. It would also become her burden to be a witness to the affair that would ensnare her father with Winston Churchill's daughter-in-law for the next 45 years. When Kathy died at 93 in February of this year, the *Telegraph* cut to the chase, saying, "She facilitated his affair with Winston Churchill's young daughter-in-law Pamela, but following the lovers' eventual marriage, sued her stepmother for millions."

The *Telegraph* overlooked the real essence of her life: Kathleen Harriman was a link to a vanished world that prided itself on discretion and distinction. The names in her diary represent the pantheon of that historical moment: Winston Churchill, press tycoon Lord Beaverbrook, British politician Duff Cooper, even the royal family. And as her father carried on with Pamela Churchill, Gil Winant fell in love with Sarah Churchill, the prime minister's bohemian daughter. When biographers approached Kathy in later years, her answer to most of them was polite but irrevocable: *Thank you, no.*

But a curious revelation startled many who read Kathleen Harriman's *New York Times* obituary: Cleaning out the cupboards at his mother's apartment in the city a few weeks before she died, Kathy's son David Mortimer, a public-policy expert, noticed a box that held two large brown leather scrapbooks. Inside was a mix of photographs and dozens of newspaper clippings with her London byline, products of a career almost unknown to her family. Page after page had scores of her dispatches with datelines all over England. Later, presiding in Moscow when her father was made ambassador in 1943, she was, noted the *New York Herald Tribune* at the time, "with the possible exception of Eleanor Roosevelt and Deanna Durbin . . . the best-known American woman in the Soviet Union." She helped to arrange the 1945 Yalta summit, where Churchill, Roosevelt, and Stalin negotiated the end of World War II.

The *Times* detailed her summers as a child spent at Arden House, a 75-room château in upstate New York, on the 25,000-acre Harriman estate. The house, once reached by funicular, was designed by John Merven Carrère and Thomas Hastings, who also built the New York Public Library.

It was impossible to conceive that her life had a secret compartment almost unknown to her sons. "Hey, Mom, what is this about?," David asked her upon discovering the boxes. "Oh, that," she said, then changed the subject. Since her mind, sharp until her 90s, was beginning to fade, David let the matter drop.

The news of the discovery caused a frisson among those who knew of the Harriman family's celebrated history. A cluster of biographies had already mined the vast Harriman archives in the Library of Congress, but in all of them Kathy remained elusive, known from brief quotations from her letters, but little else. This was very much a part of her code. For David and his younger brothers, Jay and Averell, the sons of Stanley Mortimer, the Standard Oil heir Kathy had married at the age of 29, and for her stepdaughter, Amanda Mortimer Burden, New York City's visionary urban planner, a missing puzzle piece of Kathy's early life was mysterious and thrilling.

At first there was hesitation about showing the scrapbooks. The Mortimers are among the last of the old school, who expect to be in the papers only at birth and death. The three sons revered their tomboy mother, who taught them to jump their horses and drove through blizzards to get them to the ski slopes. She served as chair of a foundation, skied through her 70s, rode in her 80s, and supervised forums on public issues, but she always disliked the spotlight.

The letterheads on her correspondence are impressive: the Dorchester hotel, 3 Grosvenor Square (an area where so many Americans stayed that it came to be called Eisenhower Platz), Chequers (the prime minister's country house), Cherkley Court (Beaverbrook's estate). But little of this was ever part of the Mortimer family's dinner conversations. "We knew our mother had been there—and the names would come up from time to time—but she deftly changed the subject or referred us to Ave's own book," said David.

David and his brothers learned that in addition to her stint at Hearst their mother had written for *Newsweek*, spending much of the winter of 1942–43 at the London office, working 12-hour days when the bureau chief and the correspondents were transferred to the front. In Moscow, she helped run the embassy, learned a passable Russian, and enchanted Stalin and his Cabinet. Stalin gave the family two horses, Fact and Boston, which followed them home to Arden. Her father went on to become Harry Truman's secretary of commerce and, later, governor of New York, and in 1952 and 1956 he was a candidate for president. He remained an integral part of international diplomacy and Democratic Party politics until his death, at age 94.

London loved the diplomat's daughter from the first, and Kathy loved her new profession. She kept all the notes from her first real assignment, a profile of Lady Astor, the peppery American-born Nancy Langhorne, who had become a heroine to the British. Kathy typed on her Underwood portable: "'I'll stand on my head on Plymouth Hoe, if anyone thinks that will help Plymouth.' That's what Lady Astor said to me today in the course of an exclusive interview as she drove to Plymouth Station to see 200 evacuating children on their way." She also quoted Lady Astor asking her, "Child . . . come and tell me about home. What are they thinking and talking about these days?" Kathy telexed the story to the International News Service with her kicker: "If invasion comes, incidentally, I won't envy the Germans who meet her."

Ave threw his daughter into the mix from the moment she arrived. The world she had grown up in was small and tightly bound by the strictest social rules: you wore white in summer, kept Jews out of your clubs, and knew the families of everyone you might marry. If you were a Harriman, your world was expanded: you skied at Sun Valley with champions, had your Labrador on the cover of *Life*, had Jewish friends who ran networks, banks, and newspapers, or wrote plays and musical comedies. "It will make a real person out of her," Ave wrote Marie, whose mother was Jewish. On the night Puff arrived, he tossed a lavish party for her at the Savoy and invited every correspondent in town.

From his 27-room suite of offices in Grosvenor Square, Harriman pulled her into meetings with editors and generals. For the first months, Kathy lived with her father at the Dorchester, a glittering fortress during the Blitz. The dining room had a steady supply of crème caramel and lobster, champagne flowed, and an orchestra played late into the night. The novelist Somerset Maugham was also a guest at the time. During the day, Kathy wrote home, "the telephone never stops ringing in our suite. . . . Combine the war and journalism and you'll never have a moment of boredom."

Some of the best women reporters in the world were in London then—the *Chicago Daily News*'s Helen Kirkpatrick; the London *Sunday Times*'s Virginia Cowles; *Life*'s Mary Welsh, who would marry Ernest Hemingway. But Kathy's arrival was splashed in the English press. KATHLEEN HAS HAD ROYAL RECEPTION, Ave cabled. He also sent a long letter to Marie: "It is too bad she had so much publicity, but it couldn't be helped. . . . She is the only girl other than Helen Kirkpatrick reporting in London. (Two others are writing books.)"

Kathy's arrival on Fleet Street was hardly the coronation her proud father described. "Telephone all your stuff to central six seven six five, our dictaphone number, where your copy will be recorded," her editor told her, but gave her little further assistance. Thrown into a world she had no experience to handle, she worried that she would never be able to make it as a journalist. "None of the American reporters have been the least help to me on my stories," she complained to Mary, "even though they are a wonderful help in every other way." She was chilled by the staff, but Kathy was not to be deterred. "This week-end we again went to Lord Beaverbrook's, where Averell collared one Frank Owen, the most brilliant editor over here, and I at last got somewhere. Today I go to my boss Chris and he tells me the exact opposite from Frank. I almost laughed in his face So you see it is not very easy to turn overnight into a reporter."

At first, she did not stray far from the gilded ghetto. She went with her father to greet the first Lend-Lease ships and railed in her journal about the photographers who dogged her every move. Taken to Chequers to meet the Churchills, she was struck by the ease of the prime minister. She would be at Chequers many weekends in the subsequent months, "watching everyone coming in and out." Her father had quickly forged a strong relationship with Britain's wartime leader, who was desperate for Harriman's help. The half-American Churchill was drawn to Wall Street's players. Often the Harrimans' phone would ring at night and it would be Churchill's secretary asking if Ave could come for a meeting. Those meetings were the infamous games of bezique, a French card game. Harriman would remain for hours, trading confidences with Churchill, who had already placed the American in his secret war-cabinet meetings. In her letters home, Kathy wrote Marie, "Do you all appreciate what a hell of a job he's doing? I've finally decided that he ought to be triplets, one for Washington, one for London, a third for Moscow."

After three weeks in England, Kathy wrote in her diary: "Sat next to P.M. at dinner—he was in wonderful mood. Was excited to find he's good at shooting the English brand of Tommy gun. Saw *That Hamilton Woman*—with Sea Lord there, the P.M. and everyone else being in England and so close to the war made the movie mean so much more. All the C.'s cried—that impressed me too." On another occasion, they watched *Citizen Kane*, "a violent flop," Kathy wrote home. On Saturday afternoons, she often played croquet with Clementine Churchill. Kathy's private notes are filled with intimate conversations: "The P.M. was depressed at dinner tonight. Turkey is giving in. Russia won't hold out more than 6 weeks, he says. All Europe is swaying toward a Hitler victory. They are giving in. 'We need a victory.' The battle started today—we talked about Lend-Lease. What they are getting—about the censor—America won't come in til we're almost there. The P.M. knows that. 'I'd like to be a cat—without worries.'"

Kathy was beginning to understand the desperation. "Remember, I am an American," she wrote in an early dispatch. "All this is new to me. I'm not accustomed to wholesale horror." Her range of reporting expanded to refugees, gas masks, and food shortages.

When Averell took her to meet the Canadian Lord Beaverbrook, she at first found him "gruff. He overpowers you and makes you feel rather young and inexperienced (a good idea)." The son of a Presbyterian minister, Beaverbrook, born William Maxwell Aitken, owned the *Evening Standard*, but he was now the minister of aircraft production, ramping up the British effort against Hitler. He was encouraging to Kathy, telling her, "Come 'round to see the old man who taught them." He asked his top reporter, Hilde Marchant, to take Kathy under her wing. Kathy noted in her diary, "She's scathing, cynical, a disapproving socialist. I'll learn a lot from her."

Kathy was kept off breaking news until she finally submitted a dispatch that showed she might have a gift for the profession. Visiting a military hospital, she produced a sensitive portrait of soldiers with maimed hands and faces in their saline baths. "Last week, believe it or not, I wrote a story all the office seemed to like on the plastic surgery hospital," she wrote home. "Now they have given me a desk—and they are allowing me to write spot news. They want me to try to be Dorothy Kilgallen [the New York reporter]."

Harriman bragged to his wife that Kathy was at one event "chic as chic . . . in a flowered summer suit and black gloves." She was having the time of her life, borrowing her father's official car and heading for the Derby with Quentin Reynolds, the best-selling *Collier's* correspondent, telling her family, "Every night next week is booked up already. The only thing people seem scared about is being lonely."

M idway through the first album, I came upon a photograph that seemed out of place, a Cecil Beaton picture of Pamela Churchill taken for *Life* in 1940, when her son, Winston, was born.

It took Averell Harriman only one day to introduce Kathy to Pam. The day after Kathy got to London, she and her father were whisked to the country, to Leeds Castle, home of the ferocious Lady Baillie, a prominent hostess who had been largely displaced by Emerald Cunard, the very social shipping heiress. It would be Kathy's first real experience with the snide, coded society. Leeds was now an officers' hospital, and Lady Baillie, Kathy noted, was a "beautiful lady of the 1920 model—nervous and out for effect. Husband a bore—hopes I'll write a story on his place. Food all weekend amazing." And there too was the prime minister's daughter-in-law. Kathy wrote, "Pam Churchill is charming . . . a born leader in a quiet effective way—the Foxcroft type!"

No higher praise could come from a Foxcroft girl, and it has always been believed that Kathy was smitten by her new friend, who bombarded her with invitations and favors. It seemed a natural match—Pam was 21 and Kathy

23—and they became close very fast. But there were profound differences in their personalities: Kathy had the staunch personal code of a champion athlete with a first-class education; Pam, the scheming heart of a country aristocrat who modeled herself after a great-aunt, Jane Digby, a famous 19th-century courtesan.

Known for her flirty giggle, creamy shoulders, auburn hair, and laser attention to powerful men, Pam was as irresistible as Becky Sharp. "On Wednesday, I'm going down with Pam Churchill—the one on the cover of *Life* some time ago—to see the feeding center she has set up and to talk to some of the people," Kathy wrote to Mary. "She is a wonderful girl my age, but one of the wisest young girls I've ever met."

At 21, Pam was still in formation as "the greatest courtesan of the twentieth century," as a future husband, producer Leland Hayward, reportedly called her later; but her freewheeling sexuality had already scandalized the Cliveden set. Harriman was her first major conquest of a wartime platoon that would include Edward R. Murrow, Jock Whitney, Bill Paley, and a cluster of generals. The vicarious erotic thrill of being a witness to her father's romance would become a complicated dance that required Kathy's deft navigation. "Pam is also a bitch," Kathy would later note about her new friend. "I like her and think we'll get on OK."

A part of Pam's allure was her ability to absorb and reprocess the large issues of political life. She took Kathy to a hospital, where she saw her first shell-shocked children, and later to her family's house in Dorset, a drafty hall that Kathy noted "needs interior painting." The two trips solidified their bond. Back at the Dorchester, Kathy wrote in her diary, "Came home— learned about Pam's courtship. Engagement first night—Married 10 days later—Everyone hates her husband—wonder if he's the louse they think."

Under Pam's influence, Kathy's learning curve was rapid. "The funny thing about England is that age makes no difference. Tonight Pam's dining alone with a guy Ave's age. I'm going out with Quent [Reynolds]. . . . Who do I go around with? People I've met through Pam, mostly older men. . . . You can't imagine how interesting life over here is," she wrote Mary. Pursued by Churchill's oil adviser Geoffrey Lloyd—Ave called him "an opportunist"— and Polish aristocrats in exile, Kathy's main beau was her I.N.S. colleague

Red Mueller. She described her weekend routines: Saturday at Chequers with the Churchills, then to Cherkley to be with Max Beaverbrook, who "looks like a cartoon out of Punch. Small, baldish, big stomach and from there he tapers down to two shiny yellow shoes. His idea of sport is to surround himself with intelligent men, then egg them on to argue and fight among themselves. . . . All this makes N.Y.C. seem very remote. My only regret is that I didn't get out of college a year earlier and learn the ropes about reporting."

Meanwhile, Harriman was desperately trying to solidify his own position. The newsman Edward R. Murrow, the most influential American in Europe, at first dismissed him as calculating and self-interested. The earnest [U.S.] ambassador [John Gilbert] Winant, loved by the British for his nighttime walks through bomb-torn London, complained bitterly that Harriman had ignored him to get to Churchill. Already in a power struggle with the State Department, Harriman knew his best shot was to be Churchill's inside man. He wangled a seat on the plane to tell Stalin that there would be no second front in 1942. However close they were, Churchill was still prime minister and had a chain of command. Early on, when Harriman learned of a top-secret meeting of Churchill and Roosevelt on the high seas to forge what would ultimately become the Atlantic Alliance, he pushed to be allowed to accompany the prime minister. Kathy was privy to all of this, but she lived a split-screen life, protecting her father's privacy in all matters. At press conferences, she learned to smile and say "I have no idea" when reporters asked her about her father's activities.

Kathy had a gift for sliding quickly over difficult terrain, and for doing so with remarkable detachment. "She was magnesium," said her niece Kitty Ames. Writing home after seeing bombed-out Plymouth with Lady Astor, she coolly noted, "I'm in a wonderful mood. I'm glad I went early. I think I will be able to be less emotional. A dead city filled with such alive people." One of her early dispatches starts, "It's so easy to forget there is a war going on in England." She goes on to describe the daffodils and cows and sheep you see in the country. As she wrote to Mary, "Except for the continual stream of tanks and lorries filled with soldiers, this might be the same England we saw in 1936."

That detachment would serve her well when Kathy learned that Ave was having yet another fling. From the time they were children, Kathy and Mary were aware that their father had an active romantic life. In the section of the albums in Kathy's box marked "Childhood," there are pages of photos of the girls on trips with their governess and mother, with no sign of Ave. Ave had met Kathy's mother, Kitty Lanier Lawrance, a frail debutante, at a time when his own mother was hounding him to settle down. When Kitty was out riding one day, her horse shied, and she was seriously injured. Ave proposed. She recovered but was always delicate. Soon after Kathy was born, Kitty contracted tuberculosis.

From the time their mother died, in 1936, Kathy and Mary were embraced by Marie. "Ave, stop being such a stuffed shirt!" she would berate the remote financier, to Kathy's huge amusement. Before Marie, there had been a nightclub singer and the star ballerina Vera Zorina. In fact, Marie had left her husband, Sonny Whitney, a Vanderbilt heir, to marry Ave. Glamorous and fun-loving, she presided at the Marie Harriman Gallery, on East 57th Street. On their honeymoon in Paris, she took Ave to meet Picasso and bought van Gogh's *White Roses* for their heirs. Marie pushed progressive education and accomplishment for her own children and her stepdaughters. At home, she was every bit as freewheeling as her husband, in the midst of an affair with the suave bandleader Eddy Duchin. Duchin's wife had died in childbirth, and he frequently parked his baby son, Peter, with Marie and a French nurse. All through the war, as Duchin toured with his band, Peter grew up at Arden and called Marie "Ma."

It is easy to imagine Kathy trying first to puzzle out what was going on with Ave and then making a quick decision to look the other way—as she had seen everyone else in her family do. In the London of 1941, a frenzy of sexuality, it was probably inconceivable to her that Pam was anything more than an amusement.

What Kathy intuited, almost everyone in Beaverbrook's circle already knew. Soon after Harriman had arrived in London, in March 1941, Pam was seated next to him at one of the weekly dinners given by Emerald

Cunard at the Dorchester; Pam conveniently lived in a small room on the top floor. That night she was dressed in gold. "I saw the most beautiful man I'd ever seen," she said of Ave. Pam's own marriage had been a misguided social leap. Randolph Churchill was handsome, a fiery orator, a gifted journalist, and a charmer when sober, but he was a rude drunk. He was also a heavy gambler and was known to propose to every girl he wanted to sleep with. Only one ever accepted, on her first date with him. Pamela Digby had a clear-eyed understanding that her future would be rosier as a Churchill. By the time she met Harriman, she had already given the prime minister a grandchild and seen her reckless husband off to sea, where he immediately gambled away two years of income, forcing his young wife to make herself indispensable to rich older men. What else was she to do? Beaverbrook counseled her to leave baby Winston with a nanny at his house in the country and move to London, where, he said, he would give her a job at the Ministry of Supply. Their tacit agreement, it has long been assumed, was that Pam would become his inside source for information. "There's a very rich American coming to London for Roosevelt," Beaverbrook is said to have told her, and his meaning was implicit. As the head of British war production, Beaverbrook wanted to stay well informed on the activities of the chief of Lend-Lease.

Soon Pam was put next to Harriman at dinner. "He was a hick from America. He knew nothing," she told author Christopher Ogden many years later. "Averell would never have had this close relationship with Winston and Max without me. I mean, it was just that night that Averell and I met when I went back down to his apartment in the Dorchester, because it was safer." Writing home, Harriman told Marie, "A bomb hit so close that it almost blew us back in the room. Bombs dropped all around us. The clusters of flairs coming down very slowly lit parts of the city like Broadway and 42nd." He made no mention of Pam. Did Beaverbrook know immediately what was up? "Oh yes, Max knew immediately," she later said.

Pam said that Harriman soon mentioned that his daughter Kathy was coming over, "and would I take care of her when he had to travel? So I moved into their apartment when he went off with Churchill. Then she and I took a cottage in the country together. We were already ensconced in this cottage by the time Averell came back. So that was kind of a good alibi. She was wonderful. She was the sort of typical American college girl. Long-legged and attractive-looking—totally captivating."

If Kathy captivated Pam, Pam had definitely caught her father. Like Beaverbrook, Harriman used her to pick up information and relay messages. In return, Pam had found the answer to her dire financial straits. When Kathy and her father took an apartment on Grosvenor Square, Pam moved in, and the three of them lived together for almost a year. Shocked that Randolph had left Pam without an income, Kathy gallantly volunteered to turn over her *Newsweek* salary to her new friend, biographer Sally Bedell Smith later would note. Soon Kathy would learn that Ave was also giving Pam money. Due to an overlooked accounting error, she would actually receive a monthly check for the next 30 years. When she and Averell married, in 1971, Harriman received a call from his bookkeeper: "Now may I take Mrs. Harriman off our rolls?"

"What? We've been paying her all these years?," Harriman said.

G oing through Kathy's dispatches, I came upon a dusty envelope filled with letters that had either never been sent or had been returned by the censor. At the bottom of the envelope was the black notebook that Kathy had carried from the time she got to Lisbon. In those handwritten pages, the real Kathy began to emerge. Landing in a Lisbon filled with desperate refugees and the Gestapo, her first night at dinner, she noted, "the conversation was of one Victor Sassoon—rich English Jew—who is said to own much of Shanghai." However much a Bennington girl Kathy was, she was also of her class in a time of intense parlor anti-Semitism. A few days later, in London, she was taken to another dinner, this time at a gambling club. "All tough looking Jews—women worse than men," she wrote.

While Harriman was away at the Churchill-Roosevelt summit, Pam set out to win Kathy's affections. Writing from the ship on his way to Washington, Harriman sent his first clue to Marie: Kathy "has teamed up with Pamela Churchill, the red-headed 22-year-old wife of your friend Randolph." "Your friend Randolph" was added in with an arrow as a hasty afterthought. Then he casually dropped the news of a country house the girls had rented together. The diary makes it clear how perceptive Kathy was about her new friend. On the day she escorted her father to the airport, she wrote: "Have decided Pam has a narcissist's complex—not quite—but she sure does fancy herself. E.g.— all her pictures around the room—Has C. Beaton do new ones every other week."

That entry was dated June 21, and it was clear that Kathy had already figured out what was going on: "[Pam] got very upset at Lady Baillie's re- marks about her using me as a means to get to Ave—Lady B. is a terribly frustrated bitch to be so jealous of someone else having Ave's attentions."

What happened the next day changed the course of the war, and, ulti- mately, the fortunes of Averell and Kathy Harriman. The world turned upside down as Russia was invaded by Hitler. Overnight, the Soviet Union morphed from enemy into ally. At Chequers, Harriman now spoke at length about his benighted years chasing mineral concessions in 1920s Russia and about what needed to be understood concerning Stalin and the Russian character.

One question about the Harriman-Churchill affair still remains: did Kathy ever confront Pam? Years later, Pam Harriman told Christopher Og- den the details of what had happened, but the pages conveniently vanished from a complete transcript of their interview sent to the Library of Congress. It took weeks to track down the missing pages:

C.O.: While you're there—alright, you're in the Dorchester, are you— when does Kathy catch on?

P.H.: Well . . . to show you how different things were, I mean, I never discussed it with Kathy. Kathy never discussed it with me. At one point, she and I were driving down to the country on a Friday, and something hap- pened, and she said to me, "Well, you know, I am not a total fool." I knew immediately, and I was very surprised, and I said, "Uh, what?" And she said, "I had a big decision to make. I had to either decide to go home and not be part of it or—but I thought I should protect my father, and the best way to do that was by staying."

By August, Kathy understood the state of the world. "The war hit us today—the first time it's hit me since I arrived," she wrote Mary, when a close friend, flying for the R.A.F., was shot down. Suddenly she was working

long days and spending weekends in the country. She wrote home angry letters about American friends "who still believe that we should do business
with Hitler." She wrote about the arguments Ave had with Beaverbrook on
the subject of Russia—"the only subject anyone is discussing." Soon the two
men would take off for Moscow and another conference. Harriman had become indispensable. He was finally Churchill's inside man.

One astonishing letter in the dusty envelope had never been mailed. It was
written by Kathy to her sister from Chequers sometime during the weekend
of December 7, 1941. "It's come at last—it's exciting." It was her 24th birthday, and the Churchills had given her a cake. As always, the valet brought in
a small radio so that the prime minister could hear the latest bulletin. It was
short: "The news has just been given that Japanese aircraft have raided Pearl
Harbor, the American naval base in Hawaii." Churchill, who had been deeply
depressed all weekend, bolted out of his chair. "Pearl Harbor? What is that?"
Kathy continued, "Dinner—people running back and forth until finally I was
left sitting alone in dining room. . . . P.M. came back, talked to Roosevelt. He
seemed in very good spirits. . . . Then all of us heard midnight news. . . . P.M.
pacing in dragon wrapper, danced a jig. Ave standing by the fireplace."

Kathy originally planned to stay in England for the summer, but in the
end she remained with her father for the next five years. In the spring of 1942,
Harriman was stricken with a form of typhoid so serious that it looked as if he
might not survive. Pam never left his side.

Not long after, Kathy confided to her former governess, Elsie Marshall, in
a letter, "Averell goes to the Middle East and comes back with reports of what
Pam said about him; he goes home and comes back with reports about what I
say about Pam. Life is annoying! (Averell is anyway!)" In New York, Marie
Harriman had taken a job running a volunteer corps to help the navy. Kathy
wrote her: "You're working too hard. Don't you think that a prolonged vacation is in order?" She added, "Averell is terribly proud of you . . . getting up
at the crack of dawn. . . . I was sort of hoping you might come back with him
this trip . . . I do wish you would. There are all kinds of jobs to be done."

Later in her life, Kathleen Mortimer kept out of the Library of Congress
scores of intimate letters she had written to Elsie Marshall. Mouche, as she

called her, still lived at Arden and was close to Marie. In this new stash of letters, recently discovered, Kathy seemed to want to alert Marie about Pam. Her father had put her in an untenable position, and Kathy was clearly worried about her role. With exquisite care, she had drawn a floor plan of the new apartment she and Ave had taken on Grosvenor Square. She indicated Ave's bedroom and identified hers as "my bedroom, huge." On a sitting room that adjoined hers, she wrote, "Small room—Pam's when in town." By then Kathy was working full-time at *Newsweek*, and as usual asked Mouche to send her a dress or two. Mouche was pressed into service for Pam as well, with lists of "Pam's Wants."

Marie finally reacted by firing off a cable to her husband: KEEP YOUR AF-FAIRS CLEAN AND OUT OF THE PAPERS OR YOU WILL BE FACING THE MOST COSTLY DIVORCE IN THE HISTORY OF THE REPUBLIC.

In 1943, Roosevelt pushed Harriman to become the ambassador to Russia when Leningrad was under siege. Harriman did not want the post, but the president convinced him that he was the man for the job. By this time, Harriman too was seemingly tired of Pam and asked Kathy to deliver the message. For the rest of her life, Kathy kept a note from her father in a jewelry box: "Help Pam straighten herself out—poor child. She is in a tough spot. Tell her I am sure she will do the right thing if she follows her own instinct. Give her my best love and to you. P.S. Destroy this letter or keep it locked up."

Kathy accompanied her father to Moscow, where she helped to run Spaso House, the dreary official residence. Often Harriman held meetings all night long trying to keep Roosevelt's relationship with Stalin on course. Kathy worked for the Office of War Information and placed third in the 1943 Moscow Slalom Championships. Kathy's letters to her sister, she later said, became a diary of the endless social obligations of a Moscow outpost where communication was spotty. She wrote to Pam as well, but it was clear that their friendship had cooled. On several occasions, Pam complained she had not received her monthly stipend on time. Kathy quickly arranged a wire to Max Beaverbrook, who served as the conduit. Whatever Kathy thought of this task, Pam's wants had become a dim secondary preoccupation as the news of the carnage from Germany began to seep into Moscow. Kathy wrote Mary the first moment she had news of the camps, heard from Bill Lawrence, the *New York Times* correspondent. Returning from Majdanek, Kathy wrote as if she were still reporting for *Newsweek* of Lawrence's description: "the [victims'] articles were carefully categorized, women's corsets, nail files, shaving brushes. I'm sort of glad I wasn't there to see it. Bill Lawrence, the biggest skeptic among correspondents here, told us about this with tears in his eyes."

In 1944, Harriman commandeered a private railroad car for Kathy and 11 other correspondents to cover the exhumation of mass graves at Katyn, near a former P.O.W. camp for Polish officers. "I was lucky I had a cold," she wrote, "so I could take notes seeing 1,000 corpses. . . . All of the other reporters were so ill." Kathy and her fellow journalists accepted the Russian explanation, that German soldiers had slaughtered the Polish officers. In fact, it was later learned, the Russians had. The episode would later, in the context of the Cold War, be considered a notorious international incident. At the time of the Yalta Conference, Kathy would write, "I don't trust Stalin. Nobody does."

Not long after the war, Harriman was appointed Truman's secretary of commerce. Pam went to work as a columnist for Max Beaverbrook and appeared in New York, trying one last time to get Averell to leave Marie. At [the nightclub] El Morocco, Marie stared at her and then looked the other way. Pam had kept herself busy by having a brief fling with the handsome Standard Oil heir Stanley Mortimer, who had just broken up with his wife, Babe. She was with him at El Morocco and introduced him to Kathy, then reporting on the United Nations for *Newsweek*. Later that evening he became ill. The two women helped him back to his apartment. Pam promptly twirled off into the night, but Kathy stayed. She and Stanley were married four months later. Babe Mortimer married Bill Paley, and they all remained friends; Kathy helped raise her stepchildren, Stanley III and Amanda.

Soon after Marie died, in 1970, Pamela Churchill Hayward surfaced again and rigged a seat next to Averell at a dinner. He was then 79 and deeply depressed, feeling out of the game, but Pam immediately revived their sexual chemistry. They were married in September 1971. By then she had a long list of conquests behind her—including Fiat heir Gianni Agnelli—and had developed her reputation for purloining the property of her husband's children and heirs.

Pamela Harriman created a new career for herself. She helped Bill Clinton get to the White House—he called her "the first lady of the Democratic Party." After Ave's death, in 1986, she was for years a Washington power hostess, opening her N Street town house for a merry-go-round of political-strategy sessions. As a reward, Clinton appointed her ambassador to France. In 1994, allegations of mismanagement of the Harriman trusts made front-page news when the Harriman family sued Pam and her advisers, citing egregious mismanagement of their assets. At stake was at least $30 million, lost to bad investments in a "conspiracy to breach fiduciary duties," according to the court papers. Prior to the suit, Kathy had reportedly flown to Paris and quietly presented Pam with a long letter of allegations at the American Embassy. The suit was eventually settled.

Visiting Arden [House] this past June, I found perhaps a clue to Kathy's inner fortitude. It was here among the lakes and stone cottages and 40 miles of horse paths, a world unto itself, that the extended Harriman family met often for celebrations and rituals. Entering by a long road off the Taconic Parkway, I was thrust back into an Edith Wharton childhood where Kathy grew up in a cocoon of privilege, with a private polo field, a track for trotting horses, and a dairy that had supplied nearby West Point since the Spanish-American War. Whenever Pam, as Mrs. Harriman, visited Arden, she would be besieged with dogs and the family's homey way of life. The Carrère and Hastings mansion had long ago been given to Columbia University, and the family stayed in modest cottages on the grounds, just as Averell always preferred. One Thanksgiving, Kathy had to snatch the pâté for hors d'oeuvres out of the mouth of one of the dogs. Putting it back on the platter, she turned to her stepmother without missing a beat and said, "May I make you one?"

In private, Kathy rarely complained about Pam, even when the Harriman heirs brought suit against her. At Arden, on the day I went to visit, Kathleen

Harriman Mortimer was celebrated by her family and friends as a woman from another era who never surrendered her principles.

I thought of a letter Kathy had written to Mouche from Moscow on August 8, 1945: "Tonight the Soviets declared war on Japan. I'm about to go out on the town. . . . Among other things it means that the end of my session here is in sight! What next?"

WHEN HUBERT MET AUDREY

By Amy Fine Collins | December 1995

On the subject of Audrey Hepburn, Cecil Beaton once tartly observed "Nobody ever looked like her before World War II. Now thousands of imitations have appeared. The woods are full of emaciated young ladies with rat-nibbled hair and moon pale faces." Like mushrooms after rain, suddenly a whole *new* generation of Audrey clones has sprung up in the forest. Obsessed with the waifish actress, they aspire not only to look like her but to dress the part as well. Divining the trend early, the department store Barneys launched a collection inspired by Hepburn's dresses, culled from her personal and cinematic wardrobes. Scores of fashion designers have since hopped aboard the Audrey bandwagon, peddling a head-to-heel neo-Hepburn look featuring fitted shifts and low, ladylike pumps. And this month Paramount Pictures is bringing out its remake of Billy Wilder's 1954 *Sabrina*, the Cinderellaesque Hepburn classic which defined her image for the rest of her career.

All of this Audrey revivalism has been noted with extreme curiosity by the late actress's close friend couturier Hubert de Givenchy, who first dressed the star in *Sabrina* and ended up creating her wardrobe for seven subsequent film roles, as well as for private life. Ironically, this renewed adulation of *le style* Audrey Hepburn is peaking just as Givenchy is retiring from the house he founded in 1952. This month English wunderkind John Galliano will replace the veteran couturier, who in October showed the final collection of his 43-year career.

Early one morning in his Paris studio, located just behind the Givenchy shop on Avenue George V, the master couturier sits, erect and silver-haired, at a table in a tiny conference area adjoining his workrooms. Dressed in his traditional uniform of an impeccable white linen smock, whose cuffs he has neatly rolled up, he embodies an old-world, gentlemanly ideal that is as rare today in the fashion world as a well-mounted sleeve. "The other day I was in Venice," he recalls quietly. "And Egon von Fürstenberg showed me a picture in a magazine. 'Look,' he said, 'all your work is now reappearing.' Then this week Jeannette [who has worked with him since he opened] showed me another picture, in an Italian magazine. I first started noticing it myself a year or two ago, in American magazines. I began seeing Sabrina necklines," he says, slowly tracing, with his long, large fingers, a wide horizontal above his collarbone. "And sleeves cut like this," he adds, chopping the inside of his shoulder with the edge of his hand. "I have seen I don't know how many young girls in little black dresses or little narrow trousers with black T-shirts. They seem to adore Audrey more for the clothes than the movies—maybe they don't even know the movies. In fact, last weekend I was visiting a friend in Portugal, and her daughter, who is 14, asked if I had any of Audrey's dresses. She wanted to see, to touch them."

Givenchy could easily fill the girl's request—shortly before she died of colon cancer in January 1993, Hepburn gave the designer more than 25 dresses he had made for her, which he keeps in his Paris apartment. "One by one" he is distributing them to museums around the world, though at this moment he has in the atelier a long, narrow, sleeveless pearl-embroidered tulle sheath in cream, circa 1960, which he is offering to the daughter of an Italian friend, Natalia Strozzi, to wear for her debut in Rome. Givenchy summons an assistant, who ceremoniously carries it out from the workroom. Tenderly, she releases the softly glittering gown onto the table, spreading it out before its maker like a precious treasure. A sumptuous but inanimate husk, it is as empty of life as a lovely shell abandoned long ago by the fantastic creature that once inhabited it.

———

ate in 1952, the 22-year-old neophyte actress Audrey Hepburn was preparing to embark on a national tour of her Broadway hit, *Gigi*. She had recently completed her first Hollywood picture with Paramount, *Roman Holiday*, for which she had been paid $12,500—a quantum leap from the meager $33.60-a-week salary she had commanded as a bit contract player with England's Associated British Pictures Corporation. Though *Roman Holiday* had not yet premiered, expectations were high, and Paramount executives were fishing for an appropriate follow-up project for their promising ingenue. The studio sent to its pixieish protégée a script by Samuel Taylor of a play Paramount had just purchased, *Sabrina Fair* (a name taken from a work by Milton), a frothy comedy about a chauffeur's daughter who returns from a trip to Paris so worldly and fetching that she ends up having her pick of her father's millionaire boss's two eligible sons, Linus and David Larrabee. Hepburn at once agreed to take on the title role, at a fee of $15,000. Her costars would be William Holden in the part of the rakish younger Larrabee boy and Humphrey Bogart as the sober older son who, despite his stuffy, unromantic nature, wins the girl. One of Hollywood's most distinguished talents, the obstreperous immigrant genius Billy Wilder, would direct.

In the early summer of 1953, while Hepburn was performing in the San Francisco production of *Gigi*, Paramount's autocratic wardrobe supervisor, Edith Head—who had designed the actress's Princess Anne regalia for *Roman Holiday*—flew up for a costume meeting with Hepburn. As she wrote in the 1983 memoir *Edith Head's Hollywood,* "Every designer wishes for the perfect picture in which he or she can really show off design magic. My one chance was in *Sabrina.* . . . It was the perfect setup. Three wonderful stars, and my leading lady looking like a Paris mannequin."

Head's dream of a "perfect setup," however, was abruptly shattered when Wilder announced to the wardrobe diva that he was sending Hepburn overseas to buy Paris originals from a real French designer. Head's services would be required only for a pre-Paris ragamuffin frock and two insignificant sportswear ensembles Sabrina would appear in after her return to the

Larrabees' luxurious Long Island home. Though Wilder—a man of sophisticated European tastes who fully appreciated the singular allure of French couture—was the one who informed Head of the change of plans, it was, the director says, Hepburn who had actually come up with the idea. For a clothes-mad actress with limited resources—an embroidered cotton blouse from Givenchy cost nearly $3,000 at the time—the chance to wear genuine Paris couture was a fantasy come to life. "Clothes are positively a passion with me," Hepburn confided to a journalist on the set of *Sabrina.* "I love them to the point where it is practically a vice."

Sometime later during that same summer of 1953, the lanky, aristocratic, 26-year-old Hubert de Givenchy, in the throes of preparing the fourth presentation of his career—an Oriental-themed winter collection, to be shown in late July—received an unexpected telephone call from his friend Gladys de Segonzac. Married to the Paris head of Paramount, Segonzac was also the *directrice* of Schiaparelli, where Givenchy had worked for four years before establishing his own business in 1952 on the Rue Alfred de Vigny. The reason for Segonzac's call, Givenchy learned, was that "Miss Hepburn" had arrived in Paris and wanted to see him at once. Busy as he was, the young couturier's interest was piqued—"I was thinking she meant Katharine Hepburn," he now explains. *Roman Holiday*—which would win her a *Time*-magazine cover and an Oscar for best actress—hadn't opened yet, and there was no reason for him to be familiar with the obscure newcomer who had recently created the title role in the Broadway production of *Gigi.* The actress was then merely, as Hepburn later put it, "a skinny little nobody"—dressed in an outrageously quirky manner for someone about to have her first encounter with the latest Parisian fashion sensation. Givenchy distinctly remembers greeting "this very thin person with beautiful eyes, short hair, thick eyebrows, very tiny trousers, ballerina shoes, and a little T-shirt. On her head was a straw gondolier's hat with a red ribbon around it that said VENEZIA. I thought, This is too much!" Eccentric as Hepburn's getup was, her appearance that day, recalls Dreda Mele, then the *directrice* of Givenchy (now Armani's general manager for France), "was like the arrival of a summer flower. She was *lumineuse*—radiant, in both a physical and spiritual sense. I felt immediately how lovely she was, inside and out. Though she came to Givenchy out of the blue, there is no doubt that they were made to meet. Audrey was always very definite in her taste and look. She came to him because she was attracted by the image he could give her. And she entered that image totally. She entered into his dream, too. I repeat, they were made for each other."

Hepburn respectfully explained to Givenchy that she was in pre-production for the movie *Sabrina,* a story which involved a young girl's metamorphosis, after a two-year stint in Paris to attend cooking school, from a plain, pubescent servant's daughter into a knowing, soignée siren. Though Hepburn didn't mention it, Givenchy could easily have guessed that until this moment she had (as she told *Vogue's* Paris-bureau chief Susan Train years later) "never even seen an haute couture dress, much less worn one." (She claimed on another occasion that before she met Givenchy she had been wearing homemade clothes.) Though from the start Hepburn had favored Givenchy, who was then, as she told Train, "the newest, youngest, most exciting couturier," Segonzac had initially tried to steer Hepburn to Balenciaga—but no one had had the temerity to disturb the reclusive master so close to collection time.

Captivated as he was by his unexpected caller, Givenchy demurred, explaining to Hepburn that it would be impossible to help her. "I told Audrey that I had very few workers and I needed all my hands to help me with my next collection, which I had to show very soon. But she insisted, 'Please, please, there must be something I can try on.'" Givenchy finally relented, proposing that she try on some of the samples that were still hanging about the atelier from the previous season's collection, spring/summer '53.

Hepburn began by putting on what she later described as "that jazzy suit"—an Oxford-gray wool-ottoman *tailleur* with a cinch-waisted, double-breasted scoop-necked jacket and a slim, calf-length vented skirt. The sample, which the model Colette Cerf had worn in the show, fit nearly perfectly, Givenchy remembers. "They both had the same thin waistline." Hepburn finished off the suit with the hat with which it had originally been presented, a saucy miniature turban of pleated pearl-gray chiffon, concocted by Givenchy's in-house milliner. "The change from the little girl who arrived that morning was unbelievable," Givenchy says. "The way she moved in the suit, she was so happy. She said that it was exactly what she wanted for the movie. She gave a life to the clothes—she had a way of installing herself in them that I have seen in no one else since, except maybe the model Dalma. The suit just adapted to her. Something magic happened. Suddenly she felt good—you could feel her excitement, her joy."

Audrey next selected a white strapless ball gown, down whose svelte sides and back a detachable train cascaded, culminating in a spray of black ruffles. Above the ankles and as slim as a string bean in front, it was confected of organdy and embroidered with flowers of black silk thread and jet beads on the bodice, skirt, and train. Dreda Mele, who had previously borrowed the sample and worn it to a ball, grows ecstatic at the memory of her first sight of Hepburn in the snowdrift-white dance dress: "She was something unreal—a fairy tale!" Givenchy agrees: "It gave her a very flattering line, especially pretty when she turned to move or dance."

Hepburn's final choice was a black cocktail dress, fashioned from a ribbed cotton piqué woven by the venerable fabric house Abraham. Fastened by a tiny bow at each shoulder, the dress also buttoned down its deep V back before flaring out below the fitted waist into a full, flirtatious ballerina-length skirt. Its most dramatic features, however, were its deeply carved armholes and shallow, razor-sharp horizontal neckline. "What used to be called a *décolleté bateau*," Givenchy says. "Afterward it was called the *décolleté* Sabrina." Audrey loved this neckline, he says, because it hid her "skinny collarbone but emphasized her very good shoulders"—which were as broad and powerful as the rest of her was narrow and fragile.

Though Givenchy had not shown the black cocktail dress with a hat, Hepburn found a medieval-looking toque in his atelier that perfectly suited her face, the ensemble, and the requirements of the story. As snug as a bathing cap and paved with rhinestones, it covered most of her ears and, due to the serried peaks projecting from its circumference, gave her the illusion of wearing a storybook crown. Givenchy says, "Audrey always added a twist, something piquant, amusing, to the clothes. Though of course I advised her, she knew precisely what she wanted. She knew herself very well—for example, which is her good profile and which is her bad. She was very professional. No detail ever escaped her. Billy Wilder approved of everything she chose, and so I gave them the samples to use for the movie. Billy's only concern was that the clothes adapt to the form of her face—they had to all correspond to the *visage*."

As the *Sabrina* schedule allowed Hepburn to linger a few days in Paris, Givenchy invited his sprightly new acquaintance to dinner at a "*bistro existentialiste*" on the Rue de Grenelle. "Immediately we had a great sympathy," the couturier recalls. "She told me about the beginning of her love affair with [future husband] Mel Ferrer [the actor-director-producer], and said, 'You are like my big brother.'" Before long Hepburn was calling him up "just to tell me how much she loved me—and then she'd say bye-bye and hang up. She remained from that time on absolutely, unbelievably loyal to me and everyone here at the house. The entire staff adored her, everyone had enormous respect for her—she became part of the family here. I have always considered her my sister.

"She was so disciplined, so organized, she never was once late for a fitting. When she needed things that I did not make—a sweater or maybe a trench coat—she'd take me shopping with her. Later, when she was married to Dr. [Andrea] Dotti [the psychiatrist] and living in Rome, sometimes she needed something immediately and would go to Valentino. But she'd call me up first and say, 'Hubert, please don't be furious with me!' We never together had an argument. She never considered ours a business relationship. When I launched the fragrance L'Interdit with her face as the image she never asked for any percentage or any payment." In fact, the actress's confidence in Givenchy ran so deep she asked him later in life to be her *légataire testamentaire*, a mediator of her will. Recalls Dreda Mele, "The two of them were very alike—so rigorous, well organized, concentrated on their work—and behaving so well at every moment of life."

For her part, Audrey, always ruthlessly self-critical and achingly vulnerable, found in Givenchy one of the few people in her life who could make her feel secure. In print, she referred to Givenchy as "a personality-maker" and a "psychiatrist," and, chronically unsure of her acting abilities, she went so far as to maintain that Givenchy's clothes made up for what she lacked in dramatic technique. "It was often an enormous help to know that I looked the part," she explained. "Then the rest wasn't so tough anymore. Givenchy's lovely simple clothes [gave me] the feeling of being whoever I played."

As the actress soon learned, her flawless Givenchy wardrobe was one of the few successfully resolved matters on the *Sabrina* set. Shooting was lagging months behind schedule. Ernest Lehman (brought in by the director from MGM to revise the screenplay when an exasperated Samuel Taylor bailed out) and Billy Wilder were staying up around the clock writing, or rewriting, the movie scene by scene. Some days the dialogue wasn't ready when the actors arrived on the set. Wilder was suffering from severe back pain, which made him even feistier than usual. Holden was drinking far too much. And Humphrey Bogart—indignant at having been Wilder's second choice to play Linus Larrabee (Cary Grant was unavailable), envious of William Holden's easy camaraderie with the director (they had worked together on both *Stalag 17* and *Sunset Boulevard*), and irritated to be playing opposite a novice starlet, who, he claimed, "could not do a line in less than 12 takes"—was relentlessly uncooperative. He taunted his adversaries with vicious imitations of Hepburn's trilling, singsong voice and Wilder's thick Austrian accent. He even went as far as to call Wilder, whose family members had been killed in concentration camps, a Nazi—and to tell a reporter that the whole movie was "a crock of shit." In retribution, Bogart was barred from the daily ritual of sundown cocktails. Wilder managed to keep his cantankerous player in line with the perpetual threat that he and Lehman would rewrite the ending so that Holden got the girl. Avoiding embroilment in these internecine squabbles, Hepburn bided her time learning the rules of baseball from Ernest Lehman (the World Series was on), or tooling around the set on a green bicycle (a gift from Wilder), dressed between takes in a cartoonish, candy-cane-striped top and trousers filched from her production of *Gigi*.

Lehman remembers that because of the frantic, fly-by-the-seat-of-your-pants shooting and writing schedules one of the movie's crucial scenes was nearly "written wrong." Hepburn, as Sabrina, meets in her Parisian cooking class the kindly 74-year-old Baron Saint-Fontenelle, who takes her under his wing and into French society. He sympathizes extravagantly with her heart-rending crush on David Larrabee, proposes for her an elfin new haircut, and advises her on a cosmopolitan new wardrobe. Just before her homecoming,

Sabrina writes from Paris to her chauffeur father back on Long Island, "You can meet me at the train—the 4:15. If you should have any difficulty recognizing your daughter, I shall be the most sophisticated woman at the Glen Cove station." The movie then dissolves to the solitary figure of Sabrina pacing on a deserted railroad platform, devastatingly chic in her Givenchy suit and hat. On a long leash she walks a miniature poodle, its silver-gray fur tonally compatible with her ensemble. Then William Holden's David Larrabee whizzes past in his Nash-Healey Sports roadster, screeching to a halt when his jaded playboy's eyes light upon this dazzling apparition.

"We had a set made of the Glen Cove railroad station, and the scene was already halfway shot when I told Billy to stop everything—it had to be re-done," Lehman recalls. "I was so new to Hollywood I didn't know you didn't go straight up to a director and criticize everything he was doing! It's hard to believe now, but until that moment Bill Holden was supposed to recognize Sabrina immediately as the chauffeur's daughter." Lehman's epiphany, partly inspired by the sultry elegance of Hepburn in the Givenchy suit, was to make the object of Sabrina's lifelong infatuation "think he's picking up a strange, charming, and attractive woman. The scene needed a concept, a gimmick, a trick. Before, it didn't have one." The new situation gave Lehman license to "insert all the flirtatious dialogue with double entendres." The reshooting took place on location in Glen Clove, where Paramount president Barney Balaban's neo-Tudor estate had already provided the exteriors for the Larrabee mansion. "The clothes almost made the woman," Lehman muses. "They were extremely helpful to the character, the mood, the movie. They made the transformation believable."

The movie's next pivotal scene also turned on one of the Givenchy creations—the angelic white ball gown. "A lovely evening dress!" Sabrina exclaims to David Larrabee. "Yards of skirt and way off the shoulders!" This is the cue for the film's great Cinderella moment, when Sabrina, finally a guest—not a lovesick, wistful outsider—at one of the Larrabees' fabled parties, makes an enchanted entrance onto the millionaires' lantern-lit terrace, leaving a trail of slack-jawed men in her wake. Charles, the prissy butler, breathlessly reports back to the kitchen, "You should see Sabrina! The prettiest girl, the prettiest dress, the best dancer! The belle of the ball! And such poise! As though she belonged up there!" The brunette Sabrina's nemesis, David's blonde fiancée, Elizabeth Tyson (played by Martha Hyer), appears at the dance dressed in an Edith Head gown that sets off Hepburn's all the more brilliantly. As dark and fussy as Givenchy's is pale and simple, it now seems dated—a fate that the French dress, by some miraculous legerdemain, manages to escape. Further, Hyer's ample bustline, spilling out of her plunging black bodice, appears matronly beside Hepburn's *garçon manqué* physique. No wonder Billy Wilder confidently quipped to a magazine, "This girl single-handedly could make bosoms a thing of the past!" Hyer also wears ostentatious earrings and a double-strand pearl choker, à la Barbara Bush, while Hepburn's attenuated white throat is jewel-less, her ears ornamented only by modest pearl drops. Wilder gleefully recalled, "Here was this chauffeur's daughter going to the ball and she looked more royal than all the other society people in New York!"

So resplendent was Hepburn in the glamorous Givenchy gown that when Wilder began to shoot the scene of her dancing with Bogart in the Larrabees' indoor tennis court, bit by bit her fawnlike radiance burned into the actor's dusky, rugged face. "Bogey complained that Wilder was getting only the back of his head," Lehman says. "It was true—but it wasn't planned that way in advance. You edit as you go." Bogart said to his agent, Phil Gersh, "Look, this guy is shooting the back of my head, I don't even have to put my hairpiece on; I'm not in this picture." Explains Lehman, "What happened with that scene is that Billy Wilder fell in love with Audrey's image onscreen."

Apparently, it was not just the celluloid likeness of Audrey Hepburn but also the flesh-and-blood girl herself who bewitched the men on the *Sabrina* set. William Holden, 11 years older than Hepburn and long married, became intoxicated with his co-star—who reciprocated in kind. Holden even took Hepburn home to meet his wife, Ardis, who had resigned herself to his infidelities in exchange for the dubious privilege of being Mrs. William Holden. The illicit couple became so transported by their mutual passion that they even discussed marriage—an idea Hepburn summarily rejected once she learned that her suitor had undergone an irreversible vasectomy. (This revelation freed her to resume her affair with Mel Ferrer, who would become not only her husband—the bride wore Givenchy—but her co-star, in the play *Ondine* and in her next movie, *War and Peace*.)

Hepburn wore the final Givenchy outfit—the eponymous cocktail dress—for the script's Scene 104, which opens, "INT. LINUS' OFFICE—(LATE AFTERNOON). Start on a figure spinning like a top." Out of this furiously twirling black-and-silver spiral of stardust the scintillating Sabrina materializes, enthroned on Linus's executive-suite swivel chair. Her little Givenchy princess hat is perched on her head, and her stem-like arms, sheathed in black gloves, stretch across his boardroom table. Aglow with expectation and as perky as the twin bows fastening her dress, she is, as the script demanded, "smartly groomed for a night on the town." Linus will take her out to dinner at "the darkest corner table of the Colony," then squire her to Broadway to see *The Seven Year Itch* (an in-joke—Wilder would direct the movie version a year later), and afterward lead her to the Persian Room for dancing. It is during these sequences and in this dress that Sabrina's affections drift away from the roguish David and attach themselves instead to his more responsible older brother.

In a story that has such an ethereal atmosphere of make-believe, Givenchy's real-life, up-to-the-minute dresses provided—as did the crisp, glossy cinematography—the firm rooting in the material world that the film needed. "I can't think of any other picture before *Sabrina* that made use of clothes in the same way. It was a real breakthrough," says Ernest Lehman. "The way Audrey looked in *Sabrina* had an effect on the roles she later played. It's fair to say that if she had never gone to Paris she wouldn't have had that role in *Breakfast at Tiffany's*. The *Sabrina* clothes fixed her image forever."

Hepburn invited Givenchy to come to California for a screening of *Sabrina*—his first trip to L.A.—and an introduction was made to Edith Head. "Then they showed the film—and my name was mentioned nowhere!" he says, still slightly stung at the memory. When the credits rolled, Head's name appeared next to the words "Costume Supervision," and that was it. "Imagine if I had received credit for *Sabrina* then, at the beginning of my career. It would have helped. But it doesn't matter—a few years passed, and then everyone knew. Anyway, what could I do? I didn't really care. I was so pleased to dress Miss Hepburn."

Sabrina opened to surpassingly favorable reviews in America, particularly where Hepburn's performance was concerned. In his column dated September 26, 1954, Bosley Crowther of *The New York Times* called it "a knockout . . . one of those smooth escapist films, which, when done with supreme sophistication, is one of the happiest resources in Hollywood. . . . Audrey Hepburn, the magical young lady . . . flows beautifully into the character of the chauffeur's lovely daughter." Another paper's reviewer noted that "the sight of Miss Hepburn, gazing out from the screen with a look of bewitching candor in her large and limpid eyes, is delectable indeed. . . . Sabrina [is] the plus chic of chicks." And an early, sanguine prediction of "hearty b.o. [box office] possibilities" was more than borne out. *Sabrina* was such a success, in fact, that when Hepburn signed on for *War and Peace* agent Kurt Frings inflated her salary to the stratospheric sum of $350,000—a fee that established her as the highest-paid actress in the world.

If *Sabrina* had vaulted Hepburn to the loftiest reaches of the Hollywood empyrean, her character survived the voyage intact. When her agent informed her of her new price tag, the ingenue gasped, "I'm not worth it. It's impossible! Please don't tell anyone." Nor was she about to lose track of her dear new friend in Paris, who, every bit as much as Billy Wilder, had helped define her elegant professional persona. In November 1954, as part of their honeymoon, Hepburn and Ferrer flew to her native Holland for the Dutch premiere of *Sabrina*. Among the activities Hepburn engaged in during this triumphant home-coming—all organized for the benefit of disabled Dutch veterans— were a photo-signing session at a department store attended by thousands and a teatime fashion show in which Hepburn herself modeled dresses by Givenchy. Interestingly, photos of Hepburn taken during this charitable public-relations-tour-cum-honeymoon show the actress wearing exactly the same three outfits by Givenchy that she had worn as Sabrina. For the movie opening in Amsterdam she once again slipped into the embroidered organza ball gown; for a visit to her childhood home in Arnhem she recycled the Oxford-gray suit, over which, due to the cold, she wore a short fur coat. And in a photo published in the November 1954 *Elle,* she appears at a Dutch restaurant table smiling beatifically in the black Sabrina cocktail dress, with Mel hovering at her side. Evidently, Paramount allowed her to incorporate the costumes into her personal wardrobe—a practice continued throughout her collaboration with Givenchy, which helped maintain that rare fluency between her on-screen and offscreen personae.

A publicity blitz of a different kind attended the movie's February 4, 1955, premiere in France. The Paramount machine, shrewdly hoping to capitalize on *Sabrina*'s French-fashion angle, opened the movie in Paris during collection week, on the day after Givenchy's spring/summer couture show. Not leaving anything to chance, the publicity department pressed into service purveyors of all kinds of goods. Fifty music stores in Paris displayed in their windows record albums of the songs from *Sabrina*. Clothing shops, as well as the Campagnie Générale Transatlantique, whose steamship the *Liberté* figured prominently in the film, also got into the act. Further fueling *Sabrina* fever in France, Paramount offered—through the boutique Prénatal—gifts to any mother who on February 4 gave birth to a baby girl and named her Sabrina. More cunning still, throughout France and North Africa a "Do You Look Like Sabrina?" contest was staged, in which winners were awarded prizes of both money and products. The climax of all these festivities was the arrival of "Sabrina" herself, who held court at a press conference at the Ritz.

The effect of the film on Givenchy was immediate and newsworthy. For his February presentation he hired his own Audrey look-alike, a mannequin named Jacky, as house model. Givenchy also named one of the dresses in his collection "Sabrina." *Elle* reported that the couturier had been inspired throughout his collection by his new muse's "flat chest, narrow hips, swan neck, and short hair." Not surprisingly, the French movie critics greeted this "Cinderella story *à l'americaine*" with a shade more cynicism than their Stateside counterparts and their colleagues in the fashion press. One reviewer remarked that the Larrabee servants' quarters would "bring joy to many French millionaires in search of lodgings." Another complained that Audrey Hepburn reminded him too much of certain young ladies of Saint-Germaine-des-Pres "who cut their hair with rusty scissors." Still another, apparently thinking of the scenes in which the actress wears the Sabrina dress, suggested that Miss Hepburn had been "transformed for five painful minutes into Miss Famine herself." But most had generous praise for Hepburn, who, as the newspaper *La Croix* conceded, "had become a Parisienne down to the tips of her fingernails."

More important, *Sabrina* reaped industry accolades. The Writers Guild honored the uneasy troika of Billy Wilder, Samuel Taylor, and Ernest Lehman with its "best written American comedy" award, and the screenplay also earned a Golden Globe. In their poll of fans in more than 50 countries abroad, the Foreign Press Association of Hollywood and the Hollywood Foreign Correspondents Association came up with Audrey Hepburn as the winner of the "world film favorite" award. *Sabrina* also landed a bouquet of Academy Award nominations: best actress, best director, best cinematography, best screenplay, best art direction, best costumes. Of all these potential Oscars, however, only one came through—best costumes—an award which Edith Head shamelessly accepted without even the slightest nod of acknowledgment to Givenchy. Effectively, Head had treated Paris's most admired young *créateur* as if he were just another anonymous cog chugging away in her vast wardrobe engine. Irene Heymann, Billy Wilder's longtime agent, says, "Edith always thought she designed everything in town. She was notorious for never giving an assistant credit, even if she hadn't done a thing." But Head, obviously galled at being so completely upstaged (even if she was one of the few to know it), went even further, insisting in her memoirs and even until her death that she had created (as she wrote in 1959) "the dress, whose boat neckline was tied on each shoulder—widely known and copied as the Sabrina neckline."

Givenchy today generously allows that, as moviemaking often requires duplicates of costumes in the event that a dress becomes damaged in some way, Head may have at some point executed a copy of the black cocktail dress in her Hollywood workrooms. Perhaps, then, it was this facsimile that she added to the costume collection which she began in the 40s and took on tour with her around the world.

While it is true that Seventh Avenue manufacturers knocked off the Sabrina neckline by the truckload, the phenomenon Audrey Hepburn unwittingly precipitated went far beyond garment-district profiteering, Dreda Mele maintains. "Everyone in the street was copying Audrey's hair, the way she moved, the way she acted, the way she spoke. Everybody wanted to look like Audrey Hepburn. She became a person of a whole generation. They copied her for 10 solid years after. She created an image above her movie image."

Back at the Givenchy atelier on Avenue George V, the couturier is also meditating on the enduring fashion legacy of Audrey Hepburn. "I dressed so many other stars. Jennifer Jones, Lauren Bacall, Marlene Dietrich, Elizabeth Taylor—we had such problems with her, with the timing of her fittings. Not like Audrey, she was always late. And the *essayages*—with her *poitrine*— so difficult! But no one ever wanted to copy what I made for them. I once was asked to do a wedding dress in the same style as the Sabrina ball gown. For the marriage of her son, [former couturière] Meryl Lanvin asked me to make a version of the black Sabrina dress. Then, in my last couture collection, I adapted that design for another dress, which I showed with a jacket." And for Barneys' special Givenchy collection last year, he did yet another spin on the Sabrina cocktail dress—this time in silk faille and without any bows—which immediately became the line's top seller.

"Ever since *Sabrina*," Givenchy continues, "Audrey kept exactly the same measurements. Do you want to see her mannequin?" One of Givenchy's loyal assistants fetches from an unseen region of the atelier the dress form on which Hepburn's clothes were fitted for four decades. Headless and limbless, with high little pancake breasts and black lines sectioning off the body into some obscure system of seamstress trigonometry, the dummy is an eerie yet somehow comforting evocation of the late actress—a De Chiricoesque portrait in stuffing, cloth, and metal. The dress form's unchanging measurements tally up to an impressively taut 31 1/2-22-31 1/2 (the actress stood five feet seven inches).

"Audrey's style is so strong," the designer continues, gazing reverently at the doll-like instrument of his profession. "Audrey's silhouette is so strong. It doesn't ever look passé. She is so present. It is difficult to think she is no longer with us—that I can no longer pick up the phone to call her. Her son Sean and I talk as if she is still alive. There are few people I communicate with this way—just my mother and Audrey. But I feel Audrey more strongly. Audrey is more recent. The force, the presence, the image, is so strong. I was just in Switzerland with Sean for the christening of his daughter—Emma Audrey. We were in the same church, with the same Protestant father, where Audrey was married. And where her funeral took place. Then we went back to her house. Her presence was there, too—the personality, the simplicity, the love she gave to the rooms. It was all still there. The emotion is still so strong," he adds, his eyes now brimming with tears. A discreet man, he reflexively bows his head—and then recovers to rise for a handshake. "Excuse me," he says softly. "I am needed in the atelier." He then disappears through a door to resume work on the very last collection of his career.

(Hubert de Givenchy died in 2018, at age 91.)

THE
RENEGADES

DIARY OF A MAD ARTIST

By Amy Fine Collins | September 1995

A s frenzied mourners watched the earthly remains of Frida Kahlo roll away into the crematory, the artist, known in her day for her macabre sense of mischief, played one last ghoulish trick on her audience. The sudden blast of heat from the open incinerator doors blew the bejeweled, elaborately coiffed body bolt upright. Her ignited hair blazed around her head like an infernal halo. One observer recalled that, deformed by the phantasmagoric, flickering shadows, her lips appeared to break into a grin just as the doors closed shut. Frida's postmortem chuckle—a last laugh if there ever was one—is echoing still. Half a century after her death, Kahlo, around whom a whole industry has sprung up like a garden on a grave site, grows more alive with each passing decade.

What Elvis Presley is to good old boys, Judy Garland to a generation of homosexuals, and Maria Callas to opera fanatics, Frida is to masses of late-20th-century idol seekers. Every day at the San Francisco Museum of Modern Art, the 1931 double portrait of newlyweds Frida and Diego Rivera draws a worshipful horde, as reverent as the devotees gathered daily before the Louvre's *Mona Lisa*. Says Hayden Herrera, author of the groundbreaking 1983 biography *Frida*, "Her paintings demand—fiercely—that you look at her."

Kirk Varnedoe, a chief curator of the Museum of Modern Art (which is exhibiting two of its three Kahlos in a summer show of women's art), reflects on the Frida Phenomenon: "She clicks with today's sensibilities—her psycho-obsessive concern with herself, her creation of a personal alternative world carry a voltage. Her constant remaking of her identity, her construction of a theater of the self are exactly what preoccupy such contemporary artists as Cindy Sherman or Kiki Smith and, on a more popular level, Madonna—who, of course, collects her work. Kahlo, incidentally, is more a figure for the age of Madonna than the era of Marilyn Monroe. She fits well with the odd, androgynous hormonal chemistry of our particular epoch."

In fact, a whole cross section of marginalized groups—lesbians, gays, feminists, the handicapped, Chicanos, Communists (she professed Trotskyism and, later, Stalinism), hypochondriacs, substance abusers, and even Jews (despite her indigenous Mexican identity, she was in fact half Jewish and only one-quarter Indian)—have discovered in her a politically correct heroine. The most concrete measure of Frida's nail-digging grip on the popular imagination is the number of publications on her: 87 and counting. (Though she has also been the subject of at least three documentaries and one Mexican art film, the world still awaits the movies promised by Madonna and Luis "La Bamba" Valdez.) [Salma Hayek would play Kahlo in Julie Taymor's 2002 film, *Frida*.] Says art dealer Mary-Anne Martin, who as founder of Sotheby's Latin-American department presided over the first auction of a Kahlo painting, in 1977 (it went for $19,000—$1,000 below the low estimate), "Frida has been carved up into little pieces. Everyone pulls out that one piece that means something special to them."

Just when Frida fever seemed on the verge of cooling down, the public's attention has once again been riveted by her—1995 is turning out to be yet another *annus mirabilis* in the Frida chronicles. This May her 1942 *Self-Portrait with Monkey and Parrot* (acquired in 1947, reports Kahlo expert Dr. Salomón Grimberg, by IBM from the Galería de Arte Mexicano for around $400) sold at Sotheby's for $3.2 million. This is the highest price ever paid for a Latin-American work of art, and the second-highest amount for a woman artist (Mary Cassatt holds the record). About the auction record he set, Argentinean collector and venture capitalist Eduardo Costantini states firmly, "There is a correlation between the painting's price and its quality."

And riding the wave of what Sotheby's director of Latin-American painting, August Uribe, calls "a thrilling, historical sale," next month Abrams is releasing with great fanfare what may be the publishing coup of the season: a facsimile edition of Frida Kahlo's diary, an intimate, enigmatic written and pictorial record of the last and most lurid decade of the artist's tortured life. Though this document has been on display at the Frida Kahlo Museum in Coyoacán, Mexico (formerly her house), since it opened in 1958, only a handful of researchers, such as Hayden Herrera, have been permitted to page through it. And even then it has resisted coherent interpretation. The situation has been further complicated by the fact that an executor of Kahlo's estate, wealthy Rivera patron Dolores Olmedo, has jealously guarded the diary. It took the savvy young Mexican art promoter Claudia Madrazo two years to persuade Olmedo to allow publication, in order at last to make the strange workings of Frida Kahlo's mind, quite literally, an open book.

Once she had Olmedo's blessing, Madrazo showed up at the office of New York literary agent Gloria Loomis with a fuzzy color photocopy of the diary. "I flipped," says Loomis. "It was original, moving. And I told her, yes, American publishers will be crazy about it." *The New York Times* broke the story of the diary, announcing on its publishing page that an auction would be held that week. "The next morning the phones went mad," Loomis recounts.

The Mexican press had picked up the *Times* story, and a furor erupted. In Mexico, where Kahlo is known as *la heroína del dolor*, "the heroine of pain," the artist is—like the Virgin of Guadalupe—a national idol. "They were demanding to know who is this gringa who has the right to do this to our national treasure," Loomis says. "I had to reassure the Mexicans that I was auctioning the right to reproduce the diary in facsimile, not the diary itself." Loomis invited a series of publishing houses to view the color photocopy in the Banco de Mexico's New York offices and place their bids. "I was immediately intrigued," says Abrams editor in chief Paul Gottlieb. "I dug in my heels and went for the moon—and we won!" Though Gottlieb won't divulge the amount of his successful bid, he allows that it is more than the $100,000 estimated by an insider in the *Times* article but "less than $500,000." Even before the first book is sold (the initial print run is more than 150,000) Abrams undoubtedly will have made good on its investment, for Frida-mania has a global reach. Abrams has already sold the foreign rights in nine different countries, and these editions will all be published simultaneously with the American one. "A miracle," Gottlieb declares breathlessly. Madrazo will publish the diary in Mexico under her own imprint—and her plans for Frida *objets* based on the diary are currently under way.

What is so compelling about Frida's esoteric scribblings and doodles, which are unintelligible to the casual reader (especially one with no Spanish) and, at best, puzzling to most Kahlo experts? "They're hypnotic," says art historian Sarah M. Lowe—who, in her succinct notes to the text, has valiantly endeavored to make sense of Kahlo's wild, sometimes polymorphously erotic pictographs and stream-of-consciousness ravings. (Carlos Fuentes is the author of the belletristic introduction.) "The diary is the most important work Kahlo ever did," Claudia Madrazo asserts. "It contains energy, poetry, magic. They reveal a more universal Frida." Continues Sarah Lowe, who cautions that her comments on the diary are not definitive, "In Kahlo's paintings you see only the mask. In the diary you see her unmasked. She pulls you into her world. And it's a mad universe."

Most pertinent to the diaries is an understanding of how the daughter of a lower-middle-class German-Jewish photographer and a hysterically Catholic Spanish-Indian mother became a celebrated painter, Communist, promiscuous temptress, and, later (during the diary years), a narcotic-addicted, dykish, suicidal amputee afflicted with a bizarre pathology known as Munchausen syndrome—the compulsion to be hospitalized and, in extreme cases, mutilated unnecessarily by surgery.

Thanks to an astonishing, largely unpublished body of research as complete as Hayden Herrera's exhaustive biography and complementary to it, compiled by an unlikely scholar—Dr. Salomón Grimberg, a 47-year-old Dallas child psychiatrist—it is possible to amplify these facts of Kahlo's life and even, Grimberg says, "decode 90 percent of the diary." Like Kahlo, Grimberg grew up in Mexico City, where he commenced, while still an adolescent, his rigorous investigations on the artist. A somewhat casual interest became an earnest fixation during his pre-med studies, when he started working at Kahlo's former gallery, the Galería de Arte Mexicano. There he started amassing records about every work of art she ever created, tracking down lost paintings, collecting pictures by her and other artists, and befriending anyone whose life had intersected Kahlo's. Though Grimberg is something of a pariah in the art world, where his unapologetic zeal and his affiliation with another profession are eyed with suspicion—"I am a bastard of art history," he admits—his knowledge of his subject is unrivaled and incontrovertible. He is routinely consulted by auction houses and dealers, often without compensation, who rely on him to locate, document, and authenticate art by Kahlo and others. And he has been given (again, without remuneration) the texts of other, better-known scholars' books for fact checking. He is, however, a paid consultant to Christie's, a curator of museum exhibitions, the author of numerous pioneering scholarly articles, as well as a co-author of the catalogue raisonné of Kahlo's work.

Because he has earned the complete confidence of several key players in the Frida story, Grimberg has been entrusted with some startling Kahlo documents—in particular a soul-baring clinical interview conducted over many sessions between 1949 and 1950 by a Mexican psychology student named Olga Campos (a classmate of Diego Rivera's daughter by Lupe Marín). Additionally, Grimberg has the transcripts of a full battery of psychological tests Kahlo underwent, in preparation for a book Campos planned to publish on the theory of creativity. Kahlo was, Campos writes, "cooperative" with her, not only because of their friendship but also because the young psychologist had begun her research at a devastating juncture in Frida's life. In response to a sudden announcement by Diego Rivera that he wanted a divorce to marry the Mexican film siren María Félix, Kahlo, Campos reports, overdosed.

The text of Campos's interview—in which Frida candidly discusses her life and her paintings—forms the core of Grimberg's unpublished book manuscript. Kahlo's intimate revelations are then fleshed out by Grimberg's psychobiographical account of Kahlo's life, Campos's personal reminiscences about the artist, the results of the artist's Rorschach, Bleuler-Jung, Szondi, and TAT psychological tests, Kahlo's medical records, and Grimberg's line-by-line analysis of the 170-page diary. For many years and from several sources he has been accumulating photographs of the journal pages (some barely the size of a playing card), assembling them in sequence, and studying the results nightly for hours at home after work. His reading of the diary, as outlined in his unpublished book, is a much closer, more thorough, and more accurate interpretation than the one offered by the Abrams volume. More astonishing still, his compilation of the diary pages is probably more complete than the Abrams facsimile. Grimberg has discovered three missing pages that Frida had torn from the diary and given to friends—lost leaves represented in the Abrams book only as jagged, ripped edges.

Though she gave her birth date as July 7, 1910, Frida Kahlo was actually born on July 6, 1907, in Coyoacán, Mexico, now a suburb of Mexico City. This most basic lie alone qualifies her for a name she goes by in the diary: "the Ancient Concealer." Her epileptic father, Guillermo Kahlo, and her mother, Matilde, had another daughter, Cristina, 11 months later. Before Frida arrived, Matilde had had a son who died a few days after birth. Unable, or too ambivalent, to breast-feed her, Matilde passed Frida on to two Indian wet nurses (the first, Frida told Campos, was fired for drinking). Probably because of the confusion of having three erratic caregivers, and her mother's general depression over the loss of a son (Frida called her family's household "sad"), Kahlo had from earliest infancy a very damaged sense of self.

In the absence of a Kahlo boy, Frida assumed something of a son's role in the family—certainly she was her father's favorite, and the one who identified most with him. Frida told Campos in her clinical interview, "I am in agreement with everything my father taught me and nothing my mother taught me." Lucienne Bloch, a close friend of Kahlo's and disciple of Diego Rivera's, recalls that "she loved her father very much, but Frida did not have these same feelings for her mother." In fact, in 1932, when Kahlo returned to Mexico from Detroit upon hearing that her mother was dying (Bloch accompanied her on the journey), she failed to visit Matilde or even view her body. The painfully obstetric work *My Birth* (now owned by Madonna), in which

Frida's head emerges from the vagina of a mother whose face is covered by a shroud, was most likely her painted response to Matilde Kahlo's death.

At age six or seven, Frida contracted polio, an illness not detected immediately by her parents. When her right leg began thinning, the Kahlos attributed the withering to "a wooden log that a little boy threw at my foot," Kahlo told Campos. She tried to hide the deformity by wrapping her atrophied leg in bandages, which she then concealed with thick woolen socks. The young Frida, however, never wore a leg brace or orthopedic shoe. Her unbuttressed limp led her pelvis and spinal column to twist and deform as she grew, according to Grimberg, who does not agree with another doctor's recent diagnosis that she suffered from spina bifida, a congenital condition. The etiology of her later problems with childbearing and spinal malformation, he feels, can therefore be traced all the way back to her polio. She herself presents this idea in her painting *The Broken Column*, in which a crevice opens in her body to reveal a backbone in the form of a ruined Ionic column. Says Grimberg, "The steel corset she wears in this painting is a polio corset," not the kind she later used when recuperating from back operations.

Though her peers maliciously nicknamed her "peg leg," Frida nevertheless found some solace in her disease. "My papa and mama began to spoil me a lot and love me more," Kahlo told Campos. This statement, extraordinary in its pathos, provides one sorrowful key to the artist's psyche. For the rest of her life, Kahlo would associate pain with love (she read one Rorschach as "male genitals with fire and thorns"), and use illness to extract from others the attention she so desperately craved. Family photographs from her adolescence show she found another unusual technique to gain attention and at the same time disguise her gimpy leg. Surrounded by primly dressed relatives, she appears nattily turned out in the full masculine attire of a three-piece suit and tie. Kahlo's early cross-dressing, of course, also reflects her ambiguous gender identity. In a poignant section of Campos's interview entitled "My Body," Frida responded, "The most important part of the body is the brain. Of my face I like the eyebrows and eyes. Aside from that I like nothing. My head is too small. My breasts and genitals are average. Of the opposite sex, I have the moustache and in general the face." (Lucienne Bloch says Frida always carefully groomed her mustache and unibrow with a little comb.)

Kahlo also intimated to Campos that her first sexual experience occurred at age 13 with her gym and anatomy teacher, a woman named Sara Zenil. Noticing Frida's stricken leg, Zenil declared the girl "too frail," pulled her out of sports, and initiated "a physical relationship" with her. When Kahlo's mother discovered some compromising letters, she removed Frida from the school and enrolled her instead in the National Preparatory School, where she was one of 35 girls in a student body of 2,000. Tellingly, when she had her first period it was a male friend who took her to the school nurse. And, she recounted to Campos, when she got home it was to her father, not her mother, that she reported the news. While Frida was attending the National Preparatory School, the government engaged the celebrated muralist Diego Rivera to paint the walls of its auditorium. Frida, about 15, developed an obsessive crush on the 36-year-old, internationally famous, and prodigiously fat Michelangelo of Mexico. She declared to her school friends that her ambition was to have his child.

Frida's affair with Diego would begin later, however, for the course of her life was diverted by a cruel twist of fate. In 1925, Frida, now apprenticing (and sleeping) with an artist friend of her father's, was riding in a wooden bus with her steady boyfriend, Alejandro Gómez Arias, when an electric trolley car crashed into it. Frida's boyfriend told Hayden Herrera, "The bus . . . burst into a thousand pieces." Trapped under the trolley, Gómez Arias sustained comparatively few injuries. But Frida, probably destabilized by her bad leg, was pierced by the trolley's metal handrail, which entered her lower body on the left side and exited through her vagina, tearing its left lip. Her spinal column and pelvis were each broken in three places; her collarbone and two ribs broke as well. Her right leg, the one deformed by polio, was shattered, fractured in 11 places, and her right foot was dislocated and crushed. Somehow, in the impact, Frida's clothes had also been yanked off, and she was left completely nude. Even more freakish, Gómez Arias recalled, "someone in the bus, probably a housepainter, had been carrying a packet of powdered gold. This package broke, and the gold fell all over the bleeding body of Frida." Kahlo was hospitalized for a month (her mother visited only twice), and then sent home to recuperate. During her convalescence she bombarded Gómez Arias with lovelorn letters, and took up painting. Her letters show how intertwined her anguish over Gómez Arias's waning attentions was with her physical suffering. She created her first self-portrait, a gift for her lukewarm beau, as a way to force him to think of her and look at her. "If, after her polio, Frida ever had the chance to separate the idea of love from the experience of pain, the accident destroyed that chance," says Grimberg. Beginning a pattern that would recur with the 30-odd operations performed on her in the course of her beleaguered life, Frida ended her bed rest prematurely and healed poorly.

Around 1927, through mutual Communist acquaintances, she remet Diego Rivera. Their affair began after she showed up one day while he was frescoing Mexico City's Ministry of Education building. With paintings tucked under her arm, she demanded that he critique her work. In 1929 they married, launching an obsessive, earthy, and doomed union that turned them into the Liz and Dick of the international art world. Twenty-one years older, 200 pounds heavier, and, at more than six feet, nearly 12 inches taller than she, Rivera was gargantuan in both scale and appetites. As irresistible as he was ugly, Rivera was described by Frida as "a boy frog standing on his hind legs"—women flung themselves at him. (Actress Paulette Goddard was perhaps his most famous conquest.) Casual as well as compulsive in his philandering, he compared making love to urinating and declared he could well be a lesbian because he loved women so much. Frida was hopelessly attracted to him (she returns to the theme constantly in her diaries), and developed a special fondness for his huge stomach, "drawn tight and smooth as a sphere," she wrote, and for "the sensitivity" of his pendulous, porcine breasts.

Frida altered her persona to please Diego, painting works influenced by indigenous Mexican art, dressing in the colorful, feminine costumes of the Tehuantepec peninsula, and arranging her long, black tresses in Indian-inspired styles. Frida became pregnant just before she married Diego, but she aborted at three months, supposedly because of her twisted pelvis. Her second pregnancy ended in a miscarriage—though she had in fact tried to induce an abortion by ingesting quinine. The third pregnancy was also terminated, quite possibly because it was a lover's child. It is part of the Frida myth that she could not bring a child to term, a situation which caused her much grief and which became the subject of at least two important artworks by her. Yet, in spite of her congenitally underdeveloped ovaries, she was still able to conceive. And though her pelvis had been damaged by both polio and the accident, there still remains the question of why she never considered a cesarean delivery. Diego supposedly worried that childbearing would ruin her delicate health, but, as Grimberg says, "even if she were physically capable of having a child, she was psychologically unable. It would have stood in the way of her bond with Diego," whom she babied to the point of filling his tub with toys while she bathed him.

Throughout the early 30s, Kahlo traveled with Diego to San Francisco, Detroit, and New York while he worked for American capitalists on large commissions with leftist themes. Kahlo, meanwhile, with Rivera's proud encouragement, developed her craft, honed her engagingly sassy persona, and made important contacts in the social and art worlds—from the Rockefellers and Louise Nevelson (with whom Diego probably had an affair) to that other amazon of art history, Georgia O'Keeffe. Frida's friend Lucienne Bloch remembers that Frida was "very irritated by the famous O'Keeffe" when she met her in 1933—a reaction probably provoked by competitive feelings. But Frida habitually neutralized rivals (usually Diego's mistresses) with a disarming camaraderie, which in this instance may have flowered into a physical relationship. Art dealer Mary-Anne Martin has in her possession an unpublished letter Kahlo sent to a friend in Detroit, dated "New York: April 11, 1933," which contains a revealing passage, sandwiched between jaunty gossip about mutual acquaintances: "O'Keeffe was in the hospital for three months, she went to Bermuda for a rest. She didn't made [sic] love to me that time, I think on account of her weakness. Too bad. Well that's all I can tell you until now."

Homesick in the United States, Frida persuaded the reluctant Rivera to return to Mexico. Once there, he retaliated by having an affair with her sister Cristina. (Rivera eventually paid a creepy price for his priapism; in his 60s he was diagnosed with cancer of the penis.) Devastated, Frida began painting herself wounded and bleeding. According to most Frida literature, the artist's series of vengeful extramarital affairs also date from the Cristina crisis. But Grimberg has discovered that Kahlo very quietly had been keeping up with her husband all along. Grimberg has found a letter among the papers of the handsome, womanizing [*Vanity Fair*] photographer Nickolas Muray (whom Kahlo probably met through the Mexican-born *Vanity Fair* [illustrator] Miguel Covarrubias), which proves that Frida and he had begun their passionate affair as early as May of 1931.

Kahlo tried to conceal her heterosexual liaisons from Rivera—not so difficult after they moved into his-and-hers houses, adjacent residences connected by a bridge. Once detected, these dalliances, such as her mid-1930s fling with the dapper Japanese-American sculptor Isamu Noguchi, usually ended. (In contrast, Rivera boasted to anyone who would listen of her flings with women.) Her brief liaison with Leon Trotsky—whom Rivera, with his potent political pull, had helped bring to Mexico in 1937—infuriated him most. (Kahlo also did not miss the opportunity to seduce Trotsky's secretary, Jean van Heijenoort.) Friends recall that long after Trotsky's assassination Kahlo delighted in driving Rivera into a rage by humiliating him with the memory of her affair with the great Communist. The Kahlo-Rivera duet was, a friend says, "heightened torture and heroism."

After Kahlo's successful New York exhibition at the Julien Levy Gallery in 1938, Rivera—eager for some distance from his overbearing wife—urged her to travel to Paris, where the Surrealist poet André Breton had promised to organize a show. Though Frida professed to feel alone and miserable in France, this "beautiful human magnet" (as a friend called her), decked in ethnic fiestawear, mesmerized Picasso, Duchamp, Kandinsky, and Schiaparelli (who paid homage by designing a "*robe* Mme. Rivera"). Frida found Breton insufferable, but she had discovered a soul mate in his wife, painter Jacqueline Lamba. Half a decade later Frida even copied into her diary a letter she had written to Lamba after departing France. It is possible to read through the letter's doubly crossed-out line "We were together . . ." When Grimberg asked Lamba if she and Frida had been close, she replied, "Very close, intimate." Grimberg feels that Kahlo's painting *The Bride Frightened at Seeing Life Opened* is a tribute to Lamba, who had confided in Kahlo the trauma of her wedding night. The little blond doll peering over this still life, and alluded to in the letter, resembles the elegant Lamba.

After her 1939 return from Paris, Rivera demanded a divorce from Kahlo.

(Paulette Goddard had by then moved across the street from Diego's studio.) Kahlo mourned the separation by cutting her hair as she had during the Cristina affair. She painted herself shorn and desexed (she described herself to Nickolas Muray as looking like a "fairy"), wearing a man's baggy suit capacious enough to be Diego's—a curious case of identification with the aggressor. In the 1940s, she also embarked on the series of arresting self-portraits that have seared her features so indelibly into the public's imagination. As Grimberg astutely points out, Kahlo clearly had difficulty being alone. "Even in her self-portraits she is usually accompanied—by her parrots, monkeys, dogs, or a doll," he says. "She kept mirrors in every room of her house, her patio included, as if she needed constant reassurance of her very existence."

A painting known today by the descriptive title *Two Nudes in the Jungle* (1939; originally titled *The Earth Herself*) is usually interpreted, like the contemporaneous *Two Fridas*, as a double self-portrait. Painted for [actress] Dolores Del Rio around the time of Frida's divorce, it may in fact be a slightly veiled sapphic image of Kahlo with the screen goddess. In the Campos interview Frida states that she painted a portrait of Del Rio, yet in the actress's estate only two Kahlo pictures turned up: *Girl with Death Mask* (1938) and *Two Nudes*. The fairer, recumbent nude, with her sloe-eyed, oval face, bears an undeniable, if somewhat stylized, resemblance to photos of Del Rio from the period. The painting brings to mind a salacious confession Kahlo made to Campos—that she was "attracted to dark nipples but repelled by pink nipples in a woman."

Never good, Frida's health—physical and otherwise—worsened after the divorce. Her endemic infirmity was exacerbated by her bottle-a-day brandy habit, chain-smoking, and steady diet of sweets. (When her teeth rotted she had two sets of dentures made, one in gold and a more festive pair studded with diamonds.) By 1940 not only was she racked with agonizing pain in her spine, she was also suffering from infected kidneys, a trophic ulcer on her right foot, where some gangrenous toes had already been amputated in 1934, and recurrent fungus infections on her right hand.

Rivera, who had fled to San Francisco to avoid embroilment in the Trotsky-assassination-attempt fiasco (he was briefly under suspicion), was disturbed to learn of Kahlo's debilitated condition and her two-day imprisonment for questioning after the Communist leader's eventual murder. Rivera sent for Frida, had her hospitalized in California, and, as Frida wrote to a friend, "I saw Diego, and that helped more than anything else. . . . I will marry Diego again. . . . I am very happy." These tender sentiments, however, did not prevent Frida from carrying on—from her hospital bed—an affair with the noted art collector and dealer Heinz Berggruen, then a boyish refugee from Nazi Germany. Says Herrera, "Remember, Frida's motto was 'Make love, take a bath, make love again.'" Nonetheless, the couple re-wed in San Francisco on Diego's 54th birthday, returned to Mexico, and set up housekeeping in Kahlo's childhood Coyoacán home.

In 1946, having consulted numerous Mexican doctors, she elected to undergo major surgical intervention on her spinal column in New York. There an orthopedic specialist named Dr. Philip Wilson performed a spinal fusion using a metal plate and a bone graft sliced from her pelvis. The operation filled her with an eerie euphoria. "He is so marvelous this doctor, and my body is so full of vitality," she wrote to her childhood sweetheart Alejandro Gómez Arias, in a letter illustrated with diagrams of the cuts Dr. Wilson had made into her back and pelvis. In her painting *Tree of Hope* (1946) these gaping wounds reappear, bleeding exhibitionistically on her almost Christlike body, wrapped as if in winding-sheets and resting on a hospital gurney.

There were several causes for the almost morbidly elated tone of Kahlo's note to Gómez Arias. Surgery always gave her a strange high—she gleefully soaked up the ministrations of doctors, nurses, and visitors (in bed she entertained guests like a hostess at a party). She also was receiving huge doses of morphine, which left her addicted to painkillers for the rest of her life. But, most pertinent to the genesis of her diary, she had embarked on what would be her last and most satisfying romance with a man.

In 1946, just before she left Mexico to see Dr. Wilson, Frida fell in love with a beautiful Spanish refugee, a gentleman of great discretion and a painter like herself. Still alive today, he is, as when Frida knew him, a peripatetic soul—and he remains infatuated with Frida. In an old cigar box he preserves a relic of their love, a *huipil*, the loose Mexican blouse Frida often wore. When they were both in Mexico, the couple trysted at the house of Kahlo's sister Cristina, and corresponded by means of a post-office box in Coyoacán. She confided to one of her friends, "He's the only reason why I'm alive." This confidante says that the Spaniard was the love of Frida's life. By contrast, the relationship with Diego was, she insists, an "obsession"—a kind of complicity of needy souls. An unpublished incantatory poem Frida addressed to Diego, which her reputed late-in-life lesbian lover Teresa Proenza gave him a few months before he died, bears witness to the kind of raw, perverse emotional ties that bound her to her husband: "Diego in my urine—/ Diego in my mouth /—in my heart, in my madness, in my sleep . . ." she wrote.

The diary is conventionally understood to have originated in 1944—that date, it is true, appears on one page. But Frida often referred to past events in the diary, and sometimes copied old material—such as the missive to Jacqueline Lamba—into the book. And her letters and diary entries show how frequently the imprecise Frida made chronological, and other, slips when she wrote. One date in the diary, for example, first written as "1933" is then corrected to 1953. On the opening page of the diary, Frida scrawled, "Painted from 1916," an inscription that has mystified scholars, but that Grimberg feels is merely a slip for 1946. The recollection of her Spanish lover, who met Frida that year, is, however, certain proof of the 1946 dating. He recalls that Cristina Kahlo was in the habit of buying little notebooks—for addresses, accounts, etc.—for her sister from a stationery store in Coyoacán. One day when he visited Frida at Cristina's house, he found her pasting a collage of flowers onto the first page of a dark-red leather book, larger than the others, with her initials stamped in gold on the cover. The collage in question is the frontispiece of Kahlo's diary. The memory of the initials is also accurate—and shows up the persistent blindness of most readers of the diary, who have, despite its crossbar, routinely mistaken the monogrammed *F* on the cover for a *J*. In fact, a preposterous story has even sprung up around this misreading and clung to it tenaciously—that the book had once belonged to John Keats. From cover to cover, the signals given off by the diary have been misunderstood, misinterpreted, or disregarded—as if "the

Ancient Concealer" has posthumously been covering people's eyes with her heavily beringed fingers.

Frida's Spanish flame remembers next seeing Kahlo with the diary in New York, at the hospital. A comparison of the drawings and handwriting in the book with sketches and letters she gave him at the time bears this out. What is more, several of the diary's more mysterious entries, once deciphered, clearly refer to the Spaniard, whom she saw until 1952 (the affair ended because he needed to travel and she was incapacitated). But by no means is this to say that he was the only lover referred to in the book or its sole subject. (Diego, naturally, is mentioned far more frequently; she, as always, is her own main subject.) Of particular interest, as far as the Spanish lover goes, is a page, partially obscured by a naughty French postcard, where fragmentary words are still legible on the right. The first of these, ". . . ra villa," Grimberg explains, in its entirety reads, "mara villa," a private pun. The Spaniard's nickname for Frida was "Mara"—in Hindu mysticism, the temptress who entices the soul through the senses. (Many of the strange words in the diary are in arcane languages—not only Sanskrit, but also Nahuatl, an Aztec tongue— and even Russian. Far from being a naïf, Kahlo was extremely sophisticated about language, art history, and culture.) She added the Spanish suffix *villa*, Grimberg says, because when people heard her secret lover call Kahlo by her nickname, Frida and he would pretend it was short for *maravilla*, the Spanish word for "marvel." Similarly, the word *árbol*, or "tree," clearly discernible beneath "mara villa," is a reference to the Mexican song "Tree of Hope Stand Firm" (also the title of one of her paintings), which the Spaniard had taught Frida to help her overcome her despair. "Voyage" refers to a trip her errant lover took, the one that occasioned the postcard. "There's always an underlying theme in the diary," Grimberg says. "You just need to find it."

Another coded reference to her clandestine lover appears on a page which begins with "September at night. Water from heaven, the dampness of you. waves in your hands, matter in my eyes . . ." Farther down Kahlo writes the words "Delaware and Manhattan North," an allusion, Grimberg says, to the northbound trip the Spaniard took from his home in that state to visit his paramour. Perversely, sometimes Kahlo's obscure scribblings weave several lovers together, in rebuslike fashion. A few pages after the one on which she pasted the French postcard, she writes, "Anniversary of the [Russian] Revolution / 7th of November 1947 / Tree of Hope / stand firm! I'll wait for you—b. / . . . your words which / will make me grow and / will enrich me / DIEGO I'm alone." The song and painting title "Tree of Hope," of course, evokes the Spanish lover—but so does the lowercase *b*, the first initial of one of his names. (The faintly marked *b* is left out of the Abrams transcription of that page.) Frida's plaintive invocation of her husband is obvious. Less so is the reference to Trotsky, whose birthday fell on the same autumnal day as the revolution. There is something undeniably disturbed about the way she conflated these men in the space of a few sparse lines—as if on an unconscious level they were all interchangeable.

Kaleidoscopic, dissociative, and fractured, the writing and drawings— floating networks of penises, faces, ears, mystical symbols, and anthropomorphic beasts—may be "automatic" in the Surrealist sense, and sometimes even funny, but they are hardly intellectually calculated avant-garde exercises. They demonstrate, Grimberg feels, the kind of chaos unleashed in Kahlo's psyche when she was left in the one state she could not bear—solitude. The word ICELTI, Nahuatl for "alone"—untranslated in the Abrams notations— blazes in large red letters amid the disembodied heads and eyes of one page. Left to her own devices, she often summoned up the name or image of Diego to allay her interior sense of disorder. "Diego was her organizing principle, the axis around which she spun," Grimberg says, pointing out another mantra-like diary entry: "Diego = my husband / Diego = my friend / Diego = my mother / Diego = my father / Diego = my son / Diego = me / Diego = Universe."

The psychiatrist continues: "Anything, no matter how banal, that emanated from the great Rivera was sacred to her. She picked his crumpled drawings out of the trash, and asked him to inscribe in her diary his recipe for tempera," an ancient, egg-based artist's medium. (The Abrams book mistakenly assumes this uncharacteristically orderly entry was written by Frida.) Similarly, a feverishly carnal message ("I pressed you against my breast and the prodigy of your form penetrated all my blood . . ."), addressed to "Mi Diego" and assumed in the Abrams volume to have issued directly from Frida, is in fact a medleylike pastiche of erotic poems by her intimate friend Elías Nandino (she even scrawled the poet's name up the right margin of the page). Some of these verses he later published in the collection *Poems in Loneliness*, dedicated to Kahlo.

Inevitably, Frida's profound ambivalence about her inordinate emotional dependence on Diego bubbles to the surface, along with all the other flotsam and jetsam streaming from her unconscious. "Nobody will ever know how much I love Diego. I don't want anything to hurt him. nothing to bother him or to sap the energy that he needs to live," she writes on another leaf. This is a classic case of what psychoanalysts call "negation" and what Shakespeare called "protesting too much." Why bring up "hurting," "bothering," and "sapping" at all, unless it is in fact a secret wish?

The only one whom she ever effectively "hurt" or "bothered," of course, was herself; the only vital energy Frida succeeded in sapping was her own. In the diary she obliquely compared her personal auto-da-fé to that of the Jews of the Spanish Inquisition. The Israeli art historian Gannit Ankori has detected that a cryptic drawing labeled "ghosts" has its source in an illustration of Jews (a few are weeping females with long black hair) being humiliated by Spanish soldiers that Kahlo lifted from a book about the Inquisition in her Coyoacán library. (This revelation, published in the 1993–94 issue of *Jewish Art*, is not mentioned in the Abrams book.) Kahlo had good reason to identify with these wretched victims, for her final years added up to a Passion of her own.

A 1950 examination suggested that in the 1946 New York operation the wrong vertebrae may have been fused. Kahlo's back was thus reopened and another fusion was performed, this time with a donor graft. When the incisions became abscessed, the surgeons had to operate again. She lay in the Mexican hospital for a year, her wounds once more healing badly because of a fungus infection, and her right leg exhibiting early signs of gangrene. But in her own baroque variation of the Munchausen disorder, Frida turned her hospital stay into a festival. Diego took a room next to hers, and doctors noted that on those rare occasions when he was attentive her pains disappeared. Like Christ with Saint Thomas, Frida exhorted her guests to look at her oozing sore, and when doctors drained it, Hayden Herrera wrote, she would "exclaim over the beautiful shade of green." After her release, the exhibitionism of Kahlo's illness reached a bizarre apogee when, warned against attending the opening of her first Mexican one-person show, at the Galería Arte Contemporáneo, she was ceremoniously brought in on a stretcher and installed in the room on her four-poster bed as a live display.

Whatever warped satisfaction Kahlo had habitually derived from illness and operations was unavailable to her when she underwent the most drastic of her 30-odd procedures (Kahlo had at least as many doctors as lovers) in August 1953—the amputation of her right leg. Kahlo's injured spinal column was already metaphoric proof that she was indeed "rotten at the core." But, unlike her backbone, the stump was an outwardly visible sign of her defectiveness. The incorrigible egomaniac Rivera wrote in his autobiography, "Following the loss of her leg, Frida became deeply depressed. She no longer even wanted to hear me tell her of my love affairs. . . . She had lost her will to live."

Though she painted, mostly still lifes, whenever she had the strength, and, if the occasion warranted, could summon up her diabolical humor (in a quarrel with Dolores Del Rio, she announced, "I will send her my leg on a silver tray as an act of vengeance"), she tried several times to kill herself by hanging or overdose. But even in her livelier moments, she was doped up on Demerol; between the scabs from previous injections and her surgeries, it was impossible to find a virgin spot of skin in which to insert a needle. Vain to the finish, she continued her daily makeup ritual—Coty rouge and powder on the face, Talika eye pencil on the unibrow, and magenta lipstick—but her expert touch failed her, and, like the surfaces of her last canvases, the cosmetics were grotesquely caked and smeared. Her features coarsened and thickened, giving her countenance, in the past compared to an effeminate boy's, a distinctly masculine cast.

In her delirious despair, Frida became an ardent Stalinist. The Soviet tyrant, who died not long before Kahlo, was somehow merged in her agitated mind with Rivera—and with her father. "VIVA STALIN / VIVA DIEGO," she wrote on one diary page. Her last known painting is an unfinished likeness of the Russian leader. With his brushy hair and drooping mustache, he resembles, Grimberg observes in his unpublished manuscript, the posthumous image she had made in 1951 of her father.

All signs point to the fact that Kahlo's death on July 13, 1954, was a suicide by overdose. As art historian Sarah Lowe says, "Enough was enough." Many factors, the diary not least among them, support this theory. Her last written words include a long list of doctors and companions whom she thanks, and then the lines "I hope the leaving is joyful—and I hope never to return—FRIDA." The diary's last self-portrait shows a green face, which looks like an amalgam of her features with those of Diego, under which Kahlo inscribed "ENVIOUS ONE." And the book's last image is a bleak and transcendental study of a dark winged being—the Angel of Death.

Through a doctor friend, Rivera obtained a death certificate that listed the cause as "pulmonary embolism," but Kahlo's body was cremated before an autopsy could be performed. In Grimberg's text Olga Campos recalls that when she leaned over to kiss the corpse's cheek Frida's mustache hairs bristled—for a moment the psychologist thought her friend was still alive. After the cremation, when Frida's ashes slid back out on a cart from the oven doors, Rivera, some witnesses claim, scooped up a handful and ate them.

With her diaries now bared to the world, what, finally, can we make of Frida, the Ancient Concealer? Was she victim, martyr, manipulator— or even a great artist? Certainly her pain, her tears, her misery, her talent were authentic—but so was her need to exploit them. Which is not to deny Frida the essential tragedy and heroism of her life. Says the psychologist Dr. James Bridger Harris, who interpreted the Rorschach tests administered by Olga Campos, "It is Kahlo's heroic battle in the face of feeling defective, deformed, and unloved that everyone taps into." Frida projected onto one of these Rorschach cards a poignant, metaphoric description of herself. Its ambiguous shape suggested to her "a strange butterfly. Full of hair, flying downward very fast." Her remarkable response to an even murkier gray inkblot eloquently reveals Kahlo's longing to transcend her afflictions with dignity and grace: "Very pretty. Here are two ballerinas without a head and they're missing a leg [this was several years before the amputation]. . . . They're dancing."

OUR LADY OF THE KITCHEN

By Laura Jacobs | August 2009

The mirror was always in the drawer, the little handheld signal mirror, to use if one is lost. It was standard issue for Americans working in the Office of Strategic Services (O.S.S.), the dashing precursor to the C.I.A., active during World War II. In 2001, when Julia Child's entire kitchen was relocated from her house in Cambridge, Massachusetts, to the first floor of the Smithsonian National Museum of American History, in Washington, D.C., the rescue mirror went, too. It is displayed on a wall in the exhibit, forever near the kitchen drawer where she kept it—a leap of light, an SOS, symbolic of the point in her life when she was found.

It is at this point—the two years she spent in the O.S.S.—that Noël Riley Fitch begins her 1997 biography of Julia Child, *Appetite for Life*. "I asked myself," Fitch remembers, "What's the critical moment that changed her life and initiated her into the woman we know—the adult Julia?" The answer was Paul. In early 1945, the O.S.S. had transferred Julia McWilliams from Kandy, Ceylon (now Sri Lanka), to Kunming, China, where she continued her work as head of the Registry, processing all top-secret communications. She was glad of the transfer because fellow O.S.S.-er Paul Child had been sent to China some months before. A worldly intellectual with a poetic sensibility, an artist and photographer who relished wine, women, and song, he designed war rooms for General (Lord) Mountbatten in Kandy and for General

[Albert C.] Wedemeyer in Kunming. Paul thought Julia unworldly, unfocused, and doubtless a virgin—"a hungry hayseed" is how she would describe herself—but also steady, game, a "classy dame," and "brave," he wrote his twin brother, Charlie, "about being an old maid!" He was 42 to her 32, five feet ten to her six feet two. He was looking for a soulmate, but had counted Julia out. And yet their sure-footed friendship, forged over Indo-Asian food and shared danger, was climbing, slipping, into love. Which led to bed. And then, in 1946, when the war was over, marriage.

It is at a later life-changing moment that the historian Laura Shapiro begins her biography, *Julia Child*, of 2007. She describes one of Julia's performances on *The French Chef*, a television show that first aired nine months after the 1961 publication of Child's momentous *Mastering the Art of French Cooking* (co-authored with Simone Beck and Louisette Bertholle). Presented on Boston's fledgling educational channel, WGBH, *The French Chef* was an instant success—the first cult cooking show in America. It was the only time the word "instant" would attach to this embracing, warm, spontaneous yet methodical woman, who stood firm against the priggish, frozen, in-minutes cooking of midcentury America.

"*Mastering the Art of French Cooking* is a great, great book," Shapiro explains. "And it actually has a fair amount of personality in it. But if that's all we ever had, Julia would have been over and forgotten by now. It was television that made her. The Julia that you see on television is the one who registered on the national consciousness and created a place for herself in the national heart." This, too, was a soul match, the marriage between Julia and the camera, between food and the tube. It is hardly an overstatement to say that the child of this marriage was public television as we know it today.

In a spiritual sense, however, the making of Julia Child—"Our Lady of the Ladle," as *Time* magazine would dub her in 1966—happened over lunch. It is here that the new movie *Julie & Julia*, based on Julie Powell's popular blog of 2002–2003—a year in which Powell made all 524 recipes in *Mastering the Art of French Cooking*—begins. Written and directed by Nora Ephron, and starring Meryl Streep as Child and Amy Adams as Powell, the movie starts in November of 1948, when Julia and Paul landed in France for his new post in the diplomatic corps. Straight from the ship they drove to a restaurant in Rouen called La Couronne (the Crown). For Julia's first meal on French soil, Paul ordered sole meunière, that simplest, purest, most implicitly French preparation of fresh fish. All it required was butter, flour, parsley, lemon, precision, history, and heat. "It was heaven to eat," Julia wrote in *From Julia Child's Kitchen*—"a dining experience," she remembered in *My Life in France*, "of a higher order than any I'd ever had before." One could say it was another shaft of light, not angled upward as from a signal mirror, but piercing inward—an annunciation. "Paul and I floated out the door into the brilliant sunshine and cool air. Our first lunch together in France had been absolute perfection. It was the most exciting meal of my life." Mrs. Child had received her vocation, her crown.

America's First Lady is not always the president's wife, though she does tend to be tall and tireless, and has in the past come from Wasp stock. The 20th century can count three such women, all of whom were cheerfully generous in the spotlight and wholly dedicated to causes that were democratic in character. Each of these women came into her own in middle age, and thus, to the American public, was never young, and each gave existential comfort by her very presence. The first was Emily Post, the author of 1922's *Etiquette*, and the conscience of the 20s and 30s. [*See page 95 of this volume for Laura Jacobs's profile of Post.*] The second was Eleanor Roosevelt, the wife of President Franklin Delano Roosevelt, and a moral beacon through the 40s and 50s. When Post died, in 1960, and Eleanor Roosevelt, in 1962, it was not the svelte and sloe-eyed Jacqueline Kennedy who moved into this matriarchal role—she was too young, too shy, too feathery, too fashionable. It was Julia Child, just turned 50.

Given the first 40 years of her life, begun on August 15, 1912, in Pasadena, California, the later fame of Julia Carolyn McWilliams hardly seemed fated. Her wealthy father, John McWilliams Jr., owned and managed farming and mining lands, and had a conservative vision for his daughter's life: marriage to a good Republican just like him. Her mother, Caro—an old-money Weston from Massachusetts (the family fortune came from making paper)—

was far more free-spirited in her views, but not aggressively so. Julia was the oldest of three children, and her chief distinction growing up, along with ebullient spirits reflected in a breathy, swoopy voice, was her height. Yes, she had [journalist-poet] William Cullen Bryant and [jurist] Oliver Wendell Holmes in her maternal bloodline, but she wasn't a particularly avid student, and it didn't help that her father equated intellectuals with Communists. Julia preferred sports, where she excelled because she was taller and stronger than anyone else, and theater, because she was a ham. In school plays Julia was always cast as the man or an animal—"never," Fitch writes, "the princess." In her diary, though, Julia wrote that she felt "meant for something."

As her mother had before her, Julia McWilliams went to Smith College—class of 1934. She graduated with a degree in history but not with the Mrs. that had been the ultimate four-year goal. Photographs show that Julia was lovely in her 20s, as lean as the young Kate Hepburn, with sun-streaked curls, a high brow, and penetrating blue eyes. She had dates and crushes. Still, when a woman is six feet two in size-12 flats, the view is unique, and not always in a good way. As O.S.S. friend Jack Moore told Fitch, "Looking down on all the males she ever [met]—she had to evolve a sense of herself that was different from the person who is a physically standard specimen." Julia chose to put the focus on others and to mute her own ego; she was modest, yet socially gung-ho.

Meanwhile, fitfully searching for that "something," she ping-ponged between East Coast and West, between career-girl aspirations—trying to write, doing P.R.—and the country-club life for which her upbringing had prepared her: golf, tennis, luncheons, dinner dances. When Harrison Chandler, the man who would one day run the Times Mirror printing operations, proposed to her, in 1941, Julia, lukewarm, eventually declined. Despite the plaintive lines of poetry she'd copied into the back of her diary—"Oh why do you walk through the fields in gloves, / Missing so much, so much?"—Julia wanted true love, what she called "sympatico," and was not willing to settle. Then, too, the war was on and her country was calling. She answered by heading to Washington, D.C. Too tall for the WACs or WAVES, she took a job as a typist in the Office of War Information, and two months later applied for a position in the O.S.S. Julia, it turned out, had formidable organizational skills: soon enough, she was supervising an office of 40 people. In 1944 she shipped out to India. "The war," she said, "was the change in my life."

That first meal at La Couronne wasn't just about the sole. It was also about salad served *after* a meal, and wine served *with lunch!* It was about the importance of a meal, its place in a day, in life, the at-table meeting of body and soul, and the pleasure of sharing that. In the O.S.S., the sympathy between Julia McWilliams and Paul Child was related to food, their eager explorations into Ceylonese and Chinese cuisine and culture, tastes both sensual and cerebral. Back in the States, the couple's love letters reflected the playful and frankly lusty nature of their relationship. "I want to see you," Paul wrote, "touch you, kiss you, talk with you, eat with you . . . eat you, maybe." Come 1948, could there have been a better diplomatic posting for Paul and his wife of two years than Paris?

While Paul was at the American Embassy, running the exhibits office for the United States Information Service (U.S.I.S.), Julia was shopping the markets, haunting Les Halles, taking French lessons at Berlitz so she could talk to the butcher, the fishmonger, the vegetable woman—to find out how to make the kind of food she'd eaten at La Couronne: *la cuisine bourgeoise.* In the months before she married, Julia had tried to cook and it wasn't pretty. She never forgot the first meal she'd made for her new husband: calves' brains simmered in red wine. It was "messy to look at," she later wrote, "and not very good to eat." She had 25 cookbooks but no technique, and she wasn't what anyone would call a natural. Yet Paul had lit the pilot light, and in Paris—*wooomf*—the flame.

"I loved the people, the food, the lay of the land, the civilized atmosphere, and the generous pace of life," she exclaimed in *My Life in France*, the memoir she wrote with her grandnephew Alex Prud'homme, published in 2006, two years after her death. "I fell in love with French food—the tastes, the processes, the history, the endless variations, the rigorous discipline, the creativity, the wonderful people, the equipment, the rituals."

The operative word is "love." In a video Julia made for the Smithsonian, in 2001, to run alongside the display of her famous Cambridge kitchen, she said of the house it was in, "If we could just have the kitchen and our bedroom that would be all we'd need." And that's pretty much what Paris was for Julia and Paul, a kitchen and a bedroom. The inheritance Julia had received when her mother died, and the helpful supplements sent by her father, not only meant that the couple had extra cash to sample French restaurants but also made possible Julia's leap: enrollment in the Paris cooking school Le Cordon Bleu. There, she worked with a passion she'd never known before. "I was beginning to feel *la cuisine bourgeoise* in my hands, my stomach, my soul." Though she called Paul a "Cordon Bleu widower," he wasn't really. "I would go to school in the morning," she once said in an interview, "then for lunch time, I would go home and make love to my husband."

If there is one line that sums up the Julia Child enterprise it is this one, written in *My Life in France*: "My immediate plan was to develop enough foolproof recipes so that I could begin to teach classes of my own." This was the seed of her great achievement. Julia did, in fact, teach classes in Paris. With Simone (Simca) Beck and Louisette Bertholle, the two women she would always call her "French sisters," she founded L'Ecole des Trois Gourmandes, a twice-weekly class for American women who wanted to cook French. It was merely a warm-up. With Beck and Bertholle she would write a book—*the* book—a masterpiece that almost 50 years later still stands alone.

It began as a fixer-upper in 1952, when Beck and Bertholle asked Julia to groom a 600-page cookbook they'd sold to Sumner Putnam of Ives Washburn, *French Home Cooking*. In recasting the recipes for American kitchens, Julia tested them and found every one overcomplicated or unclear. She decided that they had to start from scratch—rethinking, researching, retesting—and with American ingredients, American measurements, and cultural translations (for instance, what the French call *le carrelet*, the British call plaice, and Americans, sand dab or lemon sole). During this deconstruct/reconstruct process Putnam fell away and Houghton Mifflin signed on as the publisher; the book got bigger, its ambition deeper. Six years and 700 pages later, the manuscript was so involved and encyclopedic it scared the suits at

Houghton Mifflin. They asked for a scaled-down (dumbed-down is what they actually wanted), more user-friendly format, and this imperative brought focus. It would be, Julia told their editor, "a collection of good French dishes of the simpler sort, directed quite frankly to those who enjoy cooking and have a feeling for food."

At this point Bertholle had very little to do with the book. (Her royalties were whittled down to 18 percent, the rest split between Beck and Child.) Instinctive, inventive Simca and analytical Julia were the creators; Julia wrote the book, and it was her supreme and unrelenting powers of organization and test-kitchen rigor that gave the final manuscript its singular form and clarity. The book they produced was magisterial and yet intimate, serenely serious yet plainspoken. When it appeared, in 1961, majestically titled *Mastering the Art of French Cooking*, it was like nothing the world had ever seen before. The great James Beard wished he had written it, and Jacques Pépin, who saw it in manuscript, says he "read it like you read a novel, turning the pages fast, late into the night. . . . I couldn't believe that someone had broken it all down like that. I was jealous." The recipes were indeed foolproof.

Houghton Mifflin, to its everlasting regret, rejected the manuscript as still too formidable. But Judith Jones, a young editor at Knopf, took one look and knew it was a classic. Like Julia, she, too, had found herself—plus a future husband, the writer and editor Evan Jones—in France. She, too, was in love with French food. When she tested *Mastering*'s recipe for *boeuf bourguignon*, "my first bite told me that I had finally produced an authentic *French boeuf bourguignon*—as good as one I could get in Paris."

"It's not just a book of recipes," Jones says today. "It was a revolutionary book in the sense that Julia knew she had to translate French cooking into terms that we would understand. Lots of the recipes are Simca's, but I think even then Julia often put her imprint on them in more detail, more detail."

Also part of that imprint? Principles—a belief in a right way as opposed to a wrong way. Just as Emily Post's *Etiquette* set forth a blueprint for civilized conduct, an ethical structure, if you will, that anyone—no matter what their birth—could learn, so *Mastering* set forth the structural verities of classic French cooking, the disciplined themes and variations, tantamount to an art, that Julia had found so liberating: how to make the foundation sauces, how to do a roux, how to lay in flavor, how to be patient. The centuries-old techniques that the French learn like a language could now be learned step-by-step by Americans.

"She knew how she wanted it to look on the page," Jones says. "The ingredients appearing when you use them, instead of having to go back five pages."

Which meant one had to read the whole recipe before starting. This in itself forced a cook to take the enterprise seriously, to see in advance the architecture of the recipe, and to understand the alchemical flash points (its quickenings and transubstantiations) and the perils (what could go wrong and how to fix it). "We can't cater to the flimsies," Julia used to say to Jones, "flimsies" being people who weren't serious about food. ("Fluffies" was another Julia word, for people who were grandiose about eating, overly gourmet-ish.)

"It was an amazing book," says Nora Ephron, who still cooks Julia's lamb stew in the spring, still makes the *boeuf bourguignon* and the chicken breast with cream and mushrooms (deliciously filmed in *Julie & Julia*). "You understood cooking from having taken that book seriously."

And the timing couldn't have been better. Just as *Etiquette* punctually met America's booming Babel of the 1920s, new waves of the unwashed and the upwardly mobile in need of instruction, so *Mastering* coincided with the Kennedy presidency, which saw a decidedly liberal worldliness in the White House and a French chef in its kitchen. "There was that whole postwar Francophilia," says David Kamp, the author of *The United States of Arugula* and a *V.F.* contributing editor. "So French cooking was in the air; it would have happened. But it happened explosively with *Mastering.* It caught on like wildfire among a certain kind of educated, upper-middle-class housewife, back when 'housewife' was still the right term to use. It was a pretty significant demographic that really did drive change in how America approached food."

"It was an almost hilarious epidemic of cooking from that cookbook," says Ephron. "People would just pitch themselves into these things, and it was very much part of the fabric of all our lives in the early 60s."

"We'd called Julia Child by her Christian name the moment *Mastering the Art of French Cooking* appeared in 1961, because she seemed to be talking directly to us," writes one of those "pitchers," Betty Fussell, in her 1999 memoir, *My Kitchen Wars*. "To cook French, eat French, drink French . . .

was to become versant in the civilized tongues of Europe as opposed to America's barbaric yawp."

Mastering the Art of French Cooking sold more than 100,000 copies within one year of publication and by 1969 had sold 600,000—an astonishing number for a cookbook in the 60s. It is now in its 47th printing. The book paid for a small house Paul and Julia built and loved in Plascassier, in Provence—and it made life comfortable. Today, the royalties accrued from *Mastering*, as well as from Julia's 10 other cookbooks and other intangible property rights, go to the grant-giving Julia Child Foundation for Gastronomy and the Culinary Arts. The foundation operates with a base of around $1 million, and promotes cooking as a serious study.

In February 1962, four months after *Mastering*'s publication, Julia appeared on *I've Been Reading*, an interview program on [Boston's] WGBH, Channel 2. Paul, who had retired from government service in 1961, was now Julia's full-time, if unofficial, manager, and they arrived for the 30-minute show armed with a copper bowl, a dozen eggs, mushrooms, a whisk, and a hot plate. "I did not know what [I] could talk about for that long," Julia later said. On the show she whipped the egg whites, turned the mushrooms, and made an omelet. The station received 27 letters (unheard of!) asking for more. And so, with producer-director Russell Morash and associate producer Ruth Lockwood (who'd just finished a series featuring Eleanor Roosevelt), Julia made three pilots: "The French Omelette," "Coq au Vin," and "Soufflés." On July 26, 1962, a half-hour show called *The French Chef* was aired at 8:30 p.m., and a 49-year-old star was born.

"There I was in black and white," Julia wrote in *My Life in France*, "a large woman sloshing eggs too quickly here, too slowly there, gasping, looking at the wrong camera while talking too loudly, and so on."

She's right. The first *French Chef*s were rudimentary and self-conscious. They were also straightforward and mesmerizing. Julia wasn't flimsy or fluffy; she was simply the sum of her experiences standing there in a studio kitchen and turning *la cuisine bourgeoise* into a charmingly earnest, slyly earthy, and surprisingly droll one-woman show.

But, really, was there a face and figure that seemed less made for the unforgiving medium of television than Julia's? She was middle-aged, with a hairdo of short curls that David Kamp has called "unreconstructed Smith '34." She's frumpy in a button-up blouse of stiff cotton, like a home-ec teacher, until you notice how tall and lean she is over the low counter, her slim hips girded by a tightly wrapped apron, a towel tucked into the waistband—rather swashbuckling. She's like a knight without armor—not of the roundtable but of the dinner table—and she even has a coat of arms: the "Ecole Des 3 Gourmandes" embroidered badge (designed by Paul) that's pinned to her blouse. She could be a mezzo-soprano singing a trouser role—the Rosenkavalier, perhaps, or Cherubino. Which brings us to the voice.

Paul, when he first met Julia, in the O.S.S., described "her slight atmosphere of hysteria." No doubt he was referring to Julia's almost operatic vocal tonalities, the here floating, there plunging falsetto she seems to have been born with. Hers is one of the distinctive voices of 20th-century entertainment, and it has known myriad descriptions: "a flutey schoolmarm tone," the "Edwardian inflections of Lady Bracknell," "like a great horned owl," "two parts Broderick Crawford to one part Elizabeth II." Yet the voice is only half of it, the other half being her silence as she kneads the dough or wields the knife, the intervals of rigorous quiet, pure concentration, that give the show a spellbinding inner rhythm, an almost medieval sense of heat and light. For Julia Child, French cooking was a guild art requiring a committed apprenticeship, years of practice. And it required courage, too, or as she said to viewers after she muffed the flip of a potato cake, which fell in pieces on the stovetop, "You see when I flipped it I didn't have the courage to do it the way I should have." She proceeded to press the cake back together and uttered one of her most famous lines: "But you can always pick it up, and if you're alone in the kitchen, who is going to see?"

The French Chef officially premiered on February 11, 1963, and ran through 1973 (Julia did many other television shows, and won three Emmys). As the show caught on, a whole cult of Julia stories sprang up. That dropped potato cake soon became, in the retelling, a dropped chicken, a roast, a whole salmon on the floor, which she picked up while saying (not), "Your guests will never know." And because Julia used wine in her cooking and toasted viewers at the show's end, people thought she was drunk on-camera, not knowing her glass of wine was really Gravy Master mixed with water. In 1978, *Saturday Night Live* presented a Grand Guignol spoof of *The French Chef*, co-written by Al Franken and starring Dan Aykroyd as Julia, who slices off her thumb while making *poularde demi-désossée*, bleeds copiously, and then passes out crying, "*Save the liver.*" The skit is still aired today and still funny, a testament to Julia's continuing stature in the culture. (She herself loved the skit, and kept a videotape of it under the television in her kitchen.)

In the 10 years that *The French Chef* aired, Julia's subtext was not out of sync with the era's counterculture or its overt message of psychosexual liberation. Julia wanted her viewers to loosen up, get physical, not with controlled substances but with food, not through a glass darkly but at table, with delight. Hers was a civilized sensuality, the integration of the senses that she'd learned in France. This is why her following was legion—Julia's appetite appealed to young and old alike.

"Americans didn't come over on the *Mayflower* trusting food," says Laura Shapiro. "Julia's whole thing about food was that you had to trust it. That, to me, is her great message. Getting your hands into it—touch it, breathe it, smell it, live it. If we as Americans have overcome to any degree our fear of food, our weird neurotic thing about the body, it starts with Julia."

"I felt very related to her," says Judith Jones, "because we were both released from very traditional, middle-class American values. And it was France that released us. She wanted to bring this message to America—that we were still steeped in the Puritan attitude towards food, and what the food industry had done to make us feel that food was not for the modern woman. It's what an artist does: you want to express it so that you awaken sensibility. And she really did that."

"Her favorite point in her life was the years in France, that period of discovery and awakening," says Alex Prud'homme. "As she said, 'I felt myself opening like a flower.' It was a lovely phrase. And I think one of the reasons that—this is my personal theory—she wanted to write all these recipes down and transmit them to Americans is it was a form of distilling experience, almost like a short story or a poem. She used the recipe as a way of talking about France and its values, which are so different from ours. You know, doing things correctly and taking the time to get it right, and to work hard and learn your technique, and also to have fun."

Paul Child died at the age of 92, in 1994. Ten years later, in 2004, Julia Child died two days short of her 92nd birthday. In the last year of her life she suffered knee surgeries, kidney failure, and a stroke. On August 12, when her doctor called to say she had an infection and would need to be hospitalized, she chose not to be treated. The meal that turned out to be her last, before she went to sleep and never woke up, was *Mastering*'s recipe for French onion soup.

"Her birthday was August 15," says Alex Prud'homme. "And we had people from all over the country and around the world coming for this big party in Santa Barbara for her 92nd birthday, and she died two days beforehand. And I've always wondered, Did she do that on purpose? We'll never know. But it would be a very typical Julia move, knowing that all her favorite people were coming from all over, and wouldn't this be a nice moment for her to, as she would say, 'slip off the raft.'"

Did they still come?

"Everybody came. And it turned into a sort of three-day Irish wake, everybody telling stories and laughing and crying and eating and drinking. I think she felt very lucky to live the life she did. I think she loved it."

DECONSTRUCTING GLORIA

By Leslie Bennetts | January 1992

W ell manicured and well modulated, the lunchtime crowd at the Four Seasons hums discreetly with the usual heady mixture of business and gossip. Only the barest flick of an eye betrays interest as each new arrival is checked out by the power brokers already at their seats. But when a tall, frazzled-looking woman hurries over to my table, there is not so much as a glimmer of recognition from anyone in the vicinity. Indeed, as she struggles out of her coat, even I do a double take: who is this pleasant-looking matron, with her brown jacket and brown pants and mousy brownish hair pulled back into what looks suspiciously like a bun? Although I've known her for nearly twenty years, it is several long moments before I realize that the nondescript brown wren in front of me is one of the most famous women in the country, not to mention my tardy lunch date, Gloria Steinem. The last time I saw her, at a party some months ago, she seemed her usual glamorous self: a miniskirt riding outrageously high over those spectacular racehorse legs, a glittering gold tunic that made her stand out instantly in a crowded room, that radiant face partly obscured by the ever present curtain of blond-streaked hair. In fact, this is the first time I've ever seen her without that trademark shield carefully arranged over her cheeks. "As she has pointed out, she always hid behind her hair," says Stan Pottinger, a close friend and former longtime lover. "Now she's pulling her hair back and she's cut it short.

As a metaphor, it definitely does represent a change. The question is, why was she hiding before? And why is she not hiding now?"

Her friends are all talking about the change in Gloria. Even Gloria is talking about the change in Gloria, albeit guardedly, with her usual mixture of easy charm and reticence. Within a few weeks, a whole lot of other people will also be talking about the change in Gloria when her new book—a dense and wide-ranging synthesis of politics, sociology, history, psychology, science, cultural anthropology, New Age experimentation, and personal exploration called *Revolution from Within: A Book of Self-Esteem*—hits the stores. In many ways, this is Steinem's first book, the one she has been waiting all these years to write; despite a journalistic career that has spanned three decades, it is her first full-length statement of her philosophical take on the world.

For a woman who has lived an almost entirely public life for close to a quarter of a century, Gloria Steinem is the most private of household names— not only loath to bare her innermost feelings before the world but, in many ways, a stranger to those very feelings herself. Ever since she started to attract attention and commentary, she has been described in countless articles as remote, as lovely and cordial but somehow distant and seemingly impervious to the emotional storms that buffet ordinary mortals. It has finally occurred to Steinem, at the age of fifty-seven, how much she had to repress to achieve that preternatural poise, how much the anguish and shame of a blighted childhood had to be buried to permit the emergence of the dazzlingly self-possessed icon who won fame and admiration all over the world. If Steinem is just starting to open the door a crack to others, it is because she is just starting to open it to herself.

Not that you could tell from her demeanor, of course. "Writing this book helped me a lot, and it changed me a lot," she says, as low-key and matter-of-fact as if she were discussing the weather, her expression the same as when she was studying the lunch menu and deciding on the swordfish. "This has been a funny, shaky, full-of-tendrils-to-other-places kind of bridge into some other country for me. Partly the country has to do with age, but that may actually be the least important part of it."

Aging is definitely on her mind these days, but she leavens any discussion with her usual wry humor. The good part? "You don't have to worry about how you look, because you're past the time when it really matters," she says with a grin. On her worst day, Gloria Steinem couldn't look bad, but I have to admit there are faint spots on the front of her baggy beige sweater, and the whole getup lacks a certain Steinem-esque jolt of sex appeal.

Whatever the changes in her outward persona, however, the internal ones are far more profound—although even these Steinem describes with characteristic restraint. "In the past, I think I was being falsely cheerful much of the time," she says brightly. This realization did not come easily; it was only after a disastrous love affair with [real-estate mogul, investor, and publisher] Mort Zuckerman, a serious depression (well, maybe not by anyone else's standards, but certainly a low point by her own), and the terror of life-threatening illness combined with a devastating professional fiasco that Steinem began, slowly and laboriously, to explore new ways of approaching her own life. She had spent months researching and writing the first version of this book, but when she presented her magnum opus on self-esteem to a close friend who happened to be a therapist, the reaction was a writer's nightmare. "I don't know how to tell you this," said Carmen Robinson, "but I think you have a self-esteem problem. You forgot to put yourself in."

It took Steinem a while longer to come to terms with the fact that she'd been forgetting to put herself in for about fifty years. Slowly, however, "I began to understand with a terrible clarity that we teach what we need to learn, and write what we need to read," Steinem explains in the introduction to *Revolution*. "I had felt drawn to such a book not only because other people needed it, but because I did. I had come to the burnt-out end of my ability to travel one kind of feverish, productive, but entirely externalized road—but I had no idea why."

I t took Steinem another three years to produce a different kind of book, one that is decidedly unconventional in its category-defying form but that most definitely includes its author. Her growing understanding of her own psyche has both amused and touched her intimates. "Once that process began, she got as excited about it as a kid," says Robin Morgan, a friend for twenty years and the current editor of *Ms.* magazine. "She would fall upon platitudes with great excitement; for her, they were totally new. She would call me up and say, 'Have you read Alice Miller? Do you know that all of us, no matter how old we get, carry around the baggage of our childhood?' She was always fiercely smart, but the emotional intelligence had been so sacrificed to the intellectual intelligence."

Until recently, the idea of getting herself a good shrink seems never to have occurred to Steinem despite the obvious traumas of her impoverished childhood. Her parents separated when she was ten, and Gloria was left alone to care for a mentally ill mother who was subject to terrifying hallucinations and was rarely able to assume any kind of parental responsibility. Gloria had to become not only a premature adult but the mother to her own incapacitated mother. Steinem's lifelong way of dealing with pain has been a pull-yourself-up-by-your-own-bootstraps-and-don't-complain stoicism that some friends attribute to her Ohio origins. "She used to say it amazed her that everyone in New York had a psychiatrist, when in the Midwest, if you had a mood, something was wrong with you," says Pottinger, a lawyer and investment banker who also comes from the Midwest. "The ethos is the tradition of the pioneers: You get the job done, and all the handwringing and moaning—you just don't do it. You grease the axle and put the wheel back on and get the horses moving—but the price you pay for that is less self-awareness than you have in some other cultures. Gloria, like a lot of us, came to the values of self-awareness late."

For a long time, Steinem apparently believed her childhood hadn't had any lasting impact. "I had a midwestern bias against therapy," she admits, "a kind of survivor's pride. I understood it for other people, but to me it just always seemed sort of unnecessary." Or even harmful, since she was all too familiar with the damage inflicted on many women by the rigid sexism of strict Freudian analysts. "I solved everything through acting, through being an activist. You go on believing that if something hits a bruise from the past it's really painful in the present, rather than understanding that there's another reason why it's so painful." She pauses and then adds softly, "It's difficult for a neglected child, because it isn't that there's something wrong—it's that there's *nothing*. You experience it as a lack of reality, as invisibility. So I set about making myself real by being useful."

And so the years whirled by in an unceasing blur of activity. For two decades, Steinem spent at least three or four days a week on the road, traveling and organizing, fund-raising and lobbying, endlessly bringing the clarion call of feminism to campuses and benefits, women's conferences and community groups. Anywhere the movement called, Gloria was there to answer. It didn't even have to be the movement that beckoned. "She meets someone on a plane, he asks her to speak at his daughter's Bat Mitzvah, and she goes," says Letty Cottin Pogrebin, a feminist author and close friend. "She does not say no to these things, and they eat her life away."

Steinem deflected any questions about these habits with her usual charming self-mockery. "She used to say fliply, 'The examined life is not worth living,'" recalls Suzanne Braun Levine, a longtime editor at *Ms.* magazine who is now the editor of the *Columbia Journalism Review*. "I think a lot of her courage came from forging ahead without letting herself ask questions. If you know you have to keep pushing, it would be smart not to look too deeply into your own needs."

The brownstone apartment where Steinem has lived since 1967 was a pit stop to change clothes before running to catch another flight, a crash pad which was always open to friends from all over the world but which, with its notoriously empty refrigerator and the eternal piles of cartons stuffed with books and papers littering the floor, indisputably lacked a certain domestic appeal. Not that Steinem had ever been exactly renowned for her homemaking skills. "I had lived in the apartment for at least four or five years before I found out the oven didn't work," Steinem admits. "She can make the world's greatest tuna-fish salad, and after that, forget it," Pottinger attests.

These days Steinem is able to recognize her apartment as "a symbol of the self," and with the help of a decorator friend, she has finally made it into a cozy and welcoming place, full of kilim rugs and overstuffed furniture and big pillows in rich colors and textures. Such domestic comfort was "something I didn't experience growing up, so it felt foreign to me; it didn't feel like home," muses Steinem, who grew up in a dilapidated, rat-infested, virtually empty farmhouse a few feet from a major highway. "I don't know why it took me so long to realize you need to have a home," she adds, a trifle sheepishly. "I guess I thought it was just something other people had."

Just as it was other people who had marriages, families, children. Steinem's avoidance of such norms has always been an irritant for many observers. For thirty years, the commentary on Gloria Steinem has reflected an almost Manichaean duality, a schizoid seesawing between white and black as various analysts described her either as a Gandhi-esque saint who cared only about saving the world or as a cunning opportunist who used a succession of causes as a smoke screen for her own overweening ambition. Even before she became an international symbol of American feminism, Steinem was a lightning rod for an extraordinary degree of malice from friend and foe alike, and that has never changed; it has always been apparent that a lot of people—feminists and liberals at least as much as right-wing chauvinists—were waiting to see Steinem fall on her face.

For so many years, even as she was presenting herself as a spokesperson for Everywoman, she seemed impossibly superior: whippet-thin and gorgeous, as glamorous as a movie star while maintaining impeccable credentials as a relentlessly earnest social activist, free of the burdens of domesticity but perpetually surrounded by brilliant, powerful men who doted on her—and she didn't have to wash their socks or clean up a nightly mountain of dinner dishes. Her very existence was enough to make other women feel inadequate. Would she ever repent her refusal to marry, regret her decision not to have children, end up old and alone in belated penance for a lifetime of thumbing her nose at other people's most cherished conventions? Would the paragon finally get her comeuppance? When the facts of Steinem's life have failed to provide such a satisfying dénouement, people have invented them, and the inventions have become as immutable a part of her mythology as anything that ever happened in real life.

By the time Steinem hit her early fifties, however, some genuine problems had begun to surface, converging like so many express trains hurtling toward a collision: the frustration of her failure to produce a real book; the lifelong pattern of hopping from one man to another, which finally led her into a major romantic debacle; the critical lack of self-esteem, so carefully papered over for so long; and finally the shadow that stalks us all, manifesting itself this time as breast cancer. And as the crisis swelled to its climax, the ever present Greek chorus keened its "I-told-you-so"s with obscene glee.

———

Nobody seems to know for sure how it all began. Perhaps it was an inevitable corollary to Steinem's much-gossiped-about decision to get involved with Mort Zuckerman in the first place. Many of her friends were appalled; even then, back in the mid-eighties, the controversial real-estate developer was hardly beloved in liberal and feminist circles, and he has become less popular since. Zuckerman had only recently moved from Boston to New York, and cynical observers speculated that his sudden passion for Gloria Steinem had as much to do with her enviable social cachet and universal entrée as it did with a deeply felt commitment to her. But any dismay over Steinem's new romance was eclipsed by the fire storm of criticism that erupted when The Rumor That Ate New York burst onto the scene. Suddenly you couldn't go to a dinner party without hearing it: that the unattainable Gloria Steinem, the woman whose previous admirers had ranged from Mike Nichols to John Kenneth Galbraith, who had left an endless trail of disappointed suitors in her wake, the rich and the powerful and the famous littering her path like so much debris—that glorious Gloria had fallen at last, and not only fallen but humiliated herself, betraying the women's movement in the bargain.

Specifically, The Rumor held that Zuckerman, a perennial bachelor who never quite seems to make it to the altar, had promised he'd marry her if she could have his child, and that Steinem, already past fifty, was ricocheting from one fertility specialist to another in a desperate last-ditch attempt to land Mr. Moneybags. The Rumor was astonishing in its virulence, its pervasiveness, and the total certitude with which so many people instantly embraced it; everyone claimed they knew it was true because a friend of a friend had seen Gloria in some doctor's office. As it happened, the doctors Steinem was seeing during that period were cancer specialists, but no matter. The fact that she had spent her entire adult life politely responding to unending questions by saying she wasn't interested in getting married or in having children meant nothing. Trashing her became the favorite spectator sport of the smart set. For all those who had long hoped that Saint Gloria would turn out to be guilty of the hypocrisy and venality they had always suspected but never been able to prove, that period provided an undreamed-of bonanza; so much venom spewed forth on the island of Manhattan it's a wonder it didn't poison the water supply. By the time the talk died down, The Rumor had been accepted as historical fact by all but a few of her closest friends, and to question it publicly meant being dismissed as a foolish and naïve idealist who simply didn't know the score.

Typically, Steinem is philosophical in analyzing the reasons it happened, and her emotional reaction seems restrained. "It hurt my feelings," she acknowledges mildly. "It made it seem like I would suddenly want to do something I had shown no evidence in my life of wanting to do, just because of what some man wanted me to do." When I press her about whether she has ever sought out fertility specialists, she says firmly, "Absolutely, unequivocally not. I have never gone to a fertility doctor in my life." So why did The Rumor assume such proportions? In part, Steinem sees it as a function of Zuckerman's own reputation. "He has spent all of his adult life going around saying he wants to have a child, so whoever he goes out with is subject to this rumor," she says dryly. "What is hurtful about it is the assumption that women are so without their own power that they will do anything to marry a powerful man. I mean, I never even moved in with him, which was a bone of contention. Even at my lowest point, which was pretty tired and depressed, I didn't want to get married." [In 2000, Steinem would marry the British entrepreneur and environmentalist David Bale, who passed away in 2003.]

Steinem also points out the extent to which people's perceptions reflected the presumption of the female's lack of power in *any* equation. "If you see a man and a woman together whom you know disagree, the assumption is she's losing," Steinem says. "Well, maybe she's winning, or subverting, or spying, or humanizing!" Or trying to, anyway.

There are those who believe that Zuckerman himself may inadvertently have started The Rumor. Mutual acquaintances remember his talking hopefully about the possibility that Gloria might have his child. If he got the wrong idea, Steinem herself takes part of the blame. "I never had the nerve to look him in the eye and say, 'Even if I could do this, I wouldn't, so forget it, it's out of the question,'" she admits.

Zuckerman goes ballistic when asked about the whole subject. "I don't want to get into any discussion on any level," he says angrily. However, asked about whether Gloria ever saw fertility doctors because he had held out a promise of marriage, he does say, "Both parts of that are completely false. It's totally untrue." His current line on Gloria is eulogistic: "She's a wonderful woman. She may be the most brilliant person I've ever known in my life, one of the wittiest and one of the most dedicated to her values and beliefs, a fabulous woman who has given her whole life over to her principles and ideals. I have the most enormous admiration for her." Later, Gloria reports that after his conversation with me, Zuckerman immediately telephoned her "to gloat" over the idea that anyone might believe she had wanted to marry him. To her mind, they are no longer friendly; indeed, she generally looks as if she smelled something putrid whenever his name arises, although she tries to be diplomatic. "In a real sense, we were never friends, so we're not friends now," she says carefully. "It isn't that we dislike each other, but we don't have anything in common."

In *Revolution from Within*, Steinem actually takes on the Mort Question, although she doesn't identify him by name; while the tone of her account is neither defensive nor self-justifying, she clearly felt the need to address why she had fallen in love with "someone so obviously wrong for me," a judgment she illustrates with a slyly telling series of contrasts between his values and her own. Steinem attributes much of her initial attraction to Zuckerman to her particular vulnerability during that period, a time of "exhaustion and living on the edge," of "falling off the treadmill into bed only to get back on it the next day." When she arrived in New York at the airport late one night to find that her eager new swain had sent a car to pick her up, she writes, "its shelter loomed out of all proportion." Moreover, Zuckerman professed to be miserable with his life, thereby activating her Florence Nightingale instincts, not to mention the thought of how much happier he would be if he dedicated his resources to the causes she championed so passionately.

"So I reverted to a primordial skill that I hadn't used since feminism had helped me to make my own life: getting a man to fall in love with me," she reports. "As many women can testify, this is alarmingly easy providing you're willing to play down who you are and play up who he wants you to be. In this case, I was aided by my travel and his work and social schedule that left us with little time to find out how very different we were. And also by something

I didn't want to admit: a burn-out and an erosion of self so deep that outcroppings of a scared sixteen-year-old had begun to show through. . . . I had lost so much energy and hope that I was reexperiencing romantic rescue fantasies that had been forgotten long ago. The only problem was that, having got this man to fall in love with an inauthentic me, I had to keep on not being myself." It took her a long time to acknowledge that the situation was impossible, although she and Zuckerman give different accounts of how long they were involved: she says two years, he says four.

Zuckerman's money was the source of the other charge frequently leveled against her during that period—that after thirty years of turning down an endless parade of successful men, Steinem had suddenly metamorphosed into a gold digger. She doesn't deny that his financial assets were part of the appeal, although she was often embarrassed by his ostentatiousness. "I devoted most of my time to trying to get him to drive a van instead of a limousine," she says wryly. Perhaps so, although it often seemed to others that she was enjoying the helicopters and the servants and the assorted other perks of the super-rich. "It wasn't the money per se," she explains, "and it wasn't so much for myself as the idea that he could help the multitudes of causes that need that money—and possibly the magazine, although it was much harder for me to ask for something that was so closely associated with me." And did Zuckerman help *Ms.* magazine, which Steinem spent sixteen years trying desperately to keep alive before it was finally sold in 1987? "No," she says sourly. Nevertheless, the thought that "he could do a great deal of good with his power" remained tantalizing until the bitter end. And the end was bitter, at least for her, although Zuckerman seems to hang on to rosier memories; indeed, he still has a picture of Gloria in his bedroom, where all the other pictures are of himself. "In a way, I guess I was feeling as if, if I could change him, I could change the whole patriarchy," she says sadly.

The sun is not yet up on a dark November morning when a slight figure hurries out of her apartment to hail a taxi to the airport. Within the next few hours, many of her Upper East Side neighbors will be heading out for a leisurely Saturday brunch and a day of recreation, but Gloria Steinem has to catch a 6:45 A.M. flight to Saskatchewan to speak to a women's network about international feminism. Even now, with sixty in sight, her magazine in other hands, and the entire culture conspiring to convince women that the women's movement is dead, Steinem's commitment to changing the patriarchy shows no sign whatsoever of flagging.

She isn't even discouraged. Yes, the Clarence Thomas hearings [which preceded the Senate's confirmation of Thomas as a Supreme Court justice despite accusations of sexual misconduct, which he denied] were depressing, but sexual harassment didn't even exist as a defined problem until the last few years. "Sexual harassment is where rape was as an issue fifteen years ago," Steinem says confidently, "and sexual-harassment complaints are up 500 percent since the hearings." And besides, the reaction to the hearings has been extraordinary. "I've never seen anything like the outpouring of anger," she exclaims. "People come up to you in airports; they say, 'What can we do—it's so terrible! Why didn't anyone believe Anita Hill? We've got to get rid of these guys in Congress!'"

Indeed, Gloria Steinem is the last person you could convince that the women's movement was dead. "Ever since the movement began, it's been being declared dead," she says. "The first headline to that effect was in 1969, and there have been multitudes forever after. The backlash is there, and it may succeed, but it is because the movement is strong that there *is* a backlash. There used to be an identifiable band of twelve feminists, so the media knew where to go. Now it's everywhere—inside the Modern Language Association, the American Psychiatric Association, in caucuses in the Newspaper Guild.

"This is a democracy, so there's an assumption that Reagan or Bush represents the country. But if you look at the polls, the issues Reagan and Bush stand for are not the majority issues. If you measure things in the only way this country seems to provide us to measure, which is public-opinion polls, there's been a fairly steady growth in support for feminist issues, although that goes contrary to popular wisdom. One of the things I find so frustrating is the fact that you turn on the television set and nine-tenths of the national news is about so-called women's issues. There's battered children, domestic violence, sexual harassment, rape, sexual abuse of children, Teddy Kennedy and his apology in Cambridge, the critique of the Senate and its unresponsive nature, the defection of major contributors from the Republican Party, the fact that health and pro-choice issues provided the margin of victory for Harris Wofford's Senate race against Dick Thornburgh in Pennsylvania—but none of it is associated with the women's movement. The women's movement is alive and well; it's just not being called the women's movement." She sighs. "It's not conscious; it's beyond conspiracy. It's a definitional problem, a cultural drift, two-thirds of which is underwater. But it's very dangerous. I keep thinking of the sentence in college textbooks about how women were 'given' the vote, a phrase which ignored 150 years of struggle and hunger strikes. The changes are there, but unless we know how the changes got made, we won't know how to continue."

And so Gloria Steinem never stops talking about how the changes get made. She may have come late to feminism, but once she finally got the picture, she never lost sight of it again. She is the first to admit she was slow to catch on. "Until I was into my thirties I was stoutly maintaining I had not been discriminated against," she says with regret. "There was a well of anger so deep I just did not want to talk about it. I had difficulty renting an apartment, because if I was a single woman I wasn't financially reliable and if I was financially reliable I must be a call girl. I was having an almost impossible time getting serious journalistic assignments. I was certainly dealing with what we now call sexual harassment—but it was all so bad I just displaced it. I identified with every other group that was being discriminated against—the farm workers, the civil-rights movement—rather than other women in my situation."

And when she did finally jump on the bandwagon, she immediately became a target. After all, in those days Steinem was best known professionally for having worked as a Playboy Bunny and then written about it, and her personal reputation was that of the femme fatale every man in New York seemed to be in love with—"the intellectuals' pinup," as *Esquire* magazine called her in a snide 1971 profile, the woman "who advanced in public favor by appealing to powerful men." Her sudden emergence as a spokesperson for the women's movement proved especially galling to its putative author, Betty Friedan—particularly because, as Muriel Fox recalled in *The Sisterhood*, Marcia Cohen's history of the movement, "the minute Gloria came on the scene, the media dropped Betty like a hot potato." The fallout was ugly: by 1972, Friedan was denouncing Gloria for "ripping off the movement for private profit," by which she apparently meant fame rather than money, since Steinem donated at least 50 percent of her speaking fees to women's causes or to *Ms.* magazine, something Friedan didn't do, according to *The Sisterhood.* Steinem had never been part of the organized women's movement, Friedan claimed angrily: "The media tried to make her a celebrity, but no one should mistake her for a leader."

Other feminists cringed at the public discord, and even those who were loath to take sides were dismayed by the malignancy of the attacks on Steinem. "It is probably too easy to go on about the two of them this way—Betty as Wicked Witch of the West, Gloria as Ozma, Glinda, Dorothy—take your pick," Nora Ephron wrote in *Esquire.* "To talk this way ignores the subtleties, right? Gloria is not, after all, uninterested in power. . . . Still, it is hard to come out anywhere but squarely on her side. Betty Friedan, in her thoroughly irrational hatred of Steinem, has ceased caring whether or not the effects of that hatred are good or bad for the women's movement." Upset by such characterizations, Friedan vehemently denied "that I was jealous of Gloria because she was blonde and pretty and I was not," but she could never resist getting in another dig. "I was no match for her, not only because of that matter of looks—which somehow paralyzed me—but because I don't know how to manipulate," Friedan wrote piously.

Among those who knew her well, Steinem's conversion to feminism came as no surprise at all. "She'd always been very politically concerned; a sense of justice and a clear political stance had always been very central to her," says Robert Benton, the film director, who dated Steinem in the early 1960s. "She'd been very involved in civil rights, and the women's movement is another form of civil rights, so it was perfectly consistent. But because Gloria has always been extraordinarily glamorous, I think people were surprised that somebody like that would be a feminist, because everyone misunderstood feminism then."

But there was more to it than that. On some level, Gloria has always made other people feel guilty for being manifestly less perfect themselves; her very existence constitutes a reproach. "If I told her about a disastrous love affair, she told me about the cultural and social strains that had broken it up," Liz Smith complained humorously in 1971. "It's like getting a message from Gandhi. . . . Gloria has all the irritating qualities of a saint—she is a rebuke." Twenty years later, Smith's perception hasn't changed. "Gloria is sort of like the *Mona Lisa*, and the *Mona Lisa* is a really infuriating portrait," Smith observes. "That enigmatic little smile, that perfection! I think most of us perceive that Gloria is a better person than we are, and as I said back then, saints are really irritating. She is a really good person who just has not lived up to everyone else's venal ideals. She's true to herself, but she's ended up absolutely nowhere. She hasn't really done anything for herself, not even in what I consider would have been her own best interest. She's never taken advantage of anything, she has remained in that same little apartment, she doesn't have cars—how much of an opportunist ends up with virtually nothing?"

Steinem's unfailing political correctness irked people as well. She has always maintained that *Ms.* magazine had a hard time because advertisers wouldn't support it; as usual, patriarchy was the problem. Even among other feminists, this didn't necessarily seem to be the whole story. "Why did *Ms.* fail?" says one prominent female journalist who wrote for the magazine. "Because they had a hideously boring magazine no one could read. That's why it was not successful—it was a goddamn bore."

Of course, Steinem's looks alone were more than enough reason for jealousy, the underlying cause of much of the sniping over the years. And because she presented herself in a sexy way, other women often acted as if she must be insincere. The fact that her desirability conferred obvious privileges only exacerbated their suspicions of hypocrisy. "The thing I find most irritating about her is that I think she doesn't tell the truth," says one former editor. "When she says, 'A woman needs a man like a fish needs a bicycle,' it's a great quote, but I don't think you get to say it if you never in your life spent twenty minutes without a man."

Not that Steinem ever conformed to conventional expectations about what you were supposed to do with a man once you got him. "She had all these guys, some of them really wonderful, and she didn't marry any of them—unforgivable!" Smith says. "She didn't have any children—unforgivable! She dared to be in love with Mort Zuckerman and not marry him! I think he was really in love with her and would have married her. But what she did was impale her conscience over it, because she was in love with him and didn't want to be. She would say to me, 'Have you ever been in love with somebody who was totally inappropriate?' I said, 'I've never been in love with any other kind! Relax and enjoy it!' If I had been Gloria, I would have married him in a minute and used his money to accomplish my ends, but she didn't really approve of him. People think any woman would do anything to marry a rich guy, but she didn't want to marry him."

Steinem didn't make her detractors feel any better with remarks such as her much-quoted crack that she couldn't "mate in captivity," an image that made more conventional types feel rather like monkeys in depressing little cages. "People would like to believe she has some regret for making those choices, because otherwise maybe they should have made those choices," says Letty Pogrebin. "She doesn't seem to have suffered for them, and they would like to believe she *has* suffered for them, because otherwise they have to question their own lives."

But the most important reason Steinem never wanted to be a parent has always been clear to her intimates. "I think she's already had a child, and it was her mother, and therefore I don't believe she has an interest in doing it again," says Stan Pottinger, who was an assistant attorney general in the Civil Rights Division of the Justice Department when he and Steinem first got involved in the 1970s. "If she's ever had more than a passing regret, I've never seen it. I don't believe it's there, and if it is, it's so deeply suppressed that it's not an issue for her."

Steinem's mother was "an invalid who lay in bed with eyes closed and lips moving in occasional response to voices only she could hear; a woman to whom I brought an endless stream of toast and coffee, bologna sandwiches and dime pies, in a child's version of what meals should be," as Steinem would later write in her collection of essays, *Outrageous Acts and Everyday Rebellions*. Her mother had been a journalist who loved her newspaper career, but she gave it up after she married and had children, and from then on she struggled with the nervous breakdowns, the terrible hallucinations, the dependence on the knockout drops her doctor supplied, the fear of leaving her own house. Eventually her husband, a charming but feckless man who prided himself on never wearing a hat and never working for somebody else, couldn't take it anymore and moved to California, leaving ten-year-old Gloria to cope alone. Abandoned by her adored father and unassisted on a day-to-day basis by her sister, who was many years older and off on her own, the little girl retreated into a world of books, fantasizing that she had been adopted and that her real parents would someday find her. Eventually she escaped to Smith College, a triumph made possible when her mother managed to sell their deteriorating farmhouse, whose broken-down furnace had already been condemned by the health department; the house was bought for demolition by the church next door.

It scarcely seems surprising that such a child might grow up with a self-esteem problem, but the mere sight of Gloria always made it so hard to believe. She has often referred to her self-image as a "fat brunette from Toledo," but that vision seemed so preposterous to other people that they assumed she was being disingenuous. To Steinem, however, whose father weighed three hundred pounds and whose sister was also obese, the vision was all too real. It dictated her hairstyle—"I was always hiding behind my hair because I thought I had a fat face," she says apologetically—and her eating habits, which have always been bizarre. Steinem describes herself as a compulsive "foodaholic"; her friends say she isn't exaggerating. "There was never anything in her refrigerator, because she was afraid she would eat it," explains Suzanne Levine. "I've seen her around a jar of chocolate cookies, and she just can't stop. At *Ms.* she'd be in the office late at night and she'd go on a binge; she'd raid all the desks, and you'd come in the next morning to find these lovely little notes: 'I took your Tootsie Roll,' 'I took your Cheez Whiz,' 'I'll replace it,' 'I'm so sorry . . .'"

"She would sit down and say she didn't want any, and then she would eat it all," says Letty Pogrebin. "As time went on, I began to see that she's a person who's always on the brink of eating it all. She's got a finger in the dike—that's why she's thin—but let it out and she's instantly overwhelmed. You can't be not parented the way she was not parented and not do something with that pain. A lot of her placidity and peacefulness is papered-over pain, I'm sure—but that is not something she could have acknowledged or discussed until recently."

Ever since Steinem's cancer scare several years ago (she had a lumpectomy and has been fine ever since), she has been working on improving both the inner and the outer manifestations of her delinquent self-image. She eats differently, opting for grains instead of bologna sandwiches; she exercises; she stays home more. She still streaks her hair lightly, but the blatant stripes of an earlier era are gone. "I thought of them as rebellious," she explains. "It was just a way of saying, 'Fuck you.' Brunette ladies did not streak their hair with obvious streaks in those days, and the whole point was not to be a lady. But I'm thinking of stopping altogether." She grins. "As Alice Walker says, 'Oppressed hair puts a ceiling on the brain.'"

And the last thing Steinem wants to do anymore is put a ceiling on her brain; she's got too much to do for that. Now that *Ms.* is a reader-supported magazine owned by Lang Communications, Steinem no longer has to spend her time peddling advertising; she is a consulting editor who comes and goes as she pleases, secure in the knowledge that the magazine's future doesn't depend on her. [Today, *Ms.* is published by the Feminist Majority Foundation.] And having written her book at long last, perhaps the logjam is broken and others will stream forth. Certainly she has the energy, and the faith. "Women are lucky, in a way," she says earnestly. "We have a hope, a dream of greater justice, of what society could look like. To have a vision—we all need that. I see little miracles women perform in their everyday lives, sometimes opposed by their own families, sometimes ridiculed by their own husbands, and somehow they do it anyway. It's the cleaning woman in the airport who sees me sleeping on a bench where they've put all these armrests so you can't lie down, and she says, 'Honey, there's a broom closet over there where I sleep when the foreman isn't looking,' and who then tells me about how her husband beat her up for so many years and how she finally wouldn't put up with it anymore, and now she has this job—and that's a miracle. I think to myself, If this was all I lived to see, this would be enough. How many people have in their lives, and in their work, a number of things that make them feel, 'If I only did that!'? I realize people have that about their children, but a lot of us were motherless, because our mothers didn't have the power to protect us, so the movement is partly about being mothers to each other."

We are sitting in her living room, I on a cheerful yellow chintz armchair, she on the plush green velvet sofa; it is dusk, and the streetlights have begun to glow outside the soaring front windows. For twenty years Steinem slept on a platform loft in one corner of this room, so she could use the back of her two-room apartment as an office, but when she got the $700,000 book advance for *Revolution from Within* she bought two rooms downstairs and connected them with a spiral staircase. (The first two rooms cost her $23,000 in 1977; ten years later, the second two cost her $323,000.) Steinem jokes that she used her first book advance to buy the additional rooms, and the $500,000 advance for the next book she's agreed to write to pay the taxes on the first advance, but after a lifetime of financial precariousness there is enough of a margin that she has even established a belated pension fund for herself. And she finally has a big canopied bed irresistibly dressed in mountains of pristine white lace, a little girl's dream of a bed, a magical haven where nothing bad could ever happen to you and all your dreams would be wonderful. "It's so satisfying to feel as though I have a home!" she says. "And even when I'm by myself, I'm as real as I am when I'm being useful, or when there are other people around." There is a sardonic grin on her face. "And I occasionally ask myself the revolutionary question 'What do you want to do?' as opposed to what needs doing, what other people want me to do, or what I'm expected to do!" She sighs ruefully. "That may not sound like much, but for me it's a pretty big change."

Friends are waiting at an old-fashioned French restaurant to have dinner with her, but later on tonight Steinem will come home alone; there is no beau these days. "For the first time in my life," she says, bemused at the thought. "If I say it feels wonderful, I don't mean that I wasn't happy being involved. It feels wonderful in a different way. I suppose I'm doing something now that I should have done at sixteen." And what will her future hold? She smiles. "I feel as if now I know what I want to say, I should begin it," she says.

ADDENDUM, IN A 1991 LETTER TO THE EDITOR:

In the context of questions about the sale of *Ms.* magazine in 1987, I answered what I heard as a query about whether or not Mortimer Zuckerman had offered to save *Ms.* from sale. Since he had been among those urging a sale, I answered no. As the query was paraphrased in print, however, it was about "help." In fact, he had earlier been one of those who made contributions to the educational foundation that owned *Ms.* and also co-signed bank loans (the last of which was repaid with interest by the foundation with proceeds from *Ms.*'s sale). He also assigned his staff to give us advice.

Gloria Steinem
New York, New York

LESLIE BENNETTS'S REPLY, AT THE TIME:

Gloria Steinem was quoted as indicating that Mortimer Zuckerman had failed to help *Ms.* magazine when it was struggling for survival. Mr. Zuckerman has informed *Vanity Fair* that Ms. Steinem's statement was incorrect and that he donated a total of $406,151 to the Ms. Foundation for Women and the Ms. Foundation for Education and Communication (which operated *Ms.* magazine) in seven different contributions of varying amounts between 1984 and 1990. Mr. Zuckerman also guaranteed three separate bank loans worth a total of $995,000—all were eventually repaid with interest by *Ms.*—and guaranteed a printing contract and paper supplies. In addition he assigned his most senior executives to consult with *Ms.* and advise the magazine on its financial problems. In her December 11 [1991] letter to *Vanity Fair*, Ms. Steinem places our discussion about *Ms.* magazine "in the context of questions about the sale" of the magazine, but this was not the case. I asked her whether or not Mr. Zuckerman's financial assets were part of his appeal for her. She replied that they were a factor, not so much because she was personally interested in his money but because she hoped he might use it to help *Ms.* magazine, among other causes. I then asked whether Mr. Zuckerman had done so. "No," she replied. Contrary to what Ms. Steinem says in her letter, and as my notes show, the query was indeed about helping the magazine, not about saving it. I regret that Ms. Steinem's assertion was incorrect.

THE
MUSICIANS

CALIFORNIA DREAMGIRL

By Sheila Weller | December 2007

W hen Michelle Phillips and Denny Doherty spoke on January 18, they did as they'd done for 40 years: "We made it a point to keep things very professional and not . . . slip back," Michelle says in that arch, bemused way of hers. "Slip back" into talking like lovers, she means. Denny was about to undergo surgery for an abdominal aneurysm, and she'd called with moral support, her reliable compassion delivered with its usual frankness. "I was gung-ho and positive. 'If it has to be done, just get it over with!'"

The Mamas and the Papas had always remained a family—a shadow of the old, clamorous family, to be sure ("It was two and a half years of total melodrama," Michelle fondly recalls), but touchingly close, even through the decades of Sturm und Drang that postdated their breakup. Early on, their ranks had been thinned from four to three (in 1974, Cass Elliot died, at a tragically young 32, of a heart attack); then, much later, from three to two: in 2001, John Phillips, 65, finally succumbed, after decades of drinking and drugs, to heart failure. And so, by last January, only Denny, 66, and Michelle, then 62—like the little Indians in the children's rhyme—remained standing, their old, red-hot affair, which had nearly torn the group apart, self-protectively excised from their frequent reminiscences.

That two people in the seventh decade of their lives would need to try to bury several months of ancient lust is a testament to the mystique that has long outlived the group's thin songbook and brief domination of the pop charts. The Mamas and the Papas were cannon-shot onto the airwaves when the country was still shaking off its post-Camelot conventionality; girls were wearing go-go boots, and boys were growing out their early-Beatles haircuts. No group had ever looked like them—a magnetic fat girl, a pouty blond beauty, two sexy Ichabod Cranes in funny hats—or sounded like them: Cass's wry-beyond-her-years alto and Denny's aching choirboy tenor lacing through that creamy, 1950s-prom-worthy close harmony, kissed with all those *ba da da da*s.

The Mamas and the Papas were the first rich hippies, stripping folk rock of its last vestiges of Pete Seeger earnestness and making it ironic and sensual. They made the rock elite part and parcel of Hollywood. (Michelle's eventual serial conquest of its three top young lions—Dennis Hopper, Jack Nicholson, and Warren Beatty—nailed for her its femme fatale sweepstakes.) And then, just as fast as they'd streaked across the psychedelic sky, they burned out in some unseen solar system.

The day after her pep talk to Denny, Michelle got a phone call from Cass's daughter, Owen Elliot-Kugell. Denny was dead. He didn't survive the operation.

"I'll bury you all!," Michelle had screamed at the other three one night in 1966, when they'd (temporarily) evicted her from the group for her romantic transgressions. Now that wounded taunt revealed itself as prophecy. Michelle flew to Toronto for Denny's funeral and then to Halifax for his burial. No one loved the group more than she. For 25 years she had tried to bring a Mamas and the Papas movie to fruition. (The right script is in the process of being written.) She was the group's impeccably preserved face on a PBS tribute. Now she was the last one standing.

Yet people who have seen Michelle mature into a consummate rescuer know she's repaid her luck. According to Cass's sister, Leah Kunkel (who started out "unsure Michelle had my sister's best interests at heart"), "Michelle has rescued a lot of people over the years. I've come to really respect her." Plastic surgeon Steven Zax, Michelle's beau of eight years, says, "She is the most generous person I know. She drives hours to visit friends who are shut-ins. Every Saturday and Sunday she packs bags of fruit and sandwiches and money and takes them to the homeless, who know her by name." And those who watched her mint the shrewd-chick archetype in the midst of the reckless, sexist counterculture don't doubt her resilience. "I'm not saying Michelle was Helen of Troy, leading men to war while she remained unscathed, but that's close," says her onetime musical partner Marshall Brickman. "She was a very clever, centered girl, to have kept afloat in that environment. There's steel under that angelic smile." According to Lou Adler, the Mamas and the Papas' producer and Michelle's lifelong friend and at one time romantic interest, "Michelle is the ultimate survivor—so loyal and 'street' that John and I called her Trixie. And, unlike John—who was swept away . . . who was a *devil*, on drugs—Michelle was more logical, more constant. She had an anchor, her dad."

"My father was six foot three, dashingly handsome, and so unflappable nothing could rattle him," Michelle is saying, sitting in her picture-windowed living room in L.A.'s leafy, off-the-status-track Cheviot Hills. In pride of place on the coffee table is a photo album of her three grandchildren from daughter Chynna, 39, and actor Billy Baldwin, yet she's sipping wine in the early afternoon like any self-respecting sybarite.

Gardner "Gil" Gilliam, a movie-production assistant and self-taught intellectual, was all Michelle and her older sister, known as Rusty, had after their mother, Joyce, a Baptist minister's daughter turned bohemian bookkeeper, dropped dead of a brain aneurysm when Michelle was five. Gil took the girls to Mexico for several years, then back to L.A. There, as a county probation officer who smoked pot and never made a secret of his love affairs (he would eventually marry five more times), he seemed to model the axiom "Hedonism requires discipline." "My father had very few rules, but with those he was steadfast. 'Clean up your messes.' 'Be a good citizen.'" (The code stuck. "I have never been late for work a day in my life, I refused to ask John for alimony, I have never been in rehab," she enumerates proudly.) But young Michelle needed more than a male guide. "In retrospect, I see that I was looking for a girlfriend/mother figure." In 1958 she found, through her sister's boyfriend, a 23-year-old who had an unsurpassable store of harrowingly acquired female survival skills to impart.

Tamar Hodel was one of six children—by three different women—of the most pathologically decadent man in Los Angeles: Dr. George Hodel, the city's venereal-disease czar and a fixture in its A-list demimonde. She'd grown up in her father's Hollywood house, which resembled a Mayan temple, was designed by Frank Lloyd Wright's son, and was the site of wild parties, in which Hodel was sometimes joined by director John Huston and photographer Man Ray.

George Hodel shared with Man Ray a love for the work of the Marquis de Sade and the belief that the pursuit of personal liberty was worth everything—possibly even, for Hodel, gratuitous murder. What has recently come to light, by way of two startling investigative books (2003's *Black Dahlia Avenger*, by Hodel's ex-L.A.P.D. homicide-detective son, Steve Hodel, and—building upon it—*Exquisite Corpse*, 2006, by art writers Mark Nelson and Sarah Hudson Bayliss), is that George Hodel was a prime suspect in the notorious Black Dahlia murder. (According to *Black Dahlia Avenger*, Hodel was the killer, and the Los Angeles District Attorney's office conducted extensive surveillance of him. There were numerous arrests, but no one was ever charged with the murder.) A striking, graphic array of evidence in the two books strongly suggests that it was Hodel who, on January 15, 1947, killed actress Elizabeth Short, then surgically cut her in two and transported the halved, nude, exsanguinated corpse—the internal organs kept painstakingly intact—to a vacant lot, where he laid the pieces out as if in imitation of certain Surrealist artworks by Man Ray. [In recent years other potential suspects have emerged; in one theory a group of individuals may have been involved.]

Without knowing any of this, 13-year-old Michelle Gilliam walked through Tamar Hodel's porch into a room decorated all in lavender and beheld a sultry Kim Novak look-alike. "Tamar was the epitome of glamour," Michelle recalls. "She was someone who never got out of bed until two p.m., and she looked it. It was late afternoon, and she was dressed in a beautiful lavender suit with her hair in a beehive. I took one look and said, New best friend!" With Tamar was her cocoa-skinned daughter, Debbie, five; folk-singer Stan Wilson, an African-American, was Tamar's current husband. (She'd married her first—who was also black—at 16, in 1951.) "Tamar was instantly my idol."

Tamar's sophistication had a grotesque basis. In her father's home—where she had often "uncomfortably" posed nude, she recalls, for "dirty-old-man" Man Ray and had once wriggled free from a predatory John Huston—George Hodel had committed incest with her. "When I was 11, my father taught me to perform oral sex on him. I was terrified, I was gagging, and I was embarrassed that I had 'failed' him," Tamar says, telling her version of her long-misreported adolescence. George plied her with erotic books, grooming her for what he touted as their transcendent union. (Tamar says that she told her mother what George had done, and that, when confronted, George denied it.) He had intercourse with Tamar when she was 14. To the girl's horror, she became pregnant; to her greater horror, she says, "my father wanted me to have his baby." After a friend took her to get an abortion, an angry George—jealous, Tamar says, of some boys who'd come to see her—struck her on the head with his pistol. Her stepmother, Dorero (who was John Huston's ex-wife), rushed her into hiding.

George Hodel was arrested, and the tabloid flashbulbs popped during the sensational 1949 incest trial. Hodel's lawyers, Jerry Geisler and Robert Neeb, painted Tamar as a "troubled" girl who had "fantasies." Tamar's treatment by the defense and the press during that time wounds her to this day. George was acquitted.

When Michelle appeared on Tamar's porch, Tamar saw in her "a gorgeous little Brigitte Bardot" and sensed that she could rewrite her own hideous youth by guiding a protégée through a better one. "Meeting Michelle felt destined, as if we'd known each other in another life," says Tamar. "I wanted to champion her, because no one had championed me." Michelle says, "I moved in with Tamar; she 'adopted' me right away. Then everything started."

Tamar took the lower-middle-class bohemian's daughter and polished her. She bought her the clothes Gil couldn't afford, enrolled her in modeling school, taught her how to drive her lavender Nash Rambler, and provided her with a fake ID and amphetamines, Michelle says, "so I could make it through a day of eighth grade after staying up all night with her. Tamar introduced me to real music—Bessie Smith and Paul Robeson and Josh White and Leon Bibb. And I, who'd been listening to the Kingston Trio, was just entranced." To keep Gil from being bent out of shape by the fact that his daughter had been spirited away, Michelle says, "Tamar put on perfect airs around my dad, and when it became necessary she would sleep with him." One day Tamar's husband, Stan, made the mistake of crawling into Michelle's bed. Michelle shoved him out, and Tamar ended the marriage, leaving the two young blond beauties on their own, with sometimes a third one visiting them, Michelle's fresh-faced teen-model friend Sue Lyon. "Sue was innocent and naïve, not like us," Tamar says. Sue's mother bawled Michelle out for sneaking her daughter a copy of *Lolita*. Tamar says she had to explain the famous masturbation scene to the sheltered ingénue. (A few years later, Sue was cast in the title role in the 1962 Stanley Kubrick film of the novel—a role Tamar insisted should have been played by Michelle.)

In early 1961, Tamar and her teenage sidekick moved to San Francisco. They painted their apartment lavender, and, like two Holly Golightlys on uppers, they did the town, watching Lenny Bruce and Mort Sahl spew their subversive humor at the hungry i and the Purple Onion. They got to know the cool guys on the scene; Michelle fell for singer Travis Edmonson, of the folk duo Bud and Travis, and Tamar fell for activist comedian Dick Gregory.

Both girls thought that Scott McKenzie (original name: Phil Blondheim), the wavy-haired lead singer in a folk group called the Journeymen, was, as Michelle puts it, "very, very cute." Tamar won his heart. She took Scott back to the apartment to listen to *La Bohème*, and, as Michelle remembers it, with a laugh, they never left the bed. The Journeymen's leader, whose name was John Phillips, appeared at the door every night, annoyed to have to yank his tenor out of Tamar's arms to get him to the club by showtime. A native of Alexandria, Virginia, Phillips was tall and lean and exotically handsome: his mother was Cherokee; his secret actual father (whom he never knew) was Jewish, though he'd been raised thinking that the square-jawed Marine captain his mother had married was his father. From the moment Michelle saw him in the hungry i phone booth—long legs stretched out, ankles propped on his guitar case—she knew two things: one, he was married ("You could tell he was making The Call Home"), and, two, she had to have him. "I fell in love with his talent, his poise, his ability to be leader of the pack."

Michelle "stepped out of a dream," John Phillips would rhapsodize in his 1986 autobiography, *Papa John*. She was "the quintessential California girl. . . . She could look innocent, pouty, girlish, aloof, firey." Michelle says, "John was 25, married with two children, from an East Coast Catholic military family. He had gone to Annapolis, he performed in a suit and tie—he had never met anyone like me!" Her uniqueness in John's eyes was no small thing, since he was a habitual trend surfer ("a charismatic snake-oil salesman" is how Marshall Brickman puts it). He'd started a doo-wop group when doo-wop was in, then switched to ballads with his group the Smoothies—just in time for *American Bandstand*'s body-grinding slow-dancers—then jumped on the folk bandwagon. To John, Tamar Hodel's protégée was a fascinating hybrid just over the *Zeitgeist*'s horizon: a street girl, to be sure ("She would have fit into the Ronettes or the Shangri-Las perfectly," he'd later say), yet seasoned in high culture and political idealism—and with that angelic face. John used to tell Michelle she was the first flower child he had ever met.

Gil had recently married a 16-year-old himself, so he couldn't exactly be indignant about his 17-year-old daughter's paramour. "She hasn't finished high school, so if I were you I would throw a book at her now and again" was his paternal blessing. John and Susan Adams, a ballerina from a society family, prepared to divorce in 1962. She had put up for years with his many affairs and never thought that the teenager who'd recently knocked on her Mill Valley door and brazenly announced "I'm in love with your husband" would actually steal him. (With perfect manners, Susan had invited her little visitor in, made her a tuna sandwich—and herself a stiff drink—and then, with deft condescension, informed her that John had a girl like her in every city.)

John and Michelle moved to New York and married. He was so possessive that when he left town on Journeymen tours he'd board her at a supervised dorm for teenage professionals.

To keep her where he could see her (and because he knew her face on posters would rake in the crowds), he pulled her away from the teen-modeling contract she was about to sign and—with the help of voice lessons to shore up her thin soprano—made her a singer alongside him. Jump-starting the New Journeymen, he tapped as its third member Marshall Brickman, of the disbanded group the Tarriers. "I was the polite, grateful Jew from Brooklyn, infatuated with folk music, and now here I was, thrown without a life preserver into the cyclone—the maelstrom—that was John and Michelle," says Brickman of the day he entered their studio apartment (so tiny "both sides of the bed touched the walls"), which was filled with welcome to the group! balloons. "There were drugs, but not for me, and sex, but not for me." (Michelle, who'd soon have affairs with all of John's best friends, says jokingly, "Marshall left the group too soon.")

"John lived on his own circadian rhythm—working 40 hours straight and sleeping 10," Brickman continues. "Everyone fell into his gravitational pull, and it was very seductive and ultimately adolescent, but he emerged from the chaos with brilliant songs. In fact, John was one of the few folksingers in Greenwich Village writing his own songs in the very early 60s." Another was born-and-bred Villager John Sebastian. "One night I ran into John," says Sebastian. "We puffed on a joint and walked to his apartment. I was stunned by Michelle's beauty." They settled in and started passing a guitar around. Sebastian played the song "Do You Believe in Magic?," which combined folk with jug-band music (pre-Depression-era blues, hokeyed up for vaudeville), and which eventually launched his group, the Lovin' Spoonful. After he left, Michelle told John, "*That's* the direction we should go in."

The path from straight folk to something new got an even bigger boost about a year later, when another Village folkie, Roger McGuinn, a friend of Sebastian's and the Phillipses', inserted eight notes inspired by Bach's "Jesu, Joy of Man's Desiring" into Bob Dylan's "Mr. Tambourine Man" and played the song in the beat he says the Beatles had picked up from Phil Spector, the songwriter turned music producer. The result: McGuinn's group the Byrds' version of "Mr. Tambourine Man" helped give birth to the phenomenon known as folk rock.

Even before this signal moment, John Phillips—guitar strapped to his chest, prowling the streets on amphetamines—was coming at the folk-plus-other mix a third way: by channeling the smooth balladeers of his early teen years. One day, late in their first autumn in New York, John set a verse—"All the leaves are brown / and the sky is grey / I've been for a walk on a winter's day"—to a moody, slightly somber melody. Later, in their room in the Hotel Earl, Michelle recalls, a speed-addled John "woke me and said, 'Help me write this!'" She groggily muttered, "Tomorrow." "No," he said. "Help me now. You'll thank me for this someday."

Michelle sat up and summoned a recent visit to St. Patrick's Cathedral (her years in Mexico had given her an affection for Catholic churches) and came up with: "Stopped into a church I passed along the way / Well, I got down on my knees and I pretend to pray." John, who'd loathed parochial school, "hated the line," Michelle says, but kept it in for lack of anything better. Lucky he did; the line gave the song its arc of desperation to epiphany. Thus was born one of the first clarion calls of a changing culture, "California Dreamin'."

The more John tried to dominate his young wife, the more she rebelled. "One day when we were in Sausalito they had a fight, and Michelle just got in the car and drove to L.A.," stranding the other two, Brickman recalls. During another trip home to L.A., Michelle was even more rebellious. Her sister, Rusty, was dating a handsome 19-year-old fledgling songwriter and musician named Russ Titelman. Late one night Michelle was in Gil's kitchen when Russ walked in—"and here was the most beautiful girl I'd ever seen. We fell madly in love, standing there at the refrigerator," recalls Titelman, who later produced hits for Randy Newman, Chaka Khan, Eric Clapton, and Steve Winwood. In December 1963, Michelle moved back to New York, and Russ followed. "I was in love with Russ," Michelle says. "We put a deposit down on an apartment in Brooklyn Heights." But the in-over-his-head young man broke up—just in time—with his married girlfriend. John called, warning, "You know, a different kind of guy would be waiting outside your door with a shotgun." Still, no amount of John's anger could incite remorse or shame in Michelle, who'd grown up viewing free love as perfectly normal. In frustration, John wrote "Go Where You Wanna Go" about Michelle's affair with Russ. The narrator's incredulousness at his girlfriend's independence—"Three thousand miles, that's how far you'll go / And you said to me, 'Please don't follow'"—captured not only his blithe, guilt-free bride but also the slew of other girls like her, who'd soon tumble into the cities.

Even before Brickman quit the group to become a writer (eventually he worked on screenplays for *Annie Hall* and other Woody Allen movies and co-wrote the book for the Broadway-musical hit *Jersey Boys*), John started wooing Denny Doherty, who looked to him like some "fragile lute player in Elizabethan England," and whose poignant tenor was a legend on the folk circuit. Denny sang lead for the group John Sebastian briefly played harmonica with, the Mugwumps, whose improbable scene-stealer was the obese daughter of a Baltimore delicatessen owner; she had changed her name from Ellen Naomi Cohen to Cass Elliot. "Here was my big sister," says Leah Cohen Kunkel, "a fat girl with a 190 I.Q.—so witty she never made the same stage quip twice—who'd come to New York to try to make it on Broadway, knowing no one, living in a cockroach-filled apartment, yet believing in herself. It was her hopefulness that people loved!" John Sebastian adds, "Cass was a star. Whatever room she was in became her salon. She had this wonderful charisma. She was aware of what this moment was going to be—she'd say, 'Man, if we're here now, just think where we'll be in another five years.' And she was incredibly funny about being madly in love with Denny. I can't imagine how it took him so long to realize it."

John, Michelle, and Denny took the vacation to the Virgin Islands that would become the basis of their autobiographical "Creeque Alley" (which starts, "John and Mitchie were gettin' kind of itchy"). Every morning they drank rum from chopped-open coconuts, Michelle recalls, and then "we might do a little bit of acid and we might snorkel." Cass flew down ("We knew she'd come e-ven-tu-ally," the song goes) to waitress in the dive where the three were singing—"she sang the fourth part from the back of the room," Michelle says. In one recounting ("the *Johnist* version," says Leah, who thinks her sister's overwhelming popularity made John a little jealous), Cass begged to be let into the group. "Not true! Cass did not have to beg!" insists Michelle. According to the account in *Papa John*, Cass was catcalled "Fatty!" by the customers. Michelle says evenly, "If I had heard anyone say that to Cass, I would have lunged over the table and killed them. I adored Cass. She made our sound, while I could barely sing (although I was the only one of us who could read music). John, a genius at harmonizing, loved the four voices and that huge octave range." Maxing out their credit cards, high on acid, they got themselves to L.A. They were invited to crash at a place where Cass was staying with her musician friends. One day Cass turned on the TV and saw a biker gang calling their molls their "mamas." They had found their name: the Mamas and the Papas.

I closed my eyes and listened to 'California Dreamin','" Lou Adler is recalling, in his house atop a Malibu cliff, its wraparound windows serving up what seems like the entire Pacific Ocean. (In the next room, the most famous of his seven sons, starlet-romancing gossip-column staple Cisco Adler, is noisily recording an album.) "You never heard four-part harmony in rock 'n' roll in late 1965! They reminded me of groups I'd loved—the Hi-Lo's, the Four Freshmen, the Four Lads. And the girls' voices—you didn't have mixed quartets then! John was the tallest rock 'n' roller I'd ever auditioned; Denny reminded me of Errol Flynn; Cass was in a muumuu; Michelle was this beautiful blonde. I felt like George Martin the first time he met the Beatles."

"California Dreamin'" became a huge hit, followed by "Monday, Monday" (a song Michelle and Cass thought so dumb that they snickered over their gin-rummy game when John excitedly previewed it for them). Tamar, in San Francisco, received a postcard: "Watch us on Ed Sullivan and meet us at the Fairmont before the concert." She took her father with her—"If you're abused, you stay emotionally a little girl until someone helps," she explains. "Michelle looked him in the eye and said, 'I've heard all about you,'" Tamar recalls. Michelle says, "He knew that I knew so much that he didn't want me to know about, yet he stared at me without a flicker of guilt. He looked like he wanted to kill me—I was also his type!" The evening featured "a hash pipe being passed around, mounds of pot on the table that the dogs were eating, and people knocking on the door every 10 minutes to hand us more dope," as Tamar sums it up.

"There were so many soap operas," says Lou Adler, "but it never stopped the artistry. John was the ultimate controller, but as much as he liked to build up, he also tore down, including himself. He was so intelligent and yet so challenged. And Michelle—Mitch, Mitchie, Trixie: we had so many names for her—she could always push John's buttons."

Denny and Michelle's affair began just as fame was hitting. "The four of us would sit around, saying, 'O.K., you're gonna sing the third,' and 'You're gonna do the bop da bops,' and there'd be so much sexual energy between Denny and me that we'd be playing footsie under the table, and Cass and John didn't notice it," says Michelle. (But Cass, who had emerged as the fans' favorite, was no chump, fighting with John all the time, constantly chiding Michelle, "Why do you let him boss you around like that?" In their different ways, the two women were tough-chick bookends.) John's reaction to his wife's affair was seethingly pragmatic. Michelle recalls, "He said, 'You know, Mitch, you can do a lot of things to me, but you don't fuck my tenor!' I'm thinking, Am I really hearing this? You can fuck the mailman, the milkman, but not my tenor?" As he had with her Russ Titelman affair, John used Michelle's infidelity as material, co-writing, with Denny, "I Saw Her Again." The group got a hit out of it, just as they had with "Go Where You Wanna Go."

By now John and Michelle were temporarily living apart, and John had a girlfriend, Ann Marshall, a witty, young L.A. socialite who was working as a model and salesgirl for the trendy boutique Paraphernalia, and who would become (and remains) one of Michelle's best friends. Michelle struck back with what she calls a "quiet affair" with Gene Clark, of the Byrds. It didn't stay quiet for long. At a Mamas and Papas concert, Clark arrived in a bright-red shirt and sat smack in the middle of the front row, and Michelle (and partner in crime Cass) proceeded to sing right to his beaming-boyfriend face all night. That public cuckolding was too much; after the show, John stormed at Michelle, "I made you who you are, and I can take it away. You're fired!" The others joined in his decision; Michelle was replaced by Lou's girlfriend, Jill Gibson.

Michelle didn't take the expulsion lying down. She crashed the "new" Mamas and Papas' recording session—"They looked at me as if I'd walked in with an AK-47"—and "when Denny refused to stick up for me, I took a swing at him." That's when she screamed that she'd "bury" them all. "I sat in my car, shaking and despondent and crying hysterically. I had just been fired by my husband and my best friends. I thought my life was over." In short order, Michelle was reinstated in the group. She retaliated against Jill the best way she knew how: she marched into Lou and Jill's hotel room just as they were celebrating with Dom Pérignon and brightly announced that she was in love with Lou. "Lou and Jill sat there with their champagne flutes frozen mid-toast," Michelle recalls, laughing. "Then Lou walked over to the big silver ice bucket and stuck his head in it!" Adler says he doesn't remember the head dousing but comments with a flattered smile, "Anything is possible when she's on a mission to get even."

Michelle did eventually seduce Lou, in 1972. "I was in love with Lou," she says of their "hush-hush" affair, conducted when his serious girlfriend, the actress Britt Ekland, was living in London. "For the first time I felt like a backstreet girl. Then one day Lou said, 'Britt's back.' I said, 'I don't care.' He said, 'And she's five and a half months pregnant' "—with his first son, Nicholai. That ended the affair.

John and Michelle bought 1930s actress-singer Jeanette McDonald's grand Bel Air mansion. Lou was already living in that Old Guard hillock of estates, as was Beach Boy Brian Wilson, who'd painted his house purplish-pink. "John and Michelle kept peacocks," Lou says, "who make a sound like women being raped," and they would stroll the streets in their shimmery, sultan-worthy Profile du Monde caftans, intriguing the neighbors. They were always having big parties, for not only the Laurel Canyon rockers but also that hitherto separate species: movie stars. "Everyone came: Ryan O'Neal, Marlon Brando, Mia Farrow, Peter Sellers, even Zsa Zsa Gabor," says Michelle. "One night I had to ask Warren Beatty to leave the house because he was screwing some girl in the nursery [that was being prepared for Chynna's imminent birth]."

"I didn't feel comfortable in that house; it was dark—and so was John's vibe," says Leah Kunkel. Tamar remembers "John not letting Michelle come out, once when I went to see her." There was only one incident of domestic violence. "It was serious," Michelle says. "I ended up in the hospital. That's all I'll say about it."

Still, "spring and summer 1967, that was the moment," Michelle recalls fondly. And a brief, shining moment it was, when everything that immediately thereafter would be sale-priced as a silly cliché was suddenly wildly glamorous: beautiful sybarites wafting around in clothes from other centuries; life as a sensual, acid-fueled private joke. At a meeting at the house with Lou, John and Michelle were asked by a music promoter to perform at a 12-hour music festival he was organizing. John and Lou, along with singer-songwriters Paul Simon and Johnny Rivers and producer Terry Melcher, bought the investor out, turned the festival into a charitable event, and expanded it to three days. They secured the Monterey Fairgrounds, which had jazz and folk festivals, as the venue in order to validate rock. Michelle manned the phones at the festival's office on Sunset Boulevard every day, calling record executives, culling sponsors. There was a problem when the San Francisco groups at the heart of the new sensibility balked. "John and I represented what they didn't like about the business. [We were] slick, we were successful," and, says Lou, relatively Establishment. Only the persuasiveness of beloved Bay Area music columnist Ralph Gleason enabled the world to view the Jefferson Airplane, the Grateful Dead, and Big Brother and the Holding Company. (Janis Joplin was so much still the striving Texas naïf that she performed in a ribbed-knit pantsuit.)

The Monterey Pop Festival also premiered the electrifying sight of Seattle urchin turned 101st Airborne paratrooper turned British sensation Jimi Hendrix making love to his guitar and then immolating it. Laura Nyro, whose amazing soul operatics and zaftig, black-gowned appearance were decidedly non-psychedelic, knew that she had bombed and, worse, was sure she'd heard boos. She left the stage crying hysterically. ("Laura carried the baggage of that booing all her life," Michelle says. In a tragic irony worthy of Maupassant, in the 1990s Lou and Michelle listened closely to the tapes of Laura's performance. "It wasn't booing; it was someone whispering, 'I looove you,'" says Lou. Nyro died of ovarian cancer before they could deliver the news to her.) Michelle, who was newly pregnant, "was at her most beautiful at Monterey," recalls Lou. John wrote "San Francisco (Be Sure to Wear Flowers in Your Hair)" and Scott McKenzie recorded it. It was the Summer of Love's anthem at the dawning of the Age of Aquarius. And it had all started when

Tamar and Michelle had their excellent adventure with Scott and John in the lavender apartment.

Not long after Chynna was born, in 1968, John and Michelle divorced and the Mamas and the Papas disbanded. "I was John's muse, and now I was gone. I was the person John drew all his despair and joy from, and he didn't know where to go from here," says Michelle—self-serving, perhaps, but true. He fell in love with a blond South African gamine, Genevieve Waite, the girl-of-the-hour actress (in the 1968 film *Joanna*, she daringly starred as a white girl romancing a black man during apartheid) who socialized with the British rock and film elite. John was "like Svengali to me—I fell in love with him immediately," Genevieve admits today. Despite a weathered face, she is still credulous, fragile, and baby-voiced, years after a bruising on-and-off two-decade relationship with John that included, by her admission, four years of being addicted to drugs with him—mostly Dilaudid, a highly potent narcotic sometimes called "drugstore heroin," and, for a brief time, heroin itself. John's addiction was so out of control that once, when they were houseguesting with Keith Richards and Anita Pallenberg, and John was shooting cocaine, Genevieve says, "Keith said, 'This might sound strange coming from me, but you have to leave.'"

"Michelle didn't have those doormat tapes—the man comes first," says Genevieve with wistful admiration. Genevieve had loved the Mamas and the Papas since hearing them in South Africa ("They were bigger than the Beatles there! They played their songs in the *mines!*"), and practically from the moment she met John she thought of him as a genius. "Gen loved John to distraction—she was practically his slave," Michelle says, implying that he could lead her astray. Genevieve contends that she did not take drugs during her pregnancy, but that John did. In his autobiography John says that Genevieve "had been on a low dose of Dilaudid" and went to London for an "emergency cleanout" two months before daughter Bijou was born. (They also had a son, Tamerlane, who was born in 1971.) Genevieve says, "I just wish I had lived in another time, when there were not so many drugs. The early 70s was really a bad time to be a mother. I've gone through so much misery over this."

(Bijou Phillips eventually became a tempestuous teenage "It girl"; she had a long-term relationship with John Lennon's son Sean; she's now a steadily working actress.) "Gen wanted to fill the void that I'd left," Michelle continues, "and John made her pay for that." Genevieve agrees: "John slept with *everyone*, and he said it was because Michelle had made him feel so bad about himself."

While John, with Genevieve in tow, was starting his long skid into the dark side, Michelle was trying to make the transition from musical stardom to acting—a task that was harder than it looked. She started to date Jack Nicholson around the time she tested for the role of Susan in Mike Nichols's *Carnal Knowledge*, which she lost to Candice Bergen. When Jack went off to star in the film, she signed on as the female lead in Dennis Hopper's *The Last Movie*. She flew to Peru to work with Hollywood's *enfant terrible*, who was fresh from directing the counterculture epic *Easy Rider*. In a madness-venerating time, Hopper was madder than most. According to his ex-wife Brooke Hayward's account in Peter Biskind's authoritative *Easy Riders, Raging Bulls*, Hopper not only struck her but also once jumped on the hood of the car she was sitting in, shattering the windshield. Hopper told Biskind that he doesn't recall the incident. (Contacted for this article, Brooke Hayward, who since 1985 has been married to the orchestra leader Peter Duchin, declined to discuss Hopper's behavior during their marriage because, she said, "we have a child together.") [In 2010, Hopper would die from complications related to prostate cancer.]

Michelle fell in love with Dennis, drawn to him in part, she says, by "this Florence Nightingale instinct. I was so overloaded emotionally by this point in my life, I didn't know what I was doing." They married in Taos in late 1970; Ann Marshall and her boyfriend, Don Everly, were visiting there, and Don bought the marriage license. (Marshall, the droll, Bel Air–raised sophisticate, had romances with both Everly brothers, the pompadoured Kentucky twangers who'd been worshipped by the Beatles. "Phil left me on my 20th birthday, and I left Don on my 30th birthday," she says. "I sent their mother a telegram: happy mother's day. and thank you for not having a third son.")

In the days after the wedding, Dennis behaved dangerously with Michelle. Whatever Hopper did was "excruciating" is all Michelle will say. She got herself and Chynna back to L.A., where "my father dragged me into his attorney's office and said, 'Men like that never change. File for divorce now. It'll be embarrassing for a few weeks, then it will be over.' It was embarrassing for more than a few weeks. Everybody had the same question: 'A divorce after eight days? What kind of tart are you?'" When she and Hopper (who married three more times) run into each other, "we are civil," Michelle says with a freighted crispness.

On the heels of her week-long marriage to Hopper, Michelle picked up with Jack Nicholson when he was casting *Drive, He Said*. She was now, along with Carly Simon, that rare thing on the early-70s entertainment scene: the female "catch." Nicholson, not yet having arrived at his Cheshire-cat-smiling Über-coolness, set out to win her. Around this same time, according to Genevieve, "Mick Jagger also had a big crush on Michelle. He was crazy about her. When she'd visit us in Bel Air, he'd come over." Genevieve pauses, squints, and waxes puzzled at a memory: "Mick and Bianca had the weirdest marriage. They were never together."

Michelle and Jack became a couple, and she and Chynna rented a house adjacent to his, making it easy for him "to spy on me," says Michelle, adding, "I only mean that as a joke. Dear Jack. He was a lovely guy: charming, sweet, and fun to be with." The relationship went well for a year, she says, "and then, one morning, Jack had a life-changing experience. I was having breakfast in bed with him when the phone rang." The caller, according to Michelle, was a man from Jack's New Jersey hometown. "I'm eating my toast and drinking my orange juice and Jack is saying, 'Mm-hmm, mm-hmm.' Then he hangs up and dials a number"—that of his sister, Lorraine, with whom he was very close. "He says, 'Lorraine! Are you my sister? Or my aunt?'" Nicholson had just been told that his and Lorraine's deceased older sister, June, was not his sister but his mother, and that the deceased woman he thought was his mother was his grandmother. Lorraine immediately confessed to the decades-long fiction. "Jack was incredulous," says Michelle.

The news, she continues, "was horrible for him. Over the weeks, the poor guy had a very, very tough time adjusting to it. He'd been raised in this loving relationship . . . surrounded by women. . . . Now I think he felt women were liars." Even though, she says, "I'm not sure I was aware of it at the time," in retrospect she believes that the news about his family contributed to a changed atmosphere between them. The actual breakup with Jack, she says, was about "something so minor—some stupid thing like a comb or the car keys—[but it was] the straw that broke the camel's back." One day soon after, Chynna recalls, her mother told Jack, " 'I'm done.' She packed up our few things, we got in the car with my nanny, and we never went back." Lou Adler says, "At this point, she'd been through John and Hopper. She probably saw the signs. She falls, but she doesn't fall so far that she can't get up."

At about this same time, summer 1974, Michelle and Cass were sitting by Cass's pool one day watching Chynna, six, and Cass's daughter, Owen, seven, swim. (By now Cass was, as Graham Nash reverentially puts it, "the Gertrude Stein of Laurel Canyon.") Cass had kept Owen's paternity a secret. "I said, 'Come on, tell me who he is,' " Michelle says. "Cass laughed and said, 'I'll tell you when I get back from London.' She never got back, of course." [In London, Cass died suddenly—of a heart attack—at age 32.] Cass's sister, Leah, and her then husband, drummer Russ Kunkel, raised Owen as their daughter.

S upporting Chynna alone, Michelle called screenwriter Robert Towne one day and asked him to let her be an extra in the party scene in Warren Beatty's new movie, *Shampoo*. After doing the scene, she says, "I went into the trailer, not to start up a romance, just to say hello." The party boy she'd evicted from Chynna's nursery now looked considerably more appealing. Beatty was still with Julie Christie. "She had Warren wrapped around her finger," says Michelle. "He adored her, because she didn't really go for the big-movie-star thing. Julie was so cool, so beyond the Hollywood scene. He took Julie and me to the *Shampoo* wrap party." Then Julie blithely moved on, and Michelle moved in with Beatty. The John-and-Denny friction was replaced by Warren-and-Jack friction. The two men were shooting *The Fortune* together. "Mike Nichols had to bar me from the set, because I would show up and disappear into the bungalow with Warren, and it was terribly painful for Jack."

Warren was The One. "I was madly in love with him," Michelle admits. "She had diamonds in her eyes when she was with Warren; I'd never seen Michelle so happy," says Tamar. Warren was a good stepfather figure to Chynna, Michelle says. "He helped her with her homework; he talked to her, and he is notorious for talking." But Michelle bumped up against his passive-aggressiveness. "I wanted to have another child, and we talked about marriage a lot, but he was very noncommittal." She pauses. "Warren is an old-fashioned man," she allows. Michelle believes Warren would have married her if she'd found herself pregnant. But whatever else Michelle had done, luring a man into marriage through an intentional "accidental" pregnancy was not even remotely in the cards. "I never pressured him to marry me. I waited for him to ask." He didn't. And despite his "carrot dangling" talk about their doing a movie together, she says, no movie materialized.

After a while, she says, "I couldn't live under the same roof with him; we were fighting all the time." (Michelle says she "fell off the couch laughing" years later when she watched Beatty tell Barbara Walters words to the effect of "They broke up with me!" "That," she says, "is what Warren makes his women do!") According to Michelle, Warren "didn't want me to act. He wanted me to be with him all the time. When I told him I was going to do *Valentino* [which would mean six months of filming], he said, 'Well, that's probably the end of our relationship.'" After she finished the movie, they broke up. On the rebound, Michelle married radio executive Bob Burch, in 1978. "I threw myself at him, as I tend to do," she says. (Michelle's last words on Beatty: "I love Annette [Bening] and I pray for her every day! She can manage the guy, and I never could. He drove me nuts!")

My mom always seemed to have a relationship going on, but she was never a chameleon, never an extension of her boyfriends—she never compromised herself," says Chynna Phillips Baldwin, sitting at a café near the Westchester County, New York, home where she lived with Billy (whom she's been with for 16 years), their daughters Brooke (known as Chay Chay) and Jameson, and their son, Vance, before they moved to California for his role in TV's *Dirty Sexy Money*. "Growing up, I always saw her as Wonder Woman, as a tough cookie. I had respect for her—and fear! She was very passionate and emotional, and I didn't want to rock the boat." Chynna's early childhood was "hard," she admits with a sigh, "because I didn't have strong, positive connections with either of my parents." Her absent father (whom she idolized) was largely on drugs and alcohol, and, though mother and daughter loved each other, Chynna feels she didn't get all the one-on-one attention she wanted. As a result, she says, "being a mom is challenging for me—my perspective is warped. How much time is enough to spend with your kids? How much is too little? Do they feel intimate with me, and I with them? Are my feelings real?"

In the 90s, Chynna was the most glamorous member of Wilson Phillips, the second-generation-rock-royalty group (Brian Wilson's daughters Carnie and Wendy were her group-mates); they had four hit songs. But she left the family business for a sensibility foreign to her parents: she's a fervent born-again Christian. She was baptized in brother-in-law Stephen Baldwin's bathtub, and she'd love to share "the power of God" with Michelle. "When Mom says she's coming to town, I say, 'I'm filling the bathtub.' We have a good giggle over that."

Michelle was with Bob Burch for two years. Then, 26 years ago, yearning for another child, she got her beau of six months, the handsome, easygoing actor Grainger Hines, "absolutely smashed on martinis," she recalls, and proposed a deal: if he fathered a baby for her, she would take full responsibility for it. "The minute you tell a guy that he doesn't have to parent, he becomes the best parent," she says of the father of her son, Austin Hines, who is 25. "Grainger has been the greatest!" Michelle purchased her house in Cheviot Hills, and in 1986 she was cast as Nicolette Sheridan's mother on *Knot's Landing*, a role that put her back in the public eye through the beginning of the 90s. Sheridan says, of their "deep and caring" friendship, "I admire Michelle's zest for life and fearless nature, and I feel blessed to be part of her intoxicating world." During these years Michelle was involved in a serious relationship with singer-songwriter Geoff Tozer.

After the relationship ended, Michelle accepted, in 1999, a dinner date with Beverly Hills plastic surgeon Steven Zax. "The little hippie chick and the surgeon don't seem like a real match, but we've been able to bring each other closer to the center," she says. They spend weekends together, and they travel frequently. Lou, Ann, and Genevieve say it's her best relationship ever. ("She'll want to slug me for [saying] this," says Chynna, "but it's her first truly mature, grown-up relationship.")

In the end, the romantic statistics of Michelle Phillips's last 30 years don't tell the story of what she has become. Something else does: "Michelle grew into her name," says Owen Elliot-Kugell. "She became everyone's Mama Michelle." As the others flamed out, her character expanded to fill the Mama/Papa role—the parent to the whole burgeoning brood.

First step: rescuing John and Genevieve's son, Tamerlane. In March 1977, Chynna came home from a visit to her father and Genevieve (who lived on the East Coast) with some pretty heavy memories. "It was your typical heroin scene," Chynna recalls. "A lot of needles and a lot of blood and very sick people. Genevieve asked me to please not tell my mom what I just saw." Chynna recalls asking Michelle, "Mommy, can drugs kill people?" Alarmed, Michelle flew out to see John and Genevieve. "I told them, 'I'd like to take care of Tam.' They put up a little bit of a fight, but not too great of a one." (Genevieve concedes that what Chynna says she saw "was right," and "I knew it would be better for Tam because John was pretty bad off." However, in her mother's heart, she says, she believes "Michelle stole Tam.") A court granted legal custody to John's sister, Rosie, with the understanding that Tam would remain in Michelle's care. Tam moved in with Michelle, Chynna, and Bob Burch, and for two years he thrived. "I was in therapy with a really nice therapist in Beverly Hills," says Tamerlane, a former mortgage broker and now a musician (his upcoming pop-rock album has three tracks produced by Sean Lennon). "His teachers were telling me how great he was doing," Michelle says. She loved the little boy, and Chynna was happily bonded with her half-brother.

But, for Genevieve, losing her child was painful. "I spent hours and days talking John into kidnapping Tam," she says. "I said, 'John, if we do, people will think you have normal feelings.'" Genevieve (who was then pregnant with Bijou) flew out to L.A. and, on a ruse to take Tam to Disneyland, spirited him to Las Vegas, where they met up with John. Then they all drove across the country. Child-stealing charges were filed against John and Genevieve in California, and an anguished Michelle flew east with Rosie to try to reclaim Tam. In the Connecticut courtroom, the tension between Michelle and Tam's parents "was thick enough to cut," Michelle recalls. "John and Genevieve convinced the judge that I was just a disgruntled ex-wife." They won custody of Tam. "I left feeling Tam was in a lot of danger. I cried on the plane the whole way home, and, partly because Bob wanted me to get over it and I couldn't get over it, we divorced soon after." (Genevieve says a psychiatrist told her that "kidnapping Tam was the best thing we could do, because otherwise he would have felt that we didn't love him.") About eight months after John regained custody, he was arrested by federal agents for narcotics trafficking. (He disclosed in his book that he had had an illegal deal with a pharmacy to buy drugs without prescriptions.) Using the promise of anti-drug media outreach, he bargained his maximum-15-year sentence down to a mere 30 days.

Michelle's next project was less fraught. At some point in the mid-80s, when Owen Elliot was in her late teens, she called Michelle and said, "You have to help me find my father!" Michelle spent a year running down leads through musician friends. Once she had pried loose the name Cass had kept so close to her vest, she placed an ad in a musicians' publication, urging the man to call an "accountant" (hers), implying a royalty windfall. Like clockwork, Cass's long-ago secret lover took the bait. When Michelle phoned him, she recalls, "he wasn't all that shocked," and, the next day, Owen says, "Michelle gave me a plane ticket and said, 'Go meet him.'" (Owen and Michelle will not reveal the name. Owen says only, "I had envisioned this Norwegian prince.") The meeting "answered a lot of questions," says Owen, who is now married to record producer Jack Kugell and has two children. Since then, she says, "there have been times when I've been devastatingly upset about things in my personal life, and I've really leaned on Michelle. She's been a mother to me in a way that would make my mom definitely chuckle."

In the late 80s, Michelle took in a boy, Aron Wilson, and became his foster mother, thereby in effect giving Austin a "twin." From that day on, Michelle regarded both boys as her sons. There were hairy times ("When the cops come to your door and say, 'Hello, again, Mrs. Phillips'—after the boys skateboarded after 10 p.m. and put a firecracker in the neighbor's mailbox—you think you're all going to jail"), but mostly good ones. And there were many baseball, soccer, and football games that Michelle—who would rather have been shopping or lunching—rooted them through. Michelle adopted Aron when he was 24. Today he is a budding chef, and Austin is an actor and a college student.

Why do you do this every weekend?" Steven Zax asked Michelle as she made her sandwiches to take to the homeless. Her answer was immediate: "To be a good citizen." The man who had instilled that motto in her, her father, died 11 years ago. He was true to form until the end. "He was a dog," Michelle says, laughing. "I'd say, 'Dad, why are you going to A.A. meetings to pick up women? You drink!' He'd say, 'So?'"

Nevertheless, Gil had given her a great foundation—as, in a different way, had another man. And so, on the night of March 17, 2001, she entered the intensive-care unit of U.C.L.A. Medical Center. "There was a blue light on, and he was lying there with his eyes closed, breathing very heavily. I knew he was dying." But he couldn't die yet, not until he saw her again. So, just as he had roused her from sleep on that long-ago night in the Hotel Earl, she says, "I woke him up. I looked him in the eye and I said, 'You made me the woman I am today.'" It was not untrue, but if she gave him a little too much credit—well, she let that be her gift.

And John Phillips smiled and closed his eyes and the next day drifted off to his final California dream.

THE LADY HAS LEGS!

By Maureen Orth | May 1993

The Rainforest Foundation benefit at Carnegie Hall on March 2 [1993] started out to be one of those preachy-hip, politically correct, dead-in-the-tundra New York evenings. The stage was littered with stars—Dustin Hoffman, James Taylor, Sting, George Michael, Ian McKellen, Herb Alpert, Canadian rocker Bryan Adams—but even though Tom Jones woke up the audience by belting out "It's Not Unusual" Vegas-style, the white boys were mostly in the tepid zone.

Then came the hurricane. "Ladies and gentlemen, Miss Tina Turner." *Yes.* The audience immediately jolted forward in their seats. The queen mother of rock 'n' roll, 53 years old, with the body of a vamp, came running out in a tight black leather cat suit with tails and high platform boots. Her hair (piece) was a flying wedge of layered copper, and her powerful voice pierced the darkness like lightning: "When I was a little girl . . . I had a rag doll." Tina Turner was singing her classic "River Deep, Mountain High," which the legendary Phil Spector had produced for her in 1966. Those trademark legs swathed in leather, the sinuous moves, those little Pony steps that allowed her to coochie-coochie up to the guys—none of her bountiful energy had dissipated in the 27 years since she first sang it. There wasn't the slightest hint of the horror she had lived with for so long as a battered wife, or of the dark memories that still cling to her.

James Taylor leapt to his feet and started shaking a tambourine, singing backup. Dustin Hoffman and Ian McKellen joined him. Pretty soon Tina Turner had relegated all the superstar males to an adoring chorus, like cross-dressed ghosts of the Ikettes, part of the R&B roots of rock 'n' roll in the old Ike and Tina Turner Revue. Talk about stealing the show. Afterward, Dustin Hoffman told her, "You've added 10 years to my life."

"The first time you see Tina is mind-boggling," Keith Richards tells me. Adds Mick Jagger, "She's so gutsy and dynamic." Tina Turner has always been an icon-mascot to the British supergroups, and even today she is revered more in Europe, where she makes her home with her younger German boy-friend, than in the States. The Rolling Stones, particularly, were pivotal in her career. Tina Turner got her first wide exposure to young white audiences in the 60s, when she and her former husband, Ike Turner, toured with the baby Rolling Stones in England. "Tina was great-looking, plus she could move and she had that voice. Usually you can have a voice but you can't move, or you're good-looking but you can't sing. How can anybody have that much?" marvels Richards. "With Tina, there it all is—it's all there."

Richards remembers that watching Ike and Tina, whom the Stones had idolized from records, was "kind of like school for us." At that point, he says, "we were one little blues band," playing bars and tiny clubs with no room to move. "Mick's stage center was a 12-inch square." Suddenly they were sur-rounded by "all these beautiful black chicks in sequins running around back-stage, and these fantastic musicians to learn from." Every night, he says, "we'd do our little bit and then we'd watch Ike and Tina and the Ikettes, and we said, 'Wow, this is show business!' They made us realize you got to do more than just stand there and play the guitar." He adds, "To me it was all just Tina Turner. Ike didn't see it that way. To him he was a Svengali, who wrote the songs; he was the producer and Tina was his ticket. He saw himself as Phil Spector, as the driving force behind the star. I saw him as the driving force behind a lot of things. It was the first time I saw a guy pistol-whip another guy in his own band." Keith Richards concludes, "Ike acted like a goddamned pimp."

———

To the outside world, however, Tina Turner appeared oblivious. "That was when I was just being led blindly, because I didn't care about anything," she says a few days after the Rainforest Foundation benefit. "I was just getting through this period." She was so under the control of Ike and immersed in his reality that she didn't have any idea who Mick Jagger was. "I saw this very white-faced boy in the corner with big lips, and I had never seen a white person with lips that big anyway, so I didn't know who he was or what race he was."

The one thing she did realize was that "he liked black women, liked to play around with them." Then she found out that he was the songwriter. "Of course, my hero. He says, 'I like how you girls dance. How are you doing that stuff?' We would all get up with Mick, and we would do things, and we would laugh, because his rhythm and his hips and how he was doing it was totally off. It wasn't teaching him; it wasn't dance classes. This is what we did backstage—we played around, because onstage he was just doing the tambourine. He wasn't even dancing. This was 1966. Afterwards Mick came to America doing the Pony. And all of us thought we had done it backstage. Well, I didn't tell people I taught him. I said we would just sit around during intermissions and have a good time."

"Later on, when Tina finally got real big, and she still looked incredible, guys would talk about her image sexually, just as a woman," Keith Richards says. "But the Tina I knew was different. Tina was somebody to take care of you. Out on the road somebody would always be sick, and she would say, 'Take care of yourself, you have a cold, here's the VapoRub, keep your scarf on, do your coat up.' I saw her like a favorite aunt or a fairy godmother. I always had other visions of Tina—of a mother-earth thing."

"I am a fun person, and when I'm onstage I act," Turner says. "I like to tease to a point. I'm not teasing men. I am playing with the girls—you know, when all the girls get together and everybody gets up and they get a little cigarette and champagne and they do little things. That's the same thing I do onstage when I'm performing for the girls and then for the guys." She is insulted that people would ever assume otherwise. "I am not a vulgar, sexy person onstage. I think that's how people perceive me, because I have a lot of vulgar videos where they want me to do the garter-belt thing."

It's more than that. Who can ever forget Tina Turner doing dirty things to a microphone when she sang "I've Been Loving You Too Long," a song she now hates, or the immortal words in her version of "Proud Mary": "We nevah, evah, do nothin' nice and easy. We always do it nice and rough."

"She has this sensual persona, but her private mores are so old-fashioned, so traditional," says Bob Krasnow, the Elektra Entertainment chairman. "Tina could be your girlfriend, your sister, your best friend—she can fulfill all these emotional niches. Yet when she gets up onstage, she has the power to stimulate you and bring words to life in a way that's uniquely her own." Krasnow has never forgotten the time in the 60s when he first walked into the Turners' house in Baldwin Hills, in Los Angeles, expecting Tina to be a hot number. "She was in the kitchen with a wet rag, down on her hands and knees wiping the floor, wearing a do-rag on her head."

Today, Tina Turner is nervously steeling herself for the Hollywood portrayal of her rise and fall and triumphant comeback. In June, Disney's Touchstone Pictures is releasing the film based on her 1986 bestselling autobiography, *I, Tina*, written with Kurt Loder. The movie, which Tina worries takes too much liberty with actual facts, is titled *What's Love Got to Do with It?* and stars Angela Bassett (the wife of Malcolm in *Malcolm X*) as Tina, and Laurence Fishburne (of *Boyz N the Hood*) as Ike. The film's sound track—Tina's old standards plus three new songs—will come out this month, just in time for her grand concert tour of America and Canada this summer, the first time she's toured the U.S. in six years.

Tina Turner is clearly testing the waters. "I don't believe that I can go and stand and sing for the people," she tells me. "I can't stand the idea of just standing there like Barbra Streisand or Ella Fitzgerald or Diana Ross. I have never been that kind of performer. I have been in rock 'n' roll all my life. You can't be a rock 'n' roll old woman. You can be a rock 'n' roll old man." "If there's anybody around who can grow up and still be a rock 'n' roll woman, it's got to be Tina," says Keith Richards, now 49 himself. "She's in the same position I and the Stones are. It's out there to find out. The area's open."

———

Tina Turner likes to spend money—oodles of it. She doesn't look at price tags. She often buys duplicates of her designer clothes in case the cleaners wreck something. She collects antique furniture, owns a house in Germany and is renovating another in the South of France, drinks Cristal champagne, drives a Mercedes jeep, and indulges herself with massages, facials, psychic readings, and holistic cures. She's sold 30 million records since 1984, when "What's Love Got to Do with It?" soared to No. 1 on the pop charts and her *Private Dancer* album spawned three additional hit singles and swept the Grammys. Although she hasn't had a hit record in the U.S. in seven years, on her last European tour, in 1990, she filled stadiums and played to 3.5 million people, outdrawing both Madonna and the Rolling Stones. So she's hardly hurting.

But not long ago her accountant called her and told her, "You've been having a good time." If she wanted to keep the perfumed bubble bath filled to overflowing, it was time to turn on the faucet again—go out and strut her stuff for millions of dollars while the movie was playing and the sound track was being released. Not that she feels particularly like singing onstage—doing that every night with her extraordinary, God-given talent is all wrapped up in her mind with hideous memories of beatings and indentured servitude. She'd rather act. "I think it's more classy to be an actress than to be a rock singer. But you don't make as much money. I ain't no dummy. I know that."

So this year Tina Turner has moved from Europe and rented a furnished house in Beverly Hills, in Benedict Canyon, a Mediterranean-style house that's all white stucco, beamed ceilings, and bleached wooden floors, with hillsides of daisies. She greets me at the door in a long tan sleeveless knit shift and brown suede Chanel ballet slippers. We go on a tour of the house, which is lovely, low-key and tasteful. The most interesting part is an enormous walk-in closet the size of a bedroom, filled with 10 pieces of Vuitton luggage, about 60 pairs of shoes, and racks and racks of designer clothes, mostly in neutral colors, which she coordinates and tends herself. Inside that closet is a smaller, cedar closet, in which a wig identical to the auburn layered short cut she has on is suspended from a wire hanger, like a spider hanging from a thread.

The house is quiet, and filled with fragrant white roses and tuberoses. It's a place where Tina Turner can be a lady. Refinement is something she has always aspired to. "I patterned myself from classy ladies. I take as much from them as I can, but I take it naturally, because I'm not going to be phony about it. I'm not going to walk around in Chanel suits or Gucci suits—that's a little bit too much, because that's not my nature. But watching my manners, caring about not being overdressed at the wrong time—it matters how I carry myself—that's what I'm concerned about as far as being a lady. Nobody would ever think that Tina Turner is a lady. I am."

Even in her bleakest years, when life was defined by driving up to 600 or 700 miles a day 365 days a year—when she might be up singing with black eyes and blood "whooshing into my mouth"—she dreamed of her idol, Jackie O. "The first time I met her, I was nearly in tears," Tina recalls. "In those days I wasn't thinking about anybody in my circle or the clubs where I was. I was thinking that nobody was at the level of what I wanted in my life— you understand?" Even stardom, when it came, did not make much differ- ence. "It was not my priority." Not at all. "Music life was not attractive," she says. "It was dirty. It was a chitlin circuit—eating on your lap. And that's why I say I was always above it. Why I don't know, but I knew I didn't want it. I'd rather go and clean a white person's house, where it is nice, than sing in dirty old places and deal with Ike and his low life."

Today, of course, it's different. Tina Turner speaks of "classy ladies" ac- knowledging *her*. "I see a lot of ladies these days in places like Armani, and even those ladies come over and say, 'You look so good.'" Does that make her feel good? "To be accepted by another class of people? I am going to say yes, absolutely."

But love also does have something to do with it. Erwin Bach, the "very private, conservative" 37-year-old managing director of the giant E.M.I. re- cording company in Germany, with whom she shares a house in Cologne, has been Tina's boyfriend for 6 years. "He doesn't like to be discussed, because he's a businessman," she says. "It took three years for us to get together—it wasn't one of those run-and-jump-in-bed situations." They met when he was sent by the record company to give her a jeep to drive around Germany in. She didn't even know his name, and for two and a half years he had no idea, when their paths crossed occasionally, that she was smitten. "Oh yeah, first sight. It's an electrical charge, really, in the body. The body responds to something," Tina explains. "Heart *boom-bama-boom*. Hands are wet. But I said no." Then again, she thought, why not?

"Something happens to you when you're secure as a woman. I began to feel, Well, I'm fine. If I don't really find anybody, I'm O.K. It's just those times when you start running the streets, and seeing couples and loving, and watching those movies where there's a lot of love, you miss being cuddled." It wasn't until Bach went to Los Angeles for a visit while Tina was at her house in Sherman Oaks that she included him in a friend's birthday party at Spago. "Afterwards everyone came to my house, and something magic started to happen. Of course, I was attracted. By then I'm sure he knew that I was. . . . I made sure I sat next to him. Because I was also analyzing him, too." She wanted to know that he wasn't into drugs, or heavy drinking. "After everyone left, I think we exchanged a few kisses. We started to talk, and I asked him about what his record company is like." Then he pulled away, saying, " 'Private life is private life.' So I didn't really push.

"What I did do, to actually get him, was I stayed in Switzerland. I rented a house in Gstaad." She had a house party at Christmastime in 1987 and invited Bach and some mutual friends. That did it, although since then, because of their work, they tend to be apart more than they are together. "It's the first time I've ever had a real comfortable relationship. I'm not threatened. He's not jealous." There are no marriage plans, but she is friendly with Bach's parents, who have retired to the country and don't speak English. (She has struggled to learn German, to no avail.) [The couple wed in 2013.] "I believe they would prefer if Erwin had a German girl or a white woman. But when they met me, well, it's the usual. Everybody likes Tina."

For good reason. There's a warmth and utter guilelessness to Tina Turner, plus an awesomely strong constitution—though her independence and sense of security have been won at a very high price. Physically, at 53, she is in superb condition. And just because "in California everyone goes under the knife," that doesn't mean Tina does. She was terribly hurt when the director of the movie implied that she must have had work done on her face. "I pulled my hair back. I showed them there were no scars. I pulled my ears. I said, 'Look, this is me.' . . .

"I almost wish I wasn't wearing a wig, because then you can see there are no scars," she tells me. "They don't take into consideration that I've been singing and dancing—and that's exercise—35 years. It's got to do something. I have muscle. From control." To prove her point. Tina Turner leaps off the sofa where we've been chatting and begins to pull her knit shift up, up, up those fabulous tawny legs, up past the knees, the thighs—"I still have little-girl legs"—up past her old-fashioned white panties to the just slightly thicker waist, up, up over the taut breasts. She's wearing no bra. With her shift now around her shoulders, she turns to the side to show off the profile of her high, rounded bottom. At that moment Roger Davies, her Australian manager, strides into the room. "Oh, Roger!" she gasps, and quickly lets the dress fall.

What's *really* remarkable about Tina Turner's face is how few scars it bears from the years of beatings she took. The one operation she did have to have was for a deviated septum in her nose, to open one nostril because it had been punched in so much. Ike Turner struck her on a regular basis for 16 years with everything from shoes to coat hangers to walking canes, plus he once put a burning cigarette to her lips and also threw boiling-hot coffee on her face. He cracked her ribs. He made her perform with jaundice, with tuberculosis, nine months pregnant, and three days after having a baby. Following her one suicide attempt, in 1968, when she thought she had timed her overdose of Valium to take effect *after* a performance so that Ike wouldn't lose the night's receipts, he tried to revive her, saying, "You wanna die, motherfucker, die!"

"She was scared to death of him—everybody around him was, in his own little cult," says Ike and Tina's longtime road manager, Rhonda Graam, who is today Tina's assistant. "It was almost like a hold he had on people."

"This was always just bruised," Tina Turner tells me, pointing to her jaw. "This was always just torn apart, because it hits the teeth," she says, showing me the inside of her lower lip. "So the mouth was always distorted, and the eyes were always black. If you look at some of the earlier pictures, my eyes were always dark. I couldn't get them clear. I thought it was the smoke or whatever. But Ike always banged me against the head." She is kneeling on the sofa now, clutching a pillow, leaning her face in close to mine. When she pushes up the bangs of her wig, you can see a tiny part of her fuzzy white hairline. "I said the same thing—how could I have survived? Only once I got knocked out. Only once. And that was when I got this," she says, and runs her finger along the outer tip of her right eye, where there is a scar about a half-inch long. "Yeah, black eyes, busted lips—somehow I just ignored it, but people knew. I thought that they thought it was a car accident. I made something up in my head in terms of the public."

Tina rarely went to the doctor after her beatings—"just those major things." The medical people who treated her were of no help. "In those days, believe me, a doctor asked you what happened and you say, 'I had a fight with my husband,' that was it. Black people fight. They didn't care about black people."

Along the way there were many people who witnessed Ike's mistreatment of Tina, but no one ever intervened. "I felt great responsibility for Tina, and I'd be there while it was going on," admits Bob Krasnow. "I was young, and I hero-worshiped Ike in a perverted way. Had I been more liberated or more experienced, I would have spoken up. I didn't." Krasnow says the horror really began after Ike discovered cocaine, in the late 60s. "The whole thing took this huge turn for ugliness. Tina was the focus for a lot of this horror, but the whole world suffered. In those days there was no Oprah Winfrey, no publicity dealing with abuse, no abuse hot lines. She was out there by herself in a man's world—she was on the road with B.B. King and Chubby Checker. She was the only woman in this world . . . a demeaning man's world."

Tina Turner hates talking about being beaten, and she can't stand the idea that people consider her a victim. In an era in which victimization is venerated and loudly proclaimed, she rejects the label and wants nobody's sympathy. She says she wrote the book to stop talking about it. "It's like going back into time, when you are trying to understand how prehistoric people lived. I am saying it one last time, and I hope people don't even think about talking to me about it anymore. If they don't understand, fine."

The problem is, Tina Turner herself is still struggling to come to grips with why exactly she stayed around a man who brought her so much misery. We spend hours discussing why she tolerated not only the physical and psychological torture but also the scores of other women Ike flaunted under her nose—Ikettes, groupies, employees, nannies for the four children in their house: his two and her two, one by a musician in Ike's band before she became involved with Ike, and one they reluctantly had together.

One minute she's defiant on the subject: "I tried to explain it to Disney [for the movie]." Lost cause. She says they see "a deep need—a woman who was a victim to a con man. How weak! How shallow! How dare you think that was what I was? I was in control every minute there. I was there because I wanted to be, because I had promised." The next minute she says, "O.K., so if I was a victim, fine. Maybe I was a victim for a short while. But give me credit for *thinking* the whole time I was there. See, I do have pride." In fact, she's stymied. "I've got to get somebody else to say, 'Yes, Tina, I do understand, and there are no buts.'" Finally, there is a moment when Tina begins to pace, and her eyes fill with tears. "What's reality sometimes is not exactly real. Because you keep saying, 'What did I do?' You get on your knees every night and you say the Lord's Prayer, and you say, 'Somebody must send some help to me, because I've never done a thing in my life to deserve this.' And that's when I started to chant."

Anna Mae Bullock never knew anything but domestic strife. She was the result of an angry, unwanted pregnancy, and by the time she arrived on November 26, 1939, her mother and father, the majordomo of a cotton plantation in Nutbush, Tennessee, were fighting constantly. One day her mother just took off, and for years never even bothered to contact her two little girls.

"My mother was not a woman who wanted children," Tina says. "She wasn't a mother mother. She was a woman who bore children." Her father tried to cope for a while, but then he too split. "I was always shifted. I was always going from one relative to another. So I didn't have any stability."

"Ann" considered herself too gawky to be desirable. "I was very skinny when I was growing up. Long, long legs and nothing like what black people really like. I must say that black people in the class where I was at the time liked heavier women." She was living part-time with a white family, doing cleaning for her board and going to high school—just singing along to the radio—when her mother appeared to take her to St. Louis, where she was working as a maid. Ann first laid eyes on Ike Turner when she was a junior in high school and went out to a club one night with her sister. She was 17, he was 25 and a badass star in East St. Louis. Ike Turner and the Kings of

Rhythm were the biggest deal around, but, Tina says, "he had a bad reputation. He was known as 'pistol-whipping Ike Turner.'" She knew he had "an uncontrollable temper," but he was also very exciting. After months of begging him to let her sing, she finally grabbed the mike one night during a break and blew his mind with her voice. "I wanted to get up there with those guys," Tina remembers. "They had people on their feet. That place was rocking. I needed to get up there with that energy, and when I got there, Ike was shocked, and he never let go."

Ike Turner, a preacher's son whose father was shot by whites who accused him of playing around with a white woman, had already walked from Mississippi to Tennessee and been recorded by Sam Phillips of Sun Records—the first company to record Elvis Presley—when he met Ann Bullock. Today, Ike Turner is credited with recording one of the first rock 'n' roll songs, "Rocket '88," in 1951, but he never got anything for it. He was a great rhythm-and-blues musician who played the piano in the boogie-woogie style that Little Richard and Jerry Lee Lewis later adopted, as well as the guitar.

At first Ike and Tina were just friends, and he confided to her that he felt small and unattractive, that in school girls would sneak out to cars with him but not be seen with him, that he was constantly being left and being ripped off of his songwriting and publishing rights. "My problem, little Ann, is people always took my songs." Wide-eyed, Tina—who was well aware that he had women, both black and white, in every neighborhood in St. Louis, that he beat those he was closest to, and that he kept guns and bragged about having robbed a bank—promised that *she* would never leave him like that; she would help him make it to the top. "I was his vehicle to get him to being a star. That's why I had no say." she declares. "He was being a star through me. I even saw it then." She would deeply regret her promise to stay, but she kept it for nearly two decades.

"Ike had some kind of innate quality about him that you really loved him," Tina says. "And if he liked you, he would take the clothes from his back, so to speak." Tina makes it clear that "I was there because I wanted to be. Ike Turner was allowing me the chance to sing. I was a little country girl from Tennessee. This man had a big house in St. Louis, and he had a Cadillac, money, diamonds, shoes—all of the stuff that a different class of blacks would look up to."

Tina got pregnant by one of Ike's musicians and had a baby boy, Craig, in 1958. The musician left before the baby was born, and Tina worked in a hospital during the day to earn more money, while continuing to sing at night. After club dates, she would sometimes spend the weekends at Ike's house, where she had her own room. "Then he offered me more money, because one of his singers had left. That's when the relationship started. I cannot tell you how wrong it felt."

Sex with Ike and shame, it seems, were always linked in Tina's mind. She says the first time he touched her felt like "child abuse." The second time, she was seeking refuge in his room because two musicians had threatened to rape her. "Something was going on—maybe the feeling he could protect me." Ann was hooked. "That's the kind of girl I am. If I go to bed with you, then you're my boyfriend." She hastens to add, however, "It wasn't love in the beginning; it was someone else who I found to give love to." Ike had a common-law wife named Lorraine Taylor, who was pregnant at the time, but he took care of Ann too. "He was giving me money for singing. He went out and bought me clothes. I was having a dental problem, and my mother didn't have money at that point for dental work. He corrected all that. And then I was a little star around him. I was loyal to this man. He was good to me." But she was never very attracted to him physically.

"I really didn't like Ike's body. I don't give a damn how big his member was," Tina says blithely. "He really was blessed, I must say, in that area. . . . Was he a good lover? What can you do except go up and down, or sideways, or whatever it is that you do with sex?"

Well, you can get pregnant, and a year later Tina was pregnant by Ike. Lorraine—who had previously threatened Tina with a gun, then shot herself instead—was still around. By then Ike and Tina's first hit, "A Fool in Love," was climbing the R&B charts. Along the way "Ike did pull a few strings that would make it difficult for me to leave." He changed Ann's name to Tina—she says it reminded him of Sheena the jungle queen from the TV series—without consulting her, and she hated it. Worse, out on the road everyone thought the two were married. From the beginning, she never really felt good about him or herself, and looking back today, she can enumerate six or seven reasons why she eventually knew in her heart that one day she would have to leave him.

One night she was crushed to hear him on the radio with an Ikette he was passing off as Tina. Then she realized he wasn't going to give her her own money. At the same time, she began to realize her importance: "I was the singer." Her sullen unhappiness inevitably brought a beating. She was stung once again when their baby, Ronnie, was born in 1960 and Ike didn't take her to the hospital—he slept through it. That was just the beginning. When Ronnie was about two, Ike and Tina moved to California. Lorraine had left Ike by then, and without warning she sent the two sons she had had by Ike to live with their father. Tina was suddenly mother to four boys under the age of six. (Until Lorraine's boys were in their teens, they didn't know Tina was not their real mother.)

Tina was not around very much, either. Ike was obsessive about work and had Tina and the band and various Ikettes out on the road year-round. It was a rough, cash business; Ike didn't believe in banks. He had a safe in the house, a safe in the car, and lots of guns to protect him. When Tina was allowed to go shopping, he would peel bills off a big wad.

They put out dozens of records, and some of their songs became hits, but they never made the top 10, only the rhythm-and-blues or soul charts. Nevertheless, Ike and Tina were becoming hip, cult favorites, regularly booked into the Fillmore West. Within five years Ike himself was able to book them where few black acts like theirs had been before, including Vegas. At the International Hotel, they were in the lounge, and Elvis Presley was the headliner.

They had gotten married in 1962, in Tijuana, primarily, Tina says, because another woman who had been married to Ike before Lorraine was after him for alimony. "As far as I'm concerned, I've never been married," Tina says. "This woman was asking for money, so Ike felt he'd better marry me so she couldn't get property." According to Tina, Ike paid the woman $15,000 to go away. For about five years, Tina says, "I was caught in his web." But about 1965, when she came home from touring alone to find that Ike had moved another woman into the house with the children, she felt defeated once again, and began to entertain thoughts of getting away.

"I had gotten to the stage where I started to think that I didn't want to be Ike's wife, and I didn't care about the money," Tina says. "I was thinking the whole time, how could I fulfill my promise and get out of it all right?" In 1966,

Phil Spector paid Ike $20,000 to let Tina record—but mostly to stay away so that he could work with Tina alone on "River Deep, Mountain High." Tina was thrilled to be able to really sing. "Nobody wanted me to sing in those days. They wanted me to do that screaming and yelling." Although the song is considered a rock 'n' roll milestone, and became a huge hit in England, it bombed here. Yet, however much Tina may have wanted to go off on her own, she didn't, for fear that "Ike would kill" anyone who tried to wrest her away.

She was trapped. "I had to get out of there because whatever I was doing didn't matter anymore. I had my house, I had my children, I had my own car. I had stuff. I shopped. But I had this horrible relationship I was hiding behind."

Then she got to the stage of not caring. "I wanted him to find a woman." She told him she wanted a business relationship. "He would really fight harder then, because he thought he was losing control." "He was afraid she'd leave him," says Rhonda Graam. "He would keep the fear going. He didn't want her to talk to anyone else—to put thoughts in her mind." Nevertheless, he kept acting like a husband, Tina says, and right up until the day she left him he expected her to massage him, give him manicures and pedicures, and have food ready for him at all times. Sometimes, after beating her, he'd force her to have sex with him. "Sex had become rape as far as I was concerned. I didn't want Ike near me. It was more than not being turned on and having to do it without being turned on. It was the fact he was sleeping around. That was not my style."

Nor were drugs. "I could not visualize putting something up my nose." But Ike was becoming a heavy cocaine user, spending thousands of dollars a week on the drug. He also began to drink. The drugs only made Ike more flagrant with women, even in front of the children. "There was all kinds of sex going on at the house, and I had caught him on the sofas, and women on their knees. I said to him, 'You can't do this in this house.' I really felt this house was mine. Ike was at a stage of showing off. He built a recording studio not far from the house. He wanted to let people know he had an apartment in the back of the recording studio, that he had recording-studio living quarters and the building next door as an agency, and he wanted to come up and show off the house, which was decorated like a bordello, with a coffee table in the shape of a guitar."

Tina attempted to leave once, but Ike caught up with her at a terminal where her bus stopped. Her suicide attempt had also failed. But the following year, 1969, Ike and Tina had toured in the U.S. once again with the now humongous Rolling Stones. What really kept Tina going, she says, was her escape into believing what psychics told her: "One day you will be among the biggest of stars and you will live across the water." In the interim, she chanted more and more every day: *Nammyo-ho-renge-kyo.*

In California in the late 60s and early 70s, this particular Buddhist chant, the mantra of a controversial Buddhist sect, Soka Gakkai, was touted as a way to achieve your goals as well as inner harmony. A woman Ike brought to the house one night shortly after Tina's suicide attempt turned her on to the chant. (Tina actually made friends with a number of Ike's women. "All of them weren't bitches or sluts.") She remembers, "I never let go of the Lord's Prayer until I was sure of those words."

Gradually Tina became convinced that chanting was her path to salvation. She was thrilled in 1974 to accept her first movie role, the Acid Queen in Ken Russell's *Tommy* (she did not know at the time that acid was a reference to LSD), and desperately hoped for more roles in films, but they did not come. She played Aunty Entity in *Mad Max Beyond Thunderdome*, with Mel Gibson, but turned down a leading role in *The Color Purple*, saying it was too much like real life to her. Today she still says, "I feel there is a calling inside me to act."

She also appeared on a television special with Ann-Margret and saw a different way of working. "I didn't want to sing anymore. I had been tired of this singing and this whole image of how I looked. I hated how I looked," Tina says of her raunchy "Proud Mary" days onstage, when she leaned back and led with her crotch and legs, and her wigs went flying. "The hair and the makeup and the sweat—I hated all of it."

In 1976 the day finally came when Tina Turner felt strong enough to get away. She realized Ike was never going to give her their house, which she had always wanted and felt she deserved. The children were graduating or getting ready to graduate from high school. Ike, meanwhile, was involved with "the nonsinging Ikette," Ann Thomas, who had had his baby and was traveling everywhere with Ike and Tina. By then Ike was doing so much coke that he would stay up for three or four days at a time, and his preferred mode of travel was to sleep on airplanes with his head on Ann's lap and his feet on Tina's.

In early July they flew to Fort Worth to perform a date at the Dallas Hilton. Tina was wearing a white Yves Saint Laurent suit on the plane, so she refused some chocolate Ike handed her. He kicked her, and later battered her again and again with his hand and shoe in the back of the limo. This time something clicked. She understood. "I knew I would never be given my freedom. I would have to take it."

She astounded Ike by fighting back. "When someone is really trying to kill you, it hurts. But this time it didn't hurt. I was angry too." Tina remembers "digging, or just hitting and kicking. By the time we got to the hotel, I had a big swollen eye. My mouth was bleeding." She refused, however, to cover the blood, as he directed her to. Ike was in sad shape himself. He had been up for days, strung out on coke, and when they got to the room she massaged his head, as she often did, until he passed out. Tina waited for his breathing to tell her he was asleep. "My heart was in my ears."

She remembers thinking, Now is the time. You are headed toward dealing with what you're going to have to deal with, with this man. "I ran down the hall, and I was afraid I was going to run into his people—his band and his bodyguards. So I went through an exit and down the steps. I was so afraid . . . because everybody was aware that Ike and Tina were supposed to be on in half an hour. Then I turned and went through a kitchen, just running. I just dashed through and went through the back door, and I remember throwing myself up onto trash cans just to rest, just to feel I had gotten away. Then I composed myself and thought, Now what? I started to run fast, just run."

She had 36 cents and a Mobil credit card.

"I needed to call somebody with money. My family didn't have the money for a ticket. That's the whole thing always. I didn't know anybody with money. They were all Ike's people."

Tina's life away from Ike began with the manager of the Ramada Inn across the freeway from the Hilton giving her a suite for the night. Ike did not take her leaving passively. For two years, people who helped her were threatened, and their houses and cars were set afire or shot into. Tina was unwavering, however: she even lived on food stamps for a while. In 1978 their divorce was final. Tina took nothing, because she didn't want to be tied to Ike in any way. What she did come away with was an astounding debt, since she had walked out on a performance. In addition, Ike always booked them solidly for months in advance, so Tina was held liable for the missed dates.

Michael Stewart, the former head of United Artists, one of the many record companies they had been under contract to, lent Tina money to get an act together, and began booking her in cabarets and hotels, where she performed in feathers and chiffon in a disco-inferno-type act. She also did guest shots on *Hollywood Squares* to pay the rent. "Tina never complained," Stewart said, adding that he knew she would be O.K., because at the height of her in-the-depths period he took her to a movie premiere "and you would have thought I was with Madonna today. The paparazzi swarmed. She was a celebrity."

Tina was probably half a million in debt when I took her on," says Roger Davies, her current manager. She worked it off by appearing in such places as Poland, Yugoslavia, Bahrain, and Singapore. Davies tried hard to get her a record contract, but Ike's reputation cast a pall. "He told me, 'I can't get you a record now, Tina. Whenever I say Tina, they say Ike.'" In 1981 the Rolling Stones came to her rescue, and she opened a few dates of their American tour. After a magic night at the Ritz club in New York in 1983, with Keith Richards, David Bowie, and Rod Stewart in the audience, her record company, Capitol, finally agreed to proceed with plans to have her cut an album. At the end of that year, she hit it big in England with the single "Let's Stay Together." Then she made *Private Dancer*. The rosy future the psychics had predicted was coming true. Meanwhile, after 11 arrests, Ike Turner finally ended up in jail in 1990, and served 18 months for cocaine possession and transportation, among other charges.

"I never had no bad thoughts about women. I think about women just like I think about my mother. And I wouldn't do no more to no woman than I would want them to do to my mother." Ike Turner is giving a bravura performance on the phone from his new home base, Carlsbad, California, outside

San Diego, where he is putting together an all new Ike Turner Revue with Ikettes he has scouted in local karaoke bars. He's 61 now, "overwhelmed about how creative I've been lately," and Tina is a sore subject. "Did I hit her all the time? That's the biggest lie ever been told by her or by anybody that say that. I didn't hit her any more than you been hit by your guy. . . . I'm not going to sit here and lie and say because I was doing dope I slapped Tina. Because it's not the reason I slapped her. If the same thing occurred again, I'd do the same thing. It's nothing that I'm proud of, because I just didn't stop and think."

Ike has been out of jail— "It was the best thing that ever happened to me"—since September 1991. According to one friend, he tried unsuccessfully to marry four different women in jail so that he could have contact visits. Today he's off drugs, lives with a 30-year-old white singer, and says he's getting his own TV movie together to tell *his* story. "Whatever happened with Ike and Tina—if we fought every day—it's just as much her fault as it was mine. Because she stayed there and took it for whatever reason she was taking it," he asserts. "Why would she stay there for 18 years? You know, I feel like I've been used. . . . Didn't nobody else grab her and put her where I put her at." Ike also denies that he hurt Tina as much as she and others say. "You know, if somebody throw coffee on your face and your skin rolls down your face, it should be some burns there, shouldn't it? Well, you look at her face real good. When you talk to her, say, 'What kind of surgery did you have on your face?' . . . I know damn well she didn't," Ike maintains. "She ain't did shit to her skin."

All those other women, he says, were not entirely his fault, either. Ever since he was "a little nappy-headed boy" in Mississippi working in a hotel, "I would see white guys pull up with their little white girls in their father's car with the mink stole, and I'd say, 'Oh, boy, one of these days I'm going to be like that.'" That he succeeded with women beyond his wildest imaginings is Tina's fault too, he says. "I blame Tina as much for that as I blame myself. Because she always acted like it didn't bother her for me being with women, unless she seen me with *this* woman every night, or something like this. . . . And this is what be wrong with her. She'd be pissed off about some girl or something, and she would lie and say she wasn't. . . . We had fights, but we was together 24 hours a day, and so, other words, she feels more like an employee than a wife, because I would tell her what words to say, what dress to wear, how to act onstage, what songs to sing. You know, it all came from me. . . . There is no Tina in reality. It's just like the story that she's written. The movie's not about her. The movie's about me!"

Ike, in fact, showed up on the movie set one day in a chauffeured white Lincoln and passed out autographed pictures of himself. He didn't get out of the car except to show Laurence Fishburne, who plays him, how he walks. Such is his fearsome reputation that the producers would not allow Angela Bassett, who plays Tina, near him. They had security guards escort her to her trailer. "By the time I figured out how to sneak out, he'd gone," Bassett says. Fishburne did ask Ike what he called Tina. He said, "I called her Ann."

Ike tells me, "Tina was my buddy. I never touched her as a woman. She was just my buddy. I would send her to go get this girl for me, go get that girl for me. And if I bought my old lady a mink coat, I would buy her one. And that's the way we were—just hope-to-die buddies. And that's why it was never no contract between us. Because I felt we had a bond, you understand, and I never did think that nobody, white or black, could come up and brainwash her. Like, right now I feel she's totally brainwashed."

"Why do you say that?" I ask him.

"Because she don't want to be black. She don't think she's black. She don't even talk black. She don't act black. Money don't make you. You make money. Do you understand what I'm saying? And I hate stars."

Ike Turner, who has a white manager and a white publicist, and who is accused by *his* old cronies, such as record producer Richard Griffin, of thinking "black people don't have any brains," has big plans for himself, including guest shots on Jay Leno and Arsenio Hall. The last time he talked to Tina, sometime in the 80s, he suggested doing a TV special. "Ike and Tina, Sonny and Cher—the broken pieces put together with Krazy Glue." Now he's thinking Vegas and beyond. "When I was with Tina, we would open up for Bill Cosby, like, in Vegas. I'm going to start by doing stuff like that. Going on tour with Elton John. Going on tour with the Stones. Going on tour with people like that." No matter that he hasn't talked to any of those people yet. Ike likes Ike. "I got a lot of friends out there," he says. "I have no shame; it took it all to make me what I am today, and I love me today."

Tina's two sons and Ike's two by Lorraine Taylor, whom Tina reared, are now all in their 30s. The chaos they grew up in has taken its toll. They are estranged from their father, and two, Michael and Ronnie, have seriously battled drugs. Ike's eldest son, Ike junior, is a musician in St. Louis. According to Tina, because of Ike junior's legal problems, "he can't come back to California." Ike's son Michael was recently living in a downtown Los Angeles shelter. Craig is learning club management. He wants his mother to open a jazz club for him. Ronnie, her son with Ike, is a bass player. One night after he was picked up for unpaid traffic tickets, he was stunned to land in the same Los Angeles jail cell as his father. "That made an impression," says Tina. "He never went to jail again." Ronnie auditioned for the role of Ike in the movie and also played bass in the movie's band. Tina has bought houses for both her sons. "I used to tell them I wasn't the Valley Bank. Now I tell them I'm not the European Bank," she says. "They call me Mother. I know they're trying."

I t's a glorious L.A. Sunday afternoon in March. Tina Turner is bouncing in and out of a chair in an upstairs den flooded with light, giving away her beauty secrets. "I do something about my life besides eating and exercising and whatever. I contact my soul. I must stay in touch with my soul. That's my connection to the universe."

"What are you?" I ask.

"I'm a Buddhist-Baptist. My training is Baptist. And I can still relate to the Ten Commandments and to the Ten Worlds. It's all very close, as long as you contact the subconscious mind. That's where the coin of the Almighty is." Every morning and evening, Tina Turner, who keeps a Buddhist shrine in her house, prays and chants. "I don't care what they feel about me and my tight pants onstage, and my lips and my hair. I am a chanter. And everyone who knows anything about chanting knows you correct everything in your life by chanting every day," she says. "People look at me and wonder, 'You look so great—what is it you do?' What can I tell them except I changed my life?"

Just when stardom finally hit big with "Let's Stay Together," in 1984, Tina Turner was suddenly subject to frequent colds and coughing fits, even onstage. A friend in London recommended an Indian doctor who practiced holistic medicine. His diagnosis: she still had TB. Tina was sent to a special empty hospital in the country for three or four days of intravenous body-toxin purification every time she finished a stretch on the road. It was a "scary place," she says. "I watch horror movies. Imagine that Frankenstein or somebody—a mummy—is coming through the door." The doctor prescribed a special low-fat diet and made his own medicines "from gold-dust powder. It is all basically from the earth." The results were dramatic. "After my second visit to the hospital, my eyes became clear. The whites of my eyes were never clear. They were always just not white. And I started to feel healthy. I had a glow, a light, about me." Most important, she says, "I started to get energy, to feel strong, to enjoy my work more."

People constantly ask Tina Turner if she will ever do any preaching or teaching. Yes, she says, but not yet. After the tour she is planning to put together a "life-style" cassette detailing her dance steps and holistic cures. Basically, it comes down to this: "I was a victim; I don't dwell on it. I was hurt. I'm not proud of being hurt; I don't need sympathy for it. Really, I'm very forgiving. I'm very analytical. I'm very patient. My endurance is very good. I learned a lot being there with that very sick man." Like Ike, she wouldn't change the past. "I am happy that I'm not like anybody else. Because I really do believe that if I was different I might not be where I am today," Tina says. "You asked me if I ever stood up for anything. Yeah, I stood up for my life."

She'd still rather act than sing. "I stepped into singing. It was hell. It's still hell *without* Ike," Tina says. "I'd like to make money some other kind of way than singing. Especially as an old woman. You can act as an old woman if you're good enough. I'll be damned if I'm going to go onstage as a gray old woman."

But right now, singing is fine enough. "What excites me is not the lights; it's that screaming thing, like when I walk onstage and they go crazy. That's what happens with Bowie and Jagger, the times I've worked with them: they've walked on my stage, the whole place went crazy, and I thought, If I'm going to be here, I want that."

(Ike Turner died in 2007, at age 76.)

IN LADY GAGA'S WAKE

By Lisa Robinson | January 2012

N*ew York City, September 11, 2011:* Cynthia Germanotta opens the door to the apartment in the beautiful building on Manhattan's Upper West Side where Lady Gaga—born Stefani Joanne Angelina Germanotta—grew up. It was here that Stefani got dressed in her school uniform every day to attend the Convent of the Sacred Heart, practiced piano, and dreamed of stardom. And it is where—despite having a suite at a nearby hotel—Lady Gaga is sleeping this weekend, on an air mattress on the floor of her old bedroom. No journalist has ever visited the Germanottas' home before, but the last time Gaga and I talked, she described the apartment to me, and when I expressed surprise that she said it had several floors, she told me her parents got a "deal" when they bought it, 18 years ago. She suggested that I see it. She also decided she wanted to cook a meal for me. I never really believed all the stuff about how she likes to cook any more than I believed that she really hung out with her old friends at dive bars on the Lower East Side. But, having done the Lower East Side bar trip with her the day before (more about that later), I was looking forward to seeing Lady Gaga at home with her family.

Lady Gaga's parents are in their mid-50s and have been married for 30 years. They're savvy and proud and protective of their famous daughter. They're involved with her business. It is apparent, seeing them all together, that Gaga's relationship with her family—as well as with her very tight management team—keeps her levelheaded.

Cynthia Germanotta, originally from West Virginia, is a graceful blonde. Forget such inspirations as David Bowie or Marilyn Monroe—it is obvious where Gaga got her sense of style. Today, Cynthia is wearing black-rimmed eyeglasses, a lacy black sweater, and black pants. She looks about 10 years younger than her age. (We discuss plastic surgery and she says, "I always tell my daughters it doesn't make you look younger. It just looks like you've had work done.") Also present are the family's two dogs—Alice, a 14-year-old beagle, and Lilu, a 3-year-old dachshund. When I arrive, Gaga's father, Joe Germanotta, is downstairs in the basement. He's from New Jersey and is the likely owner of the Bruce Springsteen *Darkness on the Edge of Town* CD boxed set on the windowsill next to the black baby-grand piano that dominates the living room. In the entrance hallway, there's a frame with photos of Gaga with Springsteen, Elton John, and Sting, at last year's Rainforest concert at Carnegie Hall. The apartment is a cozy triplex, with a large beige sofa and many framed family photos on the piano. There is a dining table by the open kitchen, a garden off the living room where Cynthia grows fennel, arugula, Italian parsley, rosemary, and oregano, and where there are small fig, olive, and lemon trees. And, at the kitchen counter by the sink, chopping cherry tomatoes in half for a spaghetti sauce she prepares from scratch, is Lady Gaga. She is wearing a black lace Chanel dress, extra-high Louboutin stiletto heels, glass earrings, full makeup, and a Daphne Guinness–inspired black-and-white wig. Just another Sunday afternoon at the Germanotta home.

Gaga removes the pink ribbon from the box of macarons I have brought from the newly opened Ladurée bakery, on Madison Avenue. She puts the Ladurée box on top of the Dunkin' Donuts box already on the counter and ties the ribbon around her hairdo. She then proceeds to take me on a tour of the apartment. On the top floor are her parents' bedroom and the bedroom she shared with her sister, Natali (who, now 19, attends art school in the city), where the red air mattress is on the floor. I note that there are no doors on the bedrooms—her parents could have heard everything she and her sister said growing up. "Yes," she says, "and I heard them, too." (Later that evening, when we're at the hotel for a lengthy chat, I ask, Why the air mattress on the floor instead of this suite with the room service, the marble bathrooms, the magnificent views of Central Park? "I'm in hotels all the time," she says, "and they're cold. None of this really matters to me. When I can, I'd much rather spend the time with my parents.")

In the apartment, I watch Gaga prepare the tomato sauce. She adds fennel, rosemary, oregano, and leeks—"My secret ingredient"—and she and her mother discuss whether we should have whole-wheat pasta. She makes a salad. All this slicing and dicing while wearing the Chanel dress seems perfectly natural in the Gaga world. People always ask me what she's really like. This is what she's really like. When we talk later, she says she feels she owes it to her fans to always look this way. "I went to an all-girls school," Gaga says, "and I was very much like my mother; she would do her hair every morning and get dressed nice. So, most of the time I would stay up all night, straightening my hair, and I would even put my makeup on before bed sometimes, so that when I woke up in the morning it would be ready for school. I just liked to be glamorous. It made me feel like a star."

Joe Germanotta comes upstairs, wearing jeans and a red polo shirt. "That's a nice dress," he says, complimenting his daughter. We talk about the Yankees, and he tells me he purchased four seats from the old Yankee Stadium to put in the garden of the restaurant he's currently renovating at 70 West 68th Street. The restaurant will be called Joanne, after his late sister, and there will be a double fireplace between the main room and the garden area; people will be able to sit outside and watch games on TV. Cynthia is in charge of the restaurant's décor; she's picked every tile, every lamp, every fabric, every painting; it's easy to see where Gaga got her attention to detail. Joe's been working with a crew for five months to get the restaurant ready, and the plan is for it to be open this month. Cynthia shows me three large U.P.S. boxes of fan mail in the living room that she gets for Gaga every week. I read aloud an e-mail a Gaga fan sent me—12-year-old Maddie P., from Maine. She wrote that Gaga inspired her to help a boy in her school who had been harshly bullied for being gay. Gaga held her mother's hand while listening to this and tears rolled down her cheeks. Cynthia shows me a letter from the White

House commending Gaga for her work on behalf of abolishing "Don't ask, don't tell," and then says that she'll head up Gaga's new Born This Way Foundation—a charity that will empower youth, with an emphasis on anti-bullying.

Joe and Cynthia take me downstairs to see the basement, which includes a space where Joe used to make his own wine. The basement is a large, wood-paneled room, with a big screen for watching TV shows, baseball games, and N.C.A.A. March Madness. All around the room, Cynthia points out, is "Gaga's stuff"—as she still has no permanent home other than this one. And, Gaga says, despite all the rumors last year of house-hunting with her on-and-off boyfriend of six years, the bartender/writer Luc Carl, she has no plans to settle down. "Gypsy queen couldn't take the leap," she says. "I'm not going to pay millions of dollars for something. I can't commit to being an adult—I'm not ready." The basement walls are covered with Gaga's framed platinum albums, posters from her concerts, and all-access backstage passes. Joe says being on the road is "a lonely life," so one or both of her parents accompany Gaga on tour when they can. We sit down at the table to eat. In addition to Gaga and her parents, we are joined by Lane Bentley, Gaga's day-to-day manager. She's worked with Gaga for three years, has traveled with her since last June, and handles literally hundreds of e-mails daily regarding Gaga's schedule. We all hold hands as Gaga says grace. And then we eat the whole-wheat spaghetti, with the delicious homemade sauce, and the salad, and drink a bottle of red wine. And, for the record, Gaga ate a lot. "You've got a hit," her father told her about the sauce. After the meal, Gaga went to the piano to play us a new song she was working on about Princess Diana—a song about fame and celebrity death. Even in its rough stages, it has her trademark catchy chorus, and she sang the sad, slightly bitter lyrics in full voice. As I watched her parents listen to her, I could see years of such tableaux: the young Gaga at the piano, singing, her parents watching. "Oh yes," Cynthia says when I ask if it had always been this way. "We didn't push it. She was just determined. But we wouldn't have encouraged her to pursue this if we didn't think she had the talent."

In the mere four years that she's had a recording contract, Gaga, now 25, has become a global phenomenon. She was No. 11 on last year's *Forbes* list of the World's 100 Most Powerful Women, coming in ahead of Oprah Winfrey. She's sold a total of 23 million albums and 63 million singles worldwide. Her net worth has been reported to be over $100 million. Her sophomore album, *Born This Way,* sold more than 1.1 million copies in its first week of release, last May. She performed for 2.4 million people in 202 shows in 28 countries on the year-and-a-half-long Monster Ball Tour. She has more than 44.5 million "Likes" on Facebook, and more than 15 million people follow her on Twitter. According to her manager, Troy Carter, initially she wasn't an easy sell, because (hard to imagine now) at first, way back in 2008, her songs were considered "dance." Radio stations wouldn't play her music. Still, Carter says, "she walked into my office in 2007 wearing fishnet stockings, a leotard, big black sunglasses, and confidence. Too much confidence. She walked in as a superstar." The producer Vincent Herbert, who has worked with Stevie Wonder, Beyoncé, Michael Jackson, Toni Braxton, and scores of others, signed Gaga to his own label at Interscope Records in 2007. "I've never met an artist so dedicated," he says. "The first time I met her, she told me, 'If you sign me, I'll be the most loyal artist you'll ever sign. I want to be the biggest pop star in the world. I want to sell 10 million albums.' That was our first meeting. I knew immediately that she'd be our new superstar, our new Michael Jackson."

I n the past year alone, Gaga has appeared on numerous television shows including *Saturday Night Live,* where she performed in skits and displayed a real comedic flair; she could easily host the show if she ever had the time. [*She would host the show in November 2013.*] She had her own HBO special: the Monster Ball concert, live from Madison Square Garden. She appeared on the red carpet at last year's Grammys inside a "vessel"—a semi-transparent egg designed by Hussein Chalayan. At the 2010 MTV Video Music Awards, she wore a dress made of actual meat (which was chemically treated and then enshrined in the Rock and Roll Hall of Fame). And this past year, she opened the MTV V.M.A.'s dressed as her alter ego, a guy named "Jo Calderone," who resembled either Ralph Macchio or Marlon Brando, depending on your age or point of view (more about that later, too). Wearing a man's Brooks Brothers suit (and prosthetic male genitalia inside her trousers), smoking a cigarette, and guzzling a bottle of beer, she shocked the audience and instantly made every female star in attendance who had pink hair or wore a contraption on her head look dated.

Since Lady Gaga's album *Born This Way* hit the charts last May, she has promoted it all over the world. She recorded "The Lady Is a Tramp" with Tony Bennett for his *Duets II* album, prompting Bennett to rave that she's one of the greatest talents he's ever seen. When she performed for the Robin Hood Foundation benefit in New York City last May, according to David Saltzman, executive director of the charity, she was one of the very few artists to ever refuse the usual high-six-figure fee, insisting instead that the money go back to help anti-poverty programs in the city. She sang at President Clinton's 65th-birthday concert at the Hollywood Bowl. She met President Obama, who said that in her 10-inch-high heels she was "intimidating," and she implored him to do something about bullying. ("Nothing with her is small," says Bobby Campbell, the head of marketing for her management company. "So if she's going to be in a room with Obama, she's going to have to talk about what she wants to achieve in the world.") And by the time this magazine is on sale, she will have published a book in collaboration with photographer Terry Richardson (*Lady Gaga X Terry Richardson*) and released the DVD of the HBO special as well as the album *Born This Way: The Remix*. She headlined an ABC-TV special the night of Thanksgiving, where she performed and cooked with Art Smith (who will be the executive chef of her parents' restaurant). She and Nicola Formichetti, her close collaborator for her every outfit and every look and the fashion director of her Haus of Gaga, created "Gaga's Workshop"—a full floor of holiday items selected or inspired by her—at Barneys on Madison Avenue. (A percentage of the profits from all that stuff will benefit the Born This Way Foundation.) She'll perform in Times Square on New Year's Eve. She continues her work as a spokesman for Viva Glam and creative director for Polaroid, and is developing a fragrance which is scheduled to debut in 2012. And she is eager to start a Born This Way tour, which could begin sometime in 2012 and will last well into 2013. When I asked Troy Carter if, after three weeks of vacation, Gaga gets antsy and wants to work, he laughed and said, "Three weeks? Or three hours?" When I suggested to Gaga that maybe she works too hard, does too many TV shows, she said, "I love to sing. I love to dance. I love show business. I need it. It's like breath." I asked her if she worries about overexposure, or backlash. She said, "I've already *had* the backlash." But, I said, you don't want to wind up some crazy casualty. "If I'm supposed to end up like some crazy casualty," she said, "then that's my destiny."

New York City, September 10, 2011: Gaga is taking me to some of her old hangouts, where, she tells me, she grew up. "This is really where I got my education," she says about the Lower East Side neighborhood where she lived alone in a walk-up apartment at 176 Stanton Street from May 2005 to May 2007, after dropping out of the Tisch School of the Arts at New York University. This is where she slept on a mattress on the floor, and where, she says, "I wore the same outfit every day. I never did laundry—I stank." It's also where she took drugs, wrote songs, and lugged her keyboard up and down several flights of stairs to do club shows. I told her that, even though she's always said she avoids celebrity parties and prefers to spend time with old friends when she's in New York, I wasn't sure I bought it. ("I don't understand that whole thing of . . . gathering . . . in tribes," she says. "Like a club of famous people. Why would I want to have champagne with celebrities?") So today she's called some of her pals to join us on an expedition. She's just finished a photo shoot, she is spray-tanned and wearing sunglasses, a Lever Couture black lace see-through dress, black underwear, very high heels, and a black lace cape that has been dipped in latex. She rides downtown in a large S.U.V. and insists on sitting in the front seat, with her legs splayed across the dashboard, "because," she says, "I don't like to feel cramped." At East Houston and Avenue B she wants to get out and walk. This foray is not like her appearance on *60 Minutes;* no camera crew follows us and no crowd gathers. With her security team a few paces behind us, we walk with Bo O'Connor—her best friend since she was four years old—Lane Bentley, and Bobby Campbell. People on the street occasionally stop and stare, say hello, or ask to take a picture with her. (She says yes every time.) But we manage to walk around fairly hassle-free. She's showing me some of the landmarks from when she lived in the area. She's upset that a favorite Mexican restaurant, on Rivington Street between Essex and Norfolk, went out of business. So has a beauty-supply store that she loved. We walk into a T-shirt store owned by a friend of hers. She points out various bars—St. Jerome's on Rivington, where her former boyfriend worked and where her friend Lady Starlight D.J.'d and go-go-danced, and 151, which some people in the neighborhood refer to as "the cave." There's a biker bar where, she says, "I used to stand outside and do drugs." We walk by a park where Dominican families hang out and listen to music and where, she says, "the rats that ran across that street were huge." She shows me the liquor store across the street from her old apartment and says, "If I was really fucked up, I would call them to deliver." She had money for liquor delivery? "Well," she says, "a $4 bottle of wine."

And then we go into the Johnsons—a small bar on Rivington. While Lane and Bobby go to the pool table in the back, Gaga, Bo, and I sit at the bar. I say it's barely five p.m., perhaps a bit early to start drinking. "Are you kidding?," Gaga says. "Back in the day, this would be *late*." Bo and I order beer, and Gaga orders a shot of Jameson's. For the next three hours, Bo, Gaga's friend Breedlove (a musician who also does the makeup for the Broadway show *Wicked*), and Lady Starlight (née Colleen Martin) sit and talk with Gaga and me about their days on the Lower East Side and their friendships. Lady Starlight, who's preparing to go on tour as the opening act for Judas Priest, gives Gaga a tie-dyed red velour dress and a velour jacket in various shades of gold. Breedlove talks about how they used to kill time in this very bar all day "waiting for Judy," their code name for cocaine. Gaga talks about how she woke up one day on her tour bus and realized what an idiot she'd been and never touched the drug again. She says that Bo made her understand that, even after working for 17 hours, or after a flight to Tokyo—no matter how exhausted she is—if her phone rings in the middle of the night and it is her parents or Bo, she has to pick it up. Gaga recalls the first time she saw Lady Starlight go-go-dance on a bench in the corner at St. Jerome's. "There was something . . . *off* about it," Gaga says of Starlight's performance, "something awkward and uncomfortable. But she was so unapologetic and interesting; I wanted to be like that."

About Gaga, Lady Starlight says, "She's such an awesome person that you can't not like her. We hung out, we started to perform together, and people thought we were sisters, or girlfriends—neither of which we ever denied. She has such positive energy; it's so inspirational to me." Gaga always credits Lady Starlight with influencing her, and Lady Starlight says, "First of all, no one else gives that kind of credit, but she always does. And I swear to you, everyone says when people get famous they don't change, and it's just not true. But she has *not* changed. [In those early days] I just tried to show her, Don't be afraid of anything. Go to whatever lengths we need to go to to get people shocked. It was, like, live it and believe it." Gaga talks about her next tour, and she talks about her fans. It always comes back to her fans. (Nicola Formichetti had told me that when he first met Gaga, three years ago, at a photo shoot early in the morning in Malibu, she showed up in full makeup, wig, heels—the whole bit. And then she took it all off and did it again for the shoot. "She always says to me, 'I don't want my fans to see me without my high heels on,'" Nicola recalls. "She says, 'They'll kill me. They need me to be like this.' People always ask me what is she really like, and you know, *this* is who she *is*.")

The *Mandarin Oriental hotel, New York City, September 11, 2011:* Following the afternoon at her parents' apartment, over the course of three hours (and before she returns to the air mattress to sleep), Gaga talks to me about her work, her fans, her politics, and her private life. She tells me she is seeing someone new (who knows if her rumored romance with *Vampire Diaries* actor Taylor Kinney will stand the test of time), but she is notoriously private about her private life. "I can't imagine that people sit and talk for hours about their marriages and their personal relationships," she says. "It seems strange to me. I always try to be honest with my fans, because I feel like I've built this goodwill with them where they know that I'm telling them the truth. The only thing I'm not always forthright with [are] my relationships, because I think it's not classy to exploit your relationships. I have a very giving heart. . . . I'm a lot like my mother. I just let people so far in. And with men, I tend to let them in so far in my heart and my soul because I'm emotionally available. The difference between being with your fans and being with a lover is that with my fans I know what I mean to them, and I will die protecting what we have. I only know the happiness of putting a smile on someone's face from the stage. But I have never felt truly cherished by a lover. I have an inability to know what happiness feels like with a man. I have this effect on people where it starts out good. Then, when I'm in these relationships with people who are also creative, or creative in their own way, what happens is the attraction is initially there and it's all unicorns and rainbows. And then they hate me.

"Perhaps it's a whose-dick-is-bigger contest. If I go to the piano and write a quick song and play it back, they are angry with how fast and effortless it is. That's who I am, and I don't apologize for it. But it's a hideous place to be in when someone that you love has convinced you that you will never be good enough for anyone. I had a man say to me, 'You will die alone in a house bigger than you know, with all your money and hit records, and you will die alone.'" I suggest that perhaps she's picked the wrong men. "That's what my mother says," she admits. "And even though I know it sounds a bit Hallmark, whenever I [was] in that kind of stressful, worthless moment, I would think, *I'll show you*. But it's more than just saying, 'Oh, they can't handle a strong woman.' 'Oh, I'm intimidating.' 'Oh, it's the money.' I think what it really is, is that I date creative people. And I think that what intimidates them is not my purse; it's my mind." I suggest that she's just going to have to find somebody more talented than she is. "Yes, please," she says.

Then she laughs and says the weird thing is, *after* she's left a few people, they've asked her to marry them. "How fuckin' romantic, you asshole. Sure, pop a ring on my finger and make it all better. I can buy myself a fuckin' ring." She continues: "I say this honestly, and this is my new thing as of the past year: when I fight with someone I'm in a relationship with, I think, What would my fans think if they knew this was happening? How would they feel about my work and about me as a female if they knew I was allowing this to go on? And then I get out. [My fans] saved me from myself, because they would never allow it—the same way I would never allow anything to hurt them. And I have always picked the music first. If anything gets in music's way, they're gone. My work has always been primary. It's not money and it's not record sales and it's not photographs. It's this invisible thing. . . . I imagine all the artists I ever loved could smell that energy."

One of the things that made Gaga more aware of how she was in relationships was the acting piece she did as "Jo Calderone" for the MTV awards. "I thought it would be an interesting cultural exercise to create someone [who's] not me," she says, "[someone] infinitely more relatable than me. A blue-collar Italian guy in a Brooks Brothers suit who just wants this girl to stay the hell home. It took a performance piece for me to understand things about who I am. And through doing this [with acting coach Larry Arancio] I learned about how I am in bed. I said, 'Isn't it strange that I feel less able to be private in private, and more able to be private in public?' And Larry said, 'Well, maybe that's the problem.' And I said, 'That's exactly the problem.' When I'm onstage, I'm so giving and so open and myself. And when the spotlight goes off, I don't know quite what to do with myself. As we were working, and talking this through, Larry told me to write everything down. And I had to get the prosthetic cock and balls hanging between my legs—how else could I walk like a guy? And I remember one of the things I said [when writing] was that I cover my face a lot when I have an orgasm. Like I'm ashamed or something." And so, when she performed this onstage as "Jo" talking about Lady Gaga, she said, "When she comes, she covers her face, like she doesn't want me to see, like she can't stand to have an honest moment when nobody's watching." She also utilized "Jo" in her video for "You and I": "It was a sweet and youthful moment in a cornfield where I could create what the most perfect relationship would be like," she says. "It was a metaphor. I haven't had it yet."

As the sun goes down and it starts to get dark in the suite, all the crudités, figs, and pomegranates are gone from the room-service tray—yes, we ate even after that meal at her parents'. We sip some red wine and the conversation turns to politics. I ask Gaga what she cares about in regard to what's happening in our country. "I care about gay marriage. I care about immigration. I care about education," she says. "I care about families and what is taught in schools and what is taught at home. And I feel liberated by my ability to be political with no political affiliation.

"I think that we're the land of the free and the home of the brave and inviting people to come in and pursue the American Dream," she continues. "And now we're kicking everybody out and essentially making citizens explain for themselves why they should be as equal to the person sitting next to them. I don't understand why anyone would interpret the Constitution as more relevant for one person over another, based on choices that have nothing to do with committing a crime." We discuss, among other things, the current presidential candidates, the Tea Party, Fundamentalists, and a woman's right to choose. "How can we create within society a sense of respect and leadership [when a woman is put in a position] where she's so young and has to make a choice," Gaga says. "The problem is not women being irresponsible. The problem is everyone being irresponsible. I talk to my sister about this a lot because she's young. Maybe sex isn't that big a deal anymore, but I don't have sex without monogamy, and maybe that's very old-fashioned. But still, the way men treat women in this society . . . How is it O.K. for a guy not to call a girl back after sex? And how can you deny a woman the right to choose [whether or not] to have a child? It's completely outrageous."

Snug Harbor Cultural Center and Botanical Garden, Staten Island, New York, October 11, 2011: Lady Gaga is directing the video for her new single, "Marry the Night." She wrote the treatment for it over a year ago and tells me it's "autobiographical." By the time you're reading this story, the video will likely be out, and while she may not spell it out, she wants people to interpret the video for themselves. But on this night, while it's being filmed on a closed set, what I see being filmed is a very, very personal story. There is footage of Gaga in a dance class, when she was just starting her career. There is a scene where she is lugging her keyboard up the flights of stairs in her old apartment building, with neighbors coming out of their apartments to stare at her. The director of photography is Darius Khondji, who did Woody Allen's *Midnight in Paris,* and Gaga speaks to Darius in fairly fluent French. She laughs when she sees the playback of her falling down the stairs—very physical, Lucille Ball–style—with her keyboard. And then there are the two scenes that she says depict the worst day of her life.

Over a year and a half ago, when she talked to me about "the worst day of my life," she said she had never talked about it before. But all she would reveal at that time was that she called her mother, who screamed into the phone and went to get her at her Stanton Street apartment, and that she was dropped by her first record label, Island Def Jam, on the same day. Soon afterward, she and her mother went to visit her grandmother in West Virginia. Now, in this video, she says, she is reliving "the worst day of my life." In one scene, Gaga, with obvious bruises on her body, looks completely drugged and out of it as she is wheeled on a gurney into a hospital—which, she pointedly tells me, is a "women's clinic." (Although, she says, laughing, in this video "the nurses are wearing Calvin Klein 'uniforms' and Yves Saint Laurent shoes.") Following the hospital scene, a woman playing the part of her best friend, Bo, takes her back to her Stanton Street apartment, where Gaga undresses and gets into bed. And then, after she's in bed, she gets a phone call informing her that she's been dropped by her record label. Prior to filming this scene, Gaga asks the few of us assembled in her trailer how far she should go with this. She decides to go all the way. "It's chaotic," she says, "and sad. But I don't want it to be safe."

Outside the set made to look like her original apartment—with a mattress on the floor, dirty dishes in the sink, a hot plate, open cereal boxes, a leather jacket draped over a chair, a keyboard—she prepares to film the scene. She has a short dark wig on and is wearing a Stéphane Rolland dress that has latex blood along the hem. She and "Bo" are wearing gloves and heels. "We look like we just came from church," she says, joking, then takes a sip out of a bottle of Jameson's. I mutter something about how the Catholic Church will view this. "What, as if I'm their pinup girl to begin with?" she says. Clearly, this was a traumatic day; now this video is a cathartic experience for her. The soundtrack comes on; she tells me it's the Beethoven sonata *Pathétique*. As she prepares to film the scene, she starts to cry, and hugs her choreographer, Richie Jackson. She's the director and the actress, and, she says, with those two jobs "I have to get my bearings." Then she adds, "I'm getting ready to relive the worst day of my life." Tears roll down her face, and she turns to me. But, I say, you won. You *won*.

The following night, motor homes and trucks are lined up on 126th Street in Harlem. Gaga is filming another scene for the "Marry the Night" video, this time on the rooftop of a parking garage. Joe Germanotta is there; Cynthia had been there earlier. Joe and I talk about how pissed off we are about the Yankees' loss in the playoffs and Alex Rodriguez in particular. Everyone is given earplugs because cars are about to be exploded. The pyrotechnic guys are wearing what look like protective fireproof suits. They set fire to three cars. The explosions are loud; it's like an action movie. Gaga, wearing a short blond wig, a skimpy black leather outfit, and thigh-high black leather boots, says in a determined voice, "I'm going in." And as the cars burst into flames and we all hold our collective breath, Gaga walks—no, she *struts*—fearlessly, up to the fire.

(Lady Gaga would go on to win two Golden Globes and nine Grammys, earning three Academy Award nominations, including a 2018 Oscar for best original song.)

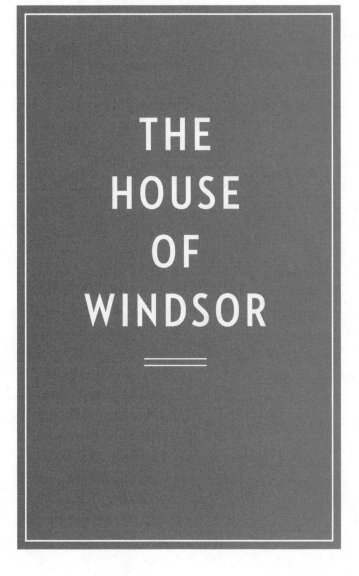

THE
HOUSE
OF
WINDSOR

LOVE AND MAJESTY

By Sally Bedell Smith | January 2012

here was a whole battalion of lively young men," recalled Lady Anne Glenconner, whose family were friends and neighbors of King George VI and Queen Elizabeth at Sandringham, their estate in Norfolk. But Princess Elizabeth, the heiress presumptive to the British throne, "realized her destiny and luckily set her heart on Prince Philip at an early age. He was ideal—good-looking and a foreign prince."

Her choice was in some respects traditional, because the princess and Philip were relatives, but not too close to raise eyebrows. They were third cousins, sharing the same great-great-grandparents, Queen Victoria and Prince Albert. Philip was in fact more royal than Elizabeth, whose mother was mere British nobility (with distant links to English and Scottish kings), while his parents were Princess Alice of Battenberg (a great-grandchild of Queen Victoria) and Prince Andrew of Greece, the descendant of a Danish prince recruited for the Greek throne in the mid-19th century. Elizabeth and Philip were both connected to most of Europe's reigning families, where consanguinity had been common for centuries. Queen Victoria and her husband had been even closer: first cousins who shared the same grandmother, the Dowager Duchess of Coburg.

In other ways, Philip was an outlier with a decidedly unconventional background. Queen Elizabeth had made no secret of her preference for one of her daughter's aristocratic English friends from a family similar to her own English-Scottish Strathmores—the future Dukes of Grafton, Rutland, and Buccleuch, or Henry Porchester, the future Earl of Carnarvon. Philip could boast none of their extensive landholdings, and in fact had very little money.

Although he was born on June 10, 1921, on the isle of Corfu, Philip spent scarcely a year in Greece before the entire royal family was expelled in a coup. His parents took him, along with his four older sisters, to Paris, where they lived rent-free in a house owned by wealthy relatives. A proud professional soldier with an extroverted personality and a quick wit, Prince Andrew found himself at loose ends, while Alice (properly known as Princess Andrew of Greece after her wedding) had difficulty managing a large family, not least because she was congenitally deaf.

After Philip's parents sent him at the age of eight to Cheam, a boarding school in England, his mother had a nervous breakdown and was committed to a sanitarium for several years, which precipitated his parents' permanent separation. She eventually moved to Athens and established a Greek Ortho-dox order of nuns.

Prince Andrew was mostly absent from his son's life as well, living as a "boulevardier" in Monte Carlo with a mistress, and subsisting on a small an-nuity, while beneficent relatives and friends paid Philip's school fees. He left Cheam in 1933 to spend one year at Salem, a boarding school in Germany run by a progressive Jewish educator named Kurt Hahn. After the Nazis briefly detained Hahn, he fled in 1934 to the North Sea coast of Scotland and founded Gordonstoun School, where Philip soon enrolled.

Once in the United Kingdom, Philip came under the wing of his relatives there, chiefly his Battenberg grandmother, the Dowager Marchioness of Mil-ford Haven, who lived in a grace-and-favor apartment in Kensington Palace, and his mother's younger brother, Louis "Dickie" Mountbatten, later the first Earl Mountbatten of Burma, who assiduously cultivated his royal relatives.

Six feet tall, with intense blue eyes, chiseled features, and blond hair, Philip was an Adonis as well as athletic and engaging, exuding confidence and a touch of impudence. He was a resourceful and energetic self-starter, yet he was also something of a loner, with a scratchy defensiveness that sprang from emotional deprivation. "Prince Philip is a more sensitive person than you would appreciate," said his first cousin Patricia Mountbatten, Dickie's older daughter. "He had a tough childhood, and his life constrained him into a hard exterior in order to survive."

As cousins, Philip and young Elizabeth had crossed paths twice, first at a family wedding in 1934 and then at the coronation of King George VI in 1937. But it wasn't until July 22, 1939, when the King and Queen took their daughters to the Royal Naval College at Dartmouth, that the 13-year-old princess spent any time with 18-year-old Philip, who was a cadet in training at the school.

At the behest of Dickie Mountbatten, an officer in the Royal Navy, Philip was invited to have lunch and tea with the royal family. Marion "Crawfie" Crawford, Princess Elizabeth's governess, observed the sparks, later writing that Lilibet, as she was called, "never took her eyes off him," although he "did not pay her any special attention"—no surprise, since he was already a man of the world, and she only on the cusp of adolescence. While everything else in the life of Lilibet was laid out for her, she made the most important decision on her own. "She never looked at anyone else," said Elizabeth's cousin Margaret Rhodes.

During the war years, Philip came to visit his cousins occasionally at Windsor Castle, and he and the princess corresponded when he was at sea, serving with the Royal Navy in the Mediterranean and the Pacific. Friends and relatives detected a flutter of romance between Philip and Elizabeth by December 1943, when he was on leave at Windsor for Christmas and watched Elizabeth, then 17, perform in the "Aladdin" pantomime. The King was quite taken by Philip, telling his mother the young man was "intelligent, has a good sense of humour and thinks about things in the right way." But both the King and Queen thought that Lilibet was too young to consider a serious suitor.

Philip visited Balmoral, the royal family's estate in the Scottish Highlands, in the summer of 1944, and he wrote Queen Elizabeth about how he savored "the simple enjoyment of family pleasures and amusements and the feeling that I am welcome to share them." That December, while Philip was away on active duty, his father died of cardiac arrest at age 62 in the room where he lived at the Hotel Metropole, in Monte Carlo. All he left his 23-year-old son were some trunks containing clothing, an ivory shaving brush, cuff links, and a signet ring that Philip would wear for the rest of his life.

While Philip was completing his deployment in the Far East, Lilibet enjoyed the freedom of the postwar period. At a party given by the Grenfell family at their Belgravia home in February 1946 to celebrate the peace, the princess impressed Laura Grenfell as "absolutely natural . . . she opens with a very easy and cosy joke or remark. . . . She had everyone in fits talking about a sentry who lost his hat while presenting arms." Elizabeth "danced every dance. . . . Thoroughly enjoying herself" as the "Guardsmen in uniform queued up."

Philip finally returned to London in March 1946. He took up residence at the Mountbatten home on Chester Street, where he relied on his uncle's butler to keep his threadbare wardrobe in good order. He was a frequent visitor to Buckingham Palace, roaring into the side entrance in a black MG sports car to join Lilibet in her sitting room for dinner, with Crawfie acting as duenna. Lilibet's younger sister, Margaret, was invariably on hand as well, and Philip included her in their high jinks, playing ball and tearing around the long corridors. Crawfie was taken with Philip's breezy charm and shirtsleeve informality—a stark contrast to the fusty courtiers surrounding the monarch.

During a month-long stay at Balmoral late in the summer of 1946, Philip proposed to Elizabeth, and she accepted on the spot, without even consulting her parents. Her father consented on the condition that they keep their engagement a secret until it could be announced after her 21st birthday, the following April. Like the princess, Philip didn't believe in public displays of affection, which made it easy to mask his feelings. But he revealed them privately in a touching letter to Queen Elizabeth in which he wondered if he deserved "all the good things which have happened to me," especially "to have fallen in love completely and unreservedly."

Palace courtiers and aristocratic friends and relatives of the royal family viewed Philip suspiciously as a penniless interloper. They were irked that he seemed to lack proper deference toward his elders. But mostly they viewed him as a foreigner, specifically a "German" or, in their less gracious moments, a "Hun," a term of deep disparagement after the bloody conflict so recently ended. Even though his mother had been born in Windsor Castle, and he had been educated in England and served admirably in the British Navy, Philip had a distinctly Continental flavor, and he lacked the clubby proclivities of the Old Etonians. What's more, the Danish royal family that had ruled in Greece was in fact predominantly German, as was his maternal grandfather, Prince Louis of Battenberg.

None of the criticisms of Philip's German blood or cheeky attitude was of any concern to Princess Elizabeth. A man of ideas and appealing complexity, he was a breath of fresh air to the heiress presumptive. It was clear that he would not be easy, but he would certainly not be boring. He shared her commitment to duty and service, but he also had an irreverence that could help lighten her official burdens at the end of a tiring day. His life had been as unfettered as hers had been structured, and he was unencumbered by the properties and competing responsibilities of a landed British aristocrat. According to their mutual cousin, Patricia Mountbatten, the princess also saw that, behind his protective shell, "Philip had a capacity for love which was waiting to be unlocked, and Elizabeth unlocked it."

The princess "would not have been a difficult person to love," said Patricia Mountbatten. "She was beautiful, amusing and gay. She was fun to take dancing or to the theater." In the seven years since their first meeting, Lilibet (which is what Philip now called her, along with "darling") had indeed become a beauty, her appeal enhanced by being petite. She did not have classical features but rather what *Time* magazine described as "pin-up" charm: big bosom (taking after her mother), narrow shoulders, a small waist, and shapely legs. Her curly brown hair framed her porcelain complexion, with cheeks that the photographer Cecil Beaton described as "sugar-pink," vivid blue eyes, an ample mouth that widened into a dazzling smile, and an infectious laugh. "She sort of expands when she laughs," said Margaret Rhodes. "She laughs with her whole face."

The press caught wind of the cousins' romance as early as October 1946, at the wedding of Patricia Mountbatten to Lord Brabourne at Romsey Abbey. Philip was an usher, and when the royal family arrived, he escorted them from their car. The princess turned as she removed her fur coat, and the cameras caught them gazing at each other lovingly. But no official confirmation followed, and the couple kept up an active social life. Elizabeth's guardsmen friends served as her escorts to restaurants and fashionable clubs, and Philip would take Elizabeth and Margaret out to a party or a play. But he was only one among many young men to dance with the heiress presumptive.

He had been working as an instructor at the Naval Staff College, in Greenwich, and with the help of Dickie Mountbatten had secured his British citizenship in February 1947, giving up his title as H.R.H. Prince Philip of Greece. Since he had no surname, Philip decided on Mountbatten, the English version of his mother's Battenberg.

The long-delayed engagement announcement came on July 9, 1947, followed by the happy couple's introduction at a Buckingham Palace garden party the next day. Philip's mother retrieved a tiara from a bank vault, and he used some of the diamonds to design an engagement ring created by Philip Antrobus, Ltd., a London jeweler. Several months later Philip was confirmed in the Church of England by the Archbishop of Canterbury.

Just before his daughter's wedding, the King gave his future son-in-law a collection of grand titles—Duke of Edinburgh, Earl of Merioneth, and Baron Greenwich—and decreed that he should be addressed as "His Royal Highness." He would be called the Duke of Edinburgh, although he would continue to be known popularly as Prince Philip and would use his Christian name for his signature.

On November 18, the King and Queen had a celebratory ball at Buckingham Palace that dramatist Noël Coward called a "sensational evening. . . . Everyone looked shiny and happy." Elizabeth and Philip were "radiant. . . . The whole thing was pictorially, dramatically and spiritually enchanting." As was his habit, the King led a conga line through the staterooms of the palace, and the festivities ended after midnight. Philip was in charge of distributing gifts to his fiancée's attendants: silver compacts in the Art Deco style with a gold crown above the bride's and groom's entwined initials and a row of five small cabochon sapphires. With typical insouciance, "he dealt them out like playing cards," recalled Lady Elizabeth Longman, one of the two non-family members among the eight bridesmaids.

The morning of the wedding, two days later, Philip gave up smoking, a habit that had kept his valet, John Dean, "busy refilling the cigarette boxes." But Philip knew how anguished Elizabeth was by her father's addiction to cigarettes, so he stopped, according to Dean, "suddenly and apparently without difficulty." Patricia Brabourne, who was also with her cousin that morning, said that Philip wondered if he was being "very brave or very foolish" by getting married, although not because he doubted his love for Lilibet. Rather, he worried that he would be relinquishing other aspects of his life that were meaningful. "Nothing was going to change for her," his cousin recalled. "Everything was going to change for him."

Outside Westminster Abbey, tens of thousands of spectators gathered in freezing temperatures to welcome the princess and her father in the Irish State Coach. Two thousand guests enjoyed the splendor of the 11:30 A.M. ceremony in the abbey, an event that Winston Churchill called "a flash of colour on the hard road we have to travel." Elizabeth's dress, which had been designed by Norman Hartnell, was of pearl-and-crystal-encrusted ivory silk satin, with a 15-foot train held by the two five-year-old pages, Prince William of Gloucester and Prince Michael of Kent, who wore Royal Stewart tartan kilts and silk shirts. Her tulle veil was embroidered with lace and secured by Queen Mary's diamond tiara, and Philip's naval uniform glinted with his new Order of the Garter insignia pinned to his jacket. The Archbishop of York, Cyril Garbett, presided, telling the young couple that they should have "patience, a ready sympathy, and forbearance."

After the hour-long service, the bride and groom led a procession down the nave that included the crowned heads of Norway, Denmark, Romania, Greece, and Holland. Noticeably absent was the King's brother, former King Edward VIII, now the Duke of Windsor, and his wife, for whom he had abdicated the throne. The estranged Windsors were living in Paris, unwelcome in London except for periodic visits. Although their exile may have seemed harsh, George VI, Queen Elizabeth, and their advisers had seen no alternative. A king and former king living in the same country would have resulted in two rival courts.

While the bells of the abbey pealed, Elizabeth and Philip were driven to Buckingham Palace in the Glass Coach, preceded and followed by two regiments of the Household Cavalry on horseback. It was the most elaborate public display since the war, and the crowds responded with ecstatic cheers.

As a concession to Britain's hard times, only 150 guests attended the "wedding breakfast," which was actually luncheon in the Ball Supper Room. The "austerity" menu featured filet de sole Mountbatten, perdreau en casserole, and bombe glacée Princess Elizabeth. The tables were decorated with pink and white carnations, as well as small keepsake bouquets of myrtle and white Balmoral heather at each place setting. The bride and groom cut the wedding cake—four tiers standing nine feet high—with Philip's Mountbatten sword.

The King didn't subject himself to the strain of making a speech, celebrating the moment instead with a raised glass of champagne to "the bride." After being showered with rose petals in the palace forecourt, the newlyweds were transported in an open carriage drawn by four horses—"the bride snugly ensconced in a nest of hot-water bottles"—to Waterloo Station.

They spent a week at Broadlands, the Mountbatten estate in Hampshire, and two weeks in snowbound seclusion at Birkhall, an early-18th-century white stone lodge on the Balmoral estate, set in the woods on the banks of the river Muick. With its Victorian décor and memories of childhood summers before her parents became King and Queen, Elizabeth could relax in a place she considered home. Dressed in army boots and a sleeveless leather jacket lined with wool, she went deerstalking with her husband, feeling "like a female Russian commando leader followed by her faithful cut-throats, all armed to the teeth with rifles," she wrote to Margaret Rhodes.

She also sent her parents tender letters thanking them for all they had given her, and the example they had set. "I only hope that I can bring up my children in the happy atmosphere of love and fairness which Margaret and I have grown up in," she wrote, adding that she and her new husband "behave as though we had belonged to each other for years! Philip is an angel—he is so kind and thoughtful." Philip revealed his carefully cloaked emotions when he wrote to his mother-in-law, "Cherish Lilibet? I wonder if that word is enough to express what is in me." He declared that his new wife was "the only 'thing' in this world which is absolutely real to me and my ambition is to weld the two of us into a new combined existence that will not only be able to withstand the shocks directed at us but will also have a positive existence for the good."

The honeymooners were back in London in time for the 52nd birthday of King George VI, on December 14, ready to begin their new life. They chose to live in Clarence House, the 19th-century residence adjacent to St. James's Palace, just down the Mall from her parents. But the house needed extensive renovations, so they moved temporarily into an apartment in Buckingham Palace. Philip had a paper-pushing job at the Admiralty, to which he would walk on weekdays. Elizabeth was kept busy by her private secretary, John "Jock" Colville.

By May 1948, Elizabeth was four months pregnant, and behind closed doors was suffering from nausea. Even so, she and Philip kept up an active social life. They went to the races at Epsom and Ascot and joined friends at restaurants, nightclubs, and dances. For a costume party at Coppins, the home of the Duchess of Kent, Elizabeth dressed "in black lace, with a large comb and mantilla, as an Infanta," wrote diarist Chips Channon, and "danced every dance until nearly 5 A.M." Philip "was wildly gay," Channon observed, in a "policeman's hat and hand-cuffs. He leapt about and jumped into the air as he greeted everybody."

When they were with friends such as Rupert and Camilla Nevill and John and Patricia Brabourne, the royal couple showed an easy affection toward each other. During a visit to the Brabournes in Kent, John said to Philip, "I never realized what lovely skin she has." "Yes," Philip replied, "she's like that all over."

In the early evening of November 14, 1948, word went out that Princess Elizabeth had gone into labor in her second-floor bedroom at Buckingham Palace, where a hospital suite had been prepared for the baby's arrival. Philip passed the time playing squash with three courtiers. Senior members of the household gathered in the Equerry's Room, a ground-floor drawing room that was equipped with a well-stocked bar, and shortly afterward were told that Elizabeth had given birth to a seven-pound-six-ounce son at 9:14. They set to work writing "Prince" on telegrams and calling the Home Office, Prime Minister Clement Attlee, and Winston Churchill, the leader of the opposition. "I knew she'd do it!" exclaimed Commander Richard Colville, press secretary to the King, exultant over the arrival of a male heir. "She'd never let us down."

Sir John Weir, one of the official physicians to the royal family, confided to Queen Elizabeth's private secretary, Major Thomas Harvey, that he'd "never been so pleased to see a male organ in all his life." Queen Elizabeth was "beaming with happiness," and George VI was "simply delighted by the success of everything." Philip, still dressed in sneakers and sports clothes, joined his wife as her anesthesia wore off, presented her with a bouquet of roses and carnations, and gave her a kiss.

Elizabeth and Philip named their son Charles Philip Arthur George. "I had no idea that one could be kept so busy in bed—there seems to be something happening all the time!," Elizabeth wrote to her cousin Lady Mary Cambridge two weeks after giving birth. "I still find it hard to believe that I really have a baby of my own!" The new mother was particularly taken with her son's "fine, long fingers—quite unlike mine and certainly unlike his father's," as she described them in a letter to her former music teacher, Mabel Lander. For nearly two months the princess breast-fed her son, until she fell ill with measles—one of several childhood diseases she had missed by being tutored at home rather than going to school with classmates—and Charles had to be sent away temporarily so that he wouldn't catch the illness.

When the family moved into Clarence House, early in the summer of 1949, Elizabeth and Philip had adjacent, connecting bedrooms. "In England the upper class always have had separate bedrooms," explained their cousin Lady Pamela Mountbatten (later Hicks). "You don't want to be bothered with snoring, or someone flinging a leg around. Then when you are feeling cozy you share your room sometimes. It is lovely to be able to choose."

That October, Philip resumed active service when he was appointed first lieutenant and second-in-command of the destroyer H.M.S. *Chequers*, based on the small island nation of Malta, in the Mediterranean, which had been part of the British Empire since 1814 and served as an important shipping center and outpost for the Mediterranean Fleet. According to John Dean, the royal couple "were advised that conditions [in Malta] were not suitable for the infant Prince." Elizabeth could have stayed in London with her son, but she decided instead to spend as much time as possible with her husband. She had been accustomed to long parental absences while she was growing up, so her decision to leave Charles wouldn't have raised eyebrows. She had expert nannies in charge, not to mention her own parents, who were eager to keep their grandson company. Elizabeth would visit Malta for long stretches of time, returning at intervals to Clarence House.

She left six days after Charles's first birthday, in time to join Philip for their second wedding anniversary. Beyond minimal royal obligations, Elizabeth was given unaccustomed freedom and anonymity. "I think her happiest time was when she was a sailor's wife in Malta," said Margaret Rhodes. "It was as nearly an ordinary a life as she got." She socialized with other officers' wives, went to the hair salon, chatted over tea, carried and spent her own cash—although shopkeepers "noticed that she was slow in handling money," according to biographer Elizabeth Longford. The royal couple lived a significant cut above the ordinary, however, in Earl Mountbatten's Villa Guardamangia, a spacious sandstone house built into a hill at the top of a narrow road, with romantic terraces, orange trees, and gardens. Dickie Mountbatten was commanding the First Cruiser Squadron, and his wife, Edwina, accompanied Elizabeth on her first flight to Malta.

Philip and Elizabeth spent Christmas of 1949 on the island, while their son stayed with his grandparents at Sandringham. After *Chequers* sailed out for duty in the Red Sea at the end of December, the princess flew back to England. She stopped first for several days in London, with a detour to Hurst Park to see her steeplechaser, Monaveen, win a race, before she was re-united with Charles in Norfolk after five weeks apart.

————

When Philip returned from naval maneuvers, Elizabeth rejoined him in Malta at the end of March 1950 for an idyllic six weeks. Much to Uncle Dickie's delight, he and his wife spent a lot of time with the royal couple, exploring the island's coves by boat, sunbathing, and picnicking. They cheered the Mountbattens' younger daughter, Pamela, when she won the ladies' race at the riding club, and in the evenings they went to the Phoenicia Hotel for dinner and dancing.

During these weeks, Elizabeth grew closer to the uncle who had taken such a prominent role in her husband's life. He gave her a polo pony and went riding with her, encouraging her to perfect her skills at sidesaddle, which she "loathed," recalled Pamela, "because she felt out of touch with the horse. She felt marooned up there and much preferred to ride astride." But in part because of Uncle Dickie's persistence, "she was a very good sidesaddle rider."

Also at Dickie's urging, Philip took up polo—"a very fast, very dangerous, very exciting game." Elizabeth shrewdly advised him how to persuade her husband: "Don't say anything. Don't push it. Don't nag. Just leave it alone."

On May 9 she flew back to London, six months pregnant and ready to resume some of her royal duties. Jock Colville had left the household the previous autumn to return to the diplomatic corps, and his replacement was 36-year-old Martin Charteris, who was enraptured by the princess on their first meeting.

Elizabeth gave birth at Clarence House on August 15, 1950, at 11:50 A.M., to her second child, Anne Elizabeth Alice Louise. Philip had returned to London two weeks earlier, which gave him time to get re-acquainted with his 21-month-old son after almost a year away. But his first command, of the frigate H.M.S. *Magpie*—and a promotion to lieutenant commander—sent him back to Malta in early September. As she had with Charles, Elizabeth breast-fed her daughter for several months. She celebrated Charles's second birthday and left shortly thereafter for Malta. Yet again the family was split at Christmas, with mother and father celebrating on their own while the children were at Sandringham with their grandparents, who unabashedly doted on them. Queen Elizabeth sent regular letters to her daughter, reporting Charles "giving himself an ecstatic hug," Anne "so pretty & neat & very feminine," and "Everybody loves them so, and they cheer us up more than I can say."

But the couple's time in the Mediterranean was coming to an end. King George VI had been in declining health since 1948, increasingly plagued by pain and numbness resulting from arteriosclerosis. In March 1949 he had undergone surgery to improve circulation in his legs. He continued to carry out his duties, but his appearance was gaunt, and by May 1951 he was seriously ill with a chronic cough that did not respond to treatment.

Elizabeth came home to stand in for her father at a variety of events, and Philip returned to London in July when it became clear that the royal couple would be needed full-time to represent the sovereign. He took an open-ended leave from the navy, but in effect the 30-year-old duke was ending his military career after only 11 months of enjoying the satisfaction of his own command—"the happiest of my sailor life." Much later Philip would say philosophically, "I thought I was going to have a career in the Navy but it became obvious there was no hope. . . . There was no choice. It just happened. You have to make compromises. That's life. I accepted it. I tried to make the best of it."

In September, George VI had a biopsy that revealed a malignancy, and surgeons removed his left lung in a three-hour operation. The cancer diagnosis was not openly discussed and certainly not given out to the press, but the family understood the severity of the King's condition.

Elizabeth and Philip had been scheduled to leave for a state visit to Canada and the United States, which they postponed by two weeks until they were reassured that her father was in no imminent danger. They departed at midnight on October 8, 1951, and arrived 16 hours later in Montreal—the beginning of a 35-day trek of more than 10,000 miles to the Pacific and back.

The essential public routine that the royal couple would use over the decades took shape in those long days: Elizabeth was the restrained presence, her smiles tentative and infrequent, which prompted criticism in some press accounts. "My face is aching with smiling," she complained to Martin Charteris when she heard the reports on her dour demeanor. Philip, always at a discreet distance behind, was already providing comic relief. Once, he went over the line, committing the first of his famous "gaffes" when he jokingly observed that Canada was "a good investment"—a remark that stuck in the Canadians' craw for its neo-imperial implication.

The scope and pace of the trip were punishing. They made more than 70 stops, and on a single day in Ontario they visited eight towns. Through it all, Elizabeth worried about the health of her father. Philip tried to keep the atmosphere light, but he clearly found the journey stressful. "He was impatient. He was restless," recalled Martin Charteris. "He hadn't yet defined his role. He was certainly very impatient with the old-style courtiers and sometimes, I think, felt that the Princess paid more attention to them than to him. He didn't like that. If he called her a 'bloody fool' now and again, it was just his way. I think others would have found it more shocking than she did."

For much of the trip, Philip wore his naval uniform, and Elizabeth favored discreetly tailored suits and close-fitting hats, as well as fur coats and capes. During their visit to Niagara Falls, they had to wear oilskin suits on the spray-lashed observation deck. Pulling her hood tight, Elizabeth exclaimed, "This will ruin my hair!"

Several weeks later, the royal couple boarded a plane for Washington and set foot on American soil for the first time on October 31. President Harry S. Truman observed that his daughter, Margaret, who had met the princess during a visit to England, "tells me when everyone becomes acquainted with you, they immediately fall in love with you." The 67-year-old president counted himself among them, calling Elizabeth a "fairy princess." Elizabeth enunciated every word of her reply, her high voice a model of cut-glass precision, proclaiming that "free men everywhere look towards the United States with affection and with hope."

At a Rose Garden ceremony, the royal couple presented the Trumans with a mirror adorned with a painting of flowers, to be hung in the refurbished Blue Room as a "welcome ornament . . . a mark of our friendship." Their visit ended with a white-tie dinner in honor of the Trumans at the Canadian Embassy.

They had a rough return trip across the North Atlantic aboard the *Empress of Scotland*. Only Elizabeth managed to avoid seasickness and show up regularly at mealtimes, and veteran sailor Philip was furious about his own weakness. On arrival at the Liverpool dockyards three days after Prince Charles's third birthday, they boarded the Royal Train for London's Euston Station. Waiting on the platform were Queen Elizabeth, Princess Margaret, and Prince Charles, who had not seen his parents in more than a month.

When the princess and duke stepped off the train, Elizabeth rushed to hug her mother and kiss her on both cheeks. For tiny Charles, she simply leaned down and gave him a peck on the top of his head before turning to kiss Margaret. "Britain's heiress presumptive puts her duty first," explained a newsreel announcer. "Motherly love must await the privacy of Clarence House." Prince Philip was even less demonstrative, touching his son on the shoulder to indicate they should move along to the waiting limousines. As they passed through the station, Prince Charles was again with his grandmother, while his parents walked ahead.

After Christmas, the ailing King deputed Elizabeth and Philip to represent him on a long-planned six-month tour of Australia, New Zealand, and Ceylon. The couple decided to add several days in the beginning of the trip to visit the British colony of Kenya, which had given them a retreat at the foot of Mount Kenya called Sagana Lodge as a wedding gift. After settling into the lodge, Elizabeth and Philip spent a night at Treetops Hotel, a three-bedroom cabin built among the branches of a large fig tree above an illuminated salt lick in a game preserve. Dressed in khaki trousers and a bush scarf, Elizabeth excitedly filmed the animals with her movie camera. At sunset, she and Philip spotted a herd of 30 elephants. "Look, Philip, they're pink!" she said, not realizing that the gray pachyderms had been rolling in pink dust.

Back at Sagana on the morning of February 6, the princess's aides learned that the 56-year-old King had died from a blood clot in his heart. Princess Elizabeth Alexandra Mary was now Queen, at age 25. When Philip was told, he muttered that it would be "the most appalling shock" for his wife, then walked into her bedroom and broke the news to her. She shed no tears, but looked "pale and worried."

"What are you going to call yourself?" asked Martin Charteris as

Elizabeth came to grips with the loss of her father. "My own name, of course. What else?" she replied. But some clarification was necessary, since her mother had been called Queen Elizabeth. The new monarch would be Queen Elizabeth II (following her 16th-century predecessor, Elizabeth I), but she would be known as the Queen. Her mother would become Queen Elizabeth the Queen Mother, rather than the fustier Dowager Queen. Elizabeth II would be Queen Regnant, and her royal cypher E II R.

"It was all very sudden," she recalled four decades later. Her task, she said, was "kind of taking it on, and making the best job you can. It's a question of maturing into something that one's got used to doing, and accepting the fact that here you are, and it's your fate, because I think continuity is important."

Dressed in a simple black coat and hat, she held her composure as she arrived at the airport in London near dusk on February 7, 1952, after a 19-hour flight. Waiting on the tarmac was a small delegation led by her uncle the Duke of Gloucester and Prime Minister Winston Churchill. She slowly shook hands with each of them, and they gave her deep bows. A Daimler bearing the sovereign's coat of arms on its roof drove her to Clarence House, where 84-year-old Queen Mary honored her by reversing roles, curtsying and kissing her hand, although she couldn't help adding, "Lilibet, your skirts are much too short for mourning."

The next day, the new Queen went to St. James's Palace, where she appeared for 20 minutes before several hundred members of the Accession Council, a ceremonial body including the Privy Council—the principal advisory group to the monarch, drawn from senior ranks of politicians, the clergy, and the judiciary—along with other prominent officials from Britain and the Commonwealth. She had been monarch since the moment of her father's death, but the council was convened to hear her proclamation and religious oath. She would not be crowned until her coronation, in 16 months, but she was fully empowered to carry out her duties as sovereign.

The men of the council bowed to the 40th monarch since William the Conqueror took the English throne after the Battle of Hastings, in 1066. Elizabeth II declared in a clear voice that "by the sudden death of my dear father,

I am called to assume the duties and responsibilities of sovereignty. My heart is too full for me to say more to you today than I shall always work, as my father did throughout his reign, to advance the happiness and prosperity of my peoples, spread as they are the world over. . . . I pray that God will help me to discharge worthily this heavy task that has been lain upon me so early in my life." As her husband escorted her out, she was in tears.

By April, the royal family had moved to Buckingham Palace, and the new Queen adapted to an office schedule that has scarcely varied throughout her reign. Adjusting to his position as the Queen's consort proved troublesome for Philip. "For a real action man, that was very hard to begin with," said Patricia Brabourne. While everything was mapped out for Elizabeth II, he had to invent his job under the scrutiny of her courtiers, and he had no role model to follow.

Prince Philip was still considered an outsider by some senior officials of the court. "Refugee husband," he mockingly referred to himself. "Philip was constantly being squashed, snubbed, ticked off, rapped over the knuckles," said John Brabourne. Much of the wariness stemmed from Philip's closeness to Dickie Mountbatten. "My father was considered pink—very progressive," Patricia Brabourne recalled. "The worry was that Prince Philip would bring into court modern ideas and make people uncomfortable."

The most hurtful rebuff had occurred in the days following the King's death, after Queen Mary heard that Dickie Mountbatten had triumphantly announced that "the House of Mountbatten now reigned." She and her daughter-in-law the Queen Mother were angered by his presumption, and the Queen shared their view that she should honor the allegiance of her grandfather and her father to the House of Windsor by keeping the Windsor name rather than taking that of her husband. Churchill and his Cabinet agreed. Philip responded with a memo to Churchill vigorously objecting to the prime minister's advice and pressing instead for the House of Mountbatten, which was ironic. It was his mother's family name, since his father had given him no surname.

The Queen failed to foresee that her actions would have a profound impact on Philip, leading to strains in their marriage. "She was very young," said Patricia Brabourne. "Churchill was elderly and experienced, and she accepted his constitutional advice. I felt that if it had been later she would have been able to say, 'I don't agree.'"

"I am the only man in the country not allowed to give his name to his children," Philip fumed to friends. "I'm nothing but a bloody amoeba." Dickie Mountbatten was even more outspoken, blaming "that old drunk Churchill" who "forced" the Queen's position. The prime minister mistrusted and resented Earl Mountbatten, largely because as India's last Viceroy, appointed by Prime Minister Clement Attlee, he had presided over that country's move to independence. "Churchill never forgave my father for 'giving away India,'" said Patricia Brabourne.

Behind the scenes, Dickie continued a campaign to reverse the decision, with his nephew's acquiescence. Meanwhile, Philip resolved to support his wife while finding his own niche, which would lead in the following decades to the active patronage of more than 800 different charities embracing sports, youth, wildlife conservation, education, and environmental causes.

Within the family, Philip also took over management of all the royal estates, to "save her a lot of time," he said. But even more significantly, as Prince Charles's official biographer Jonathan Dimbleby wrote in 1994, the Queen "would submit entirely to the father's will" in decisions concerning their children.

She made Philip the ultimate domestic arbiter, Dimbleby wrote, because "she was not indifferent so much as detached." Newspaper editor and Conservative politician William Deedes saw in Elizabeth's detachment "her struggle to be a worthy head of state, which was a heavy burden for her. The Queen in her own quiet way is immensely kind, but she had too little time to fulfill her family care. I find it totally understandable, but it led to problems."

Following her coronation, on June 2, 1953, the Queen turned her full attention to an ambitious five-and-a-half-month world tour covering 43,000 miles, from Bermuda to the Cocos Islands, by plane and ship. It was her first extended trip as sovereign, and the first time a British monarch had circled the globe.

Five-year-old Prince Charles and three-year-old Princess Anne spoke to the Queen and Prince Philip by radiotelephone, but otherwise news of their progress came in regular letters from the Queen Mother, who had them for weekends at Royal Lodge, her house in Windsor Great Park. Just as Elizabeth and Margaret had followed their parents' travels on maps, Prince Charles traced his parents' route on a globe in his nursery.

The crowds everywhere were enormous and enthusiastic. Masses of welcoming boats jammed Sydney Harbor, and by one count, three-quarters of Australia's population came out to see the Queen. At age 27 she was hailed as the "world's sweetheart." But the royal couple refused to let their celebrity go to their heads. "The level of adulation, you wouldn't believe it," Philip recalled. "It could have been corroding. It would have been very easy to play to the gallery, but I took a conscious decision not to do that. Safer not to be too popular. You can't fall too far."

The Duke of Edinburgh also helped his wife stay on an even keel when she became frustrated after endless hours of making polite conversation. Meeting and greeting thousands of people at receptions and garden parties actually gave her a temporary facial tic. But when she was watching a performance or a parade, and her face was in repose, she looked grumpy, even formidable. As the Queen herself once ruefully acknowledged, "The trouble is that, unlike my mother, I don't have a naturally smiley face." From time to time, Philip would jolly his wife. "Don't look so sad, Sausage," he said during an event in Sydney. Or he might provoke a grin by reciting Scripture at odd moments, once inquiring sotto voce, "What meaneth then this bleating of the sheep?"

At Tobruk, in Libya, the Queen and Prince Philip transferred to *Britannia*, the new, 412-foot royal yacht with a gleaming deep-blue hull, which they had designed together with architect Sir Hugh Casson. For its maiden voyage, *Britannia* took Prince Charles and Princess Anne to be re-united with their parents in early May 1954 for the first time in nearly half a year. The Queen was pleased that she would be seeing her children earlier than she had anticipated, but she worried that they wouldn't know their parents.

Still, when the moment came and the Queen was piped aboard, her strict control and conformity to protocol prevailed as it had when she met her son after her Canada trip. "No, not you, dear," she said as she greeted dignitaries first, then shook the five-year-old's extended hand. The private reunion was warm and affectionate as Charles showed his mother all around the yacht, where he had been living for more than a week. The Queen told her mother how happy she was to be with her "enchanting" children again. They had both "gravely offered us their hands," she wrote, "partly I suppose because they were somewhat overcome by the fact that we were really there and partly because they have met so many new people recently! However the ice broke very quickly and we have been subjected to a very energetic routine and innumerable questions which have left us gasping!"

In the autumn of 1957, the royal couple set off for their second trip to the United States, a state visit hosted by the 67-year-old president, Dwight D. Eisenhower, with whom the Queen had an affectionate relationship that dated back to World War II, when he was in London as supreme allied commander. Unlike the Queen's lightning visit in 1951, this would be a full-dress affair: six days in Washington, New York, and Jamestown, Virginia, where she would celebrate the 350th anniversary of the founding of the first British colony in America.

After a day-long visit to Williamsburg and Jamestown on October 16, the royal couple flew to Washington on Eisenhower's aircraft, the *Columbine III*, a swift and sleek propeller plane with four powerful engines. As they waited to take off, Philip immersed himself in a newspaper while Elizabeth unlocked her monogrammed leather writing case and began writing postcards to her children. "Philip?" she suddenly said. Her husband kept reading. "Philip!" she repeated. He glanced up, startled. "Which engines do they start first on a big plane like this?" Her husband looked momentarily perplexed. "Come on now," she said with a laugh. "Don't wait until they actually start them, Philip!" He offered a guess, which turned out to be correct. (They went in sequence, first on one wing from the inner engine to the outer, then the inner followed by the outer on the other wing.) "He was flustered," recalled Ruth Buchanan, wife of Wiley T. Buchanan Jr., Eisenhower's chief of protocol, who sat nearby. "It was so like what an ordinary wife would do when her husband wasn't paying attention."

Riding into the capital with the president and his wife, Mamie, in a bubbletop limousine, accompanied by 16 bands, they were cheered along the route into Washington by more than a million people, who were undaunted by intermittent rain showers. The royal couple spent their four nights in the most elegant guest quarters in the recently renovated White House—the Rose Suite, furnished in Federal style, for the Queen, and the Lincoln Bedroom for the Duke of Edinburgh.

Much of the visit was given over to the usual receptions, formal dinners at the White House and British Embassy (complete with gold plates flown over from Buckingham Palace), and tours of local sights. It was evident to Ruth Buchanan that the Queen was "very certain, and very comfortable in her role. She was very much in control of what she did, although she did laugh at my husband's jokes." Once, when Buchanan was waiting for her husband to escort the royal couple to their limousine, "I could hear her guffawing. You didn't realize she had that hearty laugh. But the minute she rounded the corner and saw us, she just straightened up."

Vice President Richard Nixon treated the royal couple to a luncheon with 96 guests in the orchid-bedecked Old Supreme Court Chamber, in the Capitol. Elizabeth had specifically asked to see an American football "match," so the White House arranged for her to sit in a "royal box" at the 50-yard line at the University of Maryland's Byrd Stadium for a game against the University of North Carolina. On the way she spotted a Giant supermarket and asked if a visit might be arranged so she "could see how American housewives shop for food."

To the cheers of 43,000 spectators, the Queen walked onto the field to chat with two opposing players. Dressed in a $15,000 mink coat given to her by the Mutation Mink Breeders Association, a group of American fur farmers, she watched the game intently but seemed "perturbed" whenever the players threw blocks. While the royal pair was being entertained at halftime, security men raced back to the supermarket to arrange for a royal visit on the fly. After Maryland's 21–7 victory, the motorcade arrived at the Queenstown Shopping Center at five P.M., to the amazement of hundreds of shoppers. Elizabeth and Philip had never before seen a supermarket, a phenomenon then unknown in Britain.

With the curiosity of anthropologists and an informality they had not displayed publicly in Britain, they spent 15 minutes shaking hands, quizzing customers, and inspecting the contents of shopping carts. "How nice that you can bring your children along," said Elizabeth, nodding toward the little seat in one housewife's cart. She took a particular interest in frozen chicken pot pies, while Philip nibbled on sample crackers with cheese and joked, "Good for mice!"

An exuberant welcome awaited them in New York City. The Queen had asked specifically to see Manhattan "as it should be approached," from the water, a vista she had been dreaming about since childhood. "Wheeeee!" she exclaimed as she caught her first glimpse of the Lower Manhattan skyline from the deck of a U.S. Army ferryboat. A crowd of 1.25 million lined the streets from Battery Park to City Hall and northward to the Waldorf-Astoria for their ticker-tape parade.

She had only 15 hours in the city to fulfill her wish list and shake some 3,000 hands. Wearing a dark-blue satin cocktail dress and close-fitting pink velvet hat, she addressed the representatives of 82 countries at the United Nations General Assembly. At the conclusion of her six-minute speech, the audience of 2,000 responded with "a thunderous standing ovation." During a reception with delegates, Philip talked to Soviet ambassador Andrei Gromyko about the recently launched Sputnik satellite.

The royal couple were fêted at two meals at the Waldorf: a luncheon for 1,700 hosted by Mayor Robert Wagner and a dinner for 4,500 given by the English-Speaking Union and the Pilgrims of the United States. In between, the Queen took in the "tremendous" view from the 102nd floor of the Empire State Building at twilight—another specific request. As the white-tie banquet began, in the Grand Ballroom, the punishing schedule was beginning to take its toll, even on an energetic 31-year-old Queen. *The New York Times* noted that her speech was the "one time during the program . . . when the fatigue showed through . . . She made no effort to force a smile . . . and although she stumbled over her text only once, her voice plainly showed it."

Her final stop that night was a Royal Commonwealth ball for another 4,500 guests at the Seventh Regiment Armory, on Park Avenue. One aviator blinded in World War I tried to get up from his wheelchair to greet her. "She put a gentle hand on his shoulder and told him that he should not rise," recalled Wiley Buchanan. "She spoke to him for several moments, then moved on."

"You both have captivated the people of our country by your charm and graciousness," Eisenhower wrote in his farewell letter to the royal couple.

After a hiatus of six years, the 31-year-old monarch was keen to have more children, as was her husband. Dickie Mountbatten blamed the delay on Philip's anger over the Queen's rejection of his family name after the accession. But by her own account, she had postponed her dream of having a large family primarily because she wanted to concentrate on establishing herself as an effective monarch.

During a visit to Buckingham Palace in 1957, Eleanor Roosevelt met with Elizabeth for nearly an hour the day after Prince Charles had undergone a tonsillectomy. The former First Lady found her to be "just as calm and composed as if she did not have a very unhappy little boy on her mind." Elizabeth reported that Charles had already been fed ice cream to soothe his painful throat, yet it was 6:30 in the evening, and she was compelled to entertain the widow of a former U.S. president rather than sit at the bedside of her eight-year-old son.

While the Queen certainly loved her children, she had fallen into professional habits that kept her apart from them much of the time. They benefited from nurturing nannies and a doting grandmother. But because of her dogged devotion to duty, amplified by her natural inhibitions and aversion to confrontation, Elizabeth had missed out on many maternal challenges as well as satisfactions.

In May 1959, after Philip's return from a four-month goodwill tour aboard *Britannia*, Elizabeth got pregnant at last. Once she hit the six-month mark, she withdrew from her official duties. But one bit of unfinished business needed to be resolved. When Prime Minister Harold Macmillan visited her at Sandringham in early January 1960, she told him that she needed to revisit the issue of her family name, which had been irritating her husband since she decided in 1952 to use Windsor rather than Mountbatten. "The Queen only wishes (properly enough) to do something to please her husband—with whom she is desperately in love," the prime minister wrote in his diary. "What upsets me . . . is the Prince's almost brutal attitude to the Queen over all this." Somewhat cryptically he added, "I shall never forget what she said to me that Sunday night at Sandringham."

Macmillan left shortly afterward for a trip to Africa, leaving the resolution of the Queen's tricky family problem to Rab Butler, his deputy prime minister, and Lord Kilmuir, who served as the government's legal arbiter as the lord chancellor. Butler sent a telegram to Macmillan in Johannesburg on January 27, saying that the Queen had "absolutely set her heart" on making a change for Philip's sake. By one account, Butler confided to a friend that Elizabeth had been "in tears."

Following discussions among her private secretaries and government ministers, a formula emerged in which the royal family would continue to be called "the House and Family of Windsor," but the Queen's "de-royalised" descendants—starting with any grandchildren who lacked the designation of "royal highness"—would adopt the surname "Mountbatten-Windsor." Those in the immediate line of succession, including all of the Queen's children, would continue to be called "Windsor." It seemed clear-cut, but 13 years later Princess Anne, at the urging of Dickie and Prince Charles, would contravene the policy on her wedding day by signing the marriage register as "Mountbatten-Windsor."

Elizabeth announced the compromise in a statement on February 8, 1960, saying, "The Queen has had this in mind for a long time and it is close to her heart." On February 19, at 33, she gave birth to her second son. In a gesture of wifely devotion, Elizabeth named the boy Andrew, after the father Philip had lost 15 years earlier.

THE MOUSE THAT ROARED

By Tina Brown | October 1985

When the Prince and Princess of Wales arrive in Washington next month, they step into intense curiosity about the state of their marriage. Magazines and newspapers in every capital crackle with backstairs backchat about the princess's autocratic ways. *She* has banished all his old friends. *She* has made him give up shooting. *She* throws slippers at him when she can't get his attention. *She* spends all his money on clothes. *She* forces him to live on poached eggs and spinach. *She* keeps sacking his staff. Certainly forty members of their household have resigned, including his private secretary, Edward Adeane, whose family had served the monarchy since Queen Victoria. The debonair Prince of Wales, His Royal Highness, Duke of Cornwall, heir to the throne, is, it seems, pussywhipped from here to eternity.

Can it be true? Is it possible that the girl they picked to be the Royal Mouse of Windsor has turned into Alexis Carrington [of the prime-time soap-opera *Dynasty*] in the space of four years? In the TV age it is irresistible to see such snippets of royal family life as a long-playing soap opera. Like the Ewings [of *Dallas*], most of them live in the same square mile of the royal ranch of Kensington Palace—the Wales apartments near Princess Margaret's and the Duke and Duchess of Gloucester's, and next door to Prince and Princess Michael of Kent's.

Even in the country they choose to live on top of each other in the

"Tallyho Ridge" of huntin' Gloucestershire. Recent episodes of the royal soap have starred Princess Michael, the Wagnerian blonde married to Prince Charles's cousin. She's the one whose father was revealed to be an SS officer and who, in a second burst of bad luck, was caught emerging from an Eaton Square apartment in a red wig followed by Texas millionaire John Ward Hunt. Another episode featured the royal-christening row when Princess Diana did not invite Princess Anne to be a godmother to Prince Harry. Anne snubbed the ceremony and spent the day shooting rabbits instead. (Her ratings recovered during her tour of India, when she was recast as Dame Peggy Ashcroft in *The Jewel in the Crown*.)

Back at Buck House, the Queen and Prince Philip are not amused by all this. *They're* concerned about what is happening to the future King of England since he got married. As it happens, it's a lot more interesting and complex than a scenario from Aaron Spelling Productions. Only a novelist like George Eliot, who understood that character is destiny, could fully capture the nuances of how the royal couple are acting on each other under a very peculiar set of circumstances.

A curious role reversal has taken place in the marriage.

Princess Diana, the shy introvert unable to cope with public life, has emerged as the star of the world's stage. Prince Charles, the public star unable to enjoy a satisfying private life, has made peace at last with his inner self. While he withdraws into his inner world, his wife withdraws into her outer world. Her panic attacks come when she is left alone and adulation-free on wet days at Balmoral; his come when his father tells him he must stop being such a wimp and behave like a future king. What they share is an increasing loss of reality. Ironically, both are alienated by the change in the other.

To understand why this has happened, one has to look behind the public images.

Prince Charles has for decades been presented as Action Man, jumping out of helicopters and being kissed by beauty queens in Australia. The truth is, he was always a lonely, eccentric figure haunted by self-doubt. Like the Queen, he had to work hard on his appeal, and he developed a dry sense of humor to cope with it all. He kept sane with the rigors of physical exercise and a battery of ballsy blondes who brought in refreshing gusts from the world outside. Lady Diana Spencer in 1980 was very different from most of the women Prince Charles had been attracted to in the past. Even though he looked so painfully conservative, he's always had a streak of bohemianism, however crushed by royal life. He liked the flamboyant girls of the seventies who put him in touch with that streak: Sabrina Guinness, who worked in Hollywood as Tatum O'Neal's nanny; Lady Jane Wellesley, an independent minded BBC journalist; Davina Sheffield, who went off on adventurous volunteer work to Vietnam. All were good, punchy company.

In 1980, Prince Charles was on the rebound from his affair with Anna "Whiplash" Wallace. Wallace was a dangerous version of Lady Diana—tall, blond, but a reckless horsewoman. Prince Charles was sexually obsessed by her and would probably have married her if the press hadn't revealed her past. Shortly afterward she unceremoniously dumped him.

It was following the Wallace debacle that Prince Charles began to see that he must snap up the shy little sister of his friend Sarah Spencer because the chances of another eligible virgin coming his way were slim. She was not very bright, but she had a sweet nature. At school her chief academic accolades were the Leggatt Cup for Helpfulness and the Palmer Cup for Pets' Corner (for being kind to her guinea pig, Peanuts). If he passed her up he would find himself like a royal Roman Polanski dating thirteen-year-old girls when he was forty. The press, led by Nigel Dempster, had corralled poor Lady Diana and were howling for a happy ending. His family wanted it. The public wanted it. Like the last Prince of Wales, he liked to confide in married women, and his two favorites, Lady Tryon and Camilla Parker-Bowles, wanted it. They had met the blushing little Spencer girl and deduced she was not going to give them any trouble. Better her than another fiery number like Anna Wallace. Prince Charles was exhausted. He proposed.

But Diana's famed shyness was one of her most misleading character traits. It is not the bashfulness of youth, but the statement of her whole style of operating. The generation gap between the royal couple is far more profound than a matter of age. It is the yawning sensibility gap between the Me generation and the yuppie generation. The Princess of Wales is mentally and emotionally light-years away from the career girls, the rebels, the bolters, the experimenters Prince Charles associated with in his dancing years. She is one of the new school of born-again old-fashioned girls who play it safe and breed early. Postfeminist, post-verbal, her femininity is modeled on a fifties concept of passive power. The style is all summed up by her voice, which is flat, almost gruff, with half-swallowed vowels—"Pritz Chuls" for Prince Charles, "yaw" for yes, "hice" for house. When, at a dance at Broadlands, an overenthusiastic American millionaire told her, "Your Royal Highness, I'd love a signed photograph of you," she barked, "Tough luck." With the voice goes a total absence of intellectual curiosity. Another hallmark of the type is a streak of quiet tenacity, developed, no doubt, from the age of six, when her homelife was shattered by her mother's departure with a wallpaper tycoon. She is a female type we don't often meet in the modern novel, but the Victorians knew her well. In *Middlemarch* she appears as Rosamond Vincy, the exquisite blonde with the swan's neck whose decorous extravagance in the face of her husband's pleas to desist finally breaks his spirit.

Diana's passive power chimes very well with the needs of modern royalty. What is required is an image, a symbol, a charismatic focus for Britain's inchoate feelings of nationhood in a gloomy period of history. Like the Queen Mother, another iron mouse, Diana's uninterpretative mind did not pause to analyze the mechanism of her own appeal, but she knew how to use it instinctively. That's why she began her extraordinary physical transformation from mouse to movie star. When Charles and Diana announced their engagement in 1981, they had scarcely had time to get to know each other. He had done his duty and hoped it would work out. But his feelings changed subsequently in Australia, when he saw the image of the girl he'd left behind flowering on the front page of every newspaper. Royal biographer Anthony Holden tells me that on that tour he watched Prince Charles fall in love with her before his very eyes.

Shortly after their marriage I met the Prince and Princess of Wales at a black-tie dinner at the American Embassy in London. It was Diana's most beguiling moment, when the star quality was emerging but the schoolgirl was still there. We were asked to form up in groups of four to be introduced. The playwright Tom Stoppard was in my group. It was the first time I'd ever seen him lost for words. She came first, pure and fresh and charmingly angular in her choker and senior-prom manner. She was wearing a pale-blue dress that seemed to have been spun out of moonbeams, and her skin had the pink sheen of a cultured pearl. She was startlingly more self-possessed than when I'd met her a year before, leading the small talk with a slightly pointed chin, gallantly keeping it afloat. I told her I had come back from a wonderful trip to Venice on the Orient-Express. "I can never sleep on trains, can you?" she replied. When Charles joined her, his accomplished manner was much less effective. "I've thought of a good idea for a play," he told Tom Stoppard. "It's about a hotel which caters entirely for people with phobias. It was a small item in the *Times*." "We'll go halves on the take, sir," said Stoppard kindly. "Actually, I thought it was so amusing," Prince Charles persisted, "I telephoned Spike Milligan [the British comedian] and told him. It's a most frightfully funny idea, don't you think?" His words conjured up a poignant picture: Prince Charles asking his secretary to put through a call to Milligan, who, after conquering his astonishment, had to listen politely and humor the royal desire to throw out a spark that might ignite somewhere.

They moved on to the next group. The easy chat halted as they approached. I was struck by the exhausting oddness of always approaching silent people who stood there waiting to be addressed. But even at this early stage Diana had evolved a perfect way to deal with it. Her small talk was fine, but she didn't really have to speak at all. She had perfected the art of detaching herself and being a presence. Every pair of eyes followed her hungrily as she bid the ambassador a slim, luminous good-night.

Since then the astonishing power of her fame has stamped out the schoolgirl. She is much more self-conscious about her image, much more professional. She created a fashion style in England by heightening and glamorizing the basic wardrobe requirements of the Sloane Ranger—old-fashioned pearl choker, low pumps, piecrust frills, and good earrings at all times. Now, with her shoulder pads and frosted bearskin hairdo, it's all gone Hollywood. On her Italian tour she disregarded her private advisers at British *Vogue* and belly flopped in the fashion press when she emerged in a repertoire of heinous hats. The instinctive style that carried her through is turning into a new obsession with her image. She spends hours studying her press clippings—almost as if she's trying to figure out for herself the secret of her mystique. She was furious when it was reported she spent £100,000 on her wardrobe for Italy. Like Jackie O before her, she shops compulsively to relieve the tension and is probably unaware, in the rush it gives her, of what it all costs. "Where did you get your figures?" she challenged one royal hack.

She is in that adversary mood toward the press that is the first stage in the removal from life that fame inflicts. The second stage is "Graceland," when the real world melts away altogether. There is a danger that this has started to happen to Diana. Apart from the children's tea parties at Highgrove and Kensington Palace, her social life is nonexistent. One of her closest post-marriage friends is the young Duchess of Westminster, whose children are often summoned to partake of the quivering mounds of royal Jell-O. Lately, "Tally" Westminster complains, the princess never returns her calls. Likewise, Diana's twenty-one-year-old brother, Lord Althorp, an Oxford undergraduate, is concerned with how remote she's become. With "Wills" and "Harry" looked after by three nannies, Diana spends hours cut off in her Sony Walkman, dancing on her own to Dire Straits and Wham! It's difficult for Charles to recall her from her isolation, because he's even more cut off than she is.

He doesn't seem to mind anyway. The realization that the spotlight is off him has enabled Prince Charles to relax his own arduous self-projection for the first time in his life. He has understood about Diana what Queen Elizabeth has always known about the Queen Mother—that she's a natural star. ("If it were Mummy, they would all be cheering," the Queen is said to have commented sadly at a subdued rally.) The pressure has fallen from Charles, leaving him free to be irresponsible at last. It's a release that has finally allowed him the postadolescent rebellion against the Teutonic boorishness of Prince Philip. Relations between father and son these days are so strained that when Prince Charles walks into a room Prince Philip walks out of it. He expressed his displeasure by not visiting Prince Harry until six weeks after the birth.

This suits Prince Charles, who is indulging in the luxury of being himself. It was not Diana who turned him into a fish-and-fowl freak. What he eats is not of much interest to her, since she's permanently on a diet.

It was his own brooding on biofeedback that led him up this path and also to insist that the Duchy of Cornwall farms be run on the latest organic lines. A posse of unlikely gurus have entered his life—Laurens van der Post, with his talk of mystical and religious experiences in Africa; Patrick Pietroni, a leading exponent of holistic medicine; Dr. Miriam Rothschild, an authority on fleas, who invented a seed mix of weeds and wild flowers known as "farmer's nightmare," which Charles has sown around his Highgrove acres; and a medium named Dr. Winifred Rushworth, whose books encouraged him to make contact on a Ouija board with the shade of his beloved "Uncle Dickie" Mountbatten. Again, it was not the princess who discouraged him from shooting. Perhaps he found it made a nonsense of his new conservation stance. Nor, most important, was it Diana who drove out the trusted Edward Adeane, along with Oliver Everett, Diana's private secretary, and Francis Cornish, the prince's assistant private secretary, who recently hopped it to some white man's grave in Borneo.

Adeane left because he was utterly dismayed by the motley crew of mystics, spiritualists, and self-sufficiency freaks acting as the prince's unofficial advisers. He simply could not stand working for a man whose private office had become redundant. He wanted Prince Charles to confront the need to create a serious role in British national life. He urged Charles to make Queen Elizabeth give him something real to do. With his opera interests he could, say, become chairman of the Royal Opera House. With his gardening interests he could be secretary of the Royal Horticultural Society. Dammit, there were respectable *public* outfits for Charles's new solitary passions. But Charles frustrated Adeane by refusing to push himself forward. Instead he took the chance to dismantle his office. It meant there would be no one to nag him anymore about duty. His tally of official engagements dropped off noticeably. He seemed to become obsessed with his children. Like John Lennon, who spent the last years of his life as a recluse playing with his son in the Dakota, Prince Charles has turned into a house husband.

No one is more dismayed by all this than his wife. When Diana fell in love with Charles, he was a James Bond smoothy with a glamorous sheen of metropolitan amours. Now he wants to be a farmer. It is hard to overestimate the boredom of the royal schedule she has to endure. All the royal houses are like second-rate hotels to live in, with the inmates complaining rustily that dinner was "bloody awful!" Sandringham, situated near the freezing Norfolk Broads, is the worst, but Balmoral, where Charles spends most of the summer up to his ankles in the river fishing, is also the scene of hellishly convivial family picnics and Princess Margaret playing the piano until two in the morning. It's not surprising that when she fled one autumn, Diana had only two words to say in explanation—"Boring. Raining."

Charles, for his part, was happy for his bride to evolve into the Super Sloane Ranger, but less wild about the excesses of the new princessly development. His estates bring him an income of over £1 million a year, but he is frugal to the point of meanness. One of his less endearing traits is to check the refrigerator at Highgrove for any sign the servants are overeating at his expense. Diana, appalled at the house's discomfort when she first saw it, immediately went into overdrive with the interior designer Dudley Poplak to create a comfortable, if predictably chintzy, country home.

Her lack of intellect discourages Charles. Recently he made a weekend trip to a friend's house, without Diana, to study its magnificent garden. His European hostess spoke perfect English, and he complimented her. "My father believed in educating girls," she laughed. "I wish," said Prince Charles, "that had been the philosophy in my wife's family."

If Princess Diana is a very young twenty-four, he is a very old thirty-six. Only Prince Charles could have picked a navy-blue suit to wear to the Live Aid concert. He allowed Diana to stay for only an hour before dragging her away to watch polo. ("My wife made me go to some pop jamboree," he grumbled to a friend.)

Unsurprisingly, they have few mutual cronies. There's a worthy country-bumpkin couple called the Palmer-Tomkinsons who share their skiing interests, and Lord Vestey's second wife, Celia, a senior Sloane Ranger who enjoys a certain lukewarm favor, but the old faithfuls like banker Lord Tryon and Lieutenant Colonel Andrew Parker Bowles and their frisky wives, who did so much to divert the bachelor Charles, have been banished since the marriage (a satisfyingly comic dénouement from Diana's point of view). Bonds have weakened with other inseparables like Tory M.P. Nicholas "Fatty" Soames, Winston Churchill's grandson, who offer a more sophisticated line in conversation. ("Pass the port, he's not my sort" is one of his catchphrases.) Soames recently called his son "Harry" to curry favor with Prince Charles, but Diana is unswayed and is said to find him "heavy furniture." And since Prince Charles cannot abide the Diana clones who are her old buddies, or the neo-Neanderthal Hooray Henrys who escort them, the Waleses can find very few weekend guests for house parties. For the anniversary of Handel's birth, in July, Prince Charles invited four hundred "friends" to a musical evening with the Royal Philharmonic Orchestra at Buckingham Palace. It was a private evening, but none of their peer group was present. The guests were all ambassadors, dignitaries, and assorted oldsters. The princess followed Prince Charles around looking glum.

Sometimes, through the looking glass, she sees glimpses of another life.

Earlier this year, while Prince Charles stayed at home worrying about the beet crop, Diana attended a charity fund-raiser escorted by her favorite English fashion designer, Bruce Oldfield. It was a chic, young evening. Oldfield is amusing company. The princess was supposed to leave at midnight, like Cinderella, but she stayed on and on. When Charlotte Rampling's husband, the charming French musician Jean-Michel Jarre, asked her to dance, the princess positively lit up. One guest told me, "Everyone within twenty yards got the fallout from Diana's mood that night. She was suddenly aware of everything she was missing."

It is somehow typical of Prince Charles that he was a yuppie when everyone else was a yippie, and now that everyone else has gone straight he's discovered the flower child's concern with brown rice and spiritualism. He's in just the kind of mood to fall in love with a nursery-school teacher in flat shoes who's kind to guinea pigs and babies.

If he looks hard enough, she's still there.

(The Waleses divorced in 1996 after a long separation. The following year, in Paris, Diana and her companion Dodi Fayed died, along with their chauffeur, Henri Paul, when their Mercedes S280 crashed while attempting to elude a band of paparazzi. Another passenger, bodyguard Trevor Rees-Jones, though injured, survived. Paul was later discovered to have been inebriated at the time of the accident.

Charles would marry Camilla Parker Bowles [Camilla, Duchess of Cornwall] in 2005.)

THE
STARS

GRACE KELLY'S FOREVER LOOK

By Laura Jacobs | May 2010

t may be the softest kiss in film history. The sun is setting over West Side rooftops, the sky persimmon. A man, his leg in a cast, sleeps near an open window, undisturbed by a neighbor singing scales. Just after the highest note is reached, a shadow climbs over the man's chest, shoulder, and chin. We see a face: blue eyes, red lips, skin like poured cream, pearls. Then he sees it. The kiss happens in profile, a slow-motion hallucinatory blur somewhere between myth and dream, a limbic level of consciousness. The director, Alfred Hitchcock, liked to say he got the effect by shaking the camera. In truth, this otherworldly kiss comes to us by way of a double printing. Has any muse in cinema been graced with such a perfect cameo portrait of her power?

"How's your leg?" she murmurs. "It hurts a little," Jimmy Stewart answers. Another soft kiss, more teasing questions. "Anything else bothering you?" she asks. "Uh-huh," he says. "Who are you?"

Who, indeed! In 1954, when *Rear Window* premiered, Grace Kelly had been in only four films. She was hardly known to the public, and then she was suddenly known—a star. In her first film, *Fourteen Hours*, she played an innocent bystander, on-screen for two minutes and 14 seconds. In her second, Fred Zinnemann's *High Noon*, she co-starred as the pacifist bride of embattled sheriff Gary Cooper. In her third movie, John Ford's *Mogambo*, she was the prim wife of an anthropologist (Donald Sinden) and Jane to big-game hunter Clark Gable's Tarzan. It was a steep and impressive learning curve, straight to the top. By the time Hitchcock got his hands on her, figuratively speaking, casting himself as Pygmalion to her Galatea, Grace Kelly was ready for her close-up. Hitchcock gave her one after another, in three films that placed her on a pedestal—*Dial M for Murder*, *Rear Window*, and *To Catch a Thief*—enshrining her as an archetype newly minted. "A snow-covered volcano" was how he put it. She was ladylike yet elemental, suggestive of icy Olympian heights and untouched autonomy yet, beneath it all, unblushing heat and fire. By 1956, two years, six films, and one Academy Award after *Rear Window*—while the country was still wondering, Who *are* you, Miss Kelly?—she was gone, off to Europe to marry a prince, whence she would become Her Serene Highness Princess Grace of Monaco.

The appearance and then sudden disappearance of gifted, beautiful blondes is not unknown to Hollywood. Before Grace Kelly's five-year phase of radiance in the 50s, there was Frances Farmer, whose brilliance roused the industry for six years, from 1936 to 1942. Like Kelly, Farmer was intelligent, her own person, and a serious actress wary of binding contracts. In 1957, only a year after Grace Kelly's departure, Diane Varsi took the baton, making a big impression as a sensitive ingénue in *Peyton Place*. Varsi, too, was both smart and skeptical of Hollywood, and fled the industry in 1959. (She returned in the late 60s, but without momentum.) Farmer and Varsi left, respectively, in mental and emotional disarray. The word "disarray," however, would never find its way into a sentence that included the name Grace Kelly. She was always in control. Always prepared. Always well groomed and well mannered, delightful and kind. And always, eternally it seems, beautiful.

Though it is in *Rear Window* where Grace Kelly achieves full iconic stature, answering Stewart's question by circling the room in her pure-white snowcap of a skirt, there is nothing "rear window" about her. She states her full name as she switches on three lights, and her picture-window, Park Avenue perfection is itself a kind of incandescence. Here was a white-glove glow to make men gallant and women swoon, and it was present whether she was dressed in dowdy daywear (her beloved wool skirts and cashmere cardigans) or in the confections of Hollywood designers and Paris couturiers. Hitchcock goes so far as to make a joke of it. "She's too perfect," Jimmy Stewart complains. "She's too talented. She's too beautiful. She's too sophisticated. She's too everything but what I want." And it was true, except for that last, because at the moment when Miss Kelly left Hollywood the whole world wanted her.

The story of Grace Kelly has been told and retold by friends, journalists, historians, and hacks. This April, it will be told yet again, not in words but in artifacts, when London's Victoria and Albert Museum unveils the exhibition "Grace Kelly: Style Icon." It begins as her story must, in Philadelphia, where she was born on November 12, 1929. Baby pictures aside, the image that seems to set her life in motion is one that recurs in a series of vacation snapshots. It is Grace as a little girl on the Jersey Shore, being twirled in the air by her father, who looks Herculean in a tank suit as he swings her by her legs or by an arm and a leg. The photos capture an essential dynamic: Jack Kelly was the vortex of his family, and its life revolved around him—his principles, his dreams, his drive.

Jack's goal was success in all things, pursued honestly yet relentlessly, and his drive was physical. It manifested itself both in sports—he was celebrated for winning three Olympic gold medals in sculling (one newspaper called him "the most perfectly formed American male")—and in business, where his construction company, Kelly for Brickwork, became the largest of its kind on the East Coast. His sex drive was Herculean, too. Marriage did not limit Jack's love life, which was discreet but busy. In many ways the Kellys were like the Kennedys—bright, shining, charismatic, Irish-Catholic Democrats, civically and politically engaged. (Jack once ran for Philadelphia mayor, losing by only a small margin.) Similarly, Kelly women were expected to be team players—outdoorsy, sporting, and supportive of their men.

Margaret Majer Kelly, Grace's mother, was herself an impressive physical specimen. A former cover-girl model and competitive swimmer, she was the first woman to teach physical education at the University of Pennsylvania. Her German-Protestant discipline meshed nicely with her husband's can-do spirit; when they married, she converted to Catholicism. Despite their winning energies, the Kellys were not social climbers. In the Philadelphia of those days, Irish Catholics, even rich ones, were outsiders. Thus the family never lived on the fabled Main Line, as so many Americans thought they had (because Hollywood publicists decided they had). The Kellys built a 17-room home in the Philadelphia neighborhood of East Falls, overlooking the Schuylkill River, upon which Jack rowed. And there they stayed, enviably wealthy, sailing through the Great Crash without a dip because Jack didn't play the stock market.

Grace Patricia Kelly was the third child of four and the only one without a clear definition. Peggy, extremely witty and her father's favorite, was the eldest. John junior, born second, was the only boy. ("Kell" would become a champion rower like his father, not because he wanted to but because his father expected him to.) And Lizanne was the baby. Grace was defined by what she wasn't: not athletic, not outgoing, not boisterously healthy (she suffered sinus trouble and asthma). A much-repeated family story has young Grace locked in a cupboard by tempestuous Lizanne; instead of crying to get out, Grace stayed quietly locked in, playing with her dolls, *for hours*. "She seemed to have been born with a serenity the rest of us didn't have," Lizanne later explained. Unfortunately, serenity didn't particularly impress Jack. Grace was active in a place where it didn't show: her imagination. Early on, she told her sister Peggy, "One day I'm going to be a princess."

Make-believe was where Grace excelled, both in playing with her dolls and in class theatricals, beginning with her first big role—the Virgin Mary in the Ravenhill-convent-school Nativity pageant—and continuing through high school. Years later, as she was just gaining notice in Hollywood, the *Los Angeles Times* would write that she "came seemingly out of nowhere." This was not true. Alongside the sporting blood in the Kelly clan ran a more verbal line of showmanship—the stage. Jack Kelly had two brothers who had gained fame in the theater: Walter Kelly, a successful vaudevillian, and George Kelly, a Pulitzer Prize–winning playwright. George became Grace's mentor and confidant. It was he who encouraged her dream of acting, who warned her about Hollywood's feudal studio system, and whose name helped her win late admission to the renowned American Academy of Dramatic Arts, in Manhattan. Grace's parents did not want her to leave home for New York. According to close friend Judith Balaban Quine, who would be one of Grace's six bridesmaids and later the author of *The Bridesmaids: Grace Kelly, Princess of Monaco, and Six Intimate Friends*, Jack Kelly thought acting "a slim cut above streetwalker"—not an uncommon view at the time. But Grace was adamant. "She got away from home early," her brother, Kell, once said. "None of the rest of us managed to do that."

Grace did well at the academy, and in her graduation performance played the role of Tracy Lord, the privileged heiress in *The Philadelphia Story*. This was the beginning of the potent, sometimes prophetic connection between life and art that would reverberate through the career of Grace Kelly. When in 1949 she won her first big part on Broadway—the daughter in *The Father*, with Raymond Massey in the lead—it was again a role in sync with her own situation: the loving daughter who must break away from a powerful family. Grace got good notices, which brought calls from New York television producers, but Broadway did not fall at her feet. The problem was her voice: it was too high, too flat (those sinuses), and not easily projected over the footlights. She put a clothespin on her nose and worked to bring her voice down a register, to achieve clarity and depth. The result was diction with a silver-spoon delicacy—slightly British—and the stirring lilt of afternoon tea at the Connaught. The Kellys teased Grace mercilessly, this putting on airs, but her new voice would be key.

So would her walk. Grace had studied ballet as a girl, keen on becoming a ballerina, but she grew too tall (five feet six) to be a classical dancer in that era. She never, however, lost her ballet posture or a dancer's awareness of her limbs in space. Furthermore, she'd paid her own tuition at the academy by doing lucrative work, making more than $400 a week as a commercial model for the John Robert Powers agency, selling soap, cigarettes, whatever, in print ads. This too contributed to a poise, an inner stillness, in the way she moved. Her walk became something unique: regal above the waist, shoulders back and head high, and a floating quality below, akin to a geisha's glide, or a swan's. In fact, Grace developed her acting chops not onstage but in the live "playhouse" television dramas that were a new form of entertainment in the early 50s, and one of her more than 30 TV appearances was in a shortened version of Ferenc Molnár's *The Swan*. In this play, Grace, as a princess, must choose between young love and a destiny tied to duty, a life where she will "glide like a dream on the smooth surface of the lake and never go on the shore. . . . There she must stay, out on the lake, silent, white, majestic." It's hard not to feel clairvoyance in this metaphor.

Add in the white gloves she wore to auditions—unheard of in the drafty, gypsy world of theater—and the neutral hose, the low-heeled shoes, the slim wool skirts, the camel-hair coat, the horn-rimmed glasses (she was near-sighted), and the less-is-more makeup. Well, Grace was her mother's daughter, and Margaret had never approved of frippery.

"She was fun and jolly and pretty and nice to have around," says Laura Clark, who was an editor at *Harper's Bazaar* when she met Grace, in the early 1950s, still a struggling actress. Clark remembers her style of dress as "very conservative. You know, the circle pin and the white collars. The sweater-and-tartan-skirt look. Almost schoolgirlish." Fellow actress and close friend Rita Gam described Grace's daytime style as that of a "small-town high-school teacher," while fashion designer Oleg Cassini, whom Grace would begin dating in 1954 and almost marry, called it her "Bryn Mawr look."

Maree Frisby Rambo, Grace's best friend from childhood, says that, growing up, Grace wasn't terribly interested in clothes. "We all wore about the same thing. Sweaters and skirts and loafers and socks. It was like a uniform. Dances and things, she'd wear a dress of Peggy's." That changed when Grace left home. "I remember she'd been in New York for a while," Rambo recalls. "She came to Philadelphia, and I invited her to the Cricket Club to go swimming, and she appeared, and she just looked different. Whatever she had on was so chic, as opposed to us. She looked New York, where the rest of us looked Chestnut Hill."

So the voice, the walk, the reserved bluestocking style—it all came together in a kind of crystalline equation. You couldn't say it was calculated. Grace *was* well brought up, and disciplined, and cultured, and shy. She was only highlighting what she had, just as when she took the advice of her modeling friend Carolyn Reybold, who told her to stop hiding her too square jaw under a pageboy and instead accentuate her jawline. Grace pulled back her hair and pulled on her gloves. All that was left now was for the right camera to find her.

S
he would never have had a career in the theater," Don Richardson told Robert Lacey, whose definitive biography, *Grace*, was published in 1994. Richardson was a theater director who worked with academy students, and he was also one of Grace's lovers. "Great looks and style, yes, but no vocal horsepower." One day, though, Richardson was studying some photographs he'd taken of Grace, and a headshot transfixed him. "When you looked at that picture, you were not looking at her. You were looking at the illusion of her. . . . The camera did more than love her. It was insane about her—just like I was. When I looked at that photograph, I knew that her future would have to be in pictures."

In *The Face of the World*, the photographer Cecil Beaton explains why the camera was insane for Grace Kelly. "She has, most important of all, a nice nose for photography: flat, it hardly exists at all in profile." This meant it wouldn't cast shadows that could trouble the cameraman. Furthermore, Beaton writes, "all photogenic people have square faces. . . . [Grace's] mouth, the tip of her nose, her nostrils—all are extremely sensitive. Their beauty is effective against the rugged background of the square face."

Grace's first film, *Fourteen Hours*, was not the one that set her movie career in motion. And while 1952's *High Noon* put her on the map, it was more of a spotlight than a spark. No, the touchstone was a little black-and-white screen test she shot for Twentieth Century Fox in early 1950, for a movie called *Taxi*, the part of a poor Irish girl. Grace didn't get the role, but the test hung around. In 1952 it caught the eye of John Ford, who said, "This dame has breeding, quality and class." He cast her in *Mogambo*. A year later, Alfred Hitchcock saw the test. He was in need of a leading lady for *Dial M for Murder*, having lost his previous muse, Ingrid Bergman, who'd run off with the married director Roberto Rossellini. On the basis of the *Taxi* audition, plus a scene or two of *High Noon* (in which he thought her "mousy"—a compliment), Grace was hired. "From the *Taxi* test," Hitchcock explained, "you could see Grace's potential for restraint." He liked what he called her "sexual elegance."

Grace's rise in Hollywood was swift, and her self-possession was stunning. On her own, she worked out an enviable seven-year contract with MGM, one that allowed her the freedom to live in Manhattan every other year, so she could pursue the stage, which was still her dream. She had no qualms about turning down stupid scripts, and was tight-lipped when reporters asked personal questions. Financially prudent and secure, she didn't have to accept second-rate stuff or play the publicity game. "She selects clothes and stories and directors with the same sureness," said eminent Hollywood designer Edith Head, who dressed Grace in four films. "She's always right." Grace loved the feeling of family on a movie set, and was adored by her colleagues, whether they were people behind the scenes or stars such as Ray Milland, Cary Grant, and Frank Sinatra. Oddly, the brass at MGM never seemed to understand their Miss Kelly, or value what they had in her. Of the nine movies she made after signing with MGM, five were with other studios to whom MGM lent her out. *The Country Girl*, a serious drama for which she won her best-actress Oscar, was made at Paramount.

The year 1955 was a big one for Grace. She had four films in the theaters and was the year's highest-earning female star; at the Academy Awards, not only did she win an Oscar but Bob Hope declared, "I just wanna say, they should give a special award for bravery to the producer who produced a movie *without* Grace Kelly." That same year she rose to the top of the Best-Dressed List, sharing the No.1 spot with socialite and *Über*-Wasp Babe Paley, who wore mostly Mainbocher. That Grace, who did not wear couture, could tie with Babe, who did, attests to Grace's discerning eye. "The stylish image of Grace Kelly was everywhere," writes H. Kristina Haugland in *Grace Kelly: Icon of Style to Royal Bride*, "including department store windows. In the fall of 1955, her likeness was used to create a line of mannequins." It was in 1955 and '56 that Grace ascended to something white, silent, majestic.

These were the years of her last three movies: the glorious *To Catch a Thief*, filmed on the French Riviera, all sea and sky; *The Swan*, from the play that she'd done on television in 1950, and which was now getting the lavish MGM treatment; and *High Society*, a musical remake of *The Philadelphia Story*, co-starring Bing Crosby and Frank Sinatra. Any actress would be floating with this kind of material, and Grace, almost literally, was, in fabrics that were light, airy, and ineffable (a theme that had begun with *Rear Window*). She wore chiffon, watered silk, unlined linen, and that most levitational textile, silk organza. The costumes that designers Edith Head and Helen Rose were making for these films show that everyone was on the same page, working in celestial alignment.

"Every few decades Hollywood finds a way to classicize the look of one of its stars," says film and dance critic Don Daniels. "It did it with Marlene Dietrich. It did it with Katharine Hepburn. And it eventually did it with Grace Kelly. Helen Rose specialized in this sort of thing in the 50s, in films like *Athena* and *Jupiter's Darling*. She worked on this look for Grace in both *The Swan* and *High Society*. It's every now and then a woman and her look floats into the public consciousness and can be styled so that we remember Greek goddesses."

The Swan was a costume drama and hews to an Empire line. But in *To Catch a Thief* and *High Society*, references abound to both classical draping and classical dance, an art form full of mythological creatures. Grace's gowns are columnar, with waterfall pleats and cascades of fluting, sheer trains flowing from the back (where wings would be, if she had them), and sheer scarves like soft breezes around her neck. All this pleating and fluting and floating was in tune with the Hellenistic sculpting of 50s couturiers such as Madame Grès and the Greek designer Jean Dessès. Grace's day dresses have fitted bodices and skirts blossoming from the waist—a very clever fusion of the ballerina's tutu with the American shirtwaist, and a shape that allowed her to move freely (as she did in the sensational flowered shirtwaist of *Rear Window*, in which she climbed a fire escape). As for color, Grace was given her own, Apollonian palette. Wheat-field and buttercup yellows, azure and cerulean blues, seashell pink and angel-skin coral, Sun King gold and Olympus white—no one wore white like Grace Kelly. To those with a feeling for history, beauty, and style, Grace Kelly's late-career wardrobe—the huntress Artemis during the day and Aphrodite at night—is unforgettable if not positively Delphic.

"Every time I see Grace Kelly I'm influenced by what she wears," says Janie Bryant, the costume designer for AMC's *Mad Men*. "The simplicity, it is so classic, but it's always dramatic."

"When I branched out into women's wear," says designer Tommy Hilfiger, who has an Andy Warhol silkscreen of Grace Kelly in his New York apartment, "I began to really study icons of style. Grace stood out. Style is enduring and forever. It's something you cannot buy. There is a chic-ness to conservative style done in an elegant way. You know, we did a book called *Grace Kelly: A Life in Pictures*. We did this as an inspiration book, not only for ourselves. We find that the French are obsessed with her, and the Japanese are intrigued."

"She didn't necessarily lead fashion in a new direction," says Jenny Lister, a curator of Textiles and Fashion at the Victoria and Albert Museum. "She's become shorthand for a very polished and well-accessorized look. Contemporary designers like Zac Posen have talked about her timeless appeal. I think it boils down to quite ethereal ideas, because in some of her films she almost seemed like a goddess, and because they couldn't pin her down—she was so private. That aura of mystery, she retained that. And because she stopped making films, it never changed."

"Though Grace can be very inviting," says Janie Bryant, "and her voice has a warmth to it, there's also an austerity to her. It's about the façade."

"I think Grace Kelly was someone that came along at the right time," says fashion historian June Weir. "If she had come along in the 60s, or in the 40s, I don't think it would have worked. She was the perfect 1950s beauty. Pastel colors, beautiful luxury fabrics, and very pretty necklines."

"*High Society*," says Robert Lacey, "just the whole confection of that. It was just the most extraordinary way to fly out on a new cloud. Sophia Loren, Audrey Hepburn, Grace—they were all absolute archetypes of particular sorts of beauty. They're the end of the star system and, to my mind, more beautiful than any stars of the earlier years, and more beautiful than anything since. With the newer generations we subconsciously know there's artifice involved. And we don't quite believe what we see. But we did believe what we saw with Grace."

I f we only had the woman Grace Kelly was in her films—the golden girl in the shirtwaist dress, the classical creature in white chiffon—it would be enough to place her in the pantheon. But with the biographies published after her untimely death, at 52, in 1982—when she was driving with her younger daughter, Stephanie, and their car flew off the road and down a mountainside—her symbology became more complicated, and certainly more fascinating. We learned that the volcano under the snowcap was surprisingly active and full of fire. Grace Kelly, the swan princess in white gloves, was neither a virgin when she married Prince Rainier III of Monaco, in 1956 (she'd lost it at 17, just before she left home for New York City), nor virginal in the way she had conducted her love life up until then. As the truth came out about Grace's sex life as a single girl, in books ever more salacious in their details, it was a shock, sharply at odds with her pristine screen persona. Some make it sound as if she slept with every man who crossed her path. She did not. "We were together a lot," says Maree Rambo, "and that was just not her style." And while one biographer claims Grace had affairs with almost every one of her co-stars—Cooper, Gable, Milland, Holden, Crosby, Grant, Sinatra—others believe it was only Holden for sure, probably Milland, and maybe Gable. Grace was romantic and passionate. She followed her heart, which might or might not lead to bed. All her biographers agree that she never used sex to win roles. Judged in retrospect, not by 50s standards but by feminist ones, she was as self-possessed about her sexuality as she was about her work.

"Grace was in many ways ahead of her time," says the writer Donald Spoto, whose biography *High Society: The Life of Grace Kelly* was published in November. "Her Catholic upbringing and the force of her parents' arguments and insistence on these codes of conduct were attended to but not heeded. She had an independent conscience from her earliest years. Grace said to me, 'I was constantly falling in love, and it never occurred to me that this was wrong or bad.' And when social or religious issues said otherwise, my impression is that she heard it, and then said, 'Well, thank you for your input. If you'll excuse me, I have a date.'"

"If the testimony of her succession of boyfriends is to be believed," says biographer Robert Lacey, "she was very modern and cool and relaxed and wasted no time. I think it was her rebellion against her father. In every other way she was such a good girl, and did what Daddy wanted, and of course brilliantly achieved in her field, just as Daddy brilliantly achieved in his. I'm sure she was devout, an absolutely sincere Catholic, but taking full advantage of the Catholic mechanisms for private misdemeanors."

"Grace was the daughter of a very liberated woman," says Wendy Leigh, the author of *True Grace: The Life and Times of an American Princess.* "Margaret was a healthy German blonde with no shame about her body. And then Grace's father was a great philanderer, so that she had the measure very early on about male animal instinct. And rather than walk away from it, Grace basically embraced it."

"She was shy. But physically, she was not shy," the actor Alexandre D'Arcy, who had a monthlong romance with Grace in 1948, told Robert Lacey. "She was . . . very warm indeed as far as sex was concerned. You would touch her once and she would go through the ceiling."

Gwen Robyns, who published *Princess Grace* in 1976 and then became a close friend to Grace, puts it simply: "She just adored sex. She made no bones about it. We were lying on the bed one day, and I said something about sex, and she said, 'It's heaven.'"

Grace was not unlike the ballerina Margot Fonteyn, another midcentury artist who was cherished for her aura of chastity and purity, a fairy-tale femininity girded for greater things. Fonteyn, it was later revealed, was accomplished in bed and often in bed. There is a connection between art and sex, with arousal in one realm speaking to arousal in another. Performers, like gods and goddesses, must assert themselves in space, which takes all kinds of energy pulled from all kinds of sources. While no one had a problem with this when it came to men and their muses, women of that era had to be quieter. Grace and Margot, who knew each other, were both quiet. But sex, Don Richardson remembers Grace saying, "put lights" in her eyes.

———

If Grace did not feel a societal pressure to bridle her passions, she did feel the clock ticking regarding marriage and children, for which she longed. On January 6, 1956, page one of *The New York Times* read, PRINCE OF MONACO TO WED GRACE KELLY. Unbeknownst to those who knew her, Grace, during the filming of MGM's *The Swan*, had glided into love with Rainier Grimaldi, whom she'd met in 1955 and had been exchanging letters with ever since. "She was playing in *The Swan* and she was playing a princess," says Robyns. "Along comes this prince, and, being Grace, she was carried away by dreams and things." Grace had also made it clear that she didn't want to be an aging beauty in Hollywood.

"The Wedding of the Century," as it was referred to at the time (Grace called it "the Carnival of the Century"), was arguably the first multi-media press event on a modern scale. There was a slew of reporters and photographers on the ship that took Grace and her entourage of 66 to Monaco; nearly 2,000 reporters crowded the cathedral ceremony, "more press there than guests," remembers Maree Rambo, who was a bridesmaid; and the wedding itself was filmed by MGM and broadcast live to more than 30 million viewers in Europe. It was a marriage that seemed to embody the wedding-cake ideal of postwar, 50s culture, with its emphasis on fairy-tale fertility and prosperity. The little principality of Monaco was stepped like a wedding cake, and its palace was as pink as a petit four. Even bartenders toasted the event, serving a new drink called the Princesse Cocktail: equal parts bourbon, grenadine, and fresh cream. Grace became pregnant with that precious first child (Caroline)—the offspring who would secure the Grimaldi succession in Monaco, and hence its independence from France—on her honeymoon.

It was during that first pregnancy that Grace turned an accessory by Hermès into a much-coveted cult item. Out in public, she shielded her belly with a large square handbag made of brown pigskin, the Hermès *sac à dépêches pour dames*. The descendant of a 1930s Hermès saddlebag, it was simple, sensible, and superbly made, yet another example of "always." Grace was carrying the principality's future, and she protected it with something proven from the past. In her honor, Hermès christened this bag "the Kelly." Where the Hermès Birkin bag, named for the actress Jane Birkin, has something more of bling about it, the Kelly remains *the* icon of impeccable breeding and quiet good taste.

With the same discipline, culture, and kindness that she had brought to her career as an actress, Grace fulfilled her duties as a princess. She had hoped that now and then she could return to Hollywood to make movies, because she loved and missed acting. This hope was dashed. Rainier was ambivalent, the roles on offer were problematic, and her schedule as a wife, mother, and royal was consuming. Hers turned out to be not a fairy-tale marriage but the kind of marriage anyone has, with ups and downs, joys and disappointments, and patches of marital discord. Did Rainier step out on her? Did Grace, finally, step out on him? Some of her biographers say yes and yes. Others are not so sure—as Donald Spoto cautions, "Nobody held the lamp." Her oldest friend, Maree Rambo, says today, "I don't know, but I don't think so."

As the years pulled on, Grace began to see that "disarray," the word that didn't apply to her, had a place in life. And "always"—so allied with perfection, and classicism, and her—was a kind of trap. It was with tears in her eyes that she said to her friend producer John Foreman, "I know where I am going to be every single day for the rest of my life." And sometime later, when she learned that one of her six bridesmaids had been living in a shelter, she told Judith Balaban Quine that she was strangely envious. "I know it might sound awful and insensitive," Quine remembers Grace saying, "but the thought of just getting up every day and doing what that day brings you sounds wonderful to me in certain ways."

In tiny Monaco, half the size of Manhattan's Central Park, it was as if Grace were locked back into that cupboard, but without her dolls to play with. Her life was laid out along narrow corridors, much like the corniche on which she took her last drive—rock on one side, open air on the other. It was a slim road full of hairpin turns that connected the family getaway, Roc Agel, to the pink palace where protocol reigned. "Strung like a slender thread across the clouds" is how Quine described one of these upper corniches. On that fateful day of September 13, 1982, Grace didn't let the chauffeur drive, because the car was too full. She and Stephanie were up in the front, and across the backseat she'd placed dresses that needed altering for the coming season; she didn't want them wrinkled. She was excited about new projects that were blossoming, and by all accounts she and Rainier were enjoying a renewed closeness. The best medical guess is that Grace suffered a small "warning" stroke while driving that treacherous road, which caused her to lose control of the car. A few seconds of blurred consciousness, like the kiss in *Rear Window*, and the clouds reclaimed their own.

NICOLE'S NEW LIGHT

By Ingrid Sischy | December 2002

My life collapsed," Nicole Kidman recalled recently. "People ran from me because suddenly it was 'Oh, my God! It's over for her now!'" Kidman's leper moment came last year, when her former husband, Tom Cruise, fired her as his wife—that, at least, is how the split came across to the public. But on the day this past summer when she was re-living that moment of reckoning, it all seemed like centuries ago, not only because so much has happened in her life since then, but also because we were sitting in a trailer just outside of Poiana Braşov, Romania, a spot as physically and psychologically removed from Hollywood as it gets.

Romania is where Kidman will be through the end of this year, at work on Anthony Minghella's film adaptation of *Cold Mountain*, Charles Frazier's rather turgid best-seller about the Civil War. Although some scenes have been filmed in Charleston, South Carolina, the bulk of this epic is being shot in Poiana Braşov and nearby spots in northern Romania. One quickly understands why: these are places that epitomize the phrase "going back in time." I had arrived in Poiana Braşov a day earlier, in the dead of night. After a hairy mountain ride to my hotel behind an endless stream of horse-pulled carts, and a sleepless night spent listening to wild dogs howl, I was glad to see the morning sun. So was everyone else on the set. It was the first beautiful day after weeks of relentless rain. Suddenly I heard the clippety-clop of horses' hooves, and somebody said, "Here comes Nicole." I spied the actress way up the road in costume as Ada, the book's heroine, all decked out in her corsets and petticoated skirt. She looked the height of refinement, but when she spotted me she let out a hearty laugh. "You made it," she said in her unmistakable Australian accent.

Before *Cold Mountain* is done shooting, Kidman, who stars in the film with Jude Law, will be on movie screens back home breaking audiences' hearts with her mesmerizing performance as Virginia Woolf in Stephen Daldry's adaptation of Michael Cunningham's feminist novel, *The Hours*. That movie, which also features Julianne Moore, Meryl Streep, and Ed Harris, and which doesn't betray the profound sense of aloneness that makes Cunningham's novel so moving, is scheduled to be released later this month. And just like last year—when Kidman surprised and won over moviegoers with the one-two punch of her swooningly gorgeous performance as a doomed dance-hall star in *Moulin Rouge* and her portrayal of a mother on the edge of madness in *The Others*—the studios' release schedules have decreed that she will shortly follow up *The Hours* with yet another adaptation, this time of *The Human Stain*, the tough Philip Roth novel, which has been turned into a movie gem by the director Robert Benton and which will be in theaters next year. Benton's casting of Kidman as the novel's take-no-crap, been-to-hell-and-back female janitor, opposite Anthony Hopkins, is right on the money.

And that's not all. On the heels of her breakup, Kidman spent last winter in Sweden, shooting Lars von Trier's film *Dogville*, which is scheduled for release sometime next spring. Von Trier, the director most recently of *Dancer in the Dark*, wrote this latest film for Kidman, which serves to underscore what has been happening to her career over the last few years. While the world has remained obsessed with "The Tom and Nicole Story," with what their marriage was really like—and especially with what went on between the sheets and with what truly caused the relationship to combust—Kidman has done something more useful: she has shown herself to be a major talent, a remarkable actress who can get in there with the best of them, go toe-to-toe, and come out with her credibility intact. What's more, she's proved herself to be a star with a capital *S*, the one-in-a-generation kind who, like Elizabeth Taylor, is bigger than the Hollywood system, and is also unafraid to be human and real, which only makes her more popular.

Offscreen, Kidman, like Taylor, has a love of life, a strong sense of loyalty, and a madcap sense of humor, and she seems to really know how to be a friend. (Her old buddy Naomi Watts, whose career has only recently taken off, told me, "Nicole was always there with her door open, her arms open, her ears open—just what you need.") Kidman and Taylor know how to live it up, too, and while Kidman may not share Taylor's predilection for carrying really large rocks on her mitts, she's got the rags—closets full of the hippest fashion and vintage clothes. Put this pair in a room and you'll hear two dames who really know how to laugh. In terms of their careers and their craft, there's more than coincidence in the fact that, while Taylor showed the world what she was made of when she walked the razor's edge in Edward Albee's *Who's Afraid of Virginia Woolf?*, Kidman is doing the same thing playing Woolf herself.

've gotten to know Kidman over these last couple of years, right as her life was falling apart, in my capacity as editor of *Interview* magazine. What struck me initially is that she's a person who doesn't let others down. In one way or another, I have seen her stand by her word and be thoughtful in situations that would likely bring out the worst in other stars. The more one knows her, the less "actressy" she seems. She hasn't undergone the kind of narcissistic transformation that can turn extremely famous people into absolute bores or unbearable phonies. She has gotten used to the attention that comes with being a star, but Kidman is not one of those types whom everybody else has to pamper and flatter; instead, she seems to be driven by a feeling that she has so much to learn, and so much to see. She's still curious, still hungry, and will still almost kill herself playing a part. It's like she goes into a trance on set— broken ribs and bloody knees (such as she incurred on *Moulin Rouge*) or grossly swollen ankles (*Cold Mountain*) be damned.

Nicole's childhood doesn't sound that unusual, but there are a few kinks and clues to suggest that this was a kid with big ambitions. Born in Hawaii in 1967 to Australian parents, Antony and Janelle, she grew up in an upper-middle-class suburb of Sydney, in a family that was close then and remains close today. Both parents worked, her mother as a nurse, her father as a psychologist, and it appears they passed on a strong sense of ethics and social conscience to their two daughters, Nicole and Antonia. As Nicole, the elder, remembers, "My mother would treat us as little adults. We would discuss things. I was raised to think and to question. She wanted girls who were educated, aware of everything, and opinionated. So did my father. They wanted us to be sure of being able to speak out. That's gotten me into trouble at times."

The outside world was less of an oasis, and at times Nicole felt like a bit of an oddball. She says, "My mother was a feminist in a conservative neighborhood, and my father was left-wing. I was Catholic, and most of the kids were Protestant. I looked very different from most of the other people. I was very, very tall"—she topped off at five feet ten inches—"with wild, wild curly hair, which I now try to tame. I couldn't go to the beach, because I was so fair-skinned. One of my most vivid memories is of being a child, sitting in my bedroom, and hearing the laughter from the next-door neighbors. They had a pool and you'd hear them laughing, playing. I remember feeling not included in that, just sitting in my bedroom. . . . I had a huge desire to be somebody else. I would think, I'm not living the life I want to live. I would try to come up with images before I went to sleep, to then try and live the life I wanted to live in my dreams. And I was deeply romantic."

Even today, when friends talk about Kidman they cite her love of losing herself in other worlds. She is an avid reader, frequently seen curled up with a book, oblivious to whatever's going on around her. That started a long time ago: by her teens, novels were a primary means of escape. She has said that it was thanks to characters such as Dorothea in *Middlemarch* and Natasha in *War and Peace* that she began to think about being an actor. She told me, "I wanted to be those women. I would live through them, get lost in them, and be devastated when the books ended."

Nicole also had a definite wild streak. She was hitting the clubs in Sydney by the time she was 14, drawn to the bohemian side of life, befriending the transvestites who frequented her favorite joints. Already showing her affinity for avant-garde fashion, she'd doll herself up in a tutu, fishnets, and lace-up black boots, and dye her hair like a rainbow or in even more intense shades of red than her natural coloring. Other nights she'd go vintage.

But of all the pursuits she followed in her teens, it was the drama lessons that from the age of 12 she took on weekends at Sydney's Philip Street Theater which really stirred something within her. She got some saucy parts, too, including that quintessential southern belle, Blanche du Bois, in Tennessee Williams's *Streetcar Named Desire*, played by Nicole at the ripe old age of 12. She's less amused today by the cheeseball Australian films she found herself doing a few years later, such as 1983's teen dirt-bike epic *BMX Bandits* and 1986's *Windrider*, a romance about windsurfing (with the actor Tom Burlinson, a 29-year-old who became 18-year-old Nicole's boyfriend)—but at the same time she doesn't disown them. As an actor, she says, "you're never in a position where you have an enormous amount of choices—that's why I never judge other actors' choices. One doesn't know what's behind them. Why does somebody need to do [a particular movie]? Because they have to pay the mortgage? I've certainly been in that position. *BMX Bandits*? Bring it on. I wanted to own a place. That's how I bought my apartment. After that I always knew, if everything else went to pieces, I had a floor I could crash on." As for the artistic side of the equation, such as it was, no matter how cartoony her parts, Kidman always comes off as a strong, memorable presence—and as killer sexy. Best of all her early Australian films is 1991's *Flirting*, a girls'-school classic in which she plays the alpha prefect who turns nice.

She had begun to work steadily, but at the age of 17 two events temporarily sidetracked her career. First, she decided to see a bit of the world, bagging high-school graduation for an intoxicating few months in Amsterdam and Paris. Kidman recalls, "I was like, 'Bring it on—bring on Europe!'" ("Bring it on" is a pet Kidman expression, a kind of exhortation to herself and others to let life happen.) That same year, her mother was diagnosed with breast cancer and went through chemotherapy. Kidman put everything on hold to be part of her mom's support structure. She clearly respects and loves her dad, but her relationship with her mother seems to have been the more formative one. On more than one occasion she told me, "I still think one of my motivating forces is to make her proud of me." When I asked Kidman to explain that more specifically, she answered, "She once said to me she wished she had had no children, which is a hard thing to hear from your mother. I think I stormed out of the house that day. But I understand what she meant, because she gave up a lot. She would have been an amazing doctor, she speaks French, she plays the piano, she's far more brilliant than me at everything." How many of us feel that same way about our parents' missed opportunities and end up taking on the world in their name?

What set Kidman's career in true motion was a 1986 Australian TV mini-series, *Vietnam*, which suggested she had real acting mettle. She took off in the role of Megan Goddard, an anti-war, anti-Establishment student, got nice reviews, and, out of that success, was eventually cast in 1988, at the age of 21, in the film *Dead Calm*, directed by Phillip Noyce and produced, as was *Vietnam*, by Australia's legendary Kennedy-Miller Productions. This was the project that would bring her to America and alter the trajectory of her career. A thriller, *Dead Calm* required her to outfox, outsail, and outfight a psychotic interloper—we see her together, untogether, in the altogether, and her performance never falls apart.

The 1989 film, a smash in Australia and a player in the States too, came to the attention of the screenwriter Robert Towne, who was then at work with Tom Cruise on *Days of Thunder*. Towne, who is no monkey, showed *Dead Calm* to Cruise. Kidman had already been brought to America for a publicity junket for *Dead Calm*, been signed by ICM agent Sam Cohn, and flown back across the Pacific to Tokyo, where she was doing more promotional chores, when she got a call saying Tom Cruise wanted to meet her. When I asked what her first reaction to the summons was, she laughed, saying, "I thought, Wow! This is America! Tom Cruise wants to meet me. He made *Top Gun* and *Cocktail*—the films I grew up watching." And the fairy tale began. Before she had time to straighten her hair, it seemed, she was in Daytona Beach, Florida, starring opposite Cruise in *Days of Thunder*.

Enter Cupid. Drumrolls. Music. Fireworks! Kidman was smitten: "He basically swept me off my feet. I fell madly, passionately in love. And as happens when you fall in love, my whole plan in terms of what I wanted for my life—I was like, 'Forget it. *This* is it.' I was consumed by it, willingly. And I was desperate to have a baby with him. I didn't care if we were married. That's what I wish I'd done." But that's not what happened. Instead, a few months later, Cruise's divorce from the actress Mimi Rogers came through, and America's most American leading man proposed to Australia's latest hot export.

I t's hard to imagine a more dramatic personal and sociological change than the one Kidman experienced the moment she hooked up with Cruise. She went from being an actress who had begun to taste success—and who had always insisted on living on her own, even during her various romances—to a woman inside the engine of the Hollywood machine. As for the first piece of celluloid that came out of their alliance, let's just say that time has not been kind to *Days of Thunder*. Still, it's fascinating to see how Hollywood, led by producers Don Simpson and Jerry Bruckheimer and British director Tony Scott, packaged her raw sexuality, putting a commercial gloss on it.

After *Days of Thunder*, she began working on *Billy Bathgate* for director Robert Benton, who recently teamed up with the actress again. I spent time with them this September on the Paramount lot, where they were re-recording fragments of dialogue for *The Human Stain*. It was quite an eye-opener to watch her work with Benton and the sound technicians. Kidman is a pro, but not a hack. She'll want to keep doing a line or scene until it feels true, but she also seems to have unusually direct access to all sorts of inner emotions, which she is often able to summon in a matter of seconds and articulate with authenticity.

There's a bit of a father-daughter dynamic between Benton and Kidman. When we went to lunch they both cracked up about the old days when Kidman, who married Cruise in the middle of *Billy Bathgate*, would go missing in action. Benton recalled, "One day when I couldn't find her, somebody said, 'Oh! Nicole is skydiving,' and I almost had a heart attack. I thought, God! Like I don't have enough problems." Benton sat his star down and gave her a good talking-to. She solemnly listened and, as Benton laughingly told me, was jumping out of planes again soon after with her new husband. The thrill both apparently get from a sense of danger seems to have been an aphrodisiac for Nicole and Tom, who would also amuse themselves with adrenaline-pumping fun such as spins on Cruise's Harley.

It's clear that the couple's chemistry worked big-time. When Nicole speaks of her years with Cruise she describes a devotion without clauses and without doubt. "I was willing to give up everything," she explains. "I now see that as part of me. I'm willing to do that—I do it when I do a movie too. I'm willing to go, 'Yeah, bring it on, consume me, intoxicate me.' I want to feel alive—I want to reel, basically. I was reeling with Tom and I loved it and I would have walked to the end of the earth. That meant giving up a lot of things that were very important to me." Kidman doesn't pretend that she was impervious to the glare that came with being Mrs. Cruise. "You're being watched and scrutinized, and that slowly affects you. But it's also deeply romantic, because it feels like there's only the two of you and you're in it together, as if you're in a cocoon, and you become very dependent on each other."

Apart from her role opposite Cruise in Ron Howard's immigrant drama, *Far and Away*, which was a nonstarter when it came out in 1992, Kidman's career wasn't on the front burner during the first few years of the marriage. Instead of klieg lights, her days were filled with squeals and gurgles, for it was in 1993 that the couple adopted a girl, Isabella. (In 1995 they would add to the family by adopting their son, Connor.) But ultimately the bubblelike existence had to end. This wasn't the Dark Ages. The suffragettes had come and gone, Virginia Woolf had written *A Room of One's Own* decades before, and Kidman, very much a woman of her time and of her upbringing, could not stifle her need to express herself. She started to pursue a number of parts. There was, for instance, 1995's *Batman Forever*, directed by Joel Schumacher, in which she played the love interest, Dr. Chase Meridian.

Schumacher's stories of life on the *Batman Forever* set with Kidman are telling. By that time she had become a certified member of Hollywood royalty, but it seems that that had killed off neither her sense of spontaneity nor her sense of democracy. There was, for instance, the day she got a craving for some kind of iced mocha concoction from Starbucks. As Schumacher recalls, she didn't just order one for herself. "There were hundreds of people working on *Batman*, and, sure enough, an hour later, some kind of truck arrived with all these frozen drinks, and everyone had an iced mocha thingy." But while Kidman helped to put the sass into *Batman Forever*, offering a glimpse of her flair for camp, the performance didn't do much to thaw the ice-princess image that she had by now developed in the media.

In point of fact, Kidman had never been cold or rude to the press, but somehow her perfect behavior as Mrs. Cruise—the couple was famous for their highly controlled public appearances—and the sorts of roles Americans had seen her in, along with the presumption that she was being cast only to curry favor with her husband, all combined to make it seem as if she were high-and-mighty, exquisite, but made of marble. She, too, may have bought into some of that: "I felt I didn't deserve to be there in my own right, and so throughout I wasn't there as Nicole—I was there as Tom's wife."

What finally changed this was *To Die For*, which was also released in 1995. It was not a part that was handed to her on a silver platter. Even though she had a decent track record by then and was married to such a box-office biggie, she was not considered A-list and had to work to convince the director, Gus Van Sant, that she had what it took to play Suzanne Stone-Maretto, a woman who is so obsessed with becoming a TV star that she is willing to do anything to make that happen, including seducing a weirdo high-school student (Joaquin Phoenix) and persuading him to do away with her lunkish husband (Matt Dillon). Kidman has never been the type to let pride get in the way of work she desires. Even today she'll do the requisite campaigning if she is after a role and she isn't being pursued for it; she has an instinctive grasp of the ebb and flow of fame, of the fact that you have to get up on your board if you want to ride its waves.

Van Sant, whose deadpan way with a story is almost Warholian, recalls, "She got my number somewhere. I don't know if it was hard to find it or not, but she just called me and said hi. She phoned right when Meg Ryan dropped out of the movie, which involved her knowing inside information. Our second choice was Patricia Arquette, and we even had a third choice, Jennifer Jason Leigh. Nicole was somewhere on the list. I had met her a couple of times. When she called she told me that she knew she wasn't on the top of my list, and I tried to kind of say, 'Well, I don't know about that . . . ' But she just cut me off and said, 'Look, you don't have to pretend that I am.' I said, 'O.K.,' and then she said, 'But listen, I'm destined to play this part.' That worked really well with me because I believe in destiny."

It did seem as if she had been born to play this knife-sharp black comedy, written to perfection by Buck Henry. She found humor in her character's desperation and yet also made that desperation feel painfully real. She was so wickedly funny that at the time I remember being surprised—as were many others—that there was edge and bite underneath all that Hollywood polish. This was the beginning of her transformation from perfect escort to flesh-and-blood actor. When *Portrait of a Lady*, directed by Jane Campion and featuring Kidman as the headstrong heiress, Isabel Archer, was released a year later, the project's ambition underscored the fact that Kidman might just become a big deal in her own right—even if the film itself wasn't a breakthrough for anyone.

It was inevitable that performing in these kinds of films would affect Kidman's sense of herself. She says, "I realized I could be fulfilled creatively and that I had given that up. I think this happens to women who re-enter the workforce. They go, 'Hold on, there's a world out there, and I wouldn't mind being a part of it.' I tried to deny it because it would have been so much easier for me to be satiated by being a wife. I wish it could have been part of my trajectory, but it wasn't."

Kidman imagined, like millions of women, that she'd be able to fulfill herself through her work and also be a dedicated wife and mother. Her goal was to do a worthwhile project every year or so and still have enough time and energy to give her family its due. For a while the plan worked, or at least it looked that way from the outside. The actress appeared in *The Peacemaker* in 1997 and in *Practical Magic* in 1998 (two films that ended up stiffing) while continuing to show up at her husband's side, always looking like a million bucks, for every important occasion.

And then came an opportunity that seemed heaven-sent: the late Stanley Kubrick's decision to cast Kidman and Cruise in his take on sexual obsession and jealousy, *Eyes Wide Shut*. The couple had a chance not only to work with one of the movies' true greats on a film that promised to be electrifying, but also to work together. And so, in late 1996, they picked up their household, moved to London, and dedicated themselves to implementing Kubrick's vision. It was not just a nine-to-five collaboration. Kidman and Cruise's bond with Kubrick proved to be such that their lives became intertwined with his, and the film somehow bled into their relationship.

The two actors, especially Nicole, are known for living and breathing their parts when working; this time their roles were a bored husband and wife who get caught in a web of sexual pretending that then turns dangerously real and winds up threatening their marriage. Sounds like a recipe for an emotional Molotov cocktail that would test many a couple's relationship. On top of that, the shoot, originally scheduled for 4 months, kept getting extended, and in the end Tom and Nicole would park themselves in London for 18 months. As Kidman remembers it, "Tom had such a very strong connection with Stanley, and so did I. That resonated through our lives and marriage—it had such a profound effect." Even when the actors and their director weren't actually shooting, they'd spend hours together every day. Nicole says, "Stanley saw Tom and I in the most extreme situations because of the way in which he works. He breaks you down. He challenged all of my concrete, solid bases that I'd set around myself, and basically disturbed them, and made me far more introspective." Nicole does not get literal about how this experience shook things up, but she couldn't be more clear that it did; the couple was also deeply affected by Kubrick's sudden death during postproduction. But she has an artist's acceptance of the entire experience as ultimately valuable, no matter how painful.

When we were talking I was honest with her about my reactions to the movie, which finally came out in the summer of 1999. I told her that, despite the film's visual punch, the pre-release fuss and hype seemed way overblown considering the final product, which to my mind is not the revolutionary work that was promised but rather a bourgeois attempt at titillation, an effort at illuminating truths about sexuality and relationships which have been treated with much more insight by other writers and directors. Nicole responded in a way that is characteristic of her. She was not defensive, but heard me with real interest and openness. She then stood by both her director and her leading man: "I still think Tom was mesmerizing in it, but that's partly because I know what he went through. To me, the themes are so important and so complex—and who knows what Stanley would have done [with it] if he had had more time, if he'd lived."

In the fall of 1998, Kidman was making new headlines with her performance onstage in London in *The Blue Room*, which required her to be nude for 10 seconds. One night backstage Kidman found a big bouquet of red roses in her dressing room with a note from the Australian director Baz Luhrmann that read something like: "She sings, she dances, she dies, how can you refuse?" Luhrmann was referring to Satine, the doomed heroine of the movie he was planning to shoot next, *Moulin Rouge*. He was following his gut instinct that Kidman would shine in the part of a divinely romantic showgirl who drives folks wild, sacrifices for her art, and dies tragically of tuberculosis on her beloved stage. But Kidman was still perceived by audiences as distant and cold; there was resistance to her from some of the powers behind the project. Nevertheless, Luhrmann and his casting director were passionate about their choice. They fought until the deal was done, and a role that was loaded with risk for both star and director turned out to be the best thing that ever happened to Kidman's career. Not only did it show what a multifaceted talent she is, but the part, which had her running off not with the rich producer but instead with the struggling writer, undercut her public image as a cool careerist and plainly rendered her human and warm. Whether she is flying through the air on a trapeze, singing an over-the-top love song with her leading man, Ewan McGregor, or breathing her last breath, her performance is big, bold, vulnerable when called for, and just right in terms of tone.

Like Van Sant, Luhrmann calls Kidman an ally. Recalling the *Moulin Rouge* shoot, which took place over nine months in Sydney, he says, "She never showed anything but absolute belief in the film, which I've got to say is one of the defining qualities of Nicole. She is absolutely at her best in the worst possible situations." Little did anyone know how much she would be put to the test on this front. It was during postproduction on *Moulin Rouge*, sometime in February 2001, Luhrmann remembers, that he got a call from

Kidman: "She said, 'I've broken up with Tom' or 'Tom's breaking up with me.' She told me there were helicopters flying over the house, and she was genuinely devastated and shocked."

The public's reaction to the breakup has been a lesson in how the movies and real life can converge. The timing of the marital implosion led into a period when Kidman was also in the public eye because of *Moulin Rouge*. The fact that in this film she died as a heroine passionately committed to her art, a victim of her time and her circumstances, carried over to the perception of her as a victim in real life—a perception to which there seems to be more than an element of truth. My conversations with Kidman about this tumultuous, painful time, which also included a miscarriage, showed her to be a woman genuinely struggling to understand why her marriage failed.

I doubt that legalities are the only explanation for why this couple has been so respectful to each other in public. These are two people who understand good behavior and who are committed to their children's well-being. Even though it looked at first as if they were going to land in an ugly legal battle, the couple settled out of court. Both parties have made it clear that they will not go into the nitty-gritty about what went wrong. But since their split played out publicly in such a bizarre way—with Cruise releasing cryptic tidbits to the press like "She knows why," and Kidman seeming to be in a state of shock—one can't help but still be curious. I asked Kidman point-blank, "Do you know why you broke up?" She said, "I'm starting to understand now. At the time I didn't." So I asked again, "It came as complete news?" She said yes.

Sometimes I got the feeling she'd do anything to reverse events. But I also had the sense she knew there couldn't have been any other outcome, in part, it seems, because of her own artistic needs. It's not clear how these conflicted with the marriage, but what's unusual about her, given her status as a Hollywood institution, is that she's willing to bare the confusion, the contradictions, the regret. She told me, "I didn't have to have a huge career. I would have liked to be able to make a *To Die For* occasionally and things that could stimulate me. And this makes me sad, but I still would probably choose a marriage and an intact family over my career." When I pointed out to Kidman that the beauty of living in the 21st century for women is that, one hopes, they don't have to choose between work and family, she replied, "But I think I had to choose. I think [the marriage] would have come down to it. I suppose it wasn't meant to be. What I see now is a nine-year-old little girl who [the divorce] affected and I see a seven-year-old boy, and see my duty as a mother. It means for the rest of my life I have to do things to protect and help them and make it up to them. That sounds so old-fashioned and strange. I don't know why that's in me, but it is."

While it's not unusual to worry about the kids in a divorce, Kidman is clearly wearing a kind of hair shirt; after all, she was raised as a Catholic. This leads to the role of religion in her marriage—specifically Scientology, which, as everyone knows, is Tom's thing. When I asked Kidman about her ties to the organization, she said, "Tom is a Scientologist. I'm not. I was introduced to it by him, and I explored it. But I'm not a Scientologist. I told Tom I respect his religion. I said to him, 'It is what you believe in, and it's helped you.'"

One of the most fascinating aspects of the entire story is how intrigued people are by the couple, even those who aren't normally into tabloid-type gossip. The marriage remains a kind of blank slate upon which we can all project our own ideas; people have floated so many theories, from unfaithfulness to the fallout from pre-nuptial agreements to who knows what. The speculation was endless—and still is. This sense of mystery goes way back: the marriage had always been surrounded by whispers about the couple's sexuality and questions about just what kind of transactions were taking place between them.

When I decided to face these issues directly with Nicole, she laughed at the awkwardness with which I brought them up, and then asked, "Do you want to know if I had a real marriage?" Even though I thought it was my duty as a good reporter to poke around in there, I was embarrassed by having to be so nosy. So I circled the issue of the relationship and brought up the fact that Cruise seems to call the lawyers whenever the g-word is thrown at him (and I don't mean garter). This time, she grabbed the bull by the horns and said, in a serious tone, "Look, the marriage was real. The marriage existed because it was two people in love. It's that simple. They've said I'm gay, they've said everyone's gay. I personally don't believe in doing huge lawsuits about that stuff. Tom does. That's what he wants to do, that's what he's going to do. You do not tell Tom what to do. That's it. Simple. And he's a force to be reckoned with. I have a different approach. I don't file lawsuits because I really don't care. Honestly, people have said everything under the sun. I just want to do my work, raise my kids, and hopefully find somebody who I can share my life with again, or, you know, have a number of different people at different times who come into my life. I don't know what my future is. But I really don't care what anybody else is saying."

On the same day that Kidman and I had this conversation in Los Angeles, I happened to visit the producer Lynda Obst. Philip Roth's masterpiece *American Pastoral* is on her plate as her next film project. Kidman's name came up as a possible lead. Obst and I then fell easily into the inevitable who-did-what-to-whom Tom-and-Nicole conversation. Has anyone in America *not* had this conversation? After a minute we laughed at ourselves and Obst pulled out a copy of *American Pastoral* and read a passage that says it all. The subject is "other people": You never fail to get them wrong. . . . You get them wrong before you meet them, while you're anticipating meeting them; you get them wrong while you're with them; and then you go home to tell somebody else about the meeting and you get them all wrong again. . . . The fact remains that getting people right is not what living is all about anyway. It's getting them wrong that is living, getting them wrong and wrong and wrong and then, on careful reconsideration, getting them wrong again. That's how we know we're alive: we're wrong. Maybe the best thing would be to forget being right or wrong about people and just go along for the ride.

Kidman's willingness to stay on life's ride, even when it feels like a roller coaster, is proven. She doesn't deny that doing so was hard at first after the marriage fell apart. She even told me a story about being so upset that she was lying on the ground in the fetal position, weeping, while her parents, who had arrived to help her get through the whole circus, were trying to make her snap to. "That's enough now—get up!" her mother said. She did. There were other issues to deal with, such as how the divorce was going to affect her career. Kidman remembers, "At the time, it felt like the work was going to be taken away from me. I had more things that I wanted to give, do, participate in creatively, and to have had that denied prematurely would have been awful." She saw to it that none of this happened, and she had people who were true-blue behind her. One of them is Baz Luhrmann, who spent much of the first year of the breakup's aftermath with Kidman promoting *Moulin Rouge*. Luhrmann had told Kidman that, under the circumstances, he'd understand if she bowed out of the promotional duties that can make a movie live or die. Instead, she stood by him and their work as though their lives depended on it. Luhrmann recalls, "I saw her realize the motto of the film, which is 'The show must go on.' She absolutely embodied its spirit."

Between *Moulin Rouge*, *The Others*, and even the rather kooky thriller *Birthday Girl*, released last February (Kidman plays a Russian con artist with a throat-scraping, Moscow-ready accent), she made people take her seriously. As Anthony Minghella says, "Each film is so different and distinctive. They make you feel like there's an enormously rich instrument there." When Kidman received a Golden Globe and an Academy Award nomination for *Moulin Rouge* as well as a Golden Globe nomination for *The Others*, one could feel how happy people were for her. She was finally getting recognition for who she was, not who she was with. It really didn't seem to matter to her that she didn't win a prestigious statue on Oscar night. Stepping out onto that red carpet with her sister as her date, she was a class act in a pink Chanel gown.

When *The Hours* comes out this month it is bound to cause a sensation. It's hard to imagine a finer cast of actors interpreting this remarkable book, which covers three eras—the beginning of the last century, the 1950s, and the 1990s. How appropriate that it is Kidman's job to play Virginia Woolf at the time she was writing *Mrs. Dalloway* and looking for reasons to live as she struggled with thoughts of suicide. The meaning of the role is not lost on the actress. She says, "I truly believe characters come into your life at certain periods of your life for a reason, and Virginia came into my life to help me." Her performance is nothing short of astounding. Much will be made of the aristocratic prosthetic nose she wears, which makes it difficult to recognize her. But even more amazing is the way she seems to transform herself in every possible way, from the lids of her eyes to her soulful mouth to her bony elbows to the crack in her voice, which is fragile and strong at the same time. Her portrayal of Woolf, accent and all, is so convincing it's hard not to conflate the two women's lives. When I told Kidman this she smiled and made reference to a scene in the movie in which Woolf is sitting on a bench at the Richmond, England, train station, having escaped what she saw as the suffocations of her country household. Her husband, Leonard, comes running up, afraid that she has tried to do herself in again. Virginia finally lets it all out. "The scene at the train station was the reason I wanted to do the film," Kidman told me. "It is about a woman saying, 'This isn't what I want to be. I have the right to make choices for my life that are going to fulfill me.' I loved Virginia. I just love when she says, 'I'm living a life that I have no wish to live. I'm living in a town that I have no wish to live in.'"

These were the exact lines I had written down in the dark when I first saw *The Hours*. They seemed to get at the essence of what Kidman's life has been about these last few years, a period in which she has become not just a bigger star, not just an actress who deserves to be taken seriously, but a truly daring artist. Anne Roth, the costume designer who worked with Kidman on *The Hours* and who with Conor O'Sullivan perfected the soon-to-be-famous nose, said it perfectly: "It is like she is in a new skin. She is on her own satellite. She is all alone out there and it's something you want to watch. It's as if she's an amazing piece of art."

Who knows if this would have happened if she hadn't gone through all her marital difficulties? When someone turns a potential calamity into something great we cheer. In Kidman's case, she has moved people not only because she has done that, but also because of who she's been. She's shown her feelings. She's asked for help. She hasn't come up with a bunch of phony escorts to make her life look good. She doesn't seem to mind that we can see that her life may be as messy and flawed as the rest of ours. She's even been ruefully witty, as when she remarked to David Letterman, "Now I can wear heels" (a reference to the height gap between her and her ex).

On my last night of talking to her for this article, I went over to her house in Pacific Palisades for a glass of wine. It's the same house that she lived in with Cruise, which embarrasses Kidman. She says that her friends keep saying, "Sell it! Sell it!" but that she prefers things to be done gently, not in a rushed way. She's proud, however, that she finally bit the bullet and got a place in Manhattan in the West Village. When I went by the house in L.A., it happened to be September 11, the anniversary. The kids had made a fire, and Kidman was sitting with them in the den watching the news on TV, a rerun of the day's memorials and events. When it was time for them to go to bed she said, "See, everything went O.K. today. Nothing bad happened," and turned off the TV. Relief for all of us. She came back downstairs after tucking Isabella and Connor in. We went into the living room and I noticed art, such as paintings by Ben Shahn and Milton Avery, on the walls, and photography books on the table. There was a clear sense of shared lives and interests—it felt like a home, not a set. I thought about another line from *The Hours*: "I don't think two people could have been happier than we have been." For a while.

SOMETHING ABOUT MERYL

By Leslie Bennetts | January 2010

n one of the more curious plot twists of recent industry history, Hollywood has a new box-office queen.

She's certainly not new to the industry, nor is she young. While she is fabulous by any measure, she is a babe primarily by the standards of the A.A.R.P. set. For the last 30 years, she has been venerated as the best actress of her generation, and her performances have won critical raves as well as rafts of awards—but even her most ardent fans, until recently, wouldn't have linked her name with blockbuster receipts.

And yet at an age when women have traditionally been relegated to playing old crones, Meryl Streep has become a powerhouse at the box office. Last summer's *Julie & Julia*, in which Streep played the chef Julia Child [*see a profile of Child on page 168*], has earned $121 million to date. November brought the release of *Fantastic Mr. Fox*, Wes Anderson's animated film adaptation of Roald Dahl's children's story, which co-stars George Clooney and Streep as Mr. and Mrs. Fox. And a Christmas Day opening is scheduled for *It's Complicated*, which stars Streep as the ex-wife of a cad played by Alec Baldwin, who has cheated on her, divorced her, and married a very young, very gorgeous second wife with whom he has quickly become very bored— whereupon he plunges into a torrid illicit affair with his ex, who is also being romanced by a milquetoast architect played by Steve Martin.

"It's incredible—I'm 60, and I'm playing the romantic lead in romantic comedies!" Streep marvels. "Bette Davis is rolling over in her grave. She was 42 when she did *All About Eve*, and she was 54 when she did *What Ever Happened to Baby Jane?*"

Audiences have already pegged *It's Complicated*, directed by Nancy Meyers, as a hit and Streep's performance as a must-see, thanks to an irresistible trailer that elicits peals of laughter when Streep's character tells her equally middle-aged friends about her unexpected adulterous transgressions and adds, with a priceless mixture of embarrassment and pride, "Turns out I'm a bit of a slut!"

Although her name used to be associated with such angst-ridden dramas as *Sophie's Choice*, these days Streep, the recipient of two Academy Awards— as well as 15 Oscar nominations and 23 Golden Globe nominations, more than any other actor in the history of either award—can often be found in commercial crowd-pleasers that induce hilarity instead of uncontrollable sobbing. [The current tally: 21 Oscar nominations and three Academy Awards; 31 Golden Globe nominations and eight wins.]

Mamma Mia!, the 2008 screen musical, has grossed $601 million worldwide, despite some cringe-worthy reviews (for the movie, not its much-lauded heroine) and a leading man (Pierce Brosnan) who was suitably dashing but couldn't sing as well as he acts. *The Devil Wears Prada*, released the same year to widespread acclaim, has made $324 million worldwide.

The movie business—which long assumed that success lay in making films aimed at young men—has reacted to such eye-popping numbers with bemused consternation. Many studio executives have been privately convinced that it wasn't worth even a modest budget to make films about women, particularly older ones, and they seem stunned that a series of movies about middle-aged women racked up such enviable grosses. "The problem isn't just the fact that studios forget that movies about or aimed at women have an audience—they honestly don't know how to market them," says Nora Ephron, who wrote and directed *Julie & Julia*. "What they know how to market are movies aimed at teenage boys. I don't think my movie would have been made without Meryl."

Streep's success has forced Hollywood to consider a startling hypothesis:

If you make movies that actually interest women, they will buy tickets to see them. "She broke the glass ceiling of an older woman being a big star—it has never, never happened before," says Mike Nichols, who directed Streep in *Silkwood*, *Heartburn*, *Postcards from the Edge*, and HBO's *Angels in America*. "Her crusade, at this point, is to show Hollywood how much money can be made from female-driven movies," *Entertainment Weekly* commented recently.

Although the stage version of *Mamma Mia!*—which was written, produced, and directed by women—has grossed more than $2 billion and been seen by more than 30 million people worldwide since opening in 1999, the movie was greeted with what might charitably be described as faint enthusiasm. "In press screenings, there are murmurs that to be singing karaoke Abba songs in a relentlessly cheerful Hollywood musical is a terrible career misstep," *The Guardian* noted disdainfully. "After all, Streep is renowned for much more substantial roles."

More than half a billion dollars later, the movie's success has brought sweet revenge. "It's so gratifying because it's the audience that nobody really gives a shit about," Streep has said.

Given the enormous pool of underserved baby-boomers, perennially miffed that no one makes films they want to see, the recognition that life doesn't end at 30 just seems like common sense. Streep may have redefined what Hollywood views as the peak of a woman's acting career, but the real world has always offered more possibilities than Hollywood has, and audiences have particularly responded to the passion and devotion so visible in the marriage of Julia Child and her husband, Paul—who by all accounts adored his taller, larger, and more celebrated wife—as well as to the extraordinary success she achieved in later life. "I can never get over the fact that Julia Child's famous book, *Mastering the Art of French Cooking*, was published when she was almost 50 years old," Streep observed last summer. "So she didn't really become 'Julia Child' until she was 50."

Streep's net worth is rising along with her box-office clout. She has complained in the past that the film business pays actresses far less than actors, which remains the case; according to *Forbes* magazine, Hollywood's Top 10 actors earned more than twice as much as its Top 10 actresses between June

2008 and June 2009. With $24 million in earnings during that period, Streep ranked third among the women, slightly behind Angelina Jolie, who is 34, and Jennifer Aniston, who is 40.

Streep's newfound power as a moneymaker isn't the only surprise. In "An Evening with Meryl Streep," at Toronto's Royal Ontario Museum in October, film critic Johanna Schneller commented on what she saw as "something new" in Streep's recent work, a quality the critic described as "a looseness, or what I would like to call a glee."

"Are you having more fun? Are you choosing projects that are more fun?" she asked.

Streep finessed the question by attributing her selection of roles to the increasing power of women in an industry heretofore dominated by the old boys' club. "I really don't get a choice; I don't produce my own movies. So, I'm sort of like the girl at the dance who waits to be asked," said the queen of Hollywood. "I don't seek out material, I don't buy books, I don't curry favor with producers—I just wait. I think what you're referring to is something that only happens now because there are more women in decision-making positions who are able to greenlight movies."

Streep's exuberance is palpable in her performances. "The joy of working with her is that she truly thinks, 'Oh, boy—I get to do this one more day!' and working with her you certainly feel that," says Nichols.

Audiences can see that Streep is having a devilishly good time, and her enthusiasm is contagious. "When I saw *Julie & Julia*, I just laughed and laughed and laughed," says the French photographer Brigitte Lacombe, who has photographed Streep regularly for more than three decades, amassing a formidable collection of portraits. "It was a great performance of her playing an enchanting character, but it was also the joy she was having doing it. It was exhilarating to watch. And the same year, she was doing *Doubt*, with this anger and this bitterness and all she was able to do with that."

Though Cherry Jones earned rhapsodic reviews with her portrayal of *Doubt*'s implacable Sister Aloysius on Broadway, John Patrick Shanley, who wrote the play and the screenplay and directed the film version, says that casting Streep in the movie was "kind of a no-brainer. If I had asked 20 people on the subway who should play the part, they all would have said, 'Meryl Streep.'"

Working with her lived up to every expectation. "She's rigorous, stringent, and challenging in her thinking," Shanley says. "She's completely open to free association, but she has an analytical mind that is coupled with an enormous imagination, which is unusual. Meryl is spacious in her imagination and yet clinical in her approach to the material. She asks questions—of herself, of the character, of the scene, of the director—and she doesn't assume she knows the answer. She's looking around for something, and it's not about her; it's not about power or the clash of egos. It's about the clash of ideas, which is a more fun piece of territory.

"On one level she is just like a big, mischievous cat—like a cat who sits in the corner and watches everyone and her tail twitches. She's going inward and assessing outward. She's a very interesting person to be around."

Streep's meticulousness is legendary; Nichols remembers her going so far as to have fake dandruff applied to her shoulders when she played an elderly rabbi in *Angels in America*. Having directed Streep in *Julie & Julia*, Ephron says, "I would love to take credit for that amazing performance, but the truth is that she had read everything about Julia Child, she played the cooking tapes over and over between set-ups, she worked for weeks with Ann Roth to find the character through the costumes, and she even suggested that I cast Stanley Tucci as her husband."

Streep's range has dazzled observers ever since the 1970s, when the Yale Drama School graduate began performing major Shakespearean roles with the New York Shakespeare Festival while also making movies. Lacombe first met Streep back then, and the photographer instantly recognized that the aspiring actress with the odd Dutch name was far more than the latest blond ingénue. "The minute people set an eye on her, whether they were seeing her onstage or in the movies, they knew she was someone," says Lacombe. "She was obviously different."

After visiting the set of *Kramer vs. Kramer*, Lacombe shot the movie poster of Dustin Hoffman, Streep, and Justin Henry, who played the son buffeted by their divorce. Streep's performance as the estranged wife who relinquishes her child to his father's custody earned her the Academy Award for best supporting actress in 1979, and Hoffman won best actor; the film was named best picture. Three years later, Streep won the Oscar for best actress for her harrowing portrayal of a Polish concentration-camp survivor tormented by the loss of her children in *Sophie's Choice*.

Since then, nobody has doubted Streep's ability to play anguish, but her talents as a comedienne were slower to gain recognition, even though her sense of humor is one of her most visible traits in person, continually bubbling to the surface like an irrepressible underground spring. Her first comedic film role didn't come until 1989, when she co-starred with Roseanne Barr in *She-Devil*. "Surprise! Inside the Greer Garson roles Streep usually plays, a vixenish Carole Lombard is screaming to be cut loose," reported *Time* magazine.

Streep's ability to mine the humor in unlikely places stuns even veterans like Mike Nichols. "It was always in her work," he says. "When we did *Angels in America*, I said to her, 'How in God's name did you ever think of making Ethel Rosenberg funny?' She said—and I think this is key—'You never know what you're going to do until you do it.' You tap all your unconsciousnesses. In *The French Lieutenant's Woman*, when she and Jeremy Irons are finally back together again, he says, 'How could you run out on what we had?' and he throws her to the floor. Her head hits the floor—and she giggles. Because it's like Tarzan and Jane? Because she knows they're all right now? That was one of the most miraculous acting moments I've ever seen, but the punch line is that they did six takes and she only did that once. To be able to tap your inner responses and know that's the deepest part of the character is to be a great film actress."

Streep has always interspersed her films with stage roles that ranged from Brecht to Chekhov, working steadily even as she and her husband, Don Gummer—a sculptor known for his large-scale, outdoor installations—raised four children. Henry, who is 30, is an actor and musician who uses the name Henry Wolfe. At 26, Mamie is an actress who recently announced her engagement to actor Ben Walker; her work has included *Taking Woodstock* and

HBO's *John Adams*. Grace, 23, made her Off Off Broadway debut in 2008 in *The Sexual Neuroses of Our Parents*, and Louisa, 18, graduated from high school last spring.

As the last of her children leaves the nest, Nichols sees this stage of Streep's life as another reason for her evident sense of well-being. "I think she's very happy," he says. "Anybody raising four children has worries, but they turned out so great, and you begin to relax a little bit. I think you're seeing her freedom and her strength and her relief, to have brought four kids all the way through into hot careers of their own and happy love relationships. You still have them invisibly connected to you, but she's free. At last you're not thinking, 'I have to run home,' and things happen out of that freedom that are, if not new, deeper."

Streep has consistently guarded both her family's privacy and her own, avoiding as much of the red-carpet hoopla and self-exposure in the service of publicity as she could get away with. Throughout Streep's career observers have noted, as the film critic Molly Haskell wrote in 1988, "her determination to be an actress rather than a star in the old-fashioned sense, and to do idiosyncratic, theatrical roles in a medium in which success depends on being loved by huge numbers of people. In her willingness to forgo easy identification, Streep brings to dramatic point something that has been nosing its way to the forefront of consciousness for some time: the whole issue of a woman's lovability. . . . No one has more steadfastly refused to look like a dish or ask for audience identification than Meryl Streep. . . . The determination to be different—each role not only different from the other, but different from what we assume Meryl Streep . . . to be—is the one constant in her career. An anti-star mystique seems to govern her life and her roles, a convergence, perhaps, of her seriousness as a performer and the inhibitions of a well-bred Protestant."

Any inhibitions notwithstanding, a vibrant sexuality has remained a crucial aspect of Streep's appeal, despite her advancing years and the limitations that others might try to impose in response. When Clint Eastwood cast her to star opposite him in *The Bridges of Madison County*, which won Streep an Oscar nomination for best actress, in 1996, his reason was simple: "She's the greatest actress in the world," he said with a shrug.

That said, Streep reports, "There was a big fight over how I was too old to play the part, even though Clint was nearly 20 years older than me. The part was for a 45-year-old woman, and Clint said, 'This is a 45-year-old woman.'"

When casting female roles, directors and producers have often applied a comically exaggerated double standard about age. With Streep now playing the ex-wife and current love interest of Alec Baldwin, who is actually nine years younger than she is, many observers have started wondering whether such old-fashioned biases are really changing in ways that will affect other actresses, or only in relation to Streep, who has always been *sui generis*. In any case, a good part of her aforementioned glee may have to do with her ongoing amazement that, after all these years, she's still getting away with doing what she loves. "I've been given great, weird, interesting parts well past my 'Sell by' date," she says. "I remember saying to Don when I was 38, 'Well, it's over.' And then we kicked the can down the road a little further."

She's still kicking it, but the sense lingers that there is something different about the way she has approached her career of late. At the program in Toronto, she finally described the critical shift in her attitude, both toward her work and toward herself.

In her 20s, Streep was often criticized for not being a conventional beauty. "I have a really long nose," she said merrily at the Royal Ontario Museum. One famous story has Streep auditioning for the part of the damsel in distress that was eventually won by Jessica Lange in Dino De Laurentiis's 1976 remake of *King Kong*. Streep's audition failed to impress the producer, who commented to his son, in Italian, "Why did you send me this pig? This woman is so ugly! Blech!" Having assumed that she wouldn't understand what he said, De Laurentiis was shocked when Streep replied, in fluent Italian, "I'm very sorry that I disappoint you." (De Laurentiis has denied this exchange occurred.)

Such insults were painful, but maturity and experience have freed Streep from wasting her energy on suffering over them. "So much of a young girl's life—of my life—was taken up with worrying if I was attractive enough, or appealing enough," she said in Toronto. "After a while, I got sort of tired of worrying about it. And also," she added mischievously, "I was never pretty enough."

In her recent performances, one gets the impression that Streep has finally said to herself, "Oh, the hell with it." And that feeling of personal liberation is exciting to watch. As the mother of three girls, she knows all too well how much pressure females feel to dim their light. "As girls grow up," Streep observes, "as soon as boys come into the picture, you figure out that you have to modify that assertiveness thing in order to even be acceptable, let alone appealing, within the cohort of girls as well as boys."

She has found it an enormous relief to outgrow those constraints. "I can't remember the last time I really worried about being appealing," she says with a snort of laughter. "I think it was a really long time ago. It's freeing as an actress, but whether a director likes it or not is a different thing. I remember [director and co-star] Albert Brooks saying to me in *Defending Your Life*, 'Could you just make it a little sweeter?'—and that's been repeated by other people in the years since then." This time her derisive snort is much louder. "But I don't listen to it."

So how did she free herself? "I don't think it's something anyone can tell you," Streep says. "I think you just have to get sick of hearing the accommodation in your approach to things . . . the way people have to get sick of drinking or drugs before they stop. As there begins to be less time ahead of you, you want to be exactly who you are, without making it easier for everyone else. I'm not sure I ever was really comfortable swanning around as a girl, anyway."

Given how striking she was and is, it's still difficult for others to believe that Streep could ever have agonized about her looks. "I did not realize she was thinking she wasn't beautiful enough, because to me she was so beautiful," Lacombe says. "But she was not a regular beauty; she looked different. She had some things that set her apart. That was true then, and it's true now. There's that quote from Mike Nichols—he said, 'She looks like she swallowed a lightbulb.' There's something that's completely transparent about her, a glowing quality that's quite striking and delicate. She's so fine-looking, with very fine features."

But, for the photographer, as for a director or an audience, Streep's real power emanates from a deeper level. "She has a desire to play, and she's always ready to jump in," Lacombe observes. "There's a sense of great joy and being in the moment. She's someone who is not afraid of anything, and she is not afraid of being ridiculous. She does not watch herself, in the sense of actors who try to present a certain image when they're not in character."

Streep's famous transparency allows audiences to witness everything, just as it does with the camera. "There are quick changes of mood—extraordinary, like quicksilver—and you can see them on her skin," Lacombe says. "When someone has a strong emotion or is about to cry, when the skin becomes blotchy and red and the eyes swell up—I've seen that happening with Meryl in such a subtle way. There is the ability to be in emotional places, and I think that's why she is the actress she is."

Although Streep's acting is inextricably connected with the way she looks, she has always struck Lacombe as being virtually unique among performers. "I think there is a big absence of vanity in Meryl," Lacombe says. "In *A Cry in the Dark*, she portrayed a character who was quite unsympathetic, but you never got the sense that she was trying to put you on her side, as some actors do. That's another great, endearing quality of hers—I'm sure women sense that Meryl does not have any vanity. She never acted as a woman who was entitled. You know how some beautiful women just act beautiful? There is never any of that with Meryl—never.

"With others, they are hypnotized by their own image, especially fashion people; they get completely enraptured. How many shots can you see of the same actress looking beautiful in every magazine? It's like falling into a false sense of beauty and being worshipped for all the wrong reasons. They all do it. A lot of it is huge insecurity. Many actresses won't wear their hair in a certain way, because it's not the most flattering, or they won't be photographed from a certain angle. But once someone like Meryl chooses a part, she does what is good for the character. She doesn't bring her own insecurities and fears."

As she ages, Streep's work derives additional power from her refusal to alter her face with cosmetic surgery or Botox. "If you start to do something like that, it's very hard to stop," Lacombe says. "If you understand that what makes your work good is not the way you look, as you grow older you take different parts. It's like women in real life who want to hang on to a certain part of their life, and to look younger. They miss every other stage of their life. To try to stop the time, to look young—it's such a futile, absurd way to look at life in general, and it's very detrimental to their work. They may think that it prolongs their work, and maybe they might get one or two parts more, but their face is their tool, and also what they understand about life, what they go through in life. If you alter it, you deprive yourself of some of what you need to do your work well."

Streep's disdain for such desperate measures is based on her assessment of the toll they take. "When I see it in people I meet, it's like an interruption in communication with them," she says. "It's like a flag in front of the view, and that, for an actor, is like wearing a veil—it's not a good thing."

This attitude has long made Streep the perfect photographic subject for Lacombe. "I'm so anti all the artifice," Lacombe says. "What I do is very simple; I'm not interested in transforming people."

She gestures to the enormous coffee-table book of her work, *Lacombe*, which was published in 2008 and contains several riveting pictures of Streep. "To me, that's Meryl, not an actress," Lacombe says. "But it's very rare. Even actresses in their 20s and 30s cannot look at themselves that way. They all long to be looking like a model—and then they wonder, Why am I not Meryl Streep? To me, physical beauty is not enough; it's not interesting. Beauty is *everything*. You want to have someone who will also be funny, who will also be moving, who will also be intelligent—someone who will have some contribution to bring, not just a look. Meryl is interesting; she is very funny and very smart.

"But I don't think there is ever a moment when she is enjoying the process of being photographed. Most actresses, or women, will find a moment where they enjoy being looked at, if it is in the best light and with good intent. I don't think Meryl has that moment—ever. She's not interested in looking more beautiful or making more time so we can do better. I understand not wanting to be in front of the camera; for somebody very well known, it's a complete bore and an imposition. I'm sure she sees that as Being Meryl Streep, and it's not such an interesting part to play for her. She has a lot of patience and enjoyment if she is in character, but not if she's herself."

Streep's explanation is simpler: "I hate to have my picture taken!" she exclaims.

Looking over Lacombe's photographs, which reveal Streep in a compelling array of moods and stages, another observer might remark upon her enduring beauty, her chameleon-esque ability to transform herself, or the remarkable range of her roles. But what she herself sees is very different. "I can really see when I'm pregnant," she muses. "You see the little squirrel cheeks and stuff. In the 1986 picture, I'm pregnant with Grace; my hands are on my face because I'm holding the squirrels in—holding them back!" Another hoot of laughter.

The 2002 portrait, which Lacombe took after Streep's makeup had been scrubbed off at the end of a shoot, was so unadorned that Streep's publicist was horrified to learn that the American Film Institute was using it on a Sunset Boulevard billboard to advertise its tribute to Streep. "But she loved it," the publicist says.

"It's my favorite one because they scraped all the crap off my face," Streep says, snickering. "I'm looking at Brigitte after all these years—we confront each other through the lens, and she does get it: 'Take the picture! Get it done so I can go home!'"

And now Streep is tired of talking about herself, so it's time to sum up how she feels about this stage in her life. "I'm very fucking grateful to be alive," she says fervently. "I have so many friends who are sick or gone, and I'm here. Are you kidding? No complaints!"

FOREVER CHER

By Krista Smith | December 2010

Malibu, a 21-mile stretch of oceanfront in Los Angeles County, is where many of the rich and profoundly famous members of the entertainment industry choose to live. Known as the Malibu Movie Colony in the 1920s, it has been home to everyone from Gloria Swanson to Barbra Streisand, from John McEnroe to Tom Hanks, from Britney Spears to Brad and Angelina. Locals invariably tell you that the house Bing Crosby paid around $2,500 for in the 1920s was bought by Robert Redford in 1982 for nearly $2 million. Now houses sell in the neighborhood of $45 million. Just off Pacific Coast Highway, I pull into the private driveway of one such house, a cross between a Venetian palazzo and a Moorish castle. Waiting for me inside is the most glittering Malibu resident of them all: Cher.

An assistant greets me and asks me to wait in the living room, which is suspended seemingly right over the crashing waves of the Pacific. In 2007, Cher sold all of her Gothic furnishings at auction and engaged Martyn Lawrence-Bullard to do a complete makeover. Describing their collaboration, Lawrence-Bullard says, "Cher loves all things that are Eastern—Moroccan, Syrian-inlaid furniture, Indonesian pieces, beautiful 17th- and 18th-century Chinese things. Everything has to feel very Zen, but it also has to have that bit of Cher pizzazz." The ceiling of the living room is painted in a 16th-century Moroccan design and finished in gold leaf. After a few minutes, the assistant leads me up to the star's bedroom. According to Lawrence-Bullard, the bed originally belonged to Natacha Rambova, who was the wife of Rudolph Valentino. "I bought it at an amazing Hollywood auction of all this incredible furniture that came from the MGM Studios."

Cher admits that she can't remember the last time she sat down for a lengthy interview. "What are we going to *talk* about for two hours?" she asks, sitting cross-legged on a sofa next to a wall of windows. "There's no view like it in all of Malibu," she says. "It's one of the reasons I don't sell this place. It's so big for me, but it's unbelievable." Cher has two other properties, she says, "an apartment in town—for absolutely no reason—and a house in Hawaii. When I sold my house in Aspen, I thought my kids were going to disown me." With no makeup, wearing jeans, a canary-yellow sweatshirt, and Day-Glo orange Nikes, she looks more like a teenager than the rock goddess who has sold some 100 million records. Although she has a well-known fondness for wigs, she is not wearing one today. Her hair, long and jet black, is parted in the center. She has just finished a voice lesson in order to get back into performance shape, after having taken a summer hiatus from her Las Vegas show, which began in 2008 at the Colosseum in Caesars Palace. Cher got a reported $60 million a year and a three-year contract for about 200 performances. The show will close in February.

At 64, she has been up and down too many times to count. "I feel like a bumper car. If I hit a wall, I'm backing up and going in another direction," she says, adding, "And I've hit plenty of fucking walls in my career. But I'm not stopping. I think maybe that's my best quality: I just don't stop."

Cher, who has been in show business for 46 years, has had a No. 1 record in each of the last five decades, from "I Got You Babe," in 1965, to "Song for the Lonely," in 2002. She has won an Oscar for best actress, in *Moonstruck* (1987); three Golden Globes for her performances in *The Sonny and Cher Comedy Hour* (1973), *Silkwood* (1983), and *Moonstruck*; an Emmy for her 2003 Farewell Tour special; and a 2000 Grammy for best dance recording, "Believe."

———

This fall at the 2010 MTV Video Music Awards, she stole the show in a sheer bodysuit similar to the one that got her banned from prime time 20 years ago on that same network. She was greeted with a standing ovation by the audience members, most of whom were still in diapers when her "If I Could Turn Back Time" video stretched the boundaries of what could be shown on-air. "So far tonight, I'm the oldest chick, with the biggest hair, and the littlest costume," she announced before presenting Lady Gaga—wearing a meat dress—with the Video of the Year Award. A star-struck Gaga said, "I never thought I'd be asking Cher to hold my meat purse." A week later, Cher was spoofing the exchange in the opening monologue at her Vegas show. "I thought Lady Gaga said to hold her *mink* purse—fuck, this is a *steak! [Audience laughter.]* I thought, I've seen weirder things than that in my life." She wasn't so much passing the torch as saying, *Remember, bitches, I was the original diva.*

"I know I'm not supposed to have any opinions about politics, because I'm famous," says Cher. Yet the first half of our conversation, over tea served in commemorative mugs from her 2002 tour, is about little else. Cher supported Hillary Clinton in the last election, and although she accepts the fact that Barack Obama inherited insurmountable problems, she still thinks Hillary would have done a better job. A large portion of Cher's charitable work is devoted to the veterans who have served in Iraq and Afghanistan. "I was buying helmet inserts for guys who were in Iraq. Football players have more protection on their heads than the guys over there do." One of her immediate goals is to join Obama's Veterans Task Force.

"I would be willing to pay a lot more taxes, because I make a lot more money, but I don't want to give them more to just fuck things up more," she continues. "It really should fall on people like me to get together and do things to help the people in this country. If you're not worrying about how to put food on your table, you [should be] worrying about why other people don't *have* food on *their* table. I remember a great America where we made everything. There was a time when the only thing you got from Japan was a really bad cheap transistor radio that some aunt gave you for Christmas."

Cher actively criticized the Bush administration, and she was known to call in to C-SPAN occasionally. "I got so obsessed with it that it was kind of interfering with my life. Sarah Palin came on, and I thought, Oh, fuck, this is the end. Because a dumb woman is a dumb woman." She doesn't stop there. On the subject of Arizona governor Jan Brewer, Cher says, "She was worse than Sarah Palin, if that is possible. This woman was like a deer in headlights. She's got a handle on the services of the state, and I would not let her handle the remote control."

However, she happens to have an appreciation for the conservative televangelist Joel Osteen. "He's only got kind things to say, and he's not crying or yelling or telling everybody how they're going to be damned—and send money right away. I have a problem with religion that makes it so, like, 'We are the ones. We are the chosen ones.'" I ask her if she's religious, and she confesses, "I'm just the worst little Buddhist in town. I wish that I did the things that I really believe in, because when I do, my life goes much smoother. I can get pretty wrapped up in the dramatic hysteria."

Cher has never exercised the benefit of spin; she prefers to be honest and direct. When Chastity, her daughter with the late Sonny Bono, came out as a lesbian, in 1995, Cher was angry with her at first, claiming that she felt as if she were the last to know. She admitted shortly afterward, however, that she had behaved in a very uncharacteristic way. Chastity has since gone through a gender reassignment and is now living as a man. Last May he legally changed his name to Chaz Bono. Cher says, "Well, she's a very smart girl—boy! This is where I get into trouble. My pronouns are fucked. I still don't remember to call her 'him.' She's really cool about it—such an easygoing person. Because I've hardly called her Chastity since her brother was born."

The brother is Elijah Blue Allman, 34 and an artist, Cher's son with Gregg Allman, a founding member of the very successful Allman Brothers Band, whom she impulsively married in Vegas in 1975. They divorced several years later, owing to Allman's heroin addiction. "You know, I loved him," Cher admits, "but I didn't really want Elijah around him alone. It's hard finding a drug addict who is also going to be a father."

She speaks touchingly and at length about her children, both of whom live in Los Angeles. "The moment Elijah gets in trouble, he runs to Chaz.

He just hightails his ass right there. He's doing art projects, he's had two exhibits, and he's actually sold everything. We'll see what happens. They are both very talented, both very artistic, and they are good children. They're grown-ups. They're so different. Chaz had a dad for a long time. Sonny was a great parent for a young child—even like 12, 13. But the moment you had ideas that were contrary, he was not quite as interested. Elijah didn't really have Gregory. Gregory moved off someplace else. He was the nicest person, even when he was doing drugs. But when you're doing drugs, the people you're hanging with aren't exactly. . . . You're not going to church to find these people."

Cher raised her children essentially as a single mother. "Elijah always called Chastity Da-Di-Da, so we shortened it to Da." Recently, she says, "I said to Chaz, 'I can't *not* call you Da,' and he said, 'Mom, don't be silly.' One time, when Chaz was little, we were on a field trip, and she said, 'I'm so pissed off, Mom. You can never *not* be Cher—we can never just *do* something.'" She concludes, "So your kids pay. I did the best I could do, and yet it was definitely lacking." Does she think her kids bear any residual anger? "I think Chaz is pretty much finished with it, and I think Elijah has a little longer to go, but they both really love me a lot. But it's hard."

When we get on the topic of her children's struggles with substance abuse—Chaz has been through rehab for pain medication, and Elijah for heroin—Cher doesn't blink. "It's weird, because both of my children had the same drug problems as their fathers—same drug of choice," she says. "My father was a heroin addict, and my sister's father was an alcoholic. But it jumped us. It jumped my mom, too, because my grandfather was an alcoholic. I didn't not do drugs because of moral issues. I tried a couple of drugs, but I never felt good out of control. I have the constitution of a fruit fly. I can't do coffee, but I can do Dr Pepper."

Cher seems to have arrived at an appreciation—if not a full understanding—of Chaz's choice: "If I woke up tomorrow in a guy's body, I would just kick and scream and cry and fucking rob a bank, because I cannot see myself as anything but who I am—a girl. I would not take it as well as Chaz has. I couldn't imagine it."

———

With *Burlesque*, which opens on Thanksgiving, Cher has her first lead role in a movie in a decade. Christina Aguilera, the 29-year-old pop star and songwriter, who has won four Grammys and sold 48 million records, makes her film debut opposite Cher. *Burlesque* is set in a nightclub in Los Angeles. Cher plays Tess, the proprietor; Stanley Tucci plays the stage manager; and Aguilera is a small-town aspiring dancer and singer. The poster says it all: IT TAKES A LEGEND TO MAKE A STAR.

Clint Culpepper, the president of Screen Gems, an arm of Sony Pictures, is responsible for getting Cher back into acting. Aguilera remembers, "I was the first person to sign on to the movie. When I heard that Cher was a possibility, I said, 'Clint, go after her. *Go get her!*'" Cher confirms, "It was Clint. He got down on his knees and begged. We went to the office, and [the director] Steve Antin had such a vision, and Clint had a passion. David Geffen got involved, sending me e-mails from St. Tropez saying, 'Sweetheart, you have to do this.' I was getting barraged."

Culpepper remembers describing Aguilera to Cher: "You don't understand. She adores you. She only wants to make it with you. This is a chick that would drink your bathwater." After Cher agreed to do the project, Culpepper persuaded Aguilera, who had just finished rehearsing on the Sony lot and had her baby son in her arms, to pay a surprise visit to Cher, who was on a nearby soundstage, rehearsing her Vegas show. "So we walk in, and Cher smiles and walks over to us. Christina says, 'Hi. I'm the one that would drink your bathwater.' And Cher says, 'I'm going to say to you what Meryl Streep said to me on the set of *Silkwood*: "Welcome. I'm glad you're here."'" And she hugged her."

I ask Aguilera, who was born in 1980 (the year her co-star turned 34), when she discovered Cher. "I noticed her for the first time when she was doing 'If I Could Turn Back Time.' She was in her sort of ass-less leather getup, and I think she was performing with a bunch of sailors. Maybe that was engraved in my brain and then inspired me later, for my own ass-less-chaps moment with my video 'Dirty.' I guess I remember that moment so well because I have such an appreciation for a strong woman, a woman who's been there, done everything, before everyone else—who had the guts to do it."

Stanley Tucci plays Cher's counterpart and wingman, Sean. He too admits to falling under her spell. "She's so charming, so funny, so smart, even though she always pretends she isn't. You can't help but fall in love a little bit. We were instantly comfortable with each other. I get star-struck. And I *was* star-struck. But within 10 minutes you're calling each other filthy names, and you're not star-struck anymore."

To understand Cher, you have to go back to Cherilyn Sarkisian La Piere. As David Geffen, her former lover and *consigliere* (and her current neighbor in Malibu), says, "She captured the *Zeitgeist* a very long time ago, and she never left. To do that is a miracle."

Born in El Centro, California, Cher lived most of her childhood in the Valley, a district in Los Angeles approximately 30 minutes from Hollywood. She says she always wanted to be famous. Would she have felt the same way if she had been born in Kansas? "I would have gotten my ass out of there so quickly! Driving around on my tricycle at four, I shouted to everyone, 'We've got to get *out* of here! We belong in *town*!'"

Her grandmother, who recently died at the age of 96, was 13 when she had Cher's mother, Georgia Holt, a fair-haired, green-eyed beauty, who at 84 lives just down the road from Cher in Malibu, as does Cher's half-sister, Georganne. Cher's father fled when she was just a baby, and things became so difficult at one point that she spent time in a Catholic orphanage. "My mother told me once about how she got pregnant with me and didn't want to be with my dad; she was just so young and inexperienced. My grandmother said, 'You have a bright future.' She actually suggested an abortion, so my mom was in the doctor's office—a back-alley doctor—getting on the table. And then at the last minute she said, 'I can't do this. I don't care what happens—I can't do this.'"

They had a very bohemian lifestyle. Georgia Holt married eight times (three times to Cher's biological father). "Our life was so chaotic, just one insane moment after another," recalls Cher. "They were all artists and models and dancers. I remember, once, my mother saying, 'You should have a stable future' and blah, blah, blah. I said, 'I don't think I *want* a stable future if it's going to be like our neighbors'. I don't want to be like *them*.'"

I ask her if it's the old fear of being broke that drives her to keep working, when most people her age would be resting on their laurels. She responds immediately: "I was driving today from the studio, and I looked up at this apartment building. It was kind of shabby. They had this lamppost with four lights hanging off of it, and I thought, They are really trying hard to make that unattractive two-foot part of the balcony special. I looked up at it, and for this awful chill of a moment I thought, God, I don't ever want to go back to this. Because when you're little and you live in some awful place, first of all, it's crummy, and second of all, you're ashamed. I remember being really ashamed of my clothes. I was so hard on my shoes. My mom would say, 'Jesus Christ, Cher, we can't afford shoes. Stop this!' I remember going to school with rubber bands around my shoes to keep my soles on. But it wasn't always like that. We ate a can of stew or a can of beans one week, but then sometimes we lived in Beverly Hills. It was a very strange life."

She dropped out of high school in the 11th grade and started taking acting lessons. At 16 she moved out of the house, but not before starting an affair with the heartthrob Warren Beatty, who was then 25. Soon after that, she met Sonny Bono, a songwriter and protégé of the producer Phil Spector, at a coffee shop in 1963. (Cher sang background vocals on several of Spector's biggest hits, including the Ronettes' "Be My Baby" and the Righteous Brothers' "You've Lost That Lovin' Feelin'.") "I had such a hero worship of Sonny, long after we were together. I just thought he was great." There was an 11-year age difference, but they lived together almost immediately and were rarely ever apart.

Sonny and Cher catapulted to fame in 1965 with their hit single "I Got You Babe." They charted 11 *Billboard* Top 40 hits between 1965 and 1972, including six Top 10 hits. *The Sonny and Cher Comedy Hour* was one of television's most popular shows from 1971 to 1974, landing Cher—alone—on the cover of *Time* in 1975.

Although the couple was wildly successful, they lived pretty traditionally.

Working long days on the set, never into drugs, Cher would go home almost every night and cook dinner with her husband. "I think I went out two times alone the entire time I was married to Sonny."

The couple spent a lot of time with an older Hollywood crowd that included Lucille Ball, Jack Benny, and Henry Fonda. According to Cher, "I knew Lucy since I was little. I was crazy about her. My mom was an extra on her show. One time, we were at this party, and Johnny Carson got really pissed off at me, because it was the second inauguration of Nixon. I thought Nixon was a big idiot, and Lucy thought he was a big idiot, and she was making jokes, and I was hysterically laughing. Carson got furious and said that I should get out of the room because I was being disrespectful. He would have never said boo to Lucy—she would have chewed him up and spit him out."

Sonny's domineering control of Cher strained their life together. He had married a teenager, but soon she became a woman and a mother. Although he created most of their material, Cher was the superstar, the one everyone wanted to see. She says, "He told me when we were together, 'One day you are going to leave me. You are going to go on and do great things.' He wrote me this poem, and I wish to God that I had kept it. He said, 'You are a butterfly, meant to be seen by all, not to be kept by one.' I wouldn't have left him if he hadn't had such a tight grip—*such a tight grip*."

At the start of their big success, Sonny created Cher Enterprises, of which he owned 95 percent and their lawyer owned 5 percent. "Sonny did a couple of things . . . treating me more like the golden goose than like his wife," Cher says. By 1974 the marriage was beyond repair. That's when Cher learned that she owned nothing and was prohibited from working on her own in music, television, or film.

Enter 30-year-old music mogul David Geffen, who not only became her romantic partner but also became involved in extricating her from a crippling financial contract. Today, Geffen sums it up this way: "When they broke up, she was deeply in debt and under contract to him. It was a terrible situation. It was certainly specific to their relationship. It's hard to talk about this, because of the fact that Sonny's dead. Let's just say she survived all that."

"David's one of the smartest men I've ever known," Cher tells me. "I lived with him for two years, and just on a daily basis we had a wonderful time. I *loved* him. I didn't know anything. I went from one kind of take-charge man to another. David helped me so much. I had no money and no way to live. If it wasn't for David, I don't know where I would have been. I would have been in the *street*."

She continues, "I did modeling, because that was the only thing that I could do to keep myself going." In front of the cameras of Richard Avedon and other major photographers, Cher posed for a series of what would become iconic images. Still, she was frustrated. "My friends were Jack Nicholson, Warren Beatty, Anjelica, Goldie . . . all these women and men who were working at their prime. And I couldn't take a job. I couldn't do anything."

Eventually, Cher became untangled from Sonny and their contractual arrangement, and as the 70s drew to a close, she returned to recording, brushing the charts with the disco hit "Take Me Home." She also set about re-inventing herself. She attracted the attention of filmmaker Robert Altman, who cast her in a stage play he was directing, *Come Back to the Five & Dime, Jimmy Dean, Jimmy Dean*. Her performance impressed director Mike Nichols so much that he cast her in *Silkwood* as Meryl Streep's lesbian roommate, a role that earned Cher her first Academy Award nomination.

We hung out and drank plum wine—*eww*—after work. Cher was really fun," says Streep. "I was smitten by her openness, both as an actress and as a person. It's incredibly disarming—you're a little worried for her, like: Are you sure you want to be telling me all this? Her lack of inhibition is part of what endeared her to the national audience on *The Sonny and Cher Comedy Hour*—that's where I first saw her. Most people on TV had a little TV veneer back then, a performing gloss, but her gloss was not only her beauty but how easily she wore it and dismissed it, like 'No big deal.' For a showgirl, there's not a phony bone in her body. What you see is what you get, and when she dresses up and gets gorgeous, you get *a whole lot*."

The two women are still close. "She's so good," says Cher, "and she makes me laugh hysterically. We are opposites: she takes everything so easily, and I'm so stressed about everything." She gloats, "I was responsible for Mamie [Gummer, the actress, the second of Streep's four children]! I take full credit. We were in Texas doing *Silkwood*, and Don [Gummer] was there with Henry [their son]. Meryl said, 'We need some time alone. Take Henry—it's Halloween. Please, just take him.' So I took Henry, and she got pregnant with Mamie."

Once Cher's career in film was launched, she ruled the 80s as serious actress, sex symbol, and MTV rock diva. The 90s brought more film roles, and Cher continued to evolve as an artist. As for Sonny, who had re-created himself so many times, his last metamorphosis was as a Republican congressman. In 1998, while skiing in Lake Tahoe, he was fatally injured. He was 62. Cher delivered the eulogy at his televised memorial service.

"I forgive him, I think," she says. "He hurt me in so many ways, but there was something. He was so much more than a husband—a terrible husband, but a great mentor, a great teacher. There was a bond between us that could not be broken. If he had agreed to just disband Cher Enterprises and start all over again, I would have never ever left. Just split it down the middle, 50–50." I ask her if she thought he had regretted not doing so. She replies, "I'm sure he must have."

Although Cher never remarried after her divorce from Gregg Allman, she has been far from celibate. She was the original cougar, long before Demi Moore and Susan Sarandon made it fashionable. A confessed serial monogamist, Cher dated a number of men who were significantly younger—Tom Cruise, rock guitarist Richie Sambora, and Robert Camilletti, a bartender-actor whom the tabloids named "the Bagel Boy" (because he had worked for a time in a bagel shop) and who was with her for three years. When I ask her if she still talks to any of them, she says, "Old boyfriends make good friends. Robert comes to Christmas dinner. He now flies G Vs—he is a huge pilot. He flies for all the biggest names in this town. He flew me to Jamaica."

Three weeks after talking to Cher in Malibu, I arrive at an LAX hangar to fly to Las Vegas on the private G V provided for her by Caesars Palace. Her posse includes Jen, her personal assistant for 17 years; Deb, her other assistant, who has been with her for 34 years; and Lindsay Scott, her manager. One row of seats is taken up by a spectacular Mackie costume: an enormous sunburst of golden quills over a full-length cloak. Soon Cher boards the plane, wearing sunglasses, her signature cowboy hat, a black zip-up sweatshirt, and sandals. I notice that she has bubble-gum-pink polish on her toes. She sits right in front of me, says hello, and gets a Dr Pepper.

I comment on how great her feet look. She says, "My grandmother had the most beautiful feet. When she was dying—my sister got there first, of course, because I'm always late—I opened the door and heard her laughing and joking. She's dying, she's 96 years old, and she pulls a manicured foot out from under the covers with a *decal* on it!" I ask if they were close, and she replies, "Yes. She was just a mean bitch most of the time, but I was her favorite because I was the one who could act like an adult."

Genetics have always favored Cher, who is part Armenian and part Cherokee. Her mother is still great-looking and a size 8, and Cher's body has remained impressively unchanged throughout her career. She has openly admitted to having had work done on her nose, mouth, and breasts, but, as she was once quoted as saying, "If I want to put my tits on my back, it's nobody's business but my own."

Seeing her in daylight with very little makeup on, I'm amazed at how normal she looks. It's only when she's fully decked out in wigs and costumes that she becomes The Legend. She says, "I've been screaming at the top of my lungs at my family, 'Work out! Work out! Old age is coming!' At some point you will need the strength. Who would have ever thought you would get this old?"

We talk about aging. She has always been candid about her unhappiness with getting older, feeling that she peaked at 40, and 24 years later she's still not happy. "I think Meryl is doing it great. The stupid bitch is doing it better than *all* of us!" she says, smiling. "But I don't like it. It's getting in my way. I have a job to do, and it's making my job harder."

We land in Vegas about 5:40 P.M., and two hours later Cher is descending in a gilded cage above the sold-out crowd of 4,300. Wearing a gold gown and a headpiece that must weigh 10 pounds, she waves as the lights swoop over her adoring fans. It's a tight, 90-minute show, as per Vegas rules: these people need to get back to the slot machines. During the performance, she makes 13 costume changes. She has four wardrobe attendants and gets out of each costume and into another in less than two minutes. Bob Mackie, her longtime fashion collaborator, who has been called the Sultan of Sequins, designed all the costumes, including several vintage numbers she brings out. One major crowd-pleaser is a floor-length Indian feathered headdress, with which she wears nothing but a buckskin flap and a halter to sing "Half Breed" in a montage of her greatest hits.

"She's a chameleon, but you never lose her," says Mackie. "You put a blond wig on her and you still see Cher. Forty years ago everyone thought, Oh, she's so strange, so weird, so big and gawky. Well, I saw a beautiful little girl and thought, I can work with that. That became part of the attraction of the television show: How naked was she going to be?" I ask him if he has ever told her she's going too far. "Oh, I've said it many times. But, you know, the lady gets what the lady wants."

There are 18 dancers in the Vegas show, including several aerialists. Cher confesses to longing for the giant crowds you get when you're touring. "I really miss the arenas. I won't do what I did last time [a grueling 325-performance tour that went from 2002 to 2005, from which she is rumored to have grossed $200 million]. There's an energy for me that is different than Vegas. On the road, it's like people are already having a party, and I just happen to arrive late."

Her stamina is something to behold. "It's not an easy job," she says. "You just have to make it look easy. But also, it's just a job. I'm not doing anything that's monumental. I know what I do is kind of a tonic for people. I'm either dying in my house or onstage."

One thing continues to bug her. "Sonny and I still aren't in the [Rock and Roll] Hall of Fame, and it just seems kind of rude, because we were a huge part of a certain kind of music, and we lasted for a very long time. . . . I have so much of everything that I want that those things don't usually bother me. It bothers me a little bit more because Sonny was a good writer, and we started something that no one else was doing. We were weird hippies before there was a name for it, when the Beatles were wearing sweet little haircuts and round-collared suits. The Rolling Stones were the only ones who understood us. People hated us here; we had to go to Europe to become famous. We influenced a generation, and it's like: What more do you want? Actors don't take me that seriously, either. So I always thought, I'm not an actor; I'm not a singer; I'm somewhere in between. And I've always felt like an outsider, so it doesn't bother me anymore. I like that status, truthfully."

At this point in her life Cher's sense of irony is well established. She is content to be the punch line of the joke, as long as she has the last laugh. At one point in the Vegas show, she asks the crowd, "Does this headdress make my ass look fat?" Then she turns and walks offstage.

LENA WAITHE

—

READY FOR LENA

By Jacqueline Woodson | April 2018

In your life, if you're lucky enough, you are born during a moment in time when the world is ready for the change you're bringing. So all that's left for you to do is your work. If you are a child named Lena Waithe, you find your passion on the television screen, or, as you call it, your Third Parent. Your mother, knowing that in front of the screen you're safe from the streets of Chicago, allows you unlimited watching. The Cosby Show *and* A Different World *bring you beautiful people, families you understand, and lots of laughter. And because when your grandmother watches with you she controls the remote, you watch old reruns of* The Jeffersons, Good Times, All in the Family, *and realize as you watch these people that this is what you have—words and characters and story. These are the tools these shows are giving you. So you lean into the screen. Already you know there isn't a mirror the television is holding up to you; there isn't a child like you on the screen. Not in the 1990s. Not yet. So you find your strength and a deep belief in yourself in the streets and family dinners of Chicago—a place you call home, a long way from your grandmother's own Arkansas. You're clear-eyed and queer from the womb, born as part of a larger narrative—that of the Great Migration. Already, there is resistance running through your veins. Already, at seven, you know your own dream. So you gather a posse around you. And in your 20s, you move to California, thirsty, eager, ready. Slowly, the bigger world begins to see you. We see you, Lena Waithe. We see you.*

f you haven't heard of Lena Waithe, check yourself for a pulse. She is disrupting the hell out of Hollywood. As the first black woman to nail an Emmy Award for Outstanding Writing for a Comedy Series, Lena—along with a crew of other black creatives—is sending a message to the world that Black Brilliance has arrived in Hollywood and has not come to play.

Lena and I sit down to dinner for the first time, at the Four Seasons in Beverly Hills. Having spent the past week in Utah for the Sundance Film Festival, both of us are beyond happy to be rid of our snow boots and winter coats. And because I've arrived at the restaurant a few minutes before Lena, I've had time to do what many of us do when we walk into spaces like this— count the Blacks. Now that Lena has joined me, there are two of us.

In this moment the shine is on Lena. She is all dapper and grace as she enters. Broad-shouldered and fast-walking, she flashes a smile at our hostess and emphasizes her please-and-thank-yous with our waitress. When she sits down across from me, she immediately removes her cap, and I smile, having grown up watching the boys and men around me get chastised for not removing their hats fast enough, for attempting to wear hats at the table, for even *considering* walking into someone else's home or a restaurant with their heads covered. Lena's locks are well oiled and tightly twisted, draping down past her shoulders—a femme contrast to the shaved sides of her head.

I begin to see that this is who Lena is: a woman coming at the world from many different places, quick-moving and fast-talking yet soft-spoken and thoughtful, cursing a mile a minute while bringing a new vibrancy to language. Relaxed yet ready. On the butch side of queer but with delicate edges. Star power with kindness. And it's working.

"Here's the irony of it all," she says after the conversation gets going. "I don't need an Emmy to tell me to go to work. I've *been* working. I've *been* writing, I've *been* developing, I've *been* putting pieces together and I'm bullets, you know what I'm saying?"

I do. On the critically acclaimed Netflix series *Master of None*, for which she won her Emmy, Lena, 33, also plays the role of Denise, a young lesbian and close friend of Aziz Ansari's character, Dev. While Denise was originally written for a straight woman, who would eventually become a love interest of Dev's, Waithe's character has added a depth, humor, and black-girl queerness new to the screen. She's wry, lovely, and lovable. And while Lena's Denise seems to be handpicked from Lena's life story, Waithe brings to this character something different. Denise is more reserved than Lena. It's not so much an innocence but angles smoothed over, the product of a quieter past. Many of the people in my own queer world would have blinked past the show had it not been for Waithe's character. For so many of us who have not seen an out Black lesbian front and center this way, her arrival is a small, long-awaited revelation. Her arrival is our arrival.

And then there's the Showtime hit *The Chi*, created and executive-produced by Lena, which follows inter-related characters on Chicago's South Side. With Common as an executive producer and Rick Famuyiwa directing, the show has been picked up for a second season. The credits keep on coming, though. Waithe produced the comedic dance film *Step Sisters*. She is the writer-producer of the recently green-lighted TBS television pilot *Twenties*, which is loosely based on her early years in Los Angeles and tells the stories of three black women making their way in Hollywood. And she appears this month in Steven Spielberg's *Ready Player One*, which is adapted from Ernest Cline's 2011 science-fiction novel, following contestants pitted against one another in a virtual-reality world.

When she's not producing, acting, writing, or creating, Lena is working hard to pull more people of color and queer artists into film and television both through her role as co-chair of the Committee of Black Writers at the Writers Guild and through her work with aspiring writers via Franklin Leonard's the Black List—a platform by which people can pay to get feedback on their material from established professionals.

But right now Lena is ordering an oyster appetizer, sitting back, and chatting with me about, among other things, our time at Sundance. Kindred is the vibe I'd put to this evening. Lena and I have not spent real time together before, but there's a deep knowing between us. We talk about our families, our girlfriends, East Coast versus West Coast, and the movies that didn't quite work at the festival.

Lena's family, like mine, was similar to the fictional Cosbys—not in wealth, by any means, but in the way the young people on the show were expected to respect their elders. Separated by more than 20 years, we were both raised by our mothers and grandmothers. We both came out when we were young and have amazing women helping us to stay afloat: my partner is a physician; Lena's fiancée, Alana Mayo, is the head of production and development for

Michael B. Jordan's media company. (Like me, Alana grew up a Jehovah's Witness.) By age seven, we both knew what we wanted to be. We both started our lives in the Midwest—me in Ohio, Lena in Chicago. When our parents separated, our mothers returned to their mothers' homes. My mother's mantra was: *Turn off the TV and pick up a book.* But Lena, after coming home from school, was permitted as much television as she wanted.

"I was watching a lot of movies I shouldn't have been watching," Lena tells me, laughing. "Like *Boyz N the Hood.* Also a lot of rated-R shit. *Jungle Fever.* But that's the joy of having a single mom. She was like, I can't hover over you. Watch what you want. Just don't repeat what you hear and don't do what you see."

When Lena was 12, her mother moved her and her sister to the suburbs: Evanston, just north of Chicago. "She was saving up and maybe a little bit wanted to get out of the South Side. Even though I was going to a good school [in the city], Turner-Drew, which was like an early magnet school which she found, because that's the kind of shit she did." Lena says this with true gratitude. "So half of that year I was still on the South Side and the other half I moved to Evanston and went to Chute Middle School. It was like a fuckin' Benetton ad."

At one point, Lena goes silent. It's when I ask about her father. She tells me he died when she was 14. "He had substance-abuse issues, which my mom told me about later, but . . ."

Her voice trails off. Maybe another writer would have pushed her for more. But in that moment I only want to sit with her in the quiet, to muse, wordlessly, about the strength of mothers and grandmothers and the many levels to our survival.

Growing up, I leaned into books, finding small parts of myself in the writings of Mildred Taylor, Audre Lorde, Virginia Hamilton, and Walter Dean Myers. Lena, meanwhile, found her mentors on the screen in the comedy writing of Susan Fales-Hill (*A Different World, Suddenly Susan*), Yvette Lee Bowser (*Living Single, Lush Life, Black-ish*), and Mara Brock Akil (*Moesha, Girlfriends, Being Mary Jane*). "They didn't get their shine," she says of these early black women in comedy. "They were constantly banging on the doors." In contrast, she says, "I rolled up and all I had to do was tip it and walk through."

Somewhere over the course of the two decades between us, we both found the works of James Baldwin. His writing was as relevant in the early 2000s for Lena as it was for me in the 70s—indeed, as it was for the young queer black artists coming before us in the 50s and 60s.

And still, this evening, as Lena and I talk across the table, over her truffle pasta and Sprite, and my burger and Cabernet, a deep reverence comes over us. Here we are now because Baldwin was there then. And I think about the young people who ran to their screens to watch Lena's *Master of None* episode in which her character came out to her mother. How social media blew up with her thank-you speech at the Emmys. ("I love you all and, last but certainly not least, my L.G.B.T.Q.I.A. family. . . . The things that make us different, those are our superpowers.") How her work is part of a continuum of people doing their work.

"How has the Emmy changed me? It got me all these meetings that I go in and say I'm too busy to work with you—you should have hollered at me. You can take my call when I call you about this black queer writer over here who's got a dope pilot, or this person over here who's got really cool ideas, or this actress who's really amazing but nobody's seen her."

Because we both know that, even as Hollywood's doors are being shaken, there is still so much work left to be done.

Lena came up as an assistant to director Gina Prince-Bythewood (*Love & Basketball*), whose father-in-law, an orthodontist, fixed my smile 30 years ago—just in keeping with Small Black World magic. Lena tells me she came to Hollywood in 2006 with no family, no friends, and no money. After working with Prince-Bythewood, she became a production assistant on Ava DuVernay's scripted directorial debut, *I Will Follow*. "She would make the coffee," DuVernay explains. "She would close the gate; she would take out the trash; she would run things from one part of the set to another." Through it all, the director noticed real promise.

Now that Lena is catching major fire—at a time when TV show-runners and filmmakers of color, especially women of color, are getting the opportunity to tell their tales—there seems to be a sea change. Or am I being naïve? "Is this different than any other time?," DuVernay asks me rhetorically. "It's a good time, but it's not the first good time we've had, and previous good times have not become *That*." She reminds me that a similar moment existed in the 90s, thanks to filmmakers like Prince-Bythewood and Julie Dash, the first black woman to have a theatrical release, with her groundbreaking film, *Daughters of the Dust*, not to mention Kasi Lemmons's *Eve's Bayou*, and, on the queer side, Cheryl Dunye's *The Watermelon Woman*. At that point and now in this one, DuVernay notes, you can easily count the black directors. It has been the same, she maintains, for women's creative progress through the years. "We can look at other times in the history of art where it's been the case where you've had a cluster or flurry of women who have been doing strong work that's been recognized by the mainstream and feeling like it's a moment, feeling like there's a big culture shift. But, really, when you look at it and you're sober about it, you're talking about women that you can count on two hands—and this industry has many hands."

Yes, she acknowledges, black artists are blowing up the screen, with everything from Kenya Barris's *Black-ish* to Donald Glover's *Atlanta*, to Issa Rae's *Insecure*. But this isn't yet "a moment," DuVernay reminds me. The director of *A Wrinkle in Time* (budget: $100-million-plus) says, "If no other black woman makes a film more than $100 million past me for another 10 or 15 years, if no other woman wins an Emmy for writing, for the words that come out of their head, then we're kidding ourselves that we're in a moment that makes any difference other than momentary inspiration."

Lena explores this terrain, too. "The hardest thing about being a black writer in this town is having to pitch your black story to white execs," she says. "Also, most of the time when we go into rooms to pitch, there's one token black executive that sometimes can be a friend and sometimes can be a foe. I wonder if they think it makes me more comfortable, if that makes me think that they're a woke network or studio because they've got that one black exec. It feels patronizing. I'm not against a black exec. I want there to be *more* of them."

For all that, Lena contends, "it was a symbolic moment when *Moonlight* literally took the Oscar out of *La La Land*'s hand. It is a symbolic moment when Issa Rae's poster is bigger than Sarah Jessica Parker's. Now the hands that used to pick cotton can pick the next box office. . . . See what I'm saying? There's a shift that's happening. There's a transition of power. But we still aren't in power."

When I ask Lena if she thinks we'll ever have our lesbian *Moonlight*, she is quick to tell me we've already had it. "*Pariah*," she says, referring to Dee Rees's stunningly rendered 2011 feature about a young black lesbian coming out. "I fuck with that movie really hard. I thought it was really beautiful."

I t is a few days earlier, on a cold night in January, following a blizzard. Sundance is in full swing and I'm watching Lena work magic in one of the hottest and most pumping rooms in Utah—a venue called the Blackhouse.

Co-founded by Brickson Diamond, in 2006, the Blackhouse Foundation came into being after the few black folks who'd been attending Sundance grew tired of seeing so few reflections of themselves on the Park City streets and of seeing so few black films. So Diamond, a graduate of Harvard Business School, along with two friends, Carol Ann Shine and Ryan Tarpley, created a place where their peers could gather to educate, network, and figure out how to break the white ceiling of Hollywood. During this year's festival, the Blackhouse hosted panels and parties from 10 in the morning until midnight, Friday through Monday. Its impact is evident. In 2007 there were seven black films at Sundance. Come 2018, the count was closer to 40. "If you build it," Diamond says, "they will come."

Tonight the Blackhouse is hot, the drinks are being poured, the people are excited to be here, and the D.J. is dropping beats that are hard not to move to. Outside, a long line awaits entry to the main event: a discussion examining cinematic diversity and inclusion. In attendance: Radha Blank (*Empire*, *She's Gotta Have It*), Jada Pinkett Smith, Poppy Hanks (whose production company, Macro, specializes in works by people of color and is the force behind Dee Rees's Oscar-nominated *Mudbound*)—and Lena Waithe.

As a Sundance neophyte, I try to stand out of the way of a futile attempt to clear the dance floor and set up chairs for the panel. I hesitate to inform the D.J. that, in the history of black folks, no one has ever left the floor when a Prince song was playing. And now, not even two years after his death, Prince's music in the room is a heartbreaking and sobering reminder that, as black creatives, we don't have a lot of time to get the work done.

The room is already filled with beautiful people. A woman who worked on the costumes for *Black Panther* is one of the few who are able to negotiate heels tonight. Everything she is wearing, I want. Next to her, my friend Chris Myers is discussing the Sundance debut of *Monster*, a film based on a book by his father, Walter Dean Myers. Cards are exchanged, selfies are taken, bodies are pulled into long embraces. The crowded room, filled with everyone from crew to cast to producers, feels like a family reunion.

Nearly 100 years after the Harlem Renaissance—the African-American intellectual and artistic movement of the 1920s—I can feel in this pulsing room what it must have been like to sit among the likes of Zora Neale Hurston, Countee Cullen, Langston Hughes—people who were dreaming themselves and their work beyond the moment in which they were living. Tonight feels as energized and ready as that vibrant corner of Harlem must have felt a century ago. This new Black guard is no longer fighting for a seat at the table; they're convening their own. And yet, while some call this surging West Coast energy "the Hollywood Renaissance," I am with Ava DuVernay. We need to see how far past this *now* it goes, before we can own it.

When John Amos, the dad from *Good Times*, walks into the Blackhouse, the crowd parts. People whip out phones for selfies, which he graciously allows. For so many, Lena included, *this* is where the journey into black television began—when we first saw ourselves reflected back through the characters of J.J., Michael, and Thelma. As a young child, looking for mirrors of myself in episodes of *The Brady Bunch* and *The Partridge Family*, it wasn't until shows like *Good Times* and *The Jeffersons* blued into our darkened living room that I could finally say, *Yes, some part of that is me.*

With the chairs set up and the music suspended for a while, Lena sits onstage alongside the other women. She pays homage to the creators of *A Different World* as her fellow panelists echo their agreement, tell her to say it, nod in memory and reverence. "We as artists can do whatever the fuck we want to do," she urges the audience. "We just have to do it really, really well. . . . You have to write and develop and wait for the world to catch up to your art."

Later, Justin Simien, creator of the Netflix comedy hit *Dear White People*, tells me that Lena has not only worked like mad but also "created systems, and now she's got almost 100 mentees going to writing classes, and evaluating each other's work." In fact, she recently announced an initiative with the Black List that lets upstart writers submit scripts to be judged on a point scale. "Get an 8 or above," Lena tweeted, "[and] my team will read your script."

"She turns nobody away," says Simien. The pair met at a writing workshop and became best friends. It is Waithe, he insists, who pushed him to take the leap and create *Dear White People*. "When Lena decides that something is true, it becomes true."

Lena and I meet for brunch, this time in West Hollywood. She sports her signature ensemble: hoodie, with a snapback logo cap. Today's hat says, REBEL EIGHT. Another favorite is Chance the Rapper's "3." I ask her whom she likes to wear and she quickly spits out a list of queer and black designers. Sheila Rashid; Knoxxy's brand, DVMN Pigeon; Nicole Wilson.

Lena considers her personal style her own mode of self-expression, irrespective of the circles she travels in, which, in professional Hollywood, tend to be largely white and, often, male. As much as anyone appreciates a compliment about their "look," she says she doesn't *need* it. "Being black and gay, having dreadlocks, having a certain kind of swag, and dressing the way I do," she explains, she is sometimes told by certain well-meaning admirers or fashion wannabes, "*'That's dope, you're cool.'* I don't feel validated by that. . . . I don't want to be White. I don't want to be straight. I don't want to blend in. . . . I try to wear queer designers who happen to be brown and makin' shit."

I reach out to Common—who signed on as an executive producer of *The Chi* in 2015—for his read on Lena. "There's no box you could put her in," he says. "It's not only [the fact that] I admire her, but I feel like I'm just somebody who sits and listens, looks at her work, and is like, 'Man, this is really great writing!'" He points out the pure poetry of it, the humor, the deep honesty.

Steven Spielberg echoes this. When I speak to him, he says, simply, "I adore her."

In Spielberg's new film, *Ready Player One*, Lena's character is part of a group that bands together to save a futuristic world. And while I know that sounds like every sci-fi movie ever made, this one is different. This one is *No way, did he just . . . ?* and *Wait a minute . . . did that really . . . ?* different. It's hard to say more without spoiling the plot. When I attended a screening, I was beyond surprised to walk out of the theater already planning to return with my family, saddened only by the fact that once again it was the white straight people who found love. Lena's acting chops, though, are on point here again. Spielberg says of her audition, "She was accessible at a glance. Her honesty was glaring. And she couldn't hit a wrong note, because she found a way to be herself on-camera. I suddenly felt like I had hit the jackpot. The magic hadn't walked into the room—until Lena did."

A few days before Lena is scheduled to speak at the Essence Black Women in Hollywood ceremony, where she is being honored, our talk turns to her work as an activist and in the Time's Up movement. As she reads out loud to me from her upcoming speech, her voice is a mixture of immense excitement and barely concealed fear: "Being born a gay Black female is not a revolutionary act. Being proud to be a gay Black female is."

At the event, which takes place just before the Oscars, Lena talks about the importance of coming out in Hollywood—and explains it through her love for *The Wizard of Oz*. "There's this moment in the movie," she says, "when Dorothy's presence interrupts the peace in Oz, which forces all the Munchkins to go run and hide. So Glinda the Good Witch tells them . . . to stop hiding. She tells them to come out: 'Come out, wherever you are. Don't be afraid.' It's interesting how things you hear as a kid take on a whole new meaning when you are an adult." The day after her speech, pictures of her in a beautifully tailored gold paisley suit flood social media. The country is taking notice, sending love.

"I have a ton of mentees," she tells me over the phone. "They're all people of color. Some of them are poor. And I'm just trying to help them learn how to be great writers; and for those that have become really good writers, I help them get representation; and those that have representation, I want to help get them jobs. That to me is a form of activism. I was doing this before Time's Up was created. I am doing it now. Activism is me paying for a writer to go to a television-writing class."

It is during one of these conversations that I ask her about what happened with her friend and *Master of None* co-star, Aziz Ansari, who, in a controversial online article, was accused of sexual misconduct by a woman he once went on a date with. (Ansari stated that their sexual activity was consensual.) Lena gets quieter, more thoughtful. "At the end of the day," Lena says, "what I would hope comes out of this is that we as a society . . . educate ourselves about what consent is—what it looks like, what it feels like, what it sounds like. I think there are both men and women who are still trying to figure it out. We need to be more attuned to each other, pay more attention to each other, in every scenario, and really make sure that, whatever it is we're doing with someone else, they're comfortable doing whatever that thing is, and that we're doing it together. That's just human kindness and decency."

And then, a day or two later, we hop on the phone to scream about the success of *Black Panther*. We just have to. And Lena, being Lena, has already broken down the context of this moment. "You see history books—A.D. or B.C.?," she asks. "I feel like the world felt one way before B.P. and will feel forever changed A.B.P. These execs are all looking around and saying to themselves, 'Shit, we want a *Black Panther*; we want a movie where motherfuckers come out in droves and see it multiple times and buy out movie theaters.' And because we also live in a town of copycats, there are going to be a lot of bad black superhero movies coming because everybody ain't Ryan Coogler!"

Lena, naturally, comes back to the beginning, returning to the roots of her storytelling. "I used to watch TV with my grandmother a ton. I watched a lot of old [classic sitcom] TV. And it gave me an education in using your platform to protest, but without being preachy. And how you can use TV characters, fictitious characters, as a way to speak to who we are as a society.

"I am tired of white folks telling my stories. We gotta tell our shit. Can't no one tell a black story, particularly a queer story, the way I can, because I see the God in us. James Baldwin saw the God in us. Zora saw the God in us. When I'm looking for myself, I find myself in the pages of Baldwin."

Then she adds, "I didn't realize I was born to stand out as much as I do. But I'm grateful. Because the other black or brown queer kids are like, 'Oh, we the shit.'" Lena flashes a huge smile, then shakes her head with wonder.

MICHELLE WILLIAMS

THE CHANGE AGENT

By Amanda Fortini | July 2018

A t the end of November, as Ridley Scott and the cast of *All the Money in the World* were in the midst of nine days of re-shoots in Rome and London, *The Washington Post* ran an article about pay disparities among the cast, specifically between Mark Wahlberg, the male lead, and Michelle Williams, his female co-star. Exactly how egregious the gap we would not learn until early January, when *USA Today* reported that Wahlberg, who in August 2017 was named the highest-paid actor of the year by *Forbes*, with annual earnings of $68 million, was being paid $1.5 million. Williams, on the other hand, who has been nominated for four Oscars, five Golden Globes (she won for *My Week with Marilyn* in 2012), and a Tony, was paid an $80 per diem, which amounted to less than $1,000 total. The additional filming was to re-create Kevin Spacey's scenes after the actor was accused of sexual misconduct and replaced with Christopher Plummer. "It wouldn't have occurred to me to ask for money for the re-shoots. I just wanted to do the right thing on his behalf," says Williams, referring to Anthony Rapp, the actor who accused Spacey of sexually assaulting him when he was 14 years old.

It's a muggy afternoon in June when Williams and I meet at a Williamsburg hotel that's all concrete floors and hip austerity, and sits at what might be the most hectic, throbbing corner in Brooklyn. The actress, one of the borough's better-known residents, has lived in the Boerum Hill and Red

Hook neighborhoods since 2005. On the day we meet she is about to move to a new part of Brooklyn, a location she has not yet disclosed, with a partner she has not yet made public. If you know anything about Williams, it's that she is the Thomas Pynchon of the film world—almost immaculately private.

Initially, there was talk of arranging an "activity" for us to do together. We'd look at art or visit the Cloisters, and I'd later extrapolate meaning from this or that comment, in the usual profile style. But a few days before the interview, I'm told that Williams would like to talk about income disparity in Hollywood, specifically her own. She was, after all, paid less than one-tenth of 1 percent of her male co-star's fee—a discrepancy so glaring that it caused a massive outcry online. In the end, Wahlberg donated his entire re-shoot fee to the Time's Up Legal Defense Fund, which had been established a few weeks prior, and William Morris Endeavor, the agency representing both actors, threw in an additional $500,000. It was difficult to imagine Williams discussing any of this among museum patrons and prying iPhones, so we are here, on a boat-size leather sectional sofa, in an upper-floor suite that overlooks the warehouses and luxury apartment buildings lining the East River, with a blasting air conditioner that Williams immediately turns off.

"I read somewhere that things are kept cold for men, because men prefer to be cooler while women prefer to be warmer," she says, and then moves herself, with the tensile grace of a cat, into one corner of the giant iceberg of a sofa. "Office buildings are kept colder for men." It's an apt metaphor for the many inequities, small and large—from irritatingly arctic air-conditioning to life-altering wage gaps—women contend with.

"You feel totally de-valued," she says, when I ask whether she was enraged to learn of the money Wahlberg received. Like everyone else, she read it in the paper. "But that also chimes in with pretty much every other experience you've had in your workplace, so you just learn to swallow it." She speaks deliberately, often closing her eyes as she enunciates, in what I will come to recognize as her meticulous, clear, and thoughtful manner, as though each word is put through a process of inspection. She tells me that the ultimate outcome pleased her, in that it sparked a cultural conversation and will eventually, she hopes, bring tangible change. "A private humiliation," she says, "became a public turning point."

The night before we meet, Williams worked until three a.m. She is filming Bart Freundlich's remake of the Danish film *After the Wedding*, in which she and Julianne Moore play the two formerly male lead roles, before she will fly to L.A. to do re-shoots for *Venom*, Sony's upcoming Marvel movie, in which she stars as Anne Weying, the ex-wife of Eddie Brock (Tom Hardy). She's dressed in the unadorned, vaguely vintage style specific to artsy-intellectual Brooklyn—flared jeans, a white linen shirt tied at the waist, ballet flats, straw bag, no makeup. That morning, she tells me, she awoke bone-tired and, like most women, fretful about her skin; she's been in full, pore-clogging stage makeup for two weeks running. "And I'm like, Oh well, it's O.K. It's a new world," she says. "I'm not going to walk into an interview where somebody's like, 'Her smell is blah, blah,' or 'Her skin is bare . . . ' Everything opens—at least it used to—with, like, a sexual description of the woman's worth, the exact kind or quality of her beauty. You know what I mean? It's so nice to know that I'm not walking into that."

I do know what she means, and assure her I will not be talking about her complexion or marveling that she ate a cheeseburger. We don't even order food. Instead, we drink cup after cup of room-service coffee and talk about motherhood, books, grief, her creative process, and her work.

Her recent career choices feel distinct from the independent films she's become known for, like Derek Cianfrance's gritty, close-shot *Blue Valentine* or any of Kelly Reichardt's visual tone poems. In December, she sang and danced as the wife of Hugh Jackman's P. T. Barnum in *The Greatest Showman*. This spring, in an ingenious comic turn, she played Avery LeClaire, an Aerin Lauder–esque makeup heiress with a breathy, high-pitched voice, in the Amy Schumer movie *I Feel Pretty*. Viewers and critics were delighted to see this new side of her; writing in the Huffington Post, Matthew Jacobs called her "bonkers work" in the film "delicious."

But perhaps the greatest measure that a career shift is afoot for her is that in the past year she has starred in a big-budget Ridley Scott film and, in October, will appear in a Marvel movie. "I always like to do things I haven't done before—genres, parts. I like a challenge," Williams says, pouring herself a cup of coffee. "And one of those challenges has been stepping into a bigger world." She explains that she is most at home on a small, familial set, like a Reichardt film ("where I can walk around in my underwear and say the wrong thing"), but with *All the Money in the World* and now *Venom*, she is opening herself up to "a bigger set, and strangers, and multiple monitors, and people weighing in."

W illiams's first big-screen role was in the 1994 movie *Lassie*, at the age of 14. The following year, she was emancipated from her parents and moved, by herself, from San Diego to Los Angeles. It wasn't long until she was cast as wild child Jen Lindley on *Dawson's Creek*, in 1998, a role she played for six years. "I had a steady gig, which was great," she says, "but I didn't have the thing I most wanted, which was respect and a good sense of myself—I wasn't viewed as an artist." Even back then her taste ran to the sort of arty, independent films she's become known for. She appeared in a handful of those (*Prozac Nation, The Station Agent, The United States of Leland*), but her career break came in 2004, when she was cast in Ang Lee's *Brokeback Mountain*.

For her quietly devastating portrayal of Alma, the spurned wife of a closeted gay cowboy, she earned a best-supporting-actress Oscar nomination, her first. "Her truthfulness in the part was just heartbreaking," says Lee. "This is two gay cowboys' story, but your heart breaks for the woman, and that's an effect of the fact she's so great." The cowboy husband, Ennis, was played by the late Heath Ledger, who, over the course of filming, became her real-life love. Williams was soon pregnant; their baby, Matilda, was born just before the movie opened, and the couple bought a sprawling town house in Boerum Hill. Their accelerated fairy tale was catnip for the media, and the pair were frequently photographed pushing a stroller around Brooklyn. But they split after three years together. Five months later, in January 2008, Ledger was found dead of a drug overdose in a SoHo apartment he was renting at the time.

The paparazzi descended on Williams and her two-year-old daughter, forming what one writer would call a "morbid cult." Says her friend Daphne Javitch, a holistic-nutrition coach who lived with Williams in the couple's home after Ledger died: "To have that kind of attention, in such an aggressive way, around you and your child, when so much of it is coming from what truly is tragedy for a family . . . it's a kind of violence." The actress eventually fled Brooklyn for rural upstate New York. There, she bought a house and raised Matilda—taking her on location when she was filming—for the next six years. "It was unmanageable to be stalked like that," she tells me now, "every moment of the day. So I left, in a desire to create a sane home environment." An anecdote underscores the relentlessness with which she was pursued: "I'll never forget going to the post office and seeing a sign hung on the wall for anyone with information about myself and my daughter, to please call this number." She smiles wryly. "Um, so I took that down."

Williams is an inherently private person, and being hounded pushed her further into her shell. "She always had a difficult time with the idea of doing press and what to reveal," says actress Busy Philipps, who was Williams's co-star on *Dawson's Creek* and has remained her closest friend. "And then obviously when Heath passed away, and people had this insatiable interest in her and her child and their grief, it was overwhelming and incredibly painful." When I ask Williams about this time, she makes a slight throat-clearing noise, as she does whenever the hurdle of a difficult subject presents itself. "When you're a single parent, and that element of provider and protection is missing, it's scary," she says simply.

Williams was born in Kalispell, Montana (her mom, Carla, was a homemaker and her dad, Larry, a commodities trader who twice ran unsuccessfully as the Republican candidate for U.S. Senate), and upstate she hoped to give Matilda the connection to nature she'd had as a girl. "You know, getting on a bicycle and being out and coming back for meals, and exploring snakeskins and arrowheads and cliffs and plants and abandoned houses, and having that sense of freedom and safety in the world," she remembers. (When she was nine, her family moved to San Diego in search of more temperate winters.) The natural surroundings, gardening, and planting were all a salve for her, too. "I just remember thinking, like, Hmm, maybe there's something green in me that's growing that I can't see yet," she says. But even far away from the tabloid searchlights, the narrative of Ledger's death would continue to haunt the next decade of Williams's life.

For fans of her work, the persistence of personal tragedy as the dominant

thread in almost everything written about her is understandable but also irritating. During the past 10 years, in a series of small and often unexpected
films, she has emerged as one of the most gifted actresses working today—not
a movie star who plays a version of herself in film after film but a genuine
artist, a chameleon who wholly inhabits the character at hand, in the vein of
Cate Blanchett, Meryl Streep, and Julianne Moore. "It's this unusual thing
that she has," says Bart Freundlich, "which is constant complexity with total
clarity at the same time. Even when things are simple and clear it feels like
there are layers and layers behind them."

Unlike many actors, Williams has no qualms about playing unlikable
characters without pandering to the audience; she infuses them with such authentic humanity that viewers often end up empathizing with them. There
was the tightly coiled, unhappily married nurse in *Blue Valentine* (for which
she was nominated for a best-actress Oscar) and the drugged-up, manipulative
sexpot Monroe in *My Week with Marilyn*. There are *Wendy and Lucy*, *Meek's
Cutoff*, and *Certain Women*, the trio of quiet, spare films she made with Reichardt, in which her acting is so nuanced, her performances such triumphs of
understatement, that she conveys a world of feeling with the subtlest of expressions. And then there's Kenneth Lonergan's *Manchester by the Sea*. She's in
only a handful of scenes—most memorably one in which she breaks down before her ex-husband (Casey Affleck), revealing the black, bottomless, unbearable grief of a mother who has lost three children—but they are pivotal,
providing the characters with a wrenching backstory. "Her presence pervades
the film even in her absence," says Lonergan. "Even when she's a voice on the
telephone, or a slow-motion mourner at a funeral, her sense of reality, her
strength, and her enormous gentleness change every scene she's in."

The fact that Williams is so private, her misfortune was so public, and her
film roles so intense have all contributed to what feels like a fundamental
misreading of her. When she is portrayed with any particularity, it is as a kind
of delicate bird, broken and still grieving. Instead, I find a witty, reflective,
cerebral, and precise person who is far less guarded than I expected. "We
know her as very funny and light," says Marc Silverstein, who wrote and

directed *I Feel Pretty* with Abby Kohn and is married to Philipps, "though her filmography does not suggest that at all."

She is also studiously bookish and cultured, in the way autodidacts often are. She talks in evocative, poetic metaphors. ("Single-parenting," she says, can feel like life is held together by "a thread and a paper clip.") In the course of our interviews, she refers to the work of Colson Whitehead, Andrew Solomon, Annie Dillard, Elena Ferrante, Rebecca Solnit, Maile Meloy, Jim Harrison (his poetry, she tells me, not *Dalva*), Walt Whitman, and Henry David Thoreau. She quotes one of Harrison's poems at remarkable length, and several times from soccer star Abby Wambach's recent commencement speech at Barnard. Her friends say that she is the one to discover new writers and press books on them. "She told me about Elena Ferrante before anyone fucking knew about Elena Ferrante," recalls Philipps.

As I listen to Williams, I am struck by the thought that in our bare-all era, "private" is often conflated with "sensitive" or "fragile," when in fact a fierce demand for privacy might mean a person is uncompromising and tough. Someone who moved upstate alone, raised a daughter on her own, built and navigated the vicissitudes of a high-profile career, and remained sane and solid in the process is pretty much the opposite of the way the media portrays her. "She's not like a precious fucking flower that's going to get crushed," Philipps says. "That's the thing that drives me a little bit crazy when people talk about her and write about her. She's one of the strongest people I know— one of the toughest bitches around. She's still here, she's still working, and not only is she still working, she's like the best there is."

Now, more than a decade after Ledger's death, with her career advancing in surprising new directions and her daughter entering seventh grade, Williams is inhabiting, quite intentionally, a larger, less rarefied, more vocal and open version of herself. For example, this very circumspect person was unwittingly made the poster child for pay inequity—an issue that affects women in every industry—and despite her native discomfort, she's trying to make the most of her platform. "It's a very hard thing for me to navigate," she says, "because my instinct is to keep my life very, very private. But I also need and want certain things out of my career that demand I assume a more public voice."

She quotes a line from a Joanne Kyger poem: "*That we go on, the world always goes on, breaking us with its changes until our form, exhausted, runs true.*" I listen, impressed, not wanting to interrupt. "I mean, that's definitely the place that I feel like I'm in," she says, "like I'm making a sort of developed mental leap." She pauses, then sharpens her statement, in her conscientious way. "In your 20s, you're still so jagged and fractured, and I feel like everything has sort of cohered."

Let's talk about money, I tell her. It's late afternoon now, and techno music has begun to thud-thud-thud from what seems to be a day rave below. Money, she says, was never that important to her: "It was never a motivating factor for me. It's never been the thing that's gotten me out of bed to go to work." To support herself and Matilda, Williams lived frugally "in a very simple house, with a very junky car, and went on no vacations." She drove a Prius, which she has since replaced with a mini-van with fabric-upholstered seats—"a couch on four wheels," she calls it. "They were like, 'You can get leather for an additional $4,000 or something,' and I was like, *'Why?'*" She laughs. And then, more seriously: "Keeping a life sustainable, that's really important to me."

She turns 38 in September, and as she gets older, she finds that money is becoming important to her, too. Financial success buys her freedom—like the freedom to take only films that shoot close to home or that do not require her to be away for longer than a week. She and her daughter moved back to Brooklyn six years ago, and since then Matilda, who is now 12, has been in the same private school without interruption. "She hasn't had her routine disrupted and hasn't missed class," Williams says, and it's clearly a point of pride for her. She also wants the ability to preserve summers as "undone time" ("less scheduled, less regulated, less hustle, less go go go") she spends with her daughter in their house upstate. There they live according to their inner dictates, "like animals in their natural habitat": waking when they want, eating when they want, swimming, gardening, reading, walking, spending time with friends.

Were any of her recent professional choices made with finances in mind? Like *Venom*, perhaps? It would be difficult to conceive of anything seemingly more out of character for her than a comic-book superhero movie. "You know, if something like *Venom* works, it's life-changing," she tells me. "I wanted to open myself to that possibility." She repositions herself on the couch so she's cross-legged and chooses her words even more fastidiously than usual. "Before this, I had a real fixation on . . . purity," she explains, "but I've started to address that notion as I've gotten older, and as I talk to more women, and more women artists, and I think about my long-term future, I've started to adjust my thinking about . . . how to make a life, how to support a life."

I ask her to tell me the Wahlberg story—how did the pay gulf first come to light? She inhales deeply and audibly, as though she's about to step onstage to deliver a speech or steady herself for an acrobatic feat. "The teachable moment," she says, "is that the story came out and no one cared. It didn't go anywhere. It was like it never happened, which just confirmed to me there is no recourse." But Hollywood was changing quickly in those final months of 2017. In the nearly six weeks between the publication of the two articles in *The Washington Post* and *USA Today*, Time's Up was formed, the Golden Globes ceremony was awash in somber black dresses, and a handful of actresses (Dern, Sarandon, Streep) walked the red carpet with activists. Williams, in fact, attended with Tarana Burke, the founder of the Me Too movement.

The day after the ceremony, the kindling finally caught flame. Jessica Chastain, who has 750,000 Twitter followers, is one of the most vocal advocates for equity in Hollywood, and also happens to be an old friend of Williams's (they co-starred in a 2004 stage production of *The Cherry Orchard*), texted her to ask permission to tweet about the issue. Williams responded, "Yeah, sure, go for it. But it's already out there, and nobody cared."

Regardless, Chastain went ahead. "I heard for the re-shoot she got $80 a day compared to his MILLIONS," she tweeted. "Would anyone like to clarify? I really hope that with everything coming to light, she was paid fairly. She's a brilliant actress and is wonderful in the film." Williams's crisp, lock-jawed portrayal of Gail Harris—the mother of John Paul Getty III, and the flinty moral backbone of a dissipated and depraved family—is the beating heart of the movie; that her performance garnered a Golden Globe nomination only renders her paltry fee all the more galling. (Ridley Scott, who in mid-December told *USA Today* that all the actors did the re-shoots "for nothing," could not be reached for comment.) "Please go see Michelle's performance in *All the Money in the World*," Chastain tweeted the following day, after *USA Today* reported the exact figures. "She's a brilliant Oscar nominated Golden Globe winning actress. She has been in the industry for 20 yrs. She deserves more than 1% of her male co-star's salary." The time was right. The world had shifted, and the news spread, says Williams, "like wildfire."

Her phone started blowing up. *What was she going to do? Would she leave her agency? Make a public statement?* She was acutely aware that the moment was symbolic. "I've never really been at the center of something like that, of a news cycle like that—other than, you know, traumatic death," she says. During the ensuing week, "between Jess re-breaking the bone of the story and WME offering a monetary apology," as Williams puts it, she had a series of telephone conversations with the (male) higher-ups at the agency. She called her new friend, activist Mónica Ramírez, co-founder of the National Farmworker Women's Alliance and head of the National Latina Equal Pay Day Campaign, whom she had gotten to know during the planning for the Golden Globes, to help coach her. They spoke on the phone, Williams says, "on breaks from work, after our kids went to bed, and before they woke up in the morning."

After each call with WME, Williams would notice that her hands were shaking. "But I would think about what Mónica had told me. That if it was hard to negotiate on my own behalf, I should imagine myself negotiating for *her*. Or for my daughter."

In the end, Williams chose not to leave either her agent or WME—a decision that seems, well, surprising. Later, when I press her on it, she will say that her agent, Brent Morley, is someone she "values creatively," adding, "I believe in second chances."

For her, what resonates from the experience is the power generated by women banding together. "I was one woman by myself," she says, "and I couldn't do anything about it. But in the wolf pack—the phrase Abby Wambach uses—things are possible. And that's really what it took: somebody who was at the head of the pack, Jessica Chastain, pulling me up with her, and then all these other women surrounding me, teaching me." Says Chastain, "No one should have to step out onto a limb on their own. We are all here to share the weight. It's easy to label one actress difficult, harder to label a group."

There is, of course, a lot of talk about how overcompensated all actors are, women and men alike. But, for better or worse, we do look to Hollywood actors as avatars of socio-cultural change, and in the absence of revamped industry standards, why should actresses be paid so much less than their male counterparts? "It's important not to forget that women in the entertainment industry are women workers as well, and we're trying to make things better for all women workers," says Ramírez. "It's not about the income bracket; it's about the justice."

The following evening, Williams texts me and asks to meet at a French restaurant in Fort Greene. It is a shoebox-size place, but she goes unnoticed; instead of coffee, we drink rosé. She is conscious of this time, the years before she turns 40, as "potentially being really generative," and is enjoying her work more than she ever has, with plans to play Janis Joplin in a biopic and an abortion activist in *This Is Jane.* "You're told that things get worse as you age, from the outside," she says. "But your internal experience is 'I'm hitting my stride.'" She tells me that a "shred of belief" in herself and in her acting has finally "crashed through." She shrugs, smiles. "It would be cruel not to admit it to myself."

The one subject Williams won't initially discuss is her private life. She's got a relatively new someone—or new to the media, anyway—and I can tell she's itching to mention him, the way people in love are. "I would tell you everything, in the spirit of women sharing with each other," she says, but "the Internet's an asshole." A couple of weeks later, she changes her mind and decides to talk in the hope that doing so might "take some heat and confusion" out of the situation when it finally becomes public.

By the time you read this, she and her partner, singer-songwriter Phil Elverum, whom she met through a mutual friend, will have been married in a secret ceremony in the Adirondacks, witnessed by only a handful of friends and their two daughters. Her new husband, an indie musician who records and performs under the name Mount Eerie (and, before that, the Microphones), also lost a partner in tragic circumstances while parenting a small child. His late wife, illustrator and musician Geneviève Castrée, was diagnosed with inoperable stage-4 pancreatic cancer in 2015, four months after the birth of their daughter, and the two very private artists went public with a GoFundMe page to help defray medical costs. Castrée died 13 months later, in July 2016, leaving Elverum with an 18-month-old daughter. In the past two years, he has released two raw, critically acclaimed albums, *A Crow Looked at Me* and *Now Only*, that unflinchingly explore grief, death, and the utility of art in the face of loss. Williams calls her relationship with Elverum "very sacred and very special." In July, he packed up his home in Anacortes, Washington, and drove across the country to live with her and their daughters in Brooklyn.

"I never gave up on love," she later tells me, saying that she has spent the 10 years since Ledger's death looking for the kind of "radical acceptance" she felt from him. "I always say to Matilda, 'Your dad loved me before anybody thought I was talented, or pretty, or had nice clothes.'" I can hear her voice crack. She sometimes can't believe that she's found this kind of love, at last. "Obviously I've never once in my life talked about a relationship," she says, "but Phil isn't anyone else. And that's worth something. Ultimately the way he loves me is the way I want to live my life on the whole. I work to be free inside of the moment. I parent to let Matilda feel free to be herself, and I am finally loved by someone who makes me feel free."

Williams decided to open up about her relationship, as she did about her income, on the chance that other women might find hope or instruction in her story. "I don't really want to talk about any of it," she says. "But there's that tease, that lure, that's like, What if this helps somebody? What if somebody who has always journeyed in this way, who has struggled as much as I struggled, and looked as much as I looked, finds something that helps them?" In the end, she says, what she's learned is simple: "Don't settle. Don't settle for something that feels like a prison, or is hard, or hurts you," she says. "If it doesn't feel like love, it's not love."

Back at dinner, she reaches into her purse and pulls out a small gray notebook, in which she has scribbled some thoughts about our previous interview. She wrote them in a sauna, so they're slightly smudged. "I'm going to transcribe all this much more beautifully," she tells me. Two weeks later an elegantly composed e-mail, in which she calls herself "a perfectionist Virgo, constantly qualifying and rethinking," arrives. "Women have to be watchdogs for each other. A great change has come, but if it is for me or just within my industry, it won't be enough," she writes. "Women must recognize what power we have and where—however small and dull it might feel—and use it to advocate on behalf of others for the betterment of us all." The e-mail also mentions that she was just offered a new television role and the same amount of money as the male lead without having to negotiate for it.

A few hours later, en route to a night of *Venom* re-shoots in L.A., she calls and elaborates. The show will be produced by Lin-Manuel Miranda, directed by Thomas Kail, and filmed in New York, and she'll get to sing and dance. "When they told me about it, I thought, O.K., now comes the part where I have to go in kicking and screaming and shouting about equality and transparency. . . . Then, before I could even ask for it, they said, 'They've offered you what Sam Rockwell is making.' I cried." I would, too, I tell her.

In a literary novel or an indie film, this ending wouldn't fly. True love, equal pay: it would be too neat, too contrived, too tidily wrapped up in a bow. At one point, Williams says she's "at the end of one journey and embarking on another," and then worries that phrasing sounds clichéd. But sometimes reality escapes the dictates of narrative in ways that are better and more interesting than you ever could have imagined, and language falters in the realm of the truest feelings. A few days before she elopes, we talk again, and she says, simply, that in life and in love, she's found the sense of expansiveness she's long searched for. "This kind of freedom, it's the thing that I look for. It's been a theme in my life," she says. "It's the thing that I experience in Montana, the thing that I experience onstage, the thing that I get in my work in between 'action' and 'cut.'" She pauses for a moment. "I'm free. I'm free."

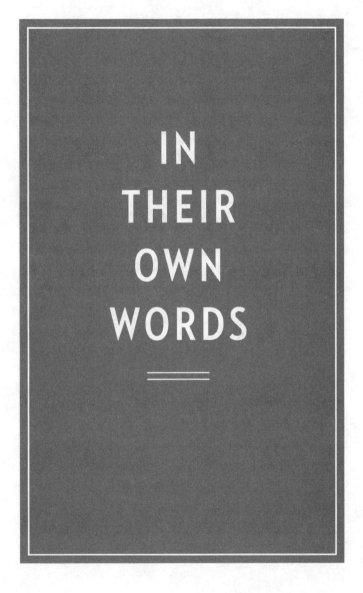

IN
THEIR
OWN
WORDS

A BOOM OF THEIR OWN

By Cari Beauchamp | Hollywood Issue 2018

The idea to convene a summit of women filmmakers was an informal, modest one, yet it was born of a deep-seated frustration. And it all began because Allison Anders was pissed.

It was late 1999, and Anders, the indie film director (*Gas Food Lodging, Grace of My Heart*) and a MacArthur "Genius" fellow, saw women being isolated and marginalized. Why did they have such trouble getting their movies produced? Why were men, after a flop, allowed to fail upward, but if a woman's film was successful, it was viewed as an aberration? And why didn't women in Hollywood know about the female pioneers who had shaped the business? Anders was devastated when she learned that Dorothy Davenport Reid, an acclaimed director in the 1920s, had died in obscurity 50 years later, "practically in my backyard in Woodland Hills," Anders now recalls.

Dorothy Davenport had not been alone. At cinema's dawn, dozens of female directors flourished in Hollywood, where they supported one another both personally and professionally. Before 1925, almost half of all films were written by women. And yet they had risen at a time when film wasn't taken seriously as a business. Once talkies arrived, in the late 20s, budgets soon tripled, Wall Street invested heavily, and moviemaking became an industry. Men muscled into high-paying positions, and women were sidelined to the point where, by the 1950s, speakers at Directors Guild meetings began their comments with "Gentlemen and Miss Lupino," as Ida Lupino was their only female member.

Anders appreciated the potential power of the camaraderie to be found among fellow creative souls, and so she e-mailed a dozen friends asking if they felt the same way. If so, what would they think of getting together, each paying her own way, to spend a weekend hashing out their concerns, strategizing, and talking about, as she put it, "what needs to happen next."

Her idea touched a nerve, and in April of 2000 more than 100 women showed up for what was billed as the "Women Filmmaker's Summit"—held at the Miramar, a run-down but still vibrant hotel between the Pacific and the railroad tracks in Santa Barbara. (The rooms shook when trains went by.) Anders knew Miramar by the Sea as "a magical place" where she occasionally holed up to write. It was on the beach, had a large conference room, and Anders secured a slight group discount.

The Miramar itself is long gone (a developer is opening a luxury hotel there this year), but that weekend still unites those who attended, and the impact of the conclave continues to ripple out in ways that few people in Hollywood realize.

Allison Anders, an innate collaborator, drew together an organically diverse and multi-generational group. Some of the women were friends. Most knew of one another only by reputation, and for many this was the first time they had come together without the support of a guild or association. The excitement was palpable and uniquely female: part reunion, part suffragette rally, part 60-hour sleepover. Maya Smukler, then working at Women Make Movies, in New York, enlisted participants from the East Coast. Publicist Kristin Borella greeted everyone upon arrival with name tags, an agenda, short bios, and Anders's original letter tucked inside a green paper folder like the ones used to turn in middle-school reports.

And what a packed agenda it was. Friday afternoon and evening were set aside for what Anders presumed would be a "very sloppy and loose" venting session. The mantra, as she recalls, was: "'We are not victims, we are survivors.' . . . There was so much anger from devastating disappointments and being fucked over—and a general feeling of injustice." Everyone crammed into the minimalist main room, with its coastal white-and-blue décor. Some sat around tables decorated with bouquets of sweet peas; others stood against the walls. Most stayed late, watching *The Wild Party*, starring Clara Bow and directed by Dorothy Arzner, who, among her many accomplishments, is one of those credited with inventing the boom mic. (As a writer of film history, I was asked to provide a primer on the women of early Hollywood and bring along some VHS tapes of films by our foremothers.)

Saturday was billed as "a day of solutions." After breakfast, speakers chaired a series of discussions, at half-hour intervals, covering almost every aspect of the professional challenges women faced. "The audience" did as much talking as the moderators. There was a sense that this was a safe space, and the candor was stunning. One woman told the crowd, "I didn't want to make small films; I want to direct epics." Another piped in, "I've been in at least 10 interviews where it was down to two of us, and every time the job went to the white male."

Some veterans were on hand, such as Polly Platt, whose visual acumen shaped her ex-husband Peter Bogdanovich's movies, and who had begun to nurture filmmakers such as Wes Anderson. Martha Coolidge had worked consistently since her first hit, *Valley Girl*, in 1983, and she was fresh from completing her groundbreaking television film, *Introducing Dorothy Dandridge*, written by a then unknown Shonda Rhimes and establishing Halle Berry as an actress to be reckoned with. Victoria Hochberg (one of the filmmakers responsible for the 1983 Directors Guild lawsuit against several studios for failing to hire women) and director Donna Deitch (*Desert Hearts*, *The Women of Brewster Place*) spoke of their struggles. Maggie Renzi, who first made it to the big screen producing and acting alongside John Sayles in their seminal film, *Return of the Secaucus 7*, had produced a dozen pictures, including *Girlfight*, by her former assistant Karyn Kusama. Renzi had come to Miramar at the encouragement of director Nancy Savoca, who had just won the Grand Jury Prize at Sundance for her first feature, *True Love*. Along with other directors such as Tamra Davis (*Billy Madison*), Sarah Jacobson (*Mary Jane's Not a Virgin Anymore*), Colette Burson (*Coming Soon*), and Gurinder Chadha (*Bend It Like Beckham*) was a smattering of critics such as Manohla Dargis, then writing for *L.A. Weekly*; *Chick Flicks* author B. Ruby Rich; agents like Shana Eddy; as well as executives, producers, and actresses, including Marianne Leone, Marina Zenovich, and Marianne Jean-Baptiste, all looking to expand into writing, directing, or producing. There were also documentarians and representatives from various film organizations. (A handful of men were welcomed, but only on Saturday. They did not spend the night.)

Then there were the young upstarts, among them: Patricia Cardoso, whose *The Water Carrier of Cucunuba* had won a Student Academy Award; Jamie Babbit, who had recently finished *But I'm a Cheerleader*; and Andrea Sperling, one of the producers of Babbit's film. Babbit arrived with Angela Robinson, just out of N.Y.U. film school, who remembers, "We tiptoed into this room full of powerful women. We were 'Wow.' Here were real live women directors—our indie heroes."

Many of the women considered themselves strong and outspoken, but few could compare to Sarah Jacobson, the activist proponent of "DIY" filmmaking, who that Saturday, with a huge smile on her face, called on the assembled to begin "fucking shit up." It became a bit of a free-for-all but never spun out of control. Woman after woman, across three generations, told tales of hurdles and harassment and dreams dashed—situations that, until then, many had thought that they alone had experienced. The confessions, helpful hints, and debates continued over long walks beside the gentle surf or back in the hotel rooms, and there was a gradual, cathartic realization that the walls they were up against weren't personal but systemic.

Almost everyone remained through Sunday, breaking into groups on the beach to discuss next steps. One of the immediate conclusions was that they would need a name. When Sarah Jacobson shouted out, "The Pussy Whippers!," Renzi responded, "That could be one faction." In the end, they settled on "50/50," summarizing their inclusionary goal. Their other mandate: to continue meeting. And as more women joined their ranks over the next few months, their forces expanded. 50/50 gatherings were held at various homes in New York and L.A. and at Martha Coolidge's ranch, in the San Fernando Valley, where everyone sat, memorably, on bales of hay. In keeping with the anonymity insisted upon by the Guerrilla Girls—feminist artists who blend humor and outrage as they expose gender inequality—a dozen or so of the Miramar women joined forces with them. Their first collaboration appeared the following year at Sundance with witty yet biting slogans on stickers posted all over town, bearing messages such as THESE DISTRIBUTORS DON'T KNOW HOW TO PICK UP WOMEN—listing companies whose rosters lacked female-directed features.

Next came a rather joyous action that required real fund-raising: A billboard trumpeting THE ANATOMICALLY CORRECT OSCAR. (HE'S WHITE & MALE, JUST LIKE THE GUYS WHO WIN!). Placed strategically on Highland Avenue in Hollywood—so that people on their way to the 2002 Academy Awards would be sure to see it—the billboard received international press coverage. (There was no social media to carry through with an #OscarsSoMale campaign.)

That same year, Miramar alum Martha Coolidge was elected president of the Directors Guild. Women were ecstatic, as were younger, minority, gay, and lesbian directors who had long felt marginalized. But while Coolidge declines to address that period and still works with the D.G.A., it was no secret her efforts to effect change were hampered by a certain segment of entrenched power at the Guild. She served for a year and remains the only woman to have held that post.

Without staff or funding, and with the pressing demands of life and work, the 50/50 meetings fell off, but loose-knit connections remained, aided by dial-up e-mail. And that community, says Coolidge, "gave rise to all these new communities now." Many a young woman in the film trade, upon encountering someone from the group, has been heard to remark, with awe, "You were at *Miramar*?" Currently, there is a bustling connectivity that evolved, in part, from the Miramar ethos. For several years, director and editor Tara Veneruso maintained a post-summit support-and-information Web site called the First Weekend (because a film's fate at the box office, in that pre-streaming era, was determined in the days right after its release). Ten years ago, Melissa Silverstein began her weekly online update, Women and Hollywood, listing films directed by and about women, along with news and interviews. Over time, film festivals such as Athena (at Barnard), Citizen Jane (at Stephens College, in Missouri), and POWFest (in Oregon) have come to provide invaluable forums for female directors.

Today there are the women's writing and directing labs at Sundance and the AFI Conservatory Directing Workshop for Women, both of which feature Miramar-alum mentors. Film Fatales is a grassroots organization for women who have directed at least one feature—with 500 members throughout the world. Female cinematographers and composers, two of the fields where women are most drastically under-represented, have their own associations.

Then there are the "quantifiers," academics who analyze the hard data on male dominance in movies, led by the woman who has been doing it for more than 20 years: Martha Lauzen and her Center for the Study of Women in Television & Film. (Full disclosure: I serve on the advisory board.) Their annual studies, such as the Celluloid Ceiling and Boxed In, reveal the shocking and continuing lack of women both in front of and behind the camera. (In 1998, 9 percent of the top 250 films were directed by women; in 2016, it was 7 percent.)

What remains unquantifiable are the films not made, the stories not told, and the careers ended early because of discouragement or harassment. It is also impossible to compute the number of hours not wasted on angst or self-doubt because of the openness and support of other women.

Nearly two decades later, the friendships forged that weekend are still a crucial part of many of the attendees' lives and careers. "Ever since," as one woman explains, "I haven't felt alone." Says another, "After the summit, I stopped asking permission." And yet another: "It opened my eyes to a lot of things that were hiding in plain sight and [from then on] I have had a different perspective."

Director Colette Burson says that weekend "appeared like an oasis in the desert" and the call for 50/50 inspired her to reach that goal for women directors on her series, *Hung*. Angela Robinson, who most recently directed *Professor Marston and the Wonder Women*, says, "I think about Miramar all the time. I thought I was ready to take on the world, but it quickly became clear that day, with so much emotion in the room and all the stories of what they were up against, that it was a mountain to scale. In particular, I think about one director who stood up and said, 'Every time I walk through a studio door, there is a white man on the other side, and I see him immediately try to put me in a box: mother, wife, daughter, or whore. Those are the categories they chose from to relate to me.' " With a laugh, Robinson explains why she passes that lesson on to the students she now teaches and why it made such a difference to her: "Because I am black and gay, when I walk through that studio door, there are still white men on the other side, but they are confused. I use that confusion to start pitching so fast they latch onto the ideas before they can figure out what box to put me in."

As is to be expected, the participants at Miramar have gone on to experience everything—from a heartbreaking lack of work to incredible success. After directing *Real Women Have Curves*, in 2002, Cardoso has just completed her second feature. Babbit is currently directing *Silicon Valley*. Coolidge teaches at Orange County's Chapman University, where her students have gone on to garner awards; Anders, after years of directing series such as *Riverdale* and *Orange Is the New Black*, is a distinguished professor in film and media studies at U.C. Santa Barbara. Shonda Rhimes—who attended follow-up 50/50 sessions—is, well, Shonda Rhimes. And Manohla Dargis, now a *New York Times* critic, notes that, even though today's directors such as Ava DuVernay, Patty Jenkins, and Kathryn Bigelow are heralded, "they are still unicorns."

Eighteen years after Miramar, the latest community of women to emerge—to find life-changing strength from standing together and speaking out—is comprised of all those who have been breaking their silence about #MeToo. Journalists ruptured the dam, but social media—and a newly energized group of determined women—created the tsunami that may yet bring about genuine change. In January, more than 300 prominent women from the film industry launched Time's Up, a multi-pronged approach to combatting sexual harassment—on the heels of a new commission headed by Anita Hill.

Andrea Sperling, now Jill Soloway's producing partner, responsible for *Transparent* and *I Love Dick*, has been in those recent meetings "with real power in the room" and reports that they are having "long conversations seeking concrete solutions." She adds, "I have been thinking about Miramar and 50/50 because one of the goals being discussed is 50/50 by 2020." When asked what she thinks is going to happen next, she responds with the same humor-tinged optimism that permeated that long-ago weekend: "The patriarchy is toppling as we speak."

WHAT HAPPENS WHEN THE RECKONING MEETS WALL STREET

Bethany McLean | March 2018

t could be the script for a movie. A brave woman comes forward to talk about the sexual harassment she's experienced in the office. She feels terrified and alone. But many others have been in similar situations, and soon her voice is joined by a chorus, backing her up and supporting her. Then it spreads. Using the hashtag #MeToo, nearly five million people generate 12 million posts, comments, and reactions on Facebook in a 24-hour period. At one of her industry's premier events, men and women alike wear black to show support for the cause, while Hollywood celebrities come together to form a group called Time's Up, to fight sexual harassment. The list of powerful, allegedly abusive men who are no longer invincible grows to include a Hollywood mogul, famous journalists, radio personalities, and even a Las Vegas casino owner. Yet no one thinks it's over.

Many believe the movement is changing the world, but in many places, including one industry that has long been regarded as a path to great wealth, there is mostly silence—in fact, it's been "eerily silent," as one woman puts it. She is talking about the world of finance. "#MeToo is not an equal-opportunity movement," says Nicole Page, a lawyer at New York's Reavis Page Jump, which handles employment cases, including those involving harassment and discrimination. Or as a recently retired senior Wall Street woman puts it, somewhat ruefully, "We all wear all black every day, and it doesn't help."

———

On the surface, this doesn't make sense. Dennis Chookaszian, an adjunct professor at the University of Chicago's Booth School of Business, recently polled his 130 students to see whether they have personally experienced harassment or observed it happening. Seventy percent of the women said they have been harassed, and roughly half the men and two-thirds of the women in the class said they've observed it or were aware of it happening. "Wall Street has to be the worst," a senior Wall Street man tells me. He says that's because of the nature of the work: the long hours, the travel, the pyramid-like structure, where there are plenty of junior women, but disproportionately fewer and fewer as you get toward the top. One woman who started on Wall Street in the late 1980s and eventually became a partner at her firm recounts having lunch with a prominent male banker, who asked her, "Did it [sexual harassment] happen to you?" "I guarantee it happened to every woman in this restaurant," she replied. "It impacts every aspect of your career."

In private groups, women, especially those who have been on Wall Street for decades, are talking about it. Some believe that a tidal wave is coming. But a close look at the industry's shameful history, and at the realities of being a woman in finance, belies that optimism.

was the only woman," recalls the woman who started on Wall Street in the late 1980s. "My very first day of work, all the men and I were given office assignments. There was an odd number. So all the men got offices to share. I got a reconfigured utility closet. I was told it was in case I needed to change my nylons. And it just went on from there."

"It was no-holds-barred," says Sallie Krawcheck, who started at a junior level at Salomon Brothers in the 1980s and rose to run wealth management at Citigroup. "One day [at Salomon Brothers], I leaned over a colleague's desk to work on a spreadsheet, and heard loud laughter from behind me; one of the guys was pretending to perform a sex act on me," she wrote in a recent op-ed piece in *The New York Times*. "Almost every day, I found a Xerox copy of male genitalia on my desk." In a recent conversation, she added that "the attitude was 'Tough it out.' You had no choice. I was 22 years old and from Charleston, South Carolina. I didn't have any money, and there wasn't anywhere to turn."

Maureen Sherry, who became the youngest managing director at Bear Stearns, in the 1990s, and fictionalized her experiences in a 2016 novel called *Opening Belle*, wrote in a *New York Times* op-ed that on her first day on Wall Street she opened up a pizza box to find unwrapped condoms instead of pepperoni slices.

"You'd hear shit every day like 'I want to lick your pussy,'" says a woman who worked on a trading floor in the 1980s. Another longtime Wall Streeter recalls being at a work dinner in Houston. On one side of her was a senior leader at her bank; on the other, a prominent politician. They simultaneously put their hands up her skirt. She recalls thinking, This is going to get really interesting when their hands touch. Thankfully, a male colleague across the table noticed her distress signals and called her out for a conference call.

On the flip side, some women who work on Wall Street say that gender has never been an issue for them, and some even say that being a woman in a mostly male world confers certain advantages for those who are strategic about it. "I will always assert that the women who are liked and who succeed in finance . . . actually see their femininity as a strength," says a close friend of mine who has worked in finance for decades. "I would also go so far as to say that for every moment when a woman feels slighted or downright harassed, there are as many opportunities where she can capitalize on her attractiveness and gain an unfair advantage over men. . . . Perhaps a controversial view, but I truly believe it."

But physical attributes can also divide women from one another. The woman who started her career in the late 1980s recalls that certain women were made fun of for the way they looked or dressed. One was dubbed "Crickets" because of the noise her stockings made when she walked. "Crickets persistently and consistently extended herself as a mentor to me and I ignored her," the woman recalls. "I felt I could intellectually muscle my way through anything on my own and . . . she was Crickets."

Other women view resorting to sex appeal as a necessary evil, but one that inevitably backfires. "Women absolutely feel compelled to use their looks," says a woman who had a successful career at a big bank. "From your first day, the deck is stacked against you," she says. "We all talk about it at every stage of our careers. As our male peers did, we attended the best universities, achieved excellent academic records, usually went to top M.B.A. programs, but as a woman, your discount rate [a financial term that measures what something is worth] is double or triple that of any man. . . . That's why women since the beginning of time have used their looks—to climb out of that very hole. These are your cards, and you play them. You have been told you don't have other cards of value. That's the beginning of how all of this happens."

At the start of my career, in 1992, when I was in my early 20s, I worked as a junior analyst at Goldman Sachs. By then, at least in the more genteel parts of Wall Street, such as investment banking at large firms, the worst forms of sexual harassment from the roaring 80s had been toned down. There was still a lot of socializing after hours, but stories of lunchtime assignations between partners and secretaries, and raunchy behavior at work, seemed to be things of the past. People were smarter than that.

The mergers-and-acquisitions department, where I worked, had been chastened. Business was slow in the aftermath of the 80s junk-bond frenzy, which had made M&A bankers Wall Street's rock stars. Even though Goldman was then making an effort to hire women, and there were many of us in my analyst class, our ranks thinned dramatically as one went up the pyramid. In M&A, as I recall, there were a few women associates, one or two female vice presidents, but no women partners. Women were forbidden to wear pants.

Our introductory program included sensitivity training—although it's hard to say the lessons sunk in. I remember asking one male associate about diversity. "We have plenty of diversity," he responded. "We have soccer players, hockey players, and football players." Not surprisingly, something of a jock ethos prevailed. There were holiday parties where partners were making out with analysts, and vice presidents with secretaries.

I was assigned to work directly for one vice president. My job was to develop presentations for consumer-products companies, a thankless task in a department that only valued deal-making. Two men had been assigned similar work, although one figured out how to get himself out of there, pronto. I could not have been less suited for that work—I was a math major looking forward to quantitative analysis—and I have no visual skills whatsoever. I was too immature not to let my unhappiness show. In return my boss made no secret that he despised me.

Our month-long training program felt like a continuation of college, with plenty of parties and lots of alcohol. But, of course, it wasn't college. Unwritten rules had very real career repercussions if you broke them, and they were very different for men and for women. Even small missteps, such as making out with a person in your class, could get a woman marked, but would enhance a man's reputation. When the real work started, almost immediately a senior man held himself to me as a mentor of sorts. I was failing at work, he told me, and I had made myself "too visible." He alone saw something redeemable in me. But, of course, his "friendship" came with strings attached (despite the fact that he had an out-of-town girlfriend). I wasn't sure how to say no.

I felt trapped—my parents, who were at home in Hibbing, Minnesota (population 19,000), were lovely, but very clear that any support was over. Perhaps because I was in search of a savior, I had a too public affair with a colleague my own age, which ended when another analyst pulled me aside and told me the man had a girlfriend. (Life lesson: Save yourself.) When another (married) senior vice president tried to get into my hotel room it was a soul-crushing moment, because I felt that I had set myself up.

All of this made it hard for me to have the kind of chipper, can-do attitude so prized in junior roles. I finally transitioned into a more quantitative role, which utilized my skills, and I distinctly remember a moment when I decided I was either going to quit or finish the job with my head held high. From that point on I did nothing but work, and I stuck it out for three years—I had something to prove. In retrospect, I think what bothered me most was the knowledge that, while we were all going to be judged for things besides the quality of our work, for women, extra-professional judgments accrued almost entirely to our disadvantage, whereas for men, at least the white-male sporty types, it was the opposite. It felt brutally unfair.

I quit and moved to a $650-a-month apartment in the far reaches of the

East Village, buzz-cut my hair, and took up boxing. I don't think the men I sparred with had a clue who it was I was punching (nor did I), but my coach told me I had a fantastically powerful right hand. I wore black biker boots (not today's chic version) and clothes that would define me as anything but feminine. I once randomly wandered into a Brooks Brothers store and the old-school saleslady looked at me, her eyes widening in horror. "Is there anything I can do to help?" she asked.

At a recent reunion for my class of analysts, a man suddenly broke off the conversation, looked at me and one of my friends, and said, "I'm so sorry." He explained that as the years went by he'd realized how hard life was for the female analysts. #MeToo has helped me see my experience through a different prism, but despite that, I will always feel in my gut that it was my fault, and the primary emotion I still feel when I think of those years is shame.

What I also know is that the potent and unique mixture of feeling that you're failing professionally while at the same time being targeted for your gender is utterly devastating to your confidence and sense of self.

With so many stories of sexual harassment spanning decades, why aren't the women on Wall Street leading the #MeToo charge? An obvious answer: the money. Wall Streeters often have a great deal of money tied up in their firms in the form of stock, and they usually have to sign non-disclosure agreements, either as a condition of employment or to get money when they depart. "For many senior women there is way too much on the table," says a retired senior woman. "That's the base reason why you haven't heard more."

But it goes beyond the money. "When you are rewarded for toughness there's a big disincentive . . . to come forward with a story that would put a dent into your armor," writes a current Wall Street woman in an e-mail. "That over time becomes identity."

"It was always just stick your head down and get the work done," says another woman. "When you are senior, you will be the change you want to see. But we weren't." In addition, there's a belief that the consequences are much worse for a woman who complains than for a man who is the subject of complaints.

Among women I spoke to, the fear was often palpable. Fear of being labeled a complainer. Fear of being ostracized. Fear of being fired. I heard current stories that I cannot print, even anonymously, because the women are terrified that someone, somehow, will figure out they talked. They wish they were braver, several say. But the consequences are too great. The stories that are printed in this piece are scrubbed of telltale details for that reason.

"If someone calls me and says they have gone to H.R., my advice is always that your future with the company is imperiled," says Dan Kaiser, a New York employment lawyer with Kaiser Saurborn & Mair. "The idea that you are staying there and living happily ever after is now unlikely. You are a complainer."

"It's a very small world, and it gets whispered around that there's a problem with her and she doesn't work again," says Maureen Sherry. "She may go entrepreneurial, but her big-league dream is dead."

A woman who sued her firm believes she was quietly blackballed from subsequent opportunities. "In our business, you either side with the boys or with the ladies—you will be forced to choose at some point," she says. "When you do, that choice is permanent, with lasting repercussions you can't possibly appreciate at the time. After years of 14- to 16-hour days and few vacations, I complained." Her previously stellar annual reviews had abruptly turned negative for no reason she could understand—other than that a man with powerful supporters wanted her book of business. "I complained once," she says. "And now I'm trapped. You know the language they use. No one says I filed a complaint—they can't. But they'll say, 'Oh, she's not a team player' or 'She's difficult.' "

Women who do complain often feel ostracized. "In the entertainment industry, it started with women, but then the industry at large showed support," Sherry says. "I do not think women on Wall Street feel that support. What they have always seen is that the person behaving badly is the powerful one and the man stays employed. The woman takes a check and where does she go? We don't know."

Nor do women always get support from the most obvious place: other women.

"The thing that hurt me the most is that fellow women peers and superiors did not have my back," says a woman who is currently an unnamed plaintiff in a suit against a large Wall Street firm. "Because the price is too high. You spend all these years trying to fit in and this [complaining] is the ultimate standing out. It's wonderful watching what's happening in Hollywood, where women are supporting other women, but that did not and does not happen in finance."

"Women are very isolated and these are very competitive jobs," says Kelly Dermody, an employment lawyer at Lieff Cabraser. "They don't want to make their career cause be fighting sexual harassment. It can be a thankless decision."

Even for those willing to take the risk of speaking out, Wall Street legal agreements make it difficult for them to be heard. Although practices vary and have changed over the years, some firms, as a condition of employment, insist that all disputes be heard in closed-door arbitrations, not in public lawsuits. Things are getting worse rather than better. Recent court rulings have determined that firms can force employees to sign waivers saying they will not participate in class-action suits (though this outcome is currently being argued). "If there were a Harvey Weinstein and he had harassed 100 women and they had all complained, they might not even know each other exists, and you would never know," says Adam Klein, an employment lawyer with the New York firm Outten & Golden.

Settlements also often require non-disclosure provisions—and settling is by far the easier route. Ann Olivarius, a longtime high-profile employment lawyer, who works in New York and London, says that when she notifies a firm of a complaint, "the firm's representatives will have a big binder with your name on it full of all sorts of details, from your personal life to your expense reports. It might all be nonsense, but it's put down as a threat. Sign and have a good life or fight us and we will destroy you. So 99 percent will take the money and go."

A recent story, told to me by a woman who was a superstar at a big firm, shows that the cost of speaking out, even internally, can be high. She was a big producer and got promoted for it. "I earned it and it was how it was supposed to be," she told me. Above all, she was loyal. "I was a fucking assassin, and I would have jumped out the window if they had told me to," she says.

That was how it was supposed to be until it wasn't. She's terrified to talk to me because she too says she'll get fired if anyone finds out, but I've already been told most of the details, and rather than duck and cover, she's willing to confirm them. When a man who joined her group made racist and sexist remarks, she reported him—because she thought she could and should. After that, "the boys' club," as she calls it, closed ranks against her. This man's boss, who was her boss as well, protected the man. She'd hear from clients and other colleagues that she was being bad-mouthed, and she was called a cunt. "I'm a tough cookie," she says, and that is clearly true. "But that is not O.K." She reported the issues to the firm's human resources department, which responded, she says, as if the problems were of her own making. "They looked at me like I'm the one on trial," she says.

As she talks, a sneaky little thought creeps into my mind: Would it have been different if she had just been . . . nicer? As soon as I think it, I realize I'm buying into some of the same stereotypes that have been so damaging to women. That a woman who is aggressive is a bitch, whereas a man is a hard-charger. That she somehow brought it on herself. But had this woman been "nicer," I realize, she never would have achieved what she had, and she would have been run over in a different way.

One of the final straws for her came when she was at an event with a client—and saw the H.R. person there with the man who was protecting the bad actor. She realized that she had nowhere to turn. She doesn't want to get fired. "I've done stuff that isn't perfect and they'd crush me," she says. So instead, she says, "I decided I'd be the sheep they wanted me to be." She works the hours that are required, but she's an assassin for the firm no longer.

I t was almost 30 years ago when a few women started bringing lawsuits alleging harassment and discrimination—the two have always gone hand in hand—in financial services. One of the first came in 1990. Teresa Contardo, who was a broker at Merrill Lynch, alleged sexual harassment—pornographic pictures had been placed at her desk—but her bigger complaint was that the men found ways to exclude her, thereby harming her ability to make money. Contardo won a $250,000 settlement. This would deter "endemic and habitual discrimination against women by undisciplined discretionary decisions in workplaces dominated by men," wrote the judge in his opinion.

In 1996, Pamela Martens and other plaintiffs sued Smith Barney, alleging both sexual harassment and discrimination. It became known as the "Boom Boom Room" case because there was a room in the firm's Garden City, New York, office where men would gather after work, and where, according to the complaint, women were "dealt with" when allowed to enter. Smith Barney eventually agreed to pay settlements to about 20,000 women, though the amounts were not disclosed.

About two years later, Allison Schieffelin, a successful bond saleswoman at Morgan Stanley, filed a claim with the Equal Employment Opportunity Commission (E.E.O.C.). She says that, as a result, she was called into her boss's office, abruptly fired, and escorted out the door. She later issued a public statement. "The campaign of retaliation that Morgan Stanley launched against me was designed not only to punish me but also to scare other women who might dare to complain of discrimination," she wrote. To settle her case, Morgan Stanley agreed to pay $54 million to as many as 340 women. The presiding judge called it a "watershed in safeguarding and promoting the rights of women on Wall Street."

In 2002, Laura Zubulake, a former saleswoman at UBS, sued, alleging that gender discrimination destroyed her career. At trial, she won her case mainly due to unassailable evidence in e-mails and other electronic communications. "There was an informal code on the street, a brotherhood. . . . No matter the allegations, managers tended to support one another," she wrote.

Three years later, Renée Fassbender Amochaev and three other women filed a class-action complaint against Smith Barney, claiming rampant discrimination in how female brokers were treated and paid. "I knew I wouldn't come out with much money, but it was the principle of the thing, and I was angry. It was about not perpetuating the problem for future women in the industry by staying silent," says Fassbender Amochaev today.

Reportedly, after she and her co-plaintiffs won their case, Jamie Dimon, then Smith Barney's co-C.E.O. (and now the C.E.O. of JPMorgan Chase), sent a memo to employees saying that the settlement "focuses on effecting real change and progress rather than simply delivering monetary rewards."

There has been change, at least on the surface. There is a widespread belief that overt sexual harassment is far less prevalent than it was, certainly at big firms such as Goldman Sachs and JPMorgan Chase. "People blame Wall Street for everything, but we're outperforming here!" says a woman who recently left a large firm. "We're better than they [the film and media industries] are!" After all, the lawsuits made financial firms aware of the risks, and one thing Wall Street is supposed to care about is managing risk.

Unlike the entrepreneurial, high-flying private partnerships of old, today's Wall Street firms are bureaucratic, somewhat stagnant, publicly traded giant institutions, with policies and procedures and diversity training and shareholders and boards of directors to whom executives must answer. The outsize characters of old are now merely life-size. "Go back 15 to 20 years, and you could name the powerful people on Wall Street," one longtime male executive says. "But who are the [Joseph] Perellas and [Bruce] Wassersteins of today? It's much more anonymous."

Put a different way: who is the Harvey Weinstein of Wall Street today? That person, in both stature in the financial sector and the egregious horror of his deeds, doesn't exist. So the firings for sexual harassment that have happened—and there have been some—have been quiet. For instance, *The Wall Street Journal* reported that Goldman Sachs fired a trader who attempted to use a female colleague to demonstrate his ability to unhook a bra.

Mores have certainly changed. "In my experience, there was no tolerance," says a senior woman, talking about a firm where she had been a managing director. "It was not presumed innocent, but presumed guilty. The irony of all ironies is that the industry to clean itself up was Wall Street."

One woman, who started her career in the 1980s, says that a few years ago she was struck by an incident at her firm's holiday party, when a senior man got drunk. The next day he was fired. She heard about it and called the

C.E.O., hoping to intervene on his behalf. The C.E.O. told her, "I had three incoming calls from women in their 20s who said they could no longer work with him. Didn't you notice what he was doing?" Her response: No! She hadn't noticed.

"It's because I was raised in the 1980s, and it was way worse then," she says. "[The younger women] thought it was so threatening that they wouldn't report to him anymore, and I called the C.E.O. to intervene! In that way, it has changed. Young women do not tolerate it."

"I think there was enough consciousness raised in the 90s and 00s that what offends young women today is so far down the list of what we went through that we wouldn't even have reacted to it," says another woman.

But overt harassment still happens, particularly in the smaller shops. One woman who worked on the investment side says that the man who ran her fund would angle his camera at her chest to take pictures, and once told her when he was leaving for a weekend in the Hamptons that he wanted to set up a camera in the office so he could watch her while he was away. "He was obsessed with me," she recalls. He encouraged rumors in the office that they were having an affair. "I do not put up with bullshit, so I never thought I would be in that predicament," she says. But she was, and she stayed because of the opportunity the job provided, until she became so physically sick she had to leave. "My body told me before my mind did," she says.

Underneath the stories are the numbers, and these show that change, in the ways that matter most, have been superficial. A Government Accountability Office report from December 2017 concluded that women had made no progress—none—in increasing their ranks in management in the financial industry from 2007 to 2015, with women in New York faring the worst in the country. The number of women in what the G.A.O. defines as "senior-level management positions" held constant at just under 30 percent. Lest education gaps be blamed, the report also pointed out that between 2011 and 2015 women in the financial industry possessed 58 percent of the bachelor's degrees, 60 percent of the master's degrees, and 45 percent of the

M.B.A.'s. According to Ariane Hegewisch, a program director at the Institute for Women's Policy Research, women in the brokerage business earn on average less than 60 percent of what men do.

"Do we really think 90 percent of the best people for these jobs are white men?" Sallie Krawcheck asks. "We are so used to it and accepting of it that we call Wall Street a meritocracy!"

The more insidious forms of discrimination are harder to stamp out than the overt ones. "It has evolved," says a lawyer who handled discrimination cases at the E.E.O.C. for many years. "[Harassment] has become more sophisticated, hidden, and subtle."

Or as the woman who tells me Wall Street is outperforming also says, "It is not a #MeToo culture, but it is a culture where it's hard for women to thrive. I think the outright sexual harassment was drummed out of the place years ago," she says about her former work environment. "But you can be excluded nonetheless, because some men have a fundamental lack of ability to work with women. That's the killer part. That's the experience most women I know have had."

That exclusion is especially devastating to women's careers. "Power in an organization is all about information and access," says Melanie Katzman, a New York psychologist who runs a consulting firm that advises corporations, including big financial firms. "If you can't speak comfortably with a woman with the door closed, that woman is being cut off from information and access."

"You get promoted via sponsors, not mentors," another woman, who was senior at a big Wall Street firm, says. "If a man can't get to know his female co-workers enough to be a sponsor, that's a problem."

Brande Stellings, who runs the advisory services at Catalyst, recently published a report on women in capital markets in Canada. Her conclusion was similar. "The majority of men at all levels are able to point to sponsors who have supported their careers, while women struggle to identify sponsors or mentors who can help them successfully navigate their careers," resulting in slower advancement for women and fewer female role models at the top.

The politically incorrect, but nonetheless widespread, fear is that #MeToo is going to make more subtle forms of discrimination even worse. Even before #MeToo, Sherry wrote in her *Times* op-ed, she was told by banks' H.R. departments that men were often afraid of hiring women because of the risk that even innocent comments could be misinterpreted and cause legal problems. "More than once I was told that it's just easier to fire a guy or—my favorite line—that 'there's just less drama with men,'" she wrote.

There's anecdotal evidence that this problem is getting worse. Katzman says she's hearing stories from men who are "really nervous about being alone with women." One client told her he wasn't taking a female colleague on a business trip, because he feared that if he fell asleep on the plane his behavior might be misinterpreted. "I'm very concerned," Katzman says, "that under the guise of protection we may be legitimizing the marginalization of women."

She adds, "Some well-intentioned men undermine women by protecting them and sometimes men use 'protection' to intentionally undermine women. Women have worked so hard in areas like trading and finance to say, 'I'm not brittle!' This is a return to the old concept of women as fragile."

"We have heard anecdotally that there is a chilling effect and that men are pulling back from sponsoring women," says Stellings. She heard that one company made a rule that men and women could not meet behind closed doors in the office. "That is the current environment," she says. "Most people think that is ridiculous, but there are some people who feel like the lines are not as clear now." Stellings says she had a conversation with a senior woman executive, whose male colleague told her, "Well, I'm just not going to take women associates out to lunch now." The woman replied, "I assume, then, that you won't take the men out, either."

An employment lawyer says, "I think the history of women in finance tells a really scary story. Unless female leadership at a firm has a voice already, I'm not terribly optimistic." She says she heard from a woman who is a member of an elite women's networking group in New York that "the people who are hiring are saying, 'We are just not going to hire women.'"

"The worst thing they could do is what they're going to do and not hire women," she adds. "How messed up is that? They won't even let us onto their playing field. What do we do?"

And yet, and yet. There are forces pushing back against this. In the past, executives spoke about the need for change because their firms had lost lawsuits. Now they speak about the need for change because it's a business imperative. "For us to deal with clients all over the world, we have to be more diverse," says David Solomon, the president and co-C.O.O. of Goldman Sachs. "We are not where we need to be. But a lot has changed in the last 10 years and we have learned along the way." Among other things, he's led a push to change how Goldman recruits, in order to have diversity from the start. He says data shows that women actually don't leave at a faster clip than men do. Reset the start button, and maybe you change the game.

And now, with a sluggish, heavily regulated Wall Street, the future might be in those entrepreneurial organizations started by women who leave big firms. Krawcheck founded Ellevest, a thriving start-up which provides investment advice for women outside of the male-dominated brokerage system.

A female hedge-fund manager who left her firm after being harassed isn't quitting, either. Far from it. The day I talk to her is the day she's launching her own fund, which will specialize in short-selling, or betting against companies that are frauds or otherwise overpriced. "It just made me angry, and anger is a great motivator," she says. "It makes me want to go after criminal companies and take no fucking prisoners in this industry. Fuck all these guys for doubting me and holding me down."

Now, that's a movie script.

HOW TO BREAK UP
THE SILICON VALLEY
BOYS' CLUB

Susan Wojcicki | March 2017

E very year around this time, we hear the same story in Silicon Valley. This year, it was Susan Fowler's distressing account of her year at Uber, followed closely by A.J. Vandermeyden's story alleging a culture of "pervasive harassment" at Tesla. Like many who read the stories, I was mad. But I was also frustrated that an industry so quick to embrace and change the future can't break free of its regrettable past.

The allegations of explicit gender discrimination that Susan and A.J. describe are unacceptable, and any report of harassment deserves a thorough examination. But implicit biases can also harm women in the workplace through more subtle forms of gender discrimination. These include being frequently interrupted or talked over; having decision-makers primarily address your male colleagues, even if they're junior to you; working harder to receive the same recognition as your male peers; having your ideas ignored unless they're rephrased by your male colleagues; worrying so much about being either "too nice" or "sharp elbowed" that it hurts your ability to be effective; frequently being asked how you manage your work-life balance; and perhaps most difficult of all, not having peers who have been through similar situations to support you during tough times.

Fortunately, there is a solution that has been proved to address gender discrimination in all its forms, both implicit and explicit: hiring more women.

Employing more women at all levels of a company, from new hires to senior leaders, creates a virtuous cycle. Companies become more attuned to the needs of their female employees, improving workplace culture while lowering attrition. They escape a cycle of men mostly hiring men. And study after study has shown that greater diversity leads to better outcomes, more innovative solutions, less groupthink, better stock performance and G.D.P. growth.

Despite this evidence, tech lags other male-dominated industries, such as finance and media, when it comes to gender balance, according to a 2016 World Economic Forum Study. So how can tech do better? Well—unlike the work of many Silicon Valley companies—it's not rocket science.

First, tech C.E.O.s need to make gender diversity a personal priority. Human Resources departments and diversity leads play a critical role, but they need the commitment and attention of the C.E.O. to succeed. Improving diversity, like any priority, requires dedicated resources, clear goals, comprehensive analytics, and company-wide transparency.

A great example of a C.E.O. taking this issue seriously is Reed Hastings of Netflix. In an effort to build a more flexible work culture, he took a strong stand on paid family leave. That policy led to a cascade effect, with companies like Microsoft and Amazon soon providing better family leave options, helping to limit the adverse effects that having children can have on a woman's career. And increasing family leave helps retain female employees; at Google, when we increased paid maternity leave from 12 to 18 weeks, the rate at which new moms left dropped by 50 percent.

Second, companies need to provide money and staff to groups that support female—or any underrepresented—employees. Women's groups have been a lifeline throughout my career, giving me a place to find inspiration, build friendships, and seek support during difficult times. But these groups take time and effort to organize, and often that burden falls on those who are already at a disadvantage. Underrepresented employees already have to overcome discriminatory barriers in their careers; they shouldn't be expected to volunteer their time to help their companies do the same. Companies should take the lead from underrepresented groups, but they also need to provide resources to help them execute on their priorities, whether it's holding trainings or off-sites, sending people to conferences or hosting social events.

Finally, addressing gender imbalance will require those who currently have power and influence to extend their privilege. In every organization, there are many people, from senior leaders to first-time managers, who have the power to elevate women in the workplace. I wouldn't be in the position I'm in today without several key people in power believing in me and giving me a chance to succeed. One of those people was Bill Campbell, the legendary coach of Silicon Valley and a crucial figure in Google's management, who passed away last April.

The most recent example of Bill's support occurred soon after I became C.E.O. of YouTube. I learned about an important invitation-only conference convening most of the top leaders in tech and media, yet my name was left off the guest list. Many of the invitees were my peers, meaning that YouTube wouldn't be represented while deals were cut and plans were made. I started to question whether I even belonged at the conference. But rather than let it go, I turned to Bill, someone I knew had a lot of influence and could help fix the situation. He immediately recognized I had a rightful place at the event and within a day he worked his magic and I received my invitation.

Bill's presence is sorely missed in the Valley, but his example should live on in the way we run our companies. At YouTube, we still have a long way to go toward improving our diversity, but we've made some progress. We've supported underrepresented groups, established a C-level Leadership Diversity Council, and ramped up our female hiring—since I joined in 2014, we've gone from a company that is 24 percent women to one that's nearly 30 percent.

Clearly, we and other companies still have a lot of work to do. But during a month when women all over the world are speaking out and rightfully asking for their contributions to be recognized, I hope Susan and A.J.'s stories can provide us a turning point. I hope this is the year in which C.E.O.s decide to take gender equality personally, give underrepresented groups the support they need, and use their positions to elevate more diverse leaders.

As someone who's been lucky to have a great career in tech, I know how creative and fulfilling a career in this industry can be for women. And I want to make sure we continue to recruit and retain great female hires. As we work to improve our company cultures, I hope next year we hear a different story in Silicon Valley, one about greater diversity making the tech industry even stronger and more innovative.

HOW MILLENNIAL WOMEN
ARE COMBATTING THE
GENDER-PAY GAP

Maya Kosoff | April 2018

t's a familiar story to almost any woman in the workforce, from minimum-wage earners to striving assistants to C.E.O.s: "Despite being a leader, I am still left off of important e-mails, left out of important decision-making processes, and left in the dark," one woman wrote in a survey conducted by theSkimm. "When the group is together or a speaker is addressing us, they tend to only look towards the men—even with things as small as eye contact . . . the 'boys' club' mentality is, unfortunately, still alive and thriving." Other women recalled similar situations: being passed over for promotions, watching their female co-workers struggle to break through, or facing sexual harassment that drove them out of their industries. Their stories are a necessary reminder that despite the advances made by the #MeToo movement, millennial women are still running up against many of the same gender dynamics faced by generations before them—even if they don't realize it themselves.

Today is Equal Pay Day—a date that marks how far into 2018 women must work to earn as much as men did the previous year. Unfortunately, substantial portions of the population don't take the problem seriously, according to a new survey conducted by [VanityFair.com's] the Hive, theSkimm, and SurveyMonkey as part of Millennial Takeover 2018, our year-long editorial project in advance of the midterm elections. As we found when investigating gender inequality in the workplace, many women don't feel empowered to elevate themselves or their concerns at work because they recognize the systemic barriers created by sexism. But they persist, in part, because of prevailing partisan divides over the extent of the issue.

These findings are critical for businesses seeking to improve their office culture and bolster their bottom line. Nearly 7 in 10 Americans say significant obstacles to gender parity in the workplace still exist, a number that rises to almost 80 percent among millennial women. Most female millennials—65 percent—believe this inequality is due to sexism, and 55 percent believe that having too few women in leadership roles contributes to the problem. Almost half of African-American millennial women cite biased interview processes as a major hurdle. A huge percentage of female millennials—68 percent—believe that women make less money than men for doing similar jobs, and 66 percent believe men have more opportunities to be promoted to top positions.

When that cohort is divided by political affiliation, however, the picture becomes more complex. In theory, equal pay shouldn't be a partisan issue, but 89 percent of Democratic and Democrat-leaning female millennial respondents say significant obstacles in the workplace exist for women, while only 60 percent of Republican and Republican-leaning millennial women say the same. A vast majority (81 percent) of Democratic and Democrat-leaning millennial women say men earn more for similar work, and the same percentage believe men have more opportunities to be promoted. Meanwhile, just 43 percent of Republican millennial women say men have more opportunities for advancement, while 45 percent say men and women are equally likely to be promoted.

Men are comparatively clueless when it comes to recognizing these disparities, with 46 percent responding that men and women earn about the same. The prevalence of male leaders appears to perpetuate the cycle of gender inequality: while the vast majority of millennial men are comfortable discussing raises, promotions, and salary information with both male and female managers, most millennial women are more comfortable covering the same topics just with female managers. "From my personal experience, men hold all the power at my company," one woman said in the Skimm survey. "While we may have a significant number of women working on the payroll, it is ultimately up to a man in charge to approve a pay increase." This creates a cycle where women hold fewer positions of power and female subordinates are less comfortable making requests in their own workplaces.

This ultimately has a major impact on businesses. We already know that diverse teams are more innovative and perform better financially than teams dominated by a single gender. According to our findings, however, gender disparities in the workplace also create a toxic feedback loop for employee retention. Thirty-two percent of female millennials (and 41 percent of Democratic and Democrat-leaning female millennials) say they would start looking for a new job if they discovered they were being paid less than a man for similar work. Nearly 60 percent of female millennials look for reasons to explain pay discrepancies at work, and sizable numbers would take action if they learned they made less than a male colleague. One-third say they would be upset upon discovering the news, while 4 in 10 would discuss the matter with human resources or try to negotiate a raise.

Millennial women appear to be seeking recourse in electoral politics. To the vast majority of female millennials—nearly 70 percent—a candidate's stance on gender equality is "extremely" or "very" important. (Among Democratic and Democrat-leaning millennial women, that number rises to 85 percent; among Republican and Republican-leaning women, it falls to 45.) "It's important to me that candidates—male or female—put significant effort into at the very least trying to sympathize with the majority of women who know and understand the daily struggle of gender inequality," wrote another Skimm survey respondent.

Almost three-quarters of female millennials don't think the Trump administration has taken adequate steps to address gender inequality during Donald Trump's first year in office, and fewer than a quarter (24 percent) think Ivanka Trump has been an effective advocate for women's issues in the White House. Those numbers are divided by party—61 percent of Republican-leaning millennial women *do* believe the Trump administration has sufficiently addressed gender inequality (among Democratic and Democrat-leaning women, just 9 percent say the same), and 63 percent of

Republican-leaning millennial women *do* think Ivanka has been an effective advocate (only 9 percent of Democratic and Democrat-leaning women agree). Already, women on the left are mobilizing to express their dismay: of the 548 women running in House primaries, according to *The New York Times*, 424 are Democrats. "I think there's a disgust," Erin Vilardi, who runs VoteRunLead, told *New York* magazine in January. "There's disgust very much about the abuse that men in power have systematically been engaging in unchecked, and disgust with the people who continue to keep those men in power."

The partisan nature of the debate suggests that while a strong stance on gender equality will attract Democratic voters, it could repel millennial women who see themselves as Republicans. But ignoring gender equality is unlikely to change those G.O.P. voters' minds—if a candidate is vocally in favor of policies that address things like pay disparity and workplace sexual harassment, they're likely to favor a whole suite of policies that are traditionally less attractive to Republicans. For most voters, then, gender equality isn't a deciding issue, but that doesn't mean it should be brushed under the rug. Instead, the challenge lies in making it a nonpartisan one.

(In 2018, a record number of women, 127, were elected or appointed to serve in the 116th Congress, including more than three dozen new members.)

WHY I DECIDED TO RUN

Lucy McBath | April 2018

We think of ourselves in different stages of life using many different adjectives. I have been a daughter, a sister, a wife, a mother, a friend. Candidate for Congress was never really part of the lexicon. Years ago, as a flight attendant with Delta Air Lines, my goals in life were much like anyone else's in America: to be a good mother, to teach my son to be a compassionate man who would share his worth with the world, and perhaps to walk him down the aisle on his wedding day. Those simple dreams ended the day after Thanksgiving of 2012. My son, Jordan Davis, was shot and killed while sitting in the back seat of a friend's car at a gas station, listening to music. The man who killed my son opened fire on four unarmed teenagers because he said the music was too loud. That man felt empowered by the stand-your-ground statute.

Overnight, I went from suburban mom to activist seeking justice for Jordan. I had witnessed what happened to [17-year-old Florida high-school student] Trayvon Martin and how, bit by bit, the defense in [neighborhood watch captain] George Zimmerman's case worked to dehumanize the young man who was walking home from a convenience store. While Jordan's shooter was initially found guilty on three counts of attempted murder, the first-degree murder charge ended in a mistrial. In an October 2014 re-trial, however, the shooter was convicted of first-degree murder and sentenced to life in prison.

Losing my son in such a senseless way fueled my lifelong commitment to community activism and my sense of the importance of political engagement, both of which run in the family. My father was the Illinois branch president of the N.A.A.C.P. for more than 20 years and served on its national board. As a child, I traveled with my family attending marches and rallies supporting the civil-rights movement and the coalitions of organizations fighting alongside Dr. Martin Luther King Jr.

After losing Jordan, I became the national spokesperson and faith and outreach leader for Everytown for Gun Safety and Moms Demand Action for Gun Sense in America. While it was terrible at first, I've learned that sharing my personal story has, thankfully, made an impact. One of the most effective ways to inform and persuade people is by telling them about your first-person experience. It's a credential I wish upon no one, but I've found solace and purpose through my fight. We need more common-sense solutions to difficult problems.

In my work, I've shared my story with Congress, governors, legislators, pastors, voters, and neighbors. The people I've spoken with, particularly in Georgia, have inspired me and taught me a lot. In their homes and churches, on their doorsteps and on the phone, over and over people have said that what's missing in politics today is leadership. Voters are looking for elected officials to have the courage to break through the blaring, divisive rhetoric and come together to forge common-sense change for the common good. In the weeks since the [school-shooting] tragedy in Parkland [Florida], we've all witnessed the reaction from Washington. It's been much the same as the response after every other mass shooting.

It's not time to have the debate.

Let's wait and see.

It isn't the time to act.

What has inspired me the most after Parkland is the students. These young folks are stepping up and have—quite literally—mobilized for their lives. From an early age, I taught Jordan that he possessed the power to effect change in a world where he might, as an African American, be unfairly judged thanks to preconceived biases. I'd like to think these students are making the change that he cannot.

So, with much prayer and reflection, I've decided to run for Congress in my home district of Georgia's 6th. I am running so that I may humbly offer my voice in this debate for the safety, security, and hope of prosperity for my neighbors in Georgia and across the country. I qualified to run on International Women's Day—a happy coincidence for me considering women are often told it isn't their "time."

My work moving the discussion forward in gun-violence prevention—through dialogue and, even more important, through listening—is how I will uniquely approach other important issues as well. My story doesn't begin or even end with one subject. I am passionate about access to women's health care; as a two-time breast cancer survivor, I know how critical it is for women to have access to preventative care, including mammograms. A more stable family—and overall society—can be measured by the health and well-being of women and children. And the economic and social advancement of women depends on coverage. On the campaign trail, I will be sharing my experience and discussing how it directly contrasts with the experience of our current member of Congress.

As a flight attendant, I've met tens of thousands of Americans from all walks of life traveling for all sorts of reasons—it's often said that the journey, and not the destination, is what matters. I know that my final destination is a reunion with my son. As for the journey, I'm constantly amazed at how my life has transformed. I am a daughter and a mother. I am a sister and a friend. I am an advocate. And now, I am a candidate. I am humbled to be all of these. There was a time when I thought my life was over. But a new path forward has opened. In sharing my story, I will embrace the journey and seek comfort in the ultimate destination.

(McBath won her Congressional race. In 2019, she began representing Georgia's 6th district in the U.S. House of Representatives.)

#METOO AND ME

Monica Lewinsky | March 2018

H*ow do I know him? Where have I seen him?* The Man in the Hat looked familiar, I thought, as I peered over at him a second time.

It was Christmas Eve 2017. My family and I were about to be seated at a quaint restaurant in Manhattan's West Village. We had just come from Gramercy Park—on the one night each year when the exclusive park (accessible only to nearby residents with special keys) opens its gates to outsiders. There had been carols. People had sung with abandon. In short, it was a magical night. I was happy.

Amid the glow of candles and soft lighting, I strained to look again at the Man in the Hat. He was part of a small group that had just exited the main dining room. They were now gathering their belongings, likely vacating what was to be our table. And then it clicked. *He looks just like . . . no, couldn't be. Could it?*

A student of Karma, I found myself seizing the moment. Whereas a decade ago I would have turned and fled the restaurant at the prospect of being in the same place as this man, many years of personal-counseling work (both trauma-specific and spiritual) had led me to a place where I now embrace opportunities to move into spaces that allow me to break out of old patterns of retreat or denial.

At the same moment I stepped toward the Man in the Hat and began to ask, "You're not . . . ?," he stepped toward me with a warm, incongruous smile and said, "Let me introduce myself. I'm Ken Starr." An introduction was indeed necessary. This was, in fact, the first time I had met him.

I found myself shaking his hand even as I struggled to decipher the warmth he evinced. After all, in 1998, this was the independent prosecutor who had investigated me, a former White House intern; the man whose staff, accompanied by a group of F.B.I. agents (Starr himself was not there), had hustled me into a hotel room near the Pentagon and informed me that unless I cooperated with them I could face 27 years in prison. This was the man who had turned my 24-year-old life into a living hell in his effort to investigate and prosecute President Bill Clinton on charges that would eventually include obstruction of justice and lying under oath—lying about having maintained a long-term extramarital relationship with me.

Ken Starr asked me several times if I was "doing O.K." A stranger might have surmised from his tone that he had actually worried about me over the years. His demeanor, almost pastoral, was somewhere between avuncular and creepy. He kept touching my arm and elbow, which made me uncomfortable.

I turned and introduced him to my family. Bizarre as it may sound, I felt determined, then and there, to remind him that, 20 years before, he and his team of prosecutors hadn't hounded and terrorized just me but also my family—threatening to prosecute my mom (if she didn't disclose the private confidences I had shared with her), hinting that they would investigate my dad's medical practice, and even deposing my aunt, with whom I was eating dinner that night. And all because the Man in the Hat, standing in front of me, had decided that a frightened young woman could be useful in his larger case against the president of the United States.

Understandably, I was a bit thrown. (It was also confusing for me to see "Ken Starr" as a human being. He was there, after all, with what appeared to be his family.) I finally gathered my wits about me—after an internal command of *Get it together.* "Though I wish I had made different choices back then," I stammered, "I wish that you and your office had made different choices, too." In hindsight, I later realized, I was paving the way for him to apologize. But he didn't. He merely said, with the same inscrutable smile, "I know. It was unfortunate."

It had been nearly 20 years since 1998. The next month would mark the

20th anniversary of the Starr investigation expanding to include me. The 20th anniversary of my name becoming public for the first time. And the 20th anniversary of an *annus horribilis* that would almost end Clinton's presidency, consume the nation's attention, and alter the course of my life.

If I have learned anything since then, it is that you cannot run away from who you are or from how you've been shaped by your experiences. Instead, you must integrate your past and present. As Salman Rushdie observed after the fatwa was issued against him, "Those who do not have power over the story that dominates their lives, power to retell it, rethink it, deconstruct it, joke about it, and change it as times change, truly are powerless, because they cannot think new thoughts." I have been working toward this realization for years. I have been trying to find that power—a particularly Sisyphean task for a person who has been gaslighted.

To be blunt, I was diagnosed several years ago with post-traumatic stress disorder, mainly from the ordeal of having been publicly outed and ostracized back then. My trauma expedition has been long, arduous, painful, and expensive. And it's not over. (I like to joke that my tombstone will read, MU-TATIS MUTANDIS—"With Changes Being Made.")

But as I find myself reflecting on what happened, I've also come to understand how my trauma has been, in a way, a microcosm of a larger, national one. Both clinically and observationally, something fundamental changed in our society in 1998, and it is changing again as we enter the second year of the Trump presidency in a post-Cosby-Ailes-O'Reilly-Weinstein-Spacey-Whoever-Is-Next world. The Starr investigation and the subsequent impeachment trial of Bill Clinton amounted to a crisis that Americans arguably endured *collectively*—some of us, obviously, more than others. It was a shambolic morass of a scandal that dragged on for 13 months, and many politicians and citizens became collateral damage—along with the nation's capacity for mercy, measure, and perspective.

Certainly, the events of that year did not constitute a war or a terrorist attack or a financial recession. They didn't constitute a natural catastrophe or a medical pandemic or what experts refer to as "Big T" traumas. But something had shifted nonetheless. And even after the Senate voted in 1999 to acquit President Clinton on two articles of impeachment, we could not escape the sense of upheaval and partisan division that lingered, settled in, and stayed.

Maybe you remember or have heard stories about how "the scandal" saturated television and radio; newspapers, magazines, and the Internet; *Saturday Night Live* and the Sunday-morning opinion programs; dinner-party conversation and watercooler discussions; late-night monologues and political talk shows (*definitely* the talk shows). In *The Washington Post* alone, there were 125 articles written about this crisis—in just the first 10 days. Many parents felt compelled to discuss sexual issues with their children earlier than they might have wanted to. They had to explain why "lying"—even if the president did it—was not acceptable behavior.

The press was navigating unexplored terrain, too. Anonymous sources seemed to emerge almost daily with new (and often false or meaningless) revelations. There was a new commingling of traditional news, talk radio, tabloid television, and online rumor mills (fake news, anyone?). With the introduction of the World Wide Web (in 1992–93) and two new cable news networks (Fox News and MSNBC in 1996), the lines began to blur between fact and opinion, news and gossip, private lives and public shaming. The Internet had become such a propulsive force driving the flow of information that when the Republican-led Judiciary Committee of the House of Representatives decided to publish Ken Starr's commission's "findings" online— just two days after he had delivered them—it meant that (for me personally) every adult with a modem could instantaneously peruse a copy and learn about my private conversations, my personal musings (lifted from my home computer), and, worse yet, my sex life.

Americans young and old, red and blue, watched day and night. We watched a beleaguered president and the embattled and often disenchanted members of his administration as they protected him. We watched a First Lady and First Daughter move through the year with grit and grace. We watched a special prosecutor get pilloried (though some thought he deserved it). We watched an American family—my family—as a mother was forced to testify against her child and as a father was forced to take his daughter to be fingerprinted at the Federal Building. We watched the wholesale dissection of a young, unknown woman—me—who, due to legal quarantine, was unable to speak out on her own behalf.

How, then, to get a handle, today, on what exactly happened back then?

One useful viewpoint is that of cognitive linguist George Lakoff. In his book *Moral Politics: What Conservatives Know That Liberals Don't,* Lakoff observes that the connective fiber of our country is often best represented through the metaphor of family: e.g., "our Founding Fathers," "Uncle Sam," the concept of sending our sons and daughters to war. Lakoff goes on to argue that, "for conservatives, the nation is conceptualized (implicitly and unconsciously) as a Strict Father family and, for liberals, as a Nurturant Parent family." Addressing the scandal itself, he asserts that Clinton was widely perceived as "the naughty child" and that, in line with the filial metaphor, "a family matter [had turned] into an affair of state." Thus, in many ways, the crack in the foundation of the presidency was also a crack in our foundation at home. Moreover, the nature of the violation—an extramarital relationship—struck at the heart of one of humanity's most complicated moral issues: infidelity. (You'll forgive me if I leave that topic right there.)

The result, I believe, was that in 1998 the person to whom we would typically turn for reassurance and comfort during a national crisis was remote and unavailable. The country, at that stage, had no consistent, Rooseveltian voice of calm or reason or empathy to make sense of the chaos. Instead, our Nurturer in Chief, because of his own actions as much as the subterfuge of his enemies, was a figurative "absent father."

As a society, we went through this together. And ever since, the scandal has had an epigenetic quality, as if our cultural DNA has slowly been altered to ensure its longevity. If you can believe it, there has been at least one significant reference in the press to that unfortunate spell in our history every day for the past 20 years. Every. Single. Day.

The fog of 1998 has lodged in our consciousness for many reasons. The Clintons have remained pivotal political figures on the global stage. Their disparagement has been vigorously abetted by "this vast right-wing conspiracy," as Hillary Clinton famously put it. And the Clinton presidency segued into a bitter electoral deadlock: the contested *Bush v. Gore* showdown, which would usher in an era so turbulent that it would leave the lessons of the Clinton years altogether murky. In succession came the unthinkable (the attacks of September 11, 2001), protracted conflicts (the wars in Iraq and Afghanistan), the Great Recession, a state of perpetual gridlock in Washington, and then the daily bedlam central to Trumpism. No matter how these subsequent events dwarfed the impeachment and subsumed our attention, maybe, just maybe, the long, unimpeded derivation of this drama, ever since, is partly the result of 1998 having been a year of unremitting crisis that we all endured but never actually resolved—a low-grade collective trauma, perhaps?

I discussed this idea with psychologist Jack Saul, founding director of New York's International Trauma Studies Program and author of *Collective Trauma, Collective Healing.* "Collective trauma," he told me, "usually refers to the shared injuries to a population's social ecology due to a major catastrophe or chronic oppression, poverty, and disease. While the events of 1998 in the United States do not fit neatly into such a definition, they may have led to some of the features we often associate with collective traumas: social rupturing and a profound sense of distress, the challenging of long-held assumptions about the world and national identity, a constricted public narrative, and a process of scapegoating and dehumanization."

Until recently (thank you, Harvey Weinstein), historians hadn't really had the perspective to fully process and acknowledge that year of shame and spectacle. And as a culture, we still haven't properly examined it. Re-framed it. Integrated it. And transformed it. My hope, given the two decades that have passed, is that we are now at a stage where we can untangle the complexities and context (maybe even with a little compassion), which might help lead to an eventual healing—and a systemic transformation. As Haruki Murakami has written, "When you come out of the storm you won't be the same person who walked in. That's what this storm's all about." *Who were we then? Who are we now?*

———

'm so sorry you were so alone." Those seven words undid me. They were written in a recent private exchange I had with one of the brave women leading the #MeToo movement. Somehow, coming from her—a recognition of sorts on a deep, soulful level—they landed in a way that cracked me open and brought me to tears. Yes, I had received many letters of support in 1998. And, yes (thank God!), I had my family and friends to support me. But by and large I had been alone. *So. Very. Alone.* Publicly Alone—abandoned most of all by the key figure in the crisis, who actually knew me well and intimately. That I had made mistakes, on that we can all agree. But swimming in that sea of Aloneness was terrifying.

Isolation is such a powerful tool to the subjugator. And yet I don't believe I would have felt so isolated had it all happened today. One of the most inspiring aspects of this newly energized movement is the sheer number of women who have spoken up in support of one another. And the volume in numbers has translated into volume of public voice. Historically, he who shapes the story (and it is so often a he) creates "the truth." But this collective rise in decibel level has provided a resonance for women's narratives. If the Internet was a bête noire to me in 1998, its stepchild—social media—has been a savior for millions of women today (notwithstanding all the cyberbullying, online harassment, doxing, and slut-shaming). Virtually anyone can share her or his #MeToo story and be instantly welcomed into a tribe. In addition, the democratizing potential of the Internet to open up support networks and penetrate what used to be closed circles of power is something that was unavailable to me back then. Power, in that case, remained in the hands of the president and his minions, the Congress, the prosecutors, and the press.

There are many more women and men whose voices and stories need to be heard before mine. (There are even some people who feel my White House experiences don't have a place in this movement, as what transpired between Bill Clinton and myself was not sexual assault, although we now recognize that it constituted a gross abuse of power.) And yet, everywhere I have gone for the past few months, I've been asked about it. My response has been the same: I am in awe of the sheer courage of the women who have stood up and begun to confront entrenched beliefs and institutions. But as for me, my history, and how I fit in personally? I'm sorry to say I don't have a definitive answer yet on the meaning of all of the events that led to the 1998 investigation; I am unpacking and reprocessing what happened to me. Over and over and over again.

For two decades, I have been working on myself, my trauma, and my healing. And, naturally, I have grappled with the rest of the world's interpretations and Bill Clinton's re-interpretations of what happened. But in truth, I have done this at arm's length. There have been so many barriers to this place of self-reckoning.

The reason this is difficult is that I've lived for such a long time in the House of Gaslight, clinging to my experiences as they unfolded in my 20s and railing against the untruths that painted me as an unstable stalker and Servicer in Chief. An inability to deviate from the internal script of what I actually experienced left little room for re-evaluation; I cleaved to what I "knew." So often have I struggled with my own sense of agency versus victimhood. (In 1998, we were living in times in which women's sexuality was a marker of their agency—"owning desire." And yet, I felt that if I saw myself as in any way a victim, it would open the door to choruses of: "See, you did merely service him.")

What it means to confront a long-held belief (one clung to like a life raft in the middle of the ocean) is to challenge your own perceptions and allow the *pentimento* painting that is hidden beneath the surface to emerge and be seen in the light of a new day.

Given my PTSD and my understanding of trauma, it's very likely that my thinking would not necessarily be changing at this time had it not been for the #MeToo movement—not only because of the new lens it has provided but also because of how it has offered new avenues toward the safety that comes from solidarity. In 2014, in an essay for *Vanity Fair*, I wrote the following: "Sure, my boss took advantage of me, but I will always remain firm on this point: it was a consensual relationship. Any 'abuse' came in the aftermath, when I was made a scapegoat in order to protect his powerful position." I now see how problematic it was that the two of us even got to a place where there was a question of consent. Instead, the road that led there was littered with inappropriate abuse of authority, station, and privilege. (Full stop.)

Now, at 44, I'm beginning (*just beginning*) to consider the implications of the power differentials that were so vast between a president and a White House intern. I'm beginning to entertain the notion that in such a circumstance the idea of consent might well be rendered moot. (Although power imbalances—and the ability to abuse them—do exist even when the sex has been consensual.)

But it's also complicated. Very, very complicated. The dictionary definition of "consent"? "To give permission for something to happen." And yet what did the "something" mean in this instance, given the power dynamics, his position, and my age? Was the "something" just about crossing a line of sexual (and later emotional) intimacy? (An intimacy I wanted—with a 22-year-old's limited understanding of the consequences.) He was my boss. He was the most powerful man on the planet. He was 27 years my senior, with enough life experience to know better. He was, at the time, at the pinnacle of his career, while I was in my first job out of college. (Note to the trolls, both Democratic and Republican: none of the above excuses me for my responsibility for what happened. I meet Regret every day.)

"This" (sigh) is as far as I've gotten in my re-evaluation; I want to be thoughtful. But I know one thing for certain: part of what has allowed me to shift is knowing I'm not alone anymore. And for that I am grateful.

I—we—owe a huge debt of gratitude to the #MeToo and Time's Up heroines. They are speaking volumes against the pernicious conspiracies of silence that have long protected powerful men when it comes to sexual assault, sexual harassment, and abuse of power.

Thankfully, Time's Up is addressing the need women have for financial resources to help defray the huge legal costs involved in speaking out. But there is another cost to consider. For many, the Reckoning has also been a *re-triggering*. Sadly, what I see with every new allegation, and with every posting of "#MeToo," is another person who may have to cope with the re-emergence of trauma. My hope is that through Time's Up (or, perhaps, another organization) we can begin to meet the need for the resources that are required for the kind of trauma therapy vital for survival and recovery. Regrettably, it's often only the privileged who can afford the time and the money to get the help they deserve.

Through all of this, during the past several months, I have been repeatedly reminded of a powerful Mexican proverb: "They tried to bury us; they didn't know we were seeds."

Spring has finally sprung.

ACKNOWLEDGMENTS

EDITOR IN CHIEF   Radhika Jones

V.F. BOOKS EDITOR   David Friend

ASSOCIATE EDITOR   Mary Alice Miller

We gratefully acknowledge our partners at Penguin Books, including Ann Godoff, president of Penguin Press; Scott Moyers, publisher; Virginia Smith Younce, editor; Caroline Sydney, editorial assistant; Colleen Boyle, publicist; and Grace Fisher, marketing specialist.

Editorial guidance was provided by Dale Brauner, David Gendelman, and Robert Walsh.

We sincerely thank Chris Mitchell, Caryn Prime, Geoff Collins, and Dan Adler (*Vanity Fair*), Christopher P. Donnellan and Tamara Kobin (Condé Nast Business Affairs and Rights Management), and Andrew Wylie, Jeffrey Posternak, Jessica Calagione, and Mia Vitale of the Wylie Agency.

CONTRIBUTORS

CARI BEAUCHAMP, a *Vanity Fair* contributor, is an author, historian, and filmmaker, who adapted her biography of screenwriter Frances Marion into the documentary film *Without Lying Down*, which earned her a Writers Guild Award nomination. Her documentary *The Day My God Died*, about Nepal and India's sex-trade industry, was nominated for an Emmy. Beauchamp, the author of six books, has written for *Variety*, *The Hollywood Reporter*, *The New York Times*, and the *Los Angeles Times*. She is currently the resident scholar of the Mary Pickford Foundation.

LESLIE BENNETTS, named a *V.F.* contributing editor in 1988, has profiled numerous celebrities for the magazine, among them Jennifer Aniston, Brad Pitt, Hillary Clinton, Julianne Moore, and Jordan's Queen Noor and Queen Rania. Her article about the sexual abuse of children by members of the Catholic clergy was nominated for a National Magazine Award. Bennetts was a longtime reporter at *The New York Times*, becoming the first woman at the publication to cover a presidential campaign. She is the author of *The Feminine Mistake* and *Last Girl Before Freeway: The Life, Loves, Losses, and Liberation of Joan Rivers*.

Since 1984, *V.F.* writer-at-large **MARIE BRENNER** has written hard-hitting profiles of public figures (such as Roy Cohn and Donald Trump), retrospective pieces (Clare Boothe [Brokaw] Luce, Pamela Harriman), and investigative stories on legal, financial, and medical scandals (Bernie Madoff, Enron, the NuvaRing contraceptive). Her article on tobacco-industry whistleblower Jeffrey Wigand became the basis for the Oscar-nominated movie *The Insider*. Her reporting on war correspondent Marie Colvin was adapted into the 2018 feature film *A Private War*. Brenner is the author of eight books, including the memoir *Apples and Oranges: My Brother and Me, Lost and Found*.

TINA BROWN was the editor in chief of *Vanity Fair* from 1984 to 1992 and of *The New Yorker* from 1992 to 1998. After her tenure in magazines, during which her publications won four George Polk Awards, five Overseas Press Club awards, and a slew of National Magazine Awards, she became the founding editor of *Talk* magazine and then *The Daily Beast*. She is the author of *Life As a Party*, *The Diana Chronicles*, and, most recently, *The Vanity Fair Diaries*. Brown, an inductee to the Magazine Editors' Hall of Fame, runs Tina Brown Live Media.

JANET COLEMAN, who began her career at *Partisan Review* and *The New York Review of Books,* is the author of *The Compass: The Improvisational Theater That Revolutionized American Comedy*; *Mingus/Mingus: Two Memoirs* (with Al Young); and many articles for publications such as *Vanity Fair* on game-changing figures in the comedy world. She is one of playwright-director Richard Maxwell's New York City Players and a producer and host for Pacifica Radio.

AMY FINE COLLINS, a *Vanity Fair* special correspondent, has been contributing to the magazine since 1990. Her beats have included style, design, larger-than-life personalities, and vintage Hollywood. She has profiled fashion legends Coco Chanel, Pauline Trigère, and Diana Vreeland, among many others, as well as golden-age movie luminaries, from Claudette Colbert to Edith Head. One of the fashion arbiters who has coordinated the International Best-Dressed List, Collins was previously style editor for *House & Garden* and style editor at large for *Harper's Bazaar*. She is the author of, among other titles, *American Impressionism* and *The God of Driving*.

MAUREEN DOWD, a *Vanity Fair* contributor, was awarded the Pulitzer Prize in Commentary for her work with *The New York Times*. She joined the staff of the *Times* in 1983 and started writing her Sunday column for the newspaper in 1995. A veteran of *The Washington Star* and *Time* magazine, she has also served as the *Times*'s White House correspondent and as a contributor to both the Style Section and *The New York Times Magazine*. Dowd is the author of *Bushworld*, *Are Men Necessary?*, and *The Year of Voting Dangerously*.

AMANDA FORTINI is a writer and a visiting lecturer at the University of Nevada, Las Vegas, as well as a contributing editor of *Elle* magazine. Her work has appeared in *Vanity Fair*, *The New York Times*, *The New Yorker*, *Rolling Stone*, *Paper*, and *California Sunday*, among other publications. She has been an editor at *Mirabella*, *The New York Review of Books*, and *Slate*, and received a James Beard Foundation Journalism Award nomination.

LAURA JACOBS served as a *Vanity Fair* contributing editor from 1995 to 2019. With a focus on culture and fashion, she has written for the magazine about film, dance, great artists of the twentieth century, and seminal mid-century American designers. She has also made a specialty of studying iconic women such as Mary McCarthy, Suzy Parker, Gypsy Rose Lee, Lilly Pulitzer, and three figures who appear in this book: Julia Child, Grace Kelly, and Emily Post. Jacobs, the author of six books of fiction and nonfiction, served as the editor in chief of *Stagebill*, writes for *The Wall Street Journal*, and is the dance critic at *The New Criterion*.

MAYA KOSOFF covered technology for *Vanity Fair*'s Hive from 2016 to 2019. Her work has appeared in *Business Insider*, *Slate*, *Inc.*, and *Entrepreneur*, and she has appeared on *Good Morning America*, *Entertainment Tonight*, CNBC's *Closing Bell*, and Huffington Post Live.

MONICA LEWINSKY is a social activist, public speaker, and a *Vanity Fair* contributing editor. As an ambassador and strategic advisor to the anti-bullying organization Bystander Revolution, she advocates for a safer social media environment and consults with companies concerned with online safety. Her P.S.A. with BBDO Studios, "In Real Life," was nominated for a 2018 Emmy. Lewinsky's 2014 *V.F.* essay, "Shame and Survival"—her first public examination of the Clinton scandal in nearly a decade—was nominated for a National Magazine Award.

LUCY McBATH is a member of the United States House of Representatives from Georgia's 6th congressional district. McBath has been the national spokesperson for Everytown for Gun Safety and for Moms Demand Action for Gun Sense in America, and served as the faith-and-outreach leader for both organizations. In 2018, McBath was a featured speaker at the *Vanity Fair* Founders Fair.

BETHANY McLEAN, a one-time investment banking analyst at Goldman Sachs and former *Fortune* editor at large, is a longtime contributing editor at *Vanity Fair*. Her most recent book is *Saudi America: The Truth About Fracking and How It's Changing the World*. Her 2001 story "Is Enron Overpriced?" was the first in a national publication to question Enron's dealings. Following the company's bankruptcy, McLean and Peter Elkind coauthored the book *The Smartest Guys in the Room*, which became the basis for the Oscar-nominated 2005 documentary of the same name.

MAUREEN ORTH, a *Vanity Fair* special correspondent, has written for the magazine since 1988. She has profiled heads of state, such as Margaret Thatcher, covered the Washington political scene, and conducted in-depth investigations that brought to light allegations of sexual abuse and child abuse. She was nominated for a National Magazine Award for her story on Michael and Arianna Huffington. Orth is the author of *The Importance of Being Famous* and *Vulgar Favors*, which grew out of her reporting for the magazine and inspired the Emmy Award–winning limited series *The Assassination of Gianni Versace: American Crime Story*.

Prior to joining *Vanity Fair* in 1999, contributing editor **LISA ROBINSON** was a long-time music columnist for the *New York Post* and *The New York Times* Syndicate, the host of syndicated radio and cable TV programs, and edited several rock magazines. From 2000 to 2006, she produced *Vanity Fair*'s music portfolios. In addition to her regular "Hot Tracks" column, she has written cover stories on figures such as Beyoncé, Katy Perry, and Kendrick Lamar; major profiles on the likes of Eminem, U2, and Serge Gains-bourg; and oral histories of Motown, disco, and Laurel Canyon. She is the author of the 2014 memoir *There Goes Gravity: A Life in Rock and Roll*.

GAIL SHEEHY became a *Vanity Fair* contributing editor in 1984. She has written character portraits of George H. W. Bush, Mikhail Gorbachev, Bill and Hillary Clinton, Robert Dole, Gary Hart, Margaret Thatcher, Jesse Jackson, Saddam Hussein, and Newt Gingrich. Her article "Hillary's Choice," which examined the relationship between President and Mrs. Clinton, won the 1999 Front Page Award and became a book. Sheehy, an original contributor to *New York*, whose work has appeared in publications such as *Esquire*, *The New York Times Magazine*, and *Parade*, is the author of *Passages*, *The Silent Passage*, and *Sex and the Seasoned Woman*, among other titles.

The late **INGRID SISCHY** was a contributing editor at *Vanity Fair* and, along with her partner, Sandra Brant, was international editor of Condé Nast's European editions. Sis-chy, who wrote photography and fashion criticism for *The New Yorker* in the 1980s and 90s, served as the editor in chief of both *ArtForum* (from 1979 to 1987) and *Interview* (from 1989 to 2008). A respected authority in the often overlapping spheres of art, fash-ion, and journalism, Sischy was the author of photography monographs, articles for publications such as *The New York Times*, and the 2018 posthumous collection *Nothing Is Lost*.

KRISTA SMITH joined *Vanity Fair* in 1988 and became the magazine's West Coast editor in 1993. She served as *Vanity Fair*'s executive West Coast editor until 2019. Smith has written cover stories on personalities such as Drew Barrymore, Jude Law, Salma Hayek, and Gwyneth Paltrow, and helped shepherd twenty-five editions of the *Vanity Fair* Hollywood Issue. She also profiled rising talent for the "Vanities" section and interviewed filmmakers and actors on camera at the Sundance and Toronto film festivals.

SALLY BEDELL SMITH, a *V.F.* contributing editor during the 1990s and 2000s, be-gan her career at *Time*, where she was a reporter-researcher from 1973 to 1977. As a staff writer for *TV Guide*, she produced feature articles and a weekly column. In 1982, Smith became a cultural news reporter for *The New York Times*. Smith's books have explored the House of Windsor, the White House years of the Kennedys and Clintons, and the lives of figures such as Pamela Harriman and William Paley.

SHEILA WELLER, a contributor to *Vanity Fair*, is an award-winning magazine journalist and a *New York Times* best-selling author of seven books, including *Girls Like Us: Carole King, Joni Mitchell, Carly Simon—and the Journey of a Generation*. She is a senior contributing editor at *Glamour* and a former contributing editor of *New York*.

The late **MARJORIE WILLIAMS** was a reporter and columnist for *The Washington Post* and *Vanity Fair*. Her *V.F.* features have included profiles of Bill Clinton, Al Gore, and Colin Powell. Her *V.F.* essay about her experience with cancer won a National Magazine Award. She is the author of two posthumous collections, edited by her husband, Timothy Noah: *The Woman at the Washington Zoo: Writings on Politics, Family, and Fate* and *Reputation: Portraits in Power*. The former book won the PEN America's Martha Albrand Award.

SUSAN WOJCICKI has been the CEO of YouTube since 2014. Wojcicki was a founding member of Google, and in 1999 became the company's first marketing manager. After tracking the success of YouTube, she proposed that Google acquire the video platform, which Google did, in 2006. Under Wojcicki's leadership, YouTube has reached 1.9 billion logged-in users per month and, on her watch, the company's percentage of female employees has risen.

JACQUELINE WOODSON won the National Book Award for *Brown Girl Dreaming*, a memoir in verse. She is the recipient of numerous citations for her children's and young adult works, including the Coretta Scott King Book Award for *Miracle's Boys*, which was adapted into a miniseries by Spike Lee; the Jane Addams Children's Book Award for *Each Kindness*; the Astrid Lindgren Memorial Award; and four Newbery Honors. Woodson, the author of adult books as well, was named the Young People's Poet Laureate by the Poetry Foundation and the 2018–19 National Ambassador for Young People's Literature by the Library of Congress.